THE EMERGENCE OF MOSCOW
1304–1359

THE EMERGENCE
OF MOSCOW
1304-1359

———

J. L. I. FENNELL

LONDON · SECKER & WARBURG

First published in England 1968 by
Martin Secker & Warburg Limited
14 Carlisle Street, London W.1

SBN 436 15250 9

Printed in Great Britain by
The Camelot Press Ltd, London and Southampton

Contents

List of Illustrations

Preface

THE PURPOSE of this book is to provide a comprehensive political history of the early stages of the principality of Moscow based on primary sources, and to provide an answer to the perennial question: Why and how did Moscow achieve supremacy over the other principalities of north-east Russia? Why not Tver', Suzdal' or Rostov?

Very little has been written on this period in English. Professor G. Vernadsky in the third volume of his history of Russia devotes some space to the political history of north-east Rus' during the first half of the fourteenth century, but his work cannot be described as a detailed study of the period, nor are his findings always based on primary sources. In Russian there are two works of capital importance which contain a close analysis of most of the available material: A. E. Presnyakov's *Obrazovanie Velikorusskogo gosudarstva* (1918) and L. V. Cherepnin's *Obrazovanie Russkogo tsentralizovannogo gosudarstva v XIV–XV vekakh* (1960). It may be pertinently asked, why not simply translate either or both into English? My answer would be that the results of my investigations frequently differ from those of Presnyakov or Cherepnin and constitute a new approach to, and solution of, certain problems.

Two more questions may be just as pertinently put: Why 1304 to 1359? And why limit the study to political history? The answer to the first question is to be found in my conclusion to this book: 1304, the year of the death of what I would call the last of the "non-parochial" grand princes of Vladimir, is also the year which marks the beginning of the struggle between Moscow and Tver'. With the death of Ivan II in 1359, which almost coincided with the death of the last of the great khans among the descendants of Baty and the beginning of the civil war in the Golden Horde, the age of Tatar-dominated Suzdalian politics came to an end and the period of Muscovite consolidation—the "gathering of the lands" and the assimilation of the thrones of Vladimir and Moscow—began.

As for my exclusion of the economic and social history of the age, I can only say that I considered it more important to limit myself to that aspect of the history of the period which is adequately documented. The available sources shed remarkably little light on economic and social conditions in the first half of the fourteenth century, and a historian studying, say, the agriculture or trade of north-east Russia during this particular period would be forced to work largely on later sources and to build up hypotheses from the most fragmentary data.[1]

I have based my work on primary sources and I have attempted where possible to establish the reliability, bias, accuracy, prejudice, originality or derivativeness of the available sources. Apart from wills and treaties, the accuracy and reliability of which are seldom open to doubt and which, as far as they concern the fourteenth century, have been sifted and studied in so masterly a manner by Cherepnin in his *Russkie feodal'nye arkhivy*, I have used the chronicles as a background on which to reconstruct the events of the period.

Now the problems facing the investigator of the available chronicle material for the period under consideration are numerous and at times insuperable. Firstly, there is the problem of contemporaneity. Only one chronicle (the older redaction of the Novgorod First Chronicle) can be said to have been written at the time of the events described; but it ends in 1330 and is concerned primarily with Novgorodian affairs. The remaining chronicles are all compilations of the fifteenth or sixteenth centuries, that is to say their date of completion is in every case more than forty years later than the end of our period. Of course these later chronicles do contain passages which were clearly written by contemporaries and which in their present state (i.e. in the state of the final edition of the chronicle) are obviously very close to the original—a good example is the period of the episcopacy of Vasily as described in the later redaction of the Novgorod First

---

[1] G. E. Kochin describes the absence of source material relevant to the history of agriculture in Russia from the 1240's to the beginning of the fifteenth century as "catastrophic". (*See* G. E. Kochin, *Sel'skoe khozyaystvo*, pp. 93 sq.)

Chronicle. But even in a case like this one cannot tell what additions, subtractions or modifications were made to the original text by later copyists or editors.

Secondly, it is often extremely difficult to establish a link between the different chronicle accounts of an event and to determine what sources could have been available to the author of one particular version or another. Did, for instance, the compiler of the Ermolinsky Chronicle account of the first half of the fourteenth century have access to the main source which was used by the compilers of the Novgorod Fourth Chronicle and the Sofiysky First Chronicle?

Finally, one is faced with the difficulty of estimating to what extent ideological considerations influenced the editing of the chronicles: how did a Tverite, a Novgorodian and a Muscovite scribe, say, writing at the time of a particular event, interpret that event to suit, flatter or justify the masters they were writing for? And how, in fifty years' time, did later editors react to the work of their predecessors? How much was censored? How much was invented at a later date?

On those occasions when the sources are sufficiently abundant to warrant it, I have attempted to show the interplay of the various chronicle accounts, to establish some hierarchy among them and to take into account the tendentiousness which is so often the hallmark of Russian provincial chronicle-compiling and which may result from local pride or from a desire to expunge from memory inglorious deeds. It is hoped that these investigations will throw more light on the events themselves than an indiscriminate use of all the available sources. In Appendix A (*see* below, pp. 315–22) I have listed the main chronicles used and have briefly described their origins, sources and what can be deduced of their history and movement.

One final remark. It will be noticed that no attempt has been made in this book to assess the personality or character of any of the main protagonists. This is because the available sources are entirely silent on such matters. No references are made to physical characteristics; there are no attempts to describe any such recreational activities as hunting or drinking which might throw even a glimmer of light on personality. Nor, alas, were there any foreign travellers in Suzdalia who left descriptions of the people they met or the places they visited. The meagre obituaries or eulogies dutifully supplied by the chroniclers are little more than a concoction of clichés which tell us nothing of the men whose piety or goodness they extol. "Pious", "Christ-loving", "humble", "meek" are adjectives which were, it seems, quite arbitrarily affixed to this or that prince or bishop. Even the sobriquets given to Ivan I, Semen and Ivan II—"Money-bag" (Ivan Kalita), "The Proud" (Semen Gordy) and "The Gentle" (Ivan Krotky)—add little to our knowledge of the personalities or characters of the early rulers of Moscow.

In transliterating Russian words I have used the "British" system of latinization advocated in the *Slavonic and East European Review* (*see* W. K. Matthews, "The Latinisation of Cyrillic Characters", *SEER*, vol. xxx, no. 75 (June 1952), pp. 531–49). I have made, however, one or two minor exceptions to this system: (i) *e* and *ё* are always transliterated *e* (thus *Evstafy*, and not *Yevstafy*); (ii) the endings -ый and -ий are always rendered by -*y* (*Sofiysky*, *novy*); (iii) the "soft sign", the letter ь, and the "hard sign", the letter ъ (when it occurs in the middle of a word) are rendered by an apostrophe (*Tver'*); (iv) in the spelling of feminine names ending in -*iya*, the spelling -*ia* has been used throughout (*Maria*, *Evpraksia*). As for the spelling of Tatar names, I have normally given the contemporary Russian version transliterated. If a Tatar name is identifiable, then it is placed in brackets after the Russian version; e.g. *Telebuga* (*Tulabugha*); *Tovluby* (*Toghlubay*). In those cases where the name has been mutilated and is difficult to relate to a known Tatar name, it is left in the original (e.g. *Istorchey*).

Note that in the text of the book patronymics in the plural are sometimes used for convenience's sake to denote the descendants of this or that prince. Thus "Konstantinovichi" denotes the descendants of Konstantin, "Monomashichi" those of Vladimir Monomakh, etc.

Appendix B 1–7 consists of genealogical tables of the main dynasties mentioned in the book. They are followed by a glossary of Russian words which occur in the text or the footnotes.

In conclusion I would like to thank all those of my colleagues in this country, the United States and the Soviet Union who have helped or advised me with various problems.

Oxford, October 1965

I

North-east Russia in the Thirteenth Century

By the beginning of the fourteenth century two princely dynasties, the houses of Tver' and Moscow, each of which considered itself strong enough to be recognized as the sole claimant for supreme power in north-east Russia, had emerged from the welter of the descendants of Grand Prince Vsevolod III of Vladimir and Suzdal'. For the past sixty years Suzdalia, that is to say the old principality of Rostov, Vladimir and Suzdal' which had been in the hands of the family of Vladimir Monomakh since the end of the eleventh century, had been subject to the Tatar khans of Kipchak. Overall power, which nominally lay with the senior prince—the grand prince of Vladimir—was largely under the control of the khans. Authority was vested in the grand princes by the rulers of Saray alone.

Throughout the thirteenth century the grand prince ruled over a federation of districts, each in its turn ruled by a member of the same princely family. Historians frequently refer to this period as the age of the disintegration of the state in north-east Russia, the period of feudal fragmentation and disunity, the "appanage period". It is true that the years between 1238, the date of the Mongol invasion, and 1304, the beginning of the struggle between Tver' and Moscow, are full of fratricidal wars, rebellions, and Tatar punitive expeditions summoned by the Russians, all of which illustrate only too well what at first sight appears to have been the aimlessness of the policy of the grand princes and the absence of any feeling of national unity amongst their relations and servants. Yet aimless and even selfish though their policies often appear, the grand princes managed to maintain their hold over the minor princes of the family and in the face of appalling odds to keep up a semblance of unity.

It cannot be denied that this strange federation of family

possessions ruled by the head of the clan was weak, ineffectual and totally incapable of resisting any demands made on it by its overlords the Tatars. The grand prince had neither the strength nor a sufficiently efficient military machine to exploit natural anti-Tatar uprisings or to shake off the more intolerable aspects of Tatar domination. Nor were they yet able or ready to extend their coalition to their extra-territorial cousins, to those descendants of Ryurik who ruled the lands beyond the borders of Suzdalia.

Several reasons can of course be found for this political and military weakness of thirteenth-century Suzdalia, not the least being the firm grip of the khans on the princes, their skill in stamping out any glimmerings of solidarity among their subjects, and the shattered economy of the country.

Less obvious perhaps, but equally important as a cause of the political impotence of Suzdalia in the thirteenth century, is the peculiar relationship which existed between sovereign power and land-ownership. The fact that none of the thirteenth-century grand princes of Vladimir was sufficiently closely tied to a particular district, or rather had not the time or the energy to build up and develop his own particular principality while ruling from Vladimir or while fighting to control Novgorod or Pereyaslavl', meant that no one of the districts belonging to the various branches of the family was strengthened at the expense of its neighbours. The grand prince ruled an amorphous group of principalities, none of which was strong enough to take over the leadership. As a result of this feeble federation the rulers of Suzdalia were unable to take advantage of any instability amongst the Tatars themselves: the period of diarchy in the Horde, for instance, which lasted for nearly a decade (1281–91) and during which two rival khans simultaneously proclaimed their supremacy, was a period not of solidarity in north-east Russia, as one would have expected, but of division; instead of grouping together under one leader, the princes formed two hostile groups, each supported by a rival khan. But at the beginning of the fourteenth century both Tver' and Moscow were emerging as the two most powerful states. Either was potentially capable of assuming leadership over all the remaining principalities, provided of course the other was suppressed and provided a benevolent khan lent his support.

Before we can discuss the question of why Tver' and Moscow, and not, say, Suzdal' or Nizhny Novgorod or Rostov, emerged as the leading principalities at this particular juncture, and before we can begin to understand the complexities of the political situation in Suzdalia at the turn of the thirteenth century, we must consider briefly the political organization of the north-east Russian principalities during the thirteenth century and examine the system of control exercised by the Tatars over their Russian subjects.

The district of Rostov–Suzdal' evidently came under the authority of the prince of Kiev as early as the end of the tenth century or the beginning of the eleventh.[1] In the south it comprised the lands watered by the middle reaches of the Moskva river and by the whole of the Klyaz'ma and Nerl' rivers. The upper waters of the Volga, from Tver' to Nizhny Novgorod, ran through the centre of the district. In the north-west it included the White Lake and the town of Beloozero; to the north-east it stretched beyond the junction of the Northern Dvina and Vychegda rivers. No princes are known to have ruled the land during most of the eleventh century, and indeed it was not until the turn of the century that Vladimir Monomakh began to take an active interest in the largest and most distant of the Kievan provinces. He founded the city of Vladimir on the Klyaz'ma in 1108[2] and placed his son Yury Dolgoruky in the new political centre of Suzdal'.

During the whole of the twelfth century Suzdalia, as it is convenient to call the Rostov–Suzdal'–Vladimir principality, was ruled efficiently and intelligently by Yury and his two sons, Andrey Bogolyubsky (d. 1174) and Vsevolod III (d. 1212); it never passed out of the hands of this particular branch of the descendants of Vladimir Monomakh. As Kiev little by little lost power, wealth, population and Western connections, so the political and economic significance of Suzdalia grew. New towns sprang up: Moscow, Yur'ev, Pereyaslavl'–Zalessky, Bogolyubovo; new monasteries were founded; an attempt was made to establish a metropolitan see in Vladimir as early as 1159; architecture, painting and literature flourished. The great princes of the

[1] See A. N. Nasonov, *Russkaya zemlya*, ch. 11.
[2] See M. N. Tikhomirov, *Drevnerusskie goroda*, pp. 401–2.

north-east, Yury, Andrey and Vsevolod, concentrated their energies not so much on seizing Kiev as on securing control of Novgorod. Trade developed along the Volga, the Klyaz'ma and the Oka, between Bolgary on the Volga to the east and Novgorod to the west. By the end of the century Kiev had yielded her economic, political and cultural supremacy to Suzdalia in the north-east and to the western principalities of Volyn' and Galich.

In 1212 Vsevolod III died leaving the grand principality of Vladimir—the title had been assumed by Andrey Bogolyubsky in the twelfth century—to those of his sons who survived him. Throughout the thirteenth century his sons, grandsons and great-grandsons succeeded one another to the grand-princely throne and ruled the lands he had ruled with only insignificant additions and subtractions.

During the thirteenth century the "grand principality of Vladimir" implied only the district of Suzdalia. All the other lands of Rus', which had at one time or other owed allegiance to the rulers of Kiev but which during the eleventh and twelfth centuries had evolved their own form of independence and established their own dynasties—such as Polotsk, Turov and Pinsk, Chernigov, Ryazan' and Murom, Galich (in south-west Rus'), Volyn', and Smolensk—were outside the power and grasp of the rulers of Suzdalia.[1] Some of these districts were too distant or too economically feeble to be of great interest to the grand princes of Vladimir; while some had long-established dynasties of their own, such as the house of Polotsk which could trace its origins to a son of Vladimir I, or had sufficient power to resist the interference of the northern princes. This does not mean, however, that the princes of Suzdalia were averse to meddling in the affairs of their immediate neighbours if it was to their

[1] Only the principality of Southern Pereyaslavl', the original patrimony of Vladimir Monomakh's father, Vsevolod I, remained in the family of Yury Dolgoruky; owing to its highly vulnerable position in the extreme south and owing to the fact that there was little room for territorial expansion, Pereyaslavl' gradually lost all importance in the eyes of the north-eastern princes. By the time of the Tatar invasions, Southern Pereyaslavl' virtually disappears from the pages of the chronicles.

THE LANDS OF RUS' IN THE EARLY THIRTEENTH CENTURY

(showing approximate inter-principality boundaries)

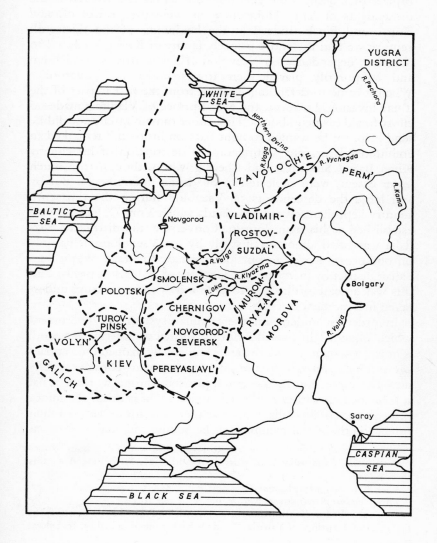

YUGRA DISTRICT

R. Pechora

WHITE SEA

Northern Dvina

R. Vaga

R. Vychegda

PERM'

ZAVOLOCH'E

R. Kama

BALTIC SEA

Novgorod

VLADIMIR-ROSTOV-SUZDAL'

R. Volga

R. Klyaz'ma

Bolgary

SMOLENSK

R. Oka

POLOTSK

MUROM

CHERNIGOV

RYAZAN'

MORDVA

R. Volga

TUROV-PINSK

VOLYN'

NOVGOROD-SEVERSK

GALICH

KIEV

PEREYASLAVL'

Saray

CASPIAN SEA

BLACK SEA

advantage to do so: the district of Ryazan', for instance, the vulnerable borderland due south of Suzdalia, was often the object of unasked-for Suzdalian solicitude and intrusion, though the princes of Ryazan' were genealogically as far removed from the descendants of Yury Dolgoruky[1] as were the princes of, say, Turov and Pinsk. Indeed at the beginning of the thirteenth century we find the entire princely family of Ryazan' reduced to complete dependence on Vsevolod III, who dispossessed them and temporarily placed their towns under his governors.[2] When it came to defending Ryazan' from the first impact of the Tatar invasion, however, the grand prince of Vladimir made no effort to aid his neighbour. "He neither came himself, nor did he send help, for he wanted to fight Baty on his own," remarked an embittered Ryazanite writing on the destruction of his city by Khan Baty.[3] Smolensk and Chernigov too, though to a much lesser extent, were subjected to Suzdalian interferences. But by and large the descendants of Vsevolod during the thirteenth century kept themselves to the lands which Yury Dolgoruky had established as his own domain. Conversely, the district of Suzdalia was ruled almost exclusively by the Vsevolodovichi; only on one occasion was an outsider permitted to take over a Suzdalian district by marrying the daughter of an heirless prince, and this was an extraordinary, probably a desperate, measure undertaken in a moment of crisis.[4]

In order to understand the peculiar system of government which obtained in Suzdalia during the whole of the thirteenth century, a system frequently, and erroneously, named the "appanage system" (*udel'naya systema*), it is necessary to consider briefly how the succession to the grand-princely throne worked, what was happening within the "patrimonies", that is to say the minor principalities of Suzdalia, what was the relationship between their rulers and the senior members of the family, and finally what was

[1] They sprang from Yaroslav Svyatoslavich, the son of Vladimir Monomakh's uncle, Svyatoslav II of Chernigov and Kiev. *See* below, Appendix B, 1, p. 324.

[2] *See* A. L. Mongayt, *Ryazanskaya zemlya*, pp. 353-5.

[3] *See Voinskie povesti drevney Rusi*, p. 9.

[4] In 1260 Fedor Rostislavich of Smolensk and Mozhaysk married the daughter of the prince of Yaroslavl' and took over the principality. *See* below, p. 20.

the attitude of the republics of Novgorod and Pskov to their eastern neighbours.

A glance at the genealogical table (*see* Appendix B, 2, p. 325) will show that throughout the thirteenth century precisely the same system of succession by seniority was in force among the descendants of Vsevolod III as that which had by and large regulated succession to the throne of Kiev from the death of Yaroslav the Wise in 1054 to the end of the twelfth century. According to this peculiar unwritten and unrecorded "law", the title of grand prince passed, not vertically, from father to son, but horizontally, from brother to brother. When one generation of brothers was defunct, then in theory, though not always in practice, the throne passed to the sons of the eldest brother, then to the sons of the second eldest brother, if there were any left, and so on. In view of the fact that after a generation or two the number of candidates for the title might be extremely large and all idea of family solidarity might disappear, some checks and limitations on this system were essential. There were two such checks possible.

First, it appears that the children of those princes who predeceased their father or their elder brothers and thus never acceded to the throne were automatically debarred from succession. They were known as *izgoi*. Thus in the post-Yaroslav Kievan period, that is to say in the second half of the eleventh and the whole of the twelfth century, none of the descendants of Yaroslav the Wise's eldest son, Vladimir, who died two years before his father, either acceded to the throne of Kiev or even claimed the throne. The same applies to the children of the two youngest sons of Yaroslav, Vyacheslav and Igor', both of whom died before their elder brothers (*see* Appendix B, 1, p. 324). Likewise in the thirteenth century the children of Konstantin Yaroslavich, who predeceased his three elder ruling brothers, were *izgoi*.[1]

The exclusion of the *izgoi* from the line of succession, however, was not sufficient to reduce the number of candidates for the throne to reasonable proportions. It became essential from time to

---

[1] Perhaps the princes of Starodub (-Ryapolovsky) were also *izgoi*. The first prince of Starodub, Ivan Vsevolodovich, certainly was never grand prince. Although the date of his death is not known, he probably predeceased his brother Svyatoslav, who was grand prince in 1247–8.

time to narrow the field by arbitrarily excluding certain branches of the family from their right to succession. Thus in 1125, when Vladimir Monomakh died and his son Mstislav was appointed grand prince out of turn, the descendants of Izyaslav and Svyato-slav, the senior sons of Yaroslav the Wise, were for the time being excluded from the grand-princely struggle, and although a branch of the Svyatoslavichi (the descendants of Oleg Svyato-slavich) managed to seize the throne of Kiev and to occupy it for short periods, they were no longer reckoned with by the *Mono-mashichi* (so the family of Vladimir Monomakh were called) as legitimate heirs to the throne (*see* Appendix B, 1, p. 324). Exactly the same narrowing-down process occurred in Suzdalia in the thirteenth century. Soon after the death of Grand Prince Yaroslav Vsevolodovich in 1246 the right of succession to the grand-princely throne of Vladimir appears to have been limited to Yaroslav's children. It is true that his brother Svyatoslav managed to hold the title for a short time (1247–8), but he was soon driven out by a Yaroslavich, Mikhail the Brave, and finally excluded by a decision of the great khan, who appointed Andrey Yaroslavich as grand prince of Vladimir. Indeed, it is probable that Yaroslav himself persuaded Khan Baty to agree to this arbitrary limitation of the right to rule to his own children.[1] Whatever the measures taken and whoever took them, all the remaining surviving grandsons of Vsevolod III—the Konstan-tinovichi of Rostov, Yaroslavl', Beloozero and Uglich, the Svyatoslavichi of Yur'ev and the Ivanovichi of Starodub[2]—appear to have been debarred from the succession to the throne; at any rate we know that not one of them ever laid claim to the title.

If we allow for the arbitrary limitation of the candidature to the Yaroslavichi in the mid-thirteenth century, we can see that the system of succession by seniority—the system of lateral succession—was almost unfailingly observed by three generations of Vsevolodovichi, from the death of Vsevolod in 1212 to the death of Grand Prince Andrey Aleksandrovich in 1304. If seizure of the throne out of order occurred, it was short-lived and due to inter-necine feuds and rivalries.

[1] Such is the opinion of Presnyakov. (*See* Presnyakov, *Obrazovanie*, p. 55.)
[2] All the sons of Grand Prince Yury were killed, like their father, in 1238 at the time of the Tatar invasion. *See* Appendix B, 2, p. 325.

As the descendants of Vsevolod III grew in number so too did the minor principalities within Suzdalia, the "patrimonies" (*otchiny*) as they were called by contemporary chroniclers. The very name *otchina* implies that these estates were hereditary—they were the possessions of separate branches of the same family and, in the main, were handed down vertically from father to son. The same principle had obtained in Kievan Rus'. There is clear evidence of the formation of patrimonies among the immediate descendants of Yaroslav the Wise on or shortly after his death: Turov, for instance, which was given to Izyaslav by Yaroslav, remained in Izyaslav's family at least until the end of the eleventh century, and probably longer; the district of Galich in south-west Rus', which Yaroslav in all probability left to his grandson Rostislav, remained in the hands of the Rostislavichi until the end of the twelfth century; Ryazan' and Murom, originally allocated by Yaroslav to his son Svyatoslav, remained in the possession of the descendants of Svyatoslav until annexed by Moscow in the sixteenth century. In like manner the north-eastern principalities within Suzdalia were formed from the beginning of the thirteenth century.

The largest of these *otchiny* was the principality of Rostov,[1] comprising, to start with, Rostov in the south, Beloozero in the north and the two towns of Yaroslavl' and Uglich on the Volga. It was granted by Vsevolod to his eldest son Konstantin in 1211, a year before the former's death. Konstantin himself, just before his death in 1218, shared out his vast patrimony between his two sons Vasil'ko and Vsevolod; the former received Rostov and probably Beloozero, while the latter was given Yaroslavl'. The third son Vladimir was four at the time, and it was only at a later date that he was given Uglich. Thus the original principality of Rostov was divided in three among the first generation of Konstantinovichi. By and large the town and district of Rostov itself remained throughout most of the thirteenth century in the hands of the eldest sons of the family— Vasil'ko, his son Boris Vasil'kovich (d. 1277) and his grandson Dmitry Borisovich (d. 1294). No attempt was made, as far as can be seen, by any of Konstantin's descendants in the thirteenth century to claim the throne of Rostov according to the law of

[1] *See* Appendix B, 3, p. 326, and Map B.

lateral succession: Vladimir Konstantinovich of Uglich, for example, after his elder brother Vasil'ko of Rostov had been killed in 1238, did not, it appears, dispute the right of Vasil'ko's son Boris to the principality of Rostov; nor did his son, Roman of Uglich, who survived all his first cousins, dispute the right of Dmitry Borisovich to succeed his father in 1277.

Although Konstantin Vsevolodovich had three sons and six grandsons, all of whom had to be settled on patrimonies carved out from the original *otchina* left by Vsevolod, nevertheless a remarkable unity was maintained in Rostov throughout the thirteenth century, and the principality was not split up into numerous semi-independent patrimonies. This was due not only to the fact that horizontal succession appears to have played no role among Konstantin's descendants, but also to the relative smallness of the princely families, the high mortality rate and the fact that many of the princes died heirless. There were bitter quarrels, especially among the descendants of Konstantin's eldest son Vasil'ko, but the dynasty survived and fragmentation of territory by the end of the thirteenth century was negligible. Uglich, which had been granted to Konstantin's youngest son, reverted to the descendants of his eldest son in 1285, when Roman Vladimirovich of Uglich died without issue. Thus when Dmitry Borisovich died (also heirless) in 1294, his brother Konstantin was sole ruler of Rostov while Konstantin's eldest son ruled in Uglich. Beloozero, which had been given to Vasil'ko's second son Gleb, remained in the latter's family. Only the town and district of Yaroslavl' were taken from the control of the Konstantinovichi when, as a result of the marriage of the only surviving child of Vasily Vsevolodovich of Yaroslavl' to Fedor Rostislavich of Mozhaysk and Smolensk, they passed to the family of the princes of Smolensk.[1]

Thus at the beginning of the fourteenth century the old patrimony of Rostov, less Yaroslavl', was divided between Konstantin Borisovich, who controlled Rostov and Uglich (his son Aleksandr ruled Uglich from 1294), and the two sons of Mikhail Glebovich, Fedor and Roman, who shared Beloozero. For a whole century the great northern principality remained virtually intact and did not pass from the hands of the direct descendants of the eldest son of Vsevolod III.

[1] *See* above, p. 16.

Far less is known about the other two patrimonies founded by princes of the first generation of Vsevolodovichi, Yur'ev-Pol'sky and Starodub. Their rulers are rarely mentioned in the chronicles and there is no indication of the size of their estates. But, to judge from the meagre information available, these two small but fertile districts situated respectively to the west and the east of the principality of Suzdal' offer an even better example of cohesion than Rostov. In 1212, after the death of Vsevolod III, his fifth eldest surviving son, Svyatoslav, was given Yur'ev-Pol'sky, formerly part of the district of Vladimir, by Grand Prince Yury Vsevolodovich.[1] Throughout the thirteenth century the principality of Yur'ev remained solely in the hands of Svyato-slav's descendants: as his son and his grandson appear to have had only one son each, there was no question of fragmentation.[2] The history of Starodub is remarkably similar: Ivan, Vsevolod's youngest son, was given the principality and left it, on his death-bed, to his only son, who in his turn left it to his only son.

At a later date, the second and third generations of the Vsevolodovichi, the children and grandchildren of Yaroslav Vsevolodovich, were settled in the principalities of Suzdal', Nizhny Novgorod and Gorodets, Tver', Galich and Dmitrov, and Moscow; and in each of these districts princely dynasties were formed.[3]

And so, by the beginning of the rule of Mikhail of Tver' as grand prince (1304), the district of Suzdalia was divided into patrimonies—into family nests, in which, as far as can be ascertained from the bare evidence of the chronicles, direct succession from father to son prevailed. There were, however, two districts which never became the permanent possessions of any one particular branch of the princely family—Pereyaslavl'-Zalessky (sandwiched between Tver', Dmitrov and Moscow in the west and Rostov, Yur'ev and Vladimir in the east) and Kostroma, to the north of Suzdal'. Various princes had held both districts

---

[1] Originally Yur'ev was given to Vladimir, Vsevolod's fourth eldest son; but Vladimir, for some unstated reason, "had no wish to be prince in Yur'ev" and fled to Volok and thence to Moscow where he settled as prince. (*See* Tikhomirov, *Drevnerusskie goroda*, pp. 412–13.)

[2] *See* N. de Baumgarten, *Généalogies*, vol. ii, pp. 72–3.

[3] *See* Appendix B, 2, p. 325.

during the thirteenth century, but never did they become the *otchiny* of any one branch of the family. At the beginning of the fourteenth century the princes of Moscow, as will be seen, attempted in the face of considerable opposition to make Pereyaslavl' part of the family territory of the house of Daniil;[1] Kostroma, which after the death of Grand Prince Vasily Yaroslavich seems to have been held by Grand Prince Andrey Aleksandrovich, was also an object of Moscow's attentions at the beginning of the civil war with Tver' in 1304.[2] The fact that neither of these districts was assimilated as *otchina* by any line of the Vsevolodovichi has led historians to look upon them both as special adjuncts to the grand-princely district of Vladimir, lands which were at the disposal of the grand prince and of the grand prince alone, in the same way as the district of Vladimir was at his disposal.[3] There is unfortunately no evidence to show that these two lands became part of the grand-princely territory. During the fourteenth century, before they were absorbed in the coalescence of the grand principality of Vladimir with the principality of Moscow, they were undoubtedly looked upon as the non-patrimonial possessions of whoever was grand prince; it may well be that they enjoyed this status throughout much of the thirteenth century as well.

What were the relations between the grand prince of Vladimir and the *otchiny* ruled by his brothers, cousins and nephews? This is a question which it is extremely difficult to answer. No written documents concerning inter-princely relations during the thirteenth century have survived; there are no copies of treaties, agreements or wills. Only an occasional indirect reference in the chronicles throws some light on the problem. Nor can we look to the Kievan period for guidance, for there again there is the same lack of documentation: we do not know what form of contract existed between the grand prince of Kiev and, say, the prince of Chernigov, or the prince of Turov. That

[1] Before this Pereyaslavl' had been held by Grand Prince Dmitry Aleksandrovich who installed his son Ivan there.

[2] *See* below, p. 62.

[3] *See*, for instance, A. N. Nasonov, *Mongoly i Rus'*, ch. 4. *Cf.* Presnyakov, *Obrazovanie*, p. 117; *Ocherki istorii SSSR I*, p. 877.

a contract existed in the Kievan age there can be no doubt, for there were periods when a certain cohesion among the princes obtained and when the state was held together by the authority of the senior prince; and it is unlikely that the ruler of any district, particularly a district exposed to attacks from external enemies, could have thought himself capable of defending his borders without the guarantee of grand-princely assistance. Indeed there is clear evidence in the Primary Chronicle of compacts between the grand prince and his "vassals"; in 1117, for example, Vladimir Monomakh, after crushing the rebellion of Yaroslav Svyatopolchich, one of the few surviving male descendants of Grand Prince Izyaslav I, forced him to make peace. The chronicler describes the incident thus, evidently quoting the actual words used: "Yaroslav subjected himself (*pokorivshyusya*) to Vladimir and bowed allegiance to him (*vdarivshyu chelom*, lit. 'struck his forehead on the ground', i.e. paid homage). And Vladimir instructed him in all things, ordering him to come to him (i.e. to lend military assistance) 'when I call you' ('*kogda tya pozovu*')."[1]

There can be little doubt that there were similar contracts between the *otchina*-rulers and their senior relatives on the throne of Vladimir throughout the thirteenth century, and it is not unlikely that the relationship between grand prince and local prince was much the same in Suzdalia as it had been in Kiev. That such contracts existed is attested by the evidence of the chronicles concerning the frequently convened inter-princely congresses (*seymy, s'ezdy* or *snemy*). These were usually summoned by the grand prince in order that as many members as possible of the princely family could meet to discuss problems affecting either a particular branch of the family or the country as a whole. A good example of such a congress convened to regulate a serious family quarrel is that recorded under the year 1229. For some unknown

---

[1] *PVL*, vol. i, p. 202. It is interesting to note that the chronicler uses similar words to describe the agreement reached between Vladimir and Gleb of Minsk in 1116: "Gleb came out of the city with his children and his *druzhina* and bowed to Vladimir [in homage]. And they discussed peace, and Gleb promised to obey Vladimir in everything. And Vladimir, having agreed to peace terms with Gleb, instructed him in all things." (*See* ibid., p. 201.)

reason Grand Prince Yury quarrelled with his eldest surviving brother Yaroslav. The latter managed to win over to his side the three sons of Konstantin: "Yaroslav Vsevolodovich listened to the false reports of certain people and removed (*otluchi*) the three sons of Konstantin, Vasil'ko, Vsevolod and Vladimir, from Yury; and he plotted to oppose his brother Yury." Clearly Yaroslav persuaded the Konstantinovichi, who had hitherto shown themselves to be the obedient subjects of the grand prince, to break their oath of allegiance to Yury and thus to destroy their contract of service. The situation, however, was rectified by Yury's action: ". . . when Prince Yury heard of this he summoned them to a *snem*, and they put right their mutual enmity and all bowed down to Yury and kissed the cross in all love to him and [promised] to hold him as their father."[1] The words "bowed down to . . . and kissed the cross" ("*poklonishasya . . . tselovasha krest*") undoubtedly refer to an act of homage, the renewal of vows binding the junior members of the family to their "elder brother". Indeed, the phraseology is strikingly similar to that used to describe the two previously-mentioned contracts enforced by Vladimir Monomakh.

As for the conditions of "service" which the junior princes obliged themselves to fulfil, we can only guess at their nature. Presumably the basic demands were military: the junior princes were required to afford armed assistance to the grand prince whenever the latter saw fit to summon them to war. As in the Kievan period, so in the thirteenth century there are frequent references in the chronicles to expeditions carried out by the grand prince with some or all of his brothers, cousins and nephews. Each prince, when called upon, was expected to produce his own army, which either he or a deputy would command, the whole army being under a commander-in-chief, who was either the grand prince himself or someone appointed by him. An excellent example of the mobilization of an army and the delegation of command is afforded by Grand Prince Yury's Bulgar campaign of 1220:

Grand Prince Yury Vsevolodovich sent his brother Svyatoslav against the godless [Volga] Bulgars and with him he sent his

[1] *PSRL*, i, cols. 451–2.

own regiments,[1] and he gave the command [over them] to Eremey Glebovich. And Yaroslav sent his regiments from Pereyaslavl', and Yury ordered Vasil'ko Konstantinovich to send his regiments; and Vasil'ko sent one from Rostov and another from Ustyug to the upper reaches of the Kama. And Yury sent also to the princes of Murom telling them to send their sons; and David [of Murom] sent his son Svyatoslav, and Yury [of Murom] sent Oleg. And all met on the Volga at the mouth of the Oka.

Later, when the expeditionary force disembarked before the battle, "Svyatoslav drew up his regiments: that from Rostov he placed on the right wing, that from Pereyaslavl' on the left. He himself took up position in the centre with the princes of Murom, and he left another regiment by the boats."[2] Thus on this occasion detachments were sent not only by the grand prince and the princes of Pereyaslavl'-Zalessky, Yur'ev-Pol'sky and Rostov, but also by two peripheral, extra-Suzdalian princelings of Murom who were presumably subject to the grand prince at the time. Of the Vsevolodovichi only Svyatoslav went on the campaign, and he went as commander-in-chief. The remaining princes entrusted their armies to their own *voevody*.[3]

This was not an isolated case. Campaigns were mounted by the grand prince against external and internal enemies, and on all occasions the junior princes appear to have obeyed the military summons of their "elder brother" unquestioningly and without complaint. It is only after the Tatar conquest and the subordination of all princes to the khan of the Golden Horde that the situation appears to have altered somewhat. Nearly all military operations carried out by the grand princes of Vladimir after the disaster of 1238 were under Tatar supervision, if not under Tatar command. Only occasionally do we find the grand prince acting independently as commander-in-chief of a force summoned from his relations and neighbours. But even on those occasions when

[1] The word *polk* is used by the chroniclers of the thirteenth and fourteenth century to designate, *inter alia*, a body of soldiers. It could be translated as force, detachment, regiment, division, corps, army. I have used "regiment" throughout with no consideration of the size of the body.

[2] *PSRL*, xxv, p. 116.

[3] Yury's *voevoda*, Eremey Glebovich, had formerly been in the service of Konstantin Vsevolodovich. (*See PSRL*, xxv, p. 112.)

Tatar representatives ordered the expedition or were in command of it, the summoning of the Russian troops was left to the grand prince and the system appears to have been the same as before. An excellent example of combined operations carried out under Tatar supervision against an external enemy is the campaign of 1269 against the lands of the Teutonic Order: "in the winter of that year [Grand Prince] Yaroslav [Yaroslavich] took council with the Novgorodians and sent Svyatoslav (his son) to the Lower lands (i.e. Suzdalia proper) to collect regiments. And he collected together all the princes (*sovokupi vsyu knyaz'yu*) and an army of innumerable size, and he led them to Novgorod; and with them was the great *baskak* (Tatar overseer) of Vladimir, Amragan by name."[1]

Our knowledge of service conditions in the thirteenth century is, then, limited to the providing of military assistance when this was demanded by the grand prince. Beyond this we cannot say what duties, if any, the local princes were obliged to perform *vis-à-vis* the grand prince. True, on occasions we find local princes acting as the grand prince's agents, as it were, at the Horde, but these were probably *ad hoc* arrangements made to suit the parties concerned and were probably not conditioned by the terms of any agreements.

As for the grand prince's obligations towards the rulers of the *otchiny*, these were limited to the defence of their lands against aggression. After the Tatar invasion his role was largely confined to the defence of the western and north-western frontiers against Germans, Swedes and Lithuanians. At the Horde he is the sole representative of all the princely families in north-east Rus', the interceder, the suppliant and the protector of their interests. True, individual princes proceeded to Saray to plead their own causes, but the collective responsibility for "all the land of Rus'" clearly lay with the grand prince alone. Presumably too, though there is no direct evidence to support the supposition, the grand princes protected the local princes against aggression by one of their number; in other words, a prince attacked by a cousin would have been able to rely on the head of the family to rectify matters, just as he had done so often in the preceding two centuries. But there grand-princely interference stopped. What

[1] *NL*, p. 88.

went on within the boundaries of the *otchiny* was the business of the local prince and only the local prince: he was free to rule his principality as he wished, and family affairs within the principality were not the concern of the grand prince. The question of succession, for example, appears to have been purely a local affair. The fate of escheats—with one notable exception[1]—was decided by the branch of the family concerned and not by the grand prince; there was no question of an escheat reverting to the grand prince, or at any rate no recorded example of this ever happening has survived.

We are left, then, with the picture of the thirteenth-century grand prince ruling a federation of independent principalities, each in its turn ruled by a member of his family. In return for the protection of their frontiers the princes agreed to answer the summons of their "elder brother" whenever he should decide that their military help was required. As generation succeeded generation, however, and as the local princes became more and more genealogically estranged from each other and from the senior prince, it might be expected that the feeling of family solidarity would disappear and that the idea of Suzdalia as a family possession would fade. This was clearly beginning to happen towards the end of the thirteenth century. And yet the authority of the grand prince was largely undiminished. Although the local prince might have been as remote as third or fourth cousin to the grand prince, yet the latter could still command his respect and obedience.

How did the grand prince manage to maintain his authority? Before answering this question, we must consider briefly the links between the grand princes and their *otchiny* or family estates, and try to estimate the extent to which purely local interests outweighed national interests in·the policies of the rulers of Vladimir. Did the grand prince of Vladimir by and large represent what can be called pan-Suzdalian views? Or was he narrowly parochial in his policy and in his actions, having at heart rather the interest of his own nest than that of the family inheritance of Vsevolod III?

Influenced no doubt by Klyuchevsky's portrayal of what he called the "appanage order" (*udel'ny poryadok*) as a period of

[1] The case of Yaroslavl'. *See* above, p. 20.

fragmentation, disunity, poverty and isolation, many historians tend to look upon the grand prince of Vladimir as a parochially-minded local prince who happened, owing to the peculiar system of lateral succession, to enjoy the title but who preferred to reside in his own patrimony and cultivate his own garden. Klyuchevsky himself, while discussing the main symptoms of the "appanage" disorder, says the following: "The shifting of ruling princes ceased: they became settled, living permanently and dying in their appanage towns, which they do not leave even when . . . they occupy the grand-princely throne."[1] This idea, which was strongly combated by Presnyakov in his history of the formation of the Russian state, is developed still further by Vernadsky, who writes: "Each of Alexander Nevsky's brothers, and then each of his sons, while becoming titular grand duke of Vladimir, preferred to stay in his own appanage, coming to Vladimir for brief visits only, to expedite those state affairs which might require his presence. We witness here the temporary victory of the apanage (udel) principle over that of the national state."[2] How much truth is there in these assertions as far as the rulers of the thirteenth century are concerned?

It is difficult to see which of the sons, grandsons or great-grandsons of Vsevolod III who acceded to the throne of Vladimir in the thirteenth century could be called parochially-minded princes and which in fact preferred to remain in their family seats rather than rule from Vladimir. Of the sons of Vsevolod, only Konstantin and Svyatoslav might be called "patrimonial princes", but then each of them ruled as grand prince for only a very short period. Yury had no territorial possessions of his own—that is to say, no family possessions—outside the grand-princely territory of Vladimir and he is not known to have made any provisions for his sons. As for Yaroslav, his links with Pereyaslavl'-Zalessky appear to have been extremely tenuous during his reign as grand prince;[3] both he and his son Aleksandr Nevsky ruled primarily

---

[1] V. O. Klyuchevsky, *Sochineniya*, vol. i, p. 338. *Cf.* Platonov's views, which bear a striking resemblance to Klyuchevsky's. (*See* S. F. Platonovo, *Lektsii*, pp. 110–18.) *Cf.* Nasonov, *Mongoly i Rus'*, p. 39.

[2] G. Vernadsky, *The Mongols and Russia*, p. 167.

[3] However, Pereyaslavl' seems to have remained in his family for three more generations. His eldest grandson Dmitry was prince of Pereyaslavl', as was his great-grandson, Ivan Dmitrievich.

from their capital city of Vladimir. Grand Prince Andrey Yaroslavich during his short reign showed little or no interest in the
otchina of Gorodets and Nizhny Novgorod which had probably
been granted him by his father.[1] Suzdal', which together with
Gorodets and Nizhny Novgorod made up the patrimony of his
descendants, was, as Presnyakov has convincingly shown, only
given him in 1257 on his return from Sweden, five years after
he had been driven out of Vladimir.[2] Even Yaroslav Yaroslavich,
the founder of the house of Tver', resided mainly in Vladimir or
Novgorod during the seven years of his rule as grand prince;
there is nothing to show that his interests were confined to his
patrimony of Tver'.[3] Nor do the chronicles indicate that his
brother Vasily and his nephews Dmitry and Andrey were in any
way tied to their "family" possessions of Kostroma, Pereyaslavl'
and Gorodets respectively; indeed, it is not known whether
Kostroma was at this period in fact an *otchina* proper, and not
merely an adjunct of the grand principality of Vladimir; and
Gorodets, as has been pointed out, originally belonged to Andrey
Aleksandrovich's uncle, Andrey Yaroslavich, and was later
claimed by the latter's descendants as part of their patrimony.

On the strength of these observations we can conclude that
there is no evidence to show that during the thirteenth century
those rulers of individual principalities who happened, largely
by accident of birth, to accede to the throne of Vladimir preferred
to reside in, and build up, their own provincial centres at the
expense of the grand principality as a whole. Nor is there any
evidence of a lack of national feeling or national responsibility—
that is to say, responsibility for Suzdalia as a whole—among the
grand princes. The policy of this or that grand prince may be
criticized as short-sighted, aimless or injurious to the interests of
Suzdalia; princes may have damaged the "national cause" by
fighting each other and calling in Tatars to assist them in the
struggle for power. But on the basis of the available evidence none

[1] *See* Presnyakov, *Obrazovanie*, p. 62, note 3.
[2] *See* ibid., pp. 62–3.
[3] *Cf.*, however, the views of B. A. Romanov, who, on the strength of
Yaroslav's treaties with Novgorod, considers him to have been a "patriot
of commercial Tver'". (*See* B. A. Romanov, "Rodina Afanasiya Nikitina",
pp. 89 sq.)

of the thirteenth-century rulers of Vladimir can be accused of narrow, selfish parochialism.

A sense of responsibility, even dedication, and a certain degree of selflessness as regards family property were not of course sufficient to maintain the authority of the grand prince. Nor was the ancient tradition of respect for the senior member of the clan as head of the state enough to ensure obedience to the ruler of Vladimir. Clearly possession of the territory of Vladimir—which in some cases was virtually the only Suzdalian district that the grand prince could exploit for troops and cash—could not provide him with sufficient military aid and financial support. What, then, gave him his power? What enabled him to summon the other princes and to command their obedience? In the second half of the thirteenth century, Tatar support of course, although this could not always be relied upon, especially during the Tatar diarchy of the 1280's. The essential adjunct to his authority and the true source of his economic strength was the republic of Novgorod. Throughout the thirteenth century the grand princes of Vladimir struggled, if not to keep Novgorod in submission, then at least to confirm and maintain some sort of control over her.

In the heyday of the Kievan state Novgorod usually had the son or a close relative of the grand prince of Kiev as prince. What the conditions existing between the prince-ruler and Novgorod were we do not know; but clearly Novgorod was militarily and economically dependent on Kiev. During the twelfth century, as the power of Kiev declined, so Novgorod worked out her own way of independence. From 1126 the all-important office of *posadnik*, the annually-appointed mayor responsible for the major portion of the city's administration, became elective; previously he had been appointed by the prince and had acted as his right hand; now he became a check on the prince's power, as did, towards the end of the twelfth century, the local commander, judge and police-chief, the *tysyatsky*. Some ten years later Novgorod won for herself the right to invite whom she wished to rule and to elect from her own clergy the nominal head of state, the bishop (archbishop from 1165). Towards the end of the twelfth century the so-called "treaty system" was inaugurated, whereby any prince invited to rule was obliged to draw up a contract with the people of Novgorod. These contracts, the first extant copy of which dates from the sixties of the thirteenth century, severely limited any autocratic tendencies on the part of the prince: they made it legally impossible for him to carry out any administrative or judicial function without the presence and the consent of the *posadnik*; they forbade him to buy, seize or own any land in Novgorod territory—and this included Novgorod's vast colonies north of the district of Rostov; and they established joint control over Novgorod's frontier outposts of Volok Lamsky and Tor-zhok,[1] previously held by garrisons commanded by the sons or brothers of the prince of Novgorod. As one historian has remarked, "The institution of the treaty system meant the con-version of Novgorod into a feudal republic."[2]

Of course the freedom to choose a ruler was often illusory and the restrictions laid upon the prince were frequently and flagrantly disregarded. Nevertheless, during much of the twelfth century the choice of dynasty depended largely on whatever group of boyars and merchants were temporarily in control. The choice fluctuated between northern and southern princely families, between the Monomashichi and the princes of Chernigov. But by the end of the twelfth century the obvious choice, both from a military and from an economic point of view, was the princely family of Suz-dalia. Vsevolod and his children not only controlled the east—

[1] *See* the treaty between Novgorod and Grand Prince Yaroslav Yaroslavich (1264). "These are the Novgorod *volosti*: Volok and all its districts—and you shall keep your *tivun* (administrator) in [one] half, and the Novgorod [official] shall be in the [other] half in all the land of Volok; and in Torzhok you shall keep your *tivun* in your part, and the Novgorod [official] shall be in his part." *GVNiP*, No. 1, p. 9.

[2] *See* A. A. Zimin, "Novgorod i Volokolamsk," p. 103. *Cf.* the opinion of V. L. Yanin, who considers that throughout most of the thirteenth century whoever was prince of Novgorod exercised considerable control over the legal, administrative and economic affairs of the republic, and that the thirteenth century was marked by the "duality of power" (*dvoevlastie*) of prince and republic. In his view, the decisive change came in the 1290's when the Novgorodian government was radically altered by the annual election of a *posadnik* from one of the permanent representatives of the five *kontsy*, or city districts, and when the power of the prince in Novgorod was drastically curtailed. The 1290's in fact represented "the most important historical boundary which separates the developed republican organization of Novgorod from the long preceding age of power shared between the republic and the prince". (*See* V. L. Yanin, *NP*, p. 175—and preceding chapter.)

west waterway of the Volga—Novgorod's principal trading route since the economic decline of Kiev—but they could also provide sufficiently powerful military aid to defend Novgorod and Pskov from the ever-growing danger of invasion from the west and the north-west, by Germans and Swedes. Thus during the thirteenth century the tendency to ask for princes from among the Vsevolodovichi virtually became the rule.

By the middle of the century it had become the established practice that the grand prince of Vladimir or his son was also prince of Novgorod: during the rule of Aleksandr Nevsky, who had been prince of Novgorod since early in his father's reign and had done much to strengthen the ties between Novgorod and Vladimir, the office of the prince of Novgorod was always held either by Aleksandr himself or by one of his two sons; when he died, the chronicler remarked: "His brother, Yaroslav Yaroslavich of Tver', became grand prince of Vladimir *and Novgorod*",[1] as though the two appointments were concomitant. And although during the last four decades of the thirteenth century, as Novgorod regained some of her lost independence and as the princes of Vladimir lost much of their power, Novgorod was ruled and defended by whoever happened to be the strongest contestant for the grand-princely throne, the right of the grand prince of Vladimir to the throne of Novgorod was a recognized principle— at any rate among the princes of Suzdalia, if not amongst the Novgorodians themselves.

It must not be assumed of course that relations between prince and republic were always smooth. They were not, especially in the early decades of the thirteenth century when the Suzdalian princes were sufficiently strong to abuse their terms of contract in an attempt to assert their authority and to subjugate Novgorod to themselves. While the princes brazenly disregarded the rules and sought to acquire ever greater control over Novgorod, the republic struggled to diminish their powers and to reduce them to the role of mere mercenaries hired to defend the frontier. It might be asked why the Novgorodians could not do without such tiresome "rulers" whose economic and political influence within the republic they were always trying to lessen. The answer is that they could not dispense entirely with the princes' military

[1] *PSRL*, x, p. 144.

aid. Novgorod was incapable of defending her own frontiers against her aggressive neighbours in the west and in the north. The more threatening the position on the frontiers, the more necessary became the presence of the prince and the more arbitrarily could he afford to behave. Nor could they refuse the offer or the demand of a prince to rule them when that prince could effectively hamper their trade and ruin their economy by simply blocking the Tvertsa river.

It might also be asked what benefit the prince-mercenary could hope to extract from controlling the turbulent republic: his powers were considerably lessened by the terms of his contract; he was unable to acquire manpower or land in Novgorod territory; he was shorn of his old rights to judge and administer; he was restricted in his dealings with foreign merchants.[1] Why then did the princes of north-east Russia struggle so desperately throughout the thirteenth and fourteenth centuries to retain even a nominal control over Novgorod? And why was control over Novgorod so indispensable an adjunct to the power and authority of the grand prince of Vladimir?

In spite of the restrictions imposed by the treaties there was still immense financial profit to be had from ruling Novgorod. Instead of enriching himself at the expense of the Novgorodians by controlling the administration and the civil law-courts, the prince received an unspecified amount of tribute (*dar*) from all the provinces of Novgorod; his *tiyun* administered half the frontier districts of Volok Lamsky and Torzhok; and, as leader of the army, he could appropriate a substantial part of all military booty. But more important still than the perquisites of his office, the prince of Novgorod derived immense benefits from the fact that Novgorod was the main transit centre, the main sorting house, for east–west trade. Most imports and exports to and from the west had to pass through Novgorod. Furs and wax from Suzdalia and the northern territories went through the transit centre of Novgorod *en route* to the west; cloth, wool, flax, salt, precious and non-ferrous metals, the basic imports from Western

---

[1] *See*, for instance, the clause in the treaty between Novgorod and Yaroslav Yaroslavich (1270): "In the German court you shall have trade only through our brothers; you shall not shut the court, nor shall you post your police agents (*pristavov*) there" (*GVNiP*, p. 13).

Europe, all filtered through Novgorod on their way to the lands of north-east Russia. It would not be an exaggeration to say that the prince who controlled Novgorod was also in a position to control the economic life of the Lower lands.

Before leaving the question of how the grand prince of Vladimir managed to maintain his authority over the other princes of Suzdalia, one other source of power which he enjoyed during the thirteenth century must be mentioned, namely the support of the Church. Unfortunately very little is known about the activities, ecclesiastical or political, of the Churchmen of the thirteenth century in Suzdalia, particularly in the period immediately following the Tatar invasions. The metropolitans' seat was situated in Kiev until 1300, and although the heads of the Church visited their dioceses in north-east Russia not infrequently,[1] there is almost no extant information on their participation in the political life of the age. One incident, however, gives some indication of the support which the Church could lend the grand prince. In 1270 Metropolitan Kirill intervened in a serious conflict which had arisen between Grand Prince Yaroslav Yaroslavich and the Tatars on the one hand and the Novgorodians on the other. After Yaroslav had been expelled following a decision of the popular assembly, the metropolitan threatened the Novgorodians with excommunication unless they complied with the wishes of the grand prince and reinstated him as their ruler. "And the men of Novgorod obeyed the metropolitan . . . and Yaroslav sat upon the throne [again]."[2]

To what extent the grand princes in the thirteenth century were able to rely on such support in general, we do not know. But it is likely that the close collaboration and friendship between the same metropolitan, Kirill, and Aleksandr Nevsky resulted in substantial political aid to the latter. He demonstratively welcomed Aleksandr back from his visit to the Horde in 1252—

[1] Metropolitan Kirill, for example, spent most of his thirty years as metropolitan (1250–80) in Vladimir. From 1250 to 1274 he resided, when in Vladimir, in the Monastery of the Nativity of the Mother of God (Rozhdestvensky Monastery). (See Yu. K. Begunov, *Pamyatnik russkoy literatury xiii veka*, pp. 58–9.)

[2] *PSRL*, xxv, p. 149.

a visit which coincided with, if it did not actually result in, the despatch of two Tatar punitive forces against his brothers Grand Prince Andrey and Yaroslav and against Daniil of Galich (in south-west Rus')—and crowned him in Vladimir. "The metropolitan met him by the Golden Gates with crosses, together with all the priestly orders, and placed him upon the throne of his father Yaroslav."[1] With equal solemnity and ostentation he buried him and pronounced the funeral oration over him. It was undoubtedly one of his close associates who wrote the remarkable and tendentious *vita* of the prince[2]—remarkable in that it skilfully combined the genres of traditional hagiography and military tale, and tendentious in that it carefully camouflaged Aleksandr's more dubious acts of collaboration with the Tatars.

How significant the support of the Church was and to what extent this support aided the grand princes to maintain their power over the local princes throughout the thirteenth century can best be understood by considering the immense authority and respect enjoyed by the metropolitans, the subordination of all local bishops to them and the fact that the majority of those most influential moulders of political opinion, the compilers of chronicles, were employed by them. It might also be added that the Church, by the very fact that it recognized no political boundaries in so far as the landed possessions of abbots and bishops were scattered throughout Suzdalia, helped the grand prince to transcend frontiers within his state and in no small way to combat separatism among the principalities. As the princes of Moscow were later to learn to their great advantage, the support of the Church, particularly of the head of the Church, could be of great political value to whoever enjoyed it.

One final question remains to be answered before we can discuss the emergence of Tver' and Moscow as the leading principalities

---

[1] *PSRL*, xxv, p. 142.

[2] D. S. Likhachev has shown Metropolitan Kirill's close connection with the *Life* of Aleksandr Nevsky, by indicating the south-west Russian traits in the work (Kirill, before his consecration as metropolitan, was probably Daniil of Galich's chancellor). *See* D. S. Likhachev, "Galitskaya literaturnaya traditsiya". Yu. K. Begunov considers that the *Life* was written in 1282–3 in the Rozhdestvensky Monastery in Vladimir where Metropolitan Kirill had lived. (*See* Begunov, op. cit., p. 61.)

in Suzdalia at the turn of the century: how did the Tatars control and keep in subjection the north-east Russian lands during the first sixty years of their domination? This is a subject on which there is a large literature,[1] and it is not proposed to study the whole question here. It may, however, be helpful for the understanding of political conditions in the fourteenth century to consider certain aspects of the problem.

One of the deciding factors in the conflict between Moscow and Tver' was, as will be discussed in later chapters of this book, the attitude of the khans of the Golden Horde to the question of princely power in north-east Rus' and the degree of support they were prepared to lend to their vassals. Far more is known of the interrelation of khan and prince in the fourteenth century than in the previous period, but nevertheless we can obtain some idea of the control exercised by the khans over the princes of Suzdalia in the thirteenth century by piecing together fragmentary information from the chronicles, and by bearing in mind that while the policy of the khans *vis-à-vis* Suzdalia changed constantly in the light of the changing international situation, their method and technique of control remained fundamentally the same throughout the thirteenth and the fourteenth centuries.

No prince of Suzdalia was able to assume the title of grand prince of Vladimir without the permission of the khan of Kipchak, in some cases of the great khan, himself. The system of appointment was simple: at the death or murder of the ruling grand prince the prince who was next in line of succession presented himself at the Horde and was given the *yarlyk*,[2] or patent, to the throne of Vladimir. He was accompanied back to the capital by the khan's representatives (*posly*), who solemnly invested him with his dignity of office. The chronicles give a graphic, though somewhat embellished, picture of the first visit made by a prince to the Horde. In 1243 Yaroslav Vsevolodovich "went to the Tatars, to Baty, and sent his son Konstantin to the

---

[1] The leading works on the subject are: B. Spuler, *Die Goldene Horde*; B. D. Grekov and A. Yu. Yakubovsky, *Zolotaya Orda i ee padenie*; A. N. Nasonov, *Mongoly i Rus'*; G. Vernadsky, *The Mongols and Russia*.

[2] The term is not found until the fourteenth century. However, on the back of Yaroslav of Tver''s treaty with Novgorod (1270) are found the words: "*Posly* from Khan Mangu Timur arrived to enthrone (*sazhat*) Yaroslav *with a document* (*s gramotoyu*)" (*GVNiP*, No. 3, p. 11).

great khan [in Karakorum]. And Baty treated Yaroslav the Great and all his men with honour and let him go saying: 'O Yaroslav, be the senior amongst all the princes in the land of Rus'.'"[1] This was not the only visit a grand prince was obliged to make to Saray. He had to go whenever he was summoned by the khan, and also whenever a khan of the Golden Horde died: sometimes even the death of the great khan necessitated a trip to Karakorum in Mongolia. The ostensible aim of these visits was to congratulate the new khan and to renew the patent for the throne. At the same time it looks as though many, if not all, of the local princes were also required to visit Saray for the same purpose—to obtain permission to rule or at any rate to get a ratification for their title.[2]

Such obligatory visits to the Horde did not mean that the khans determined who should be grand prince. This was left almost entirely to the Russians to decide for themselves. The system of accession by seniority was allowed to function un- hampered. Only on one occasion was a prince given the *yarlyk* for Vladimir in preference to his elder brother—when Andrey Yaroslavich was made grand prince in 1249. But even then the circumstances were exceptional: on the death of Yaroslav Vsevolodovich (1246) Khan Baty gave his brother Svyatoslav the *yarlyk*. The widow of the great khan, however, disagreed with Baty's choice. She summoned Aleksandr and Andrey, Yaroslav's two eldest sons, to Karakorum. There Andrey was appointed grand prince of Vladimir, while Aleksandr was given "Kiev and all the land of Rus'".[3] No satisfactory explanation for this curious divison of power between the two eldest sons of Yaroslav has yet been given by historians; but it is evident that the breach of tradition can be ascribed exclusively to abnormal circumstances (the hostility between the great khan's widow Oghul-Gaymish and Baty) and not to the arbitrary decision of a khan to appoint a prince of his own choice.[4]

[1] *PSRL*, i, col. 470; *TL*, p. 321. *Cf.* the soberer account in *PSRL*, xxiii, p. 80, and xxv, p. 136.

[2] In 1244 three of the princes of Rostov went to Baty "about their patri- mony (*pro svoyu otchinu*)". "And Baty paid them due honour and dismissed them, having assigned (*rasudiv*) them each to his own patrimony" (*PSRL*, i, col. 470; *TL*, p. 321).

[3] *PSRL*, i, col. 472; *TL*, p. 322.

[4] V. T. Pashuto thinks that Oghul-Gaymish, the widow of Güyük and

The khans of the Golden Horde, then, were content in principle to permit their Russian subjects to choose who should rule. Of course there were certain limitations to this apparently liberal freedom of choice. Whoever was elected must be amenable to the khan and his advisers; the grand prince must rule in strict conformity with the desires of the khan; and above all he must countenance no signs of disobedience or revolt among his subjects. This is evident from the immediate punishment meted out to anyone who was not prepared to conform with the policy of the Horde. The best example of such action occurred in 1252 when Grand Prince Andrey was chased from Suzdalia by a Tatar expedition despatched by Baty's son and co-ruler Sartak. Some historians, in their anxiety not to tarnish the reputation of Aleksandr Nevsky, see in Andrey's expulsion merely a reversal of Mongol policy at the highest level: Oghul-Gaymish, Andrey's sponsor, was overthrown in 1251 or 1252 by Khan Mangu (Möngke), friend and creature of Baty. At the same time they attribute the support given to Aleksandr Nevsky to his rejection of the overtures of the pope.[1] These may well be valid reasons for the expedition of Nevryuy, as the Tatar general sent to oust Andrey was called; but the chronicles indicate that there was a far more cogent cause for Baty's decision: Andrey, according to the Laurentian Chronicle, "took council with his boyars [and decided] to flee rather than serve the khans";[2] they add that the

---

enemy of Baty, appointed Andrey over the heads of his uncle Svyatoslav, and his elder brother Aleksandr, because Baty had approved the accession of the former and because of Baty's links with the latter. (*See* V. T. Pashuto, *Ocherki*, p. 271.) Vernadsky, following Nasonov (*Mongoly i Rus'*, p. 33), thinks that Güyük appointed Andrey to Vladimir and Aleksandr to Kiev because he "wanted someone dependent on him to rule in West Russia". (*See* Vernadsky, *The Mongols and Russia*, p. 147.)

Note that the appointment of Andrey Aleksandrovich as grand prince in 1282 was due again to exceptional circumstances and must be ascribed to the diarchy within the Horde.

[1] Such are the views of Pashuto and Nasonov. (*See* Pashuto, *Ocherki*, pp. 271–2; Nasonov, *Mongoly i Rus'*, p. 34.) *Cf.* Vernadsky's explanation of the overthrow of Andrey (*Mongols*, p. 148).

[2] *PSRL*, i, col. 473; *TL*, p. 324. The plight of Andrey is deliberately heightened by the compiler of the sixteenth-century Nikon Chronicle, who puts the following words into his mouth: "O Lord, why do we quarrel amongst ourselves and lead the Tatars against one another! It would be

Tatars chased him as far as Pereyaslavl'-Zalessky, where they "seized the princess and children of Yaroslav (Yaroslavich of Tver')"; and they killed Yaroslav's *voevoda* Zhidislav there."[1] Other chronicles mention a fierce battle between Andrey and the Tatars at Pereyaslavl' and Andrey's flight first to Novgorod where he was not admitted and then to Sweden where he was received "with honour".[2] From this evidence it would appear that Andrey was determined to resist the Tatars and that he had at least one ally in the person of his brother, Prince Yaroslav Yaroslavich of Tver', the commander of whose army was killed at the battle of Pereyaslavl'. If we take into consideration the fact that in 1250 Andrey had allied himself with the staunchest enemy of the Tatars, Daniil of Galich, by marrying his daughter,[3] and the fact that at the same time as Nevryuy was attacking Andrey another Tatar expeditionary force under Kuremsa was marching against Daniil, it will become clear that Andrey, if he was not at the head of an anti-Tatar coalition, was at least unwilling to comply with Tatar demands, for which he was punished, and had two of the strongest Russian princes as his allies.[4]

Andrey was the exception. None of the other grand princes of the thirteenth century showed the slightest inclination to rebel against the overlordship of the Tatars. The Soviet historian Nasonov has, it is true, attempted to prove that Aleksandr Nevsky was the leader and inspirer of the great anti-Tatar uprisings of 1262,[5] but his arguments are unconvincing: Aleksandr's intimate connections with the khans of the Golden Horde, his uncompromising fulfilment of all their commands, his

---

better for me to flee to a foreign land than to be friends with, and serve, the Tatars" (*PSRL*, x, p. 138).

[1] *PSRL*, i, col. 473; *TL*, p. 324.

[2] *See PSRL*, xxiii, pp. 83–4; xxv, pp. 141–2. *Cf. NL*, p. 304 ("He fled to the Swedish land and they killed him(!)"). Note that there is no mention of Nevryuy's expedition and Andrey's expulsion in the older recension of the Novgorod First Chronicle.

[3] *See PSRL*, i, col. 472; *TL*, p. 323.

[4] Presnyakov is inclined to think that the betrothal of the daughter of Prince Vasily of Yaroslavl' to Fedor of Mozhaysk was "linked with the plans of Prince Andrey Yaroslavich, who sought a union of Russian princes against the Tatars". (Presnyakov, *Obrazovanie*, p. 61, note 1.)

[5] *See* Nasonov, *Mongoly i Rus'*, pp. 52–3.

possible collusion with them in the despatch of Tatar punitive forces against Andrey and Daniil, his close collaboration with Tatar officials in north-east Russia, all make him an improbable rebel leader. Indeed it is more likely that his last trip to the Horde in 1262 was made to beg Khan Berke not to punish the Russians for the rebellions, a mission in which he was eminently successful.

The amenability of the grand princes was one valid reason why the khans refrained from meddling in their vassals' system of succession. Provided the grand princes were prepared to rule as the khans wanted them to, the khans for their part were prepared to allow them to adhere to the old traditions of handing down the throne. They were prepared to go even farther and to assist the rulers of Vladimir by physically removing their rivals, particularly if the latter had dangerous links with the enemies of the Horde. Yaroslav Vsevolodovich, for example, was rid of his most intelligent, imaginative and powerful rival, Mikhail of Chernigov, whose considerable connections with the Hungarian and Polish courts led indirectly to his execution at the Horde in 1246, an execution in which Yaroslav probably played a role.[1] And it may well be that one of the causes of Andrey Yaroslavich's removal was his alliance with a West-Russian prince of known pro-Catholic sympathies.

A second reason for the Tatars' willingness to allow the Russians to choose their candidates for the throne and their readiness to strengthen their position once they were appointed is the fact that the grand princes were territorially and militarily weak. None of them had sufficient strength to offer effective opposition to the Horde; none of them, with the possible exception of Andrey Yaroslavich, ever looked like being capable of uniting all Suzdalia under one strong principality. The explanation for this has been given above: the grand princes did not have sufficiently strong links with their own *otchiny* to allow them to develop them at the expense of the other family possessions. Consequently there was no need for the khans to play off one principality against another; better to have a relatively strong, efficient, and, at the same time, amenable grand prince ruling a relatively weak federation of principalities, each as powerless as

[1] *See* Pashuto, *Ocherki*, p. 270.

its neighbour, than to support one prince at the expense of his brother or cousin. A civil war in Suzdalia at this stage was of no use to the Horde. It was only when two sufficiently powerful principalities arose that the khan found it necessary to adjust the balance between the two rival leaders by supporting now the one, now the other. Later, when the menace of Lithuania became a reality, the Tatars were obliged to revert to their old policy of the thirteenth century and to lend support to one prince of Suzdalia, and to one prince alone, in order to provide a bulwark against the West. But by then circumstances had changed: the prince in question, Ivan I, was not merely grand prince of Vladimir; he was also prince of Moscow.

Although it is possible to form some idea of the overall control exercised by the khans and their agents over the system of government in north-east Russia, the details of this control are unfortunately missing. We know that the princes applied to the khan for permission to rule and that his plenipotentiaries (*posly*) accompanied the princes to their capitals where they not only enthroned them but presumably remained permanently at their courts, keeping a watching brief for the khan; we know that Tatar officials called *baskaki* were stationed in various centres of strategic importance and that as commanders of small part-Tatar part-Russian detachments they were responsible for maintaining order in troublesome districts, quelling rebellions and supporting tax-collectors[1] with force if needs be; we know that they or their representatives were present at all princely conventions. But we do not know to what extent the princes were obliged to consult the khan or his representatives before undertaking any military or political venture. There were, as has been pointed out above,[2] occasional instances of Russian expeditionary forces under Russian commanders—i.e. with no Tatar troops or Tatar generals attached—but it would be naïve to imagine that there was no Tatar supervision on such occasions, no Tatar

[1] For the vexed question of when the princes acquired the right to collect Tatar tribute from their own subjects, *see* Nasonov, *Mongoly i Rus'*, pp. 77–8. Nasonov is of the opinion that Grand Prince Dmitry Aleksandrovich was the first grand prince to collect tribute, which he sent to Nogay. For Ivan I's collection of tribute from the Novgorod colonies of Vychegda and Pechora, *see* below, p. 140, note 3.

[2] *See* above, p. 25.

agents attached to the various headquarters, or that the expedition had not the approval of the khan. Indeed, we must assume that no independent military or political undertaking could be carried out without consultation with Tatar officials; there could be no independent relations with extra-Suzdalian districts, and above all with the West, without the permission of the khan. An independent policy, in fact, was impossible. The grand princes of the second half of the thirteenth century ruled, fought their wars, summoned their relatives to congresses and mustered their troops, only with the knowledge and the approval of the khans.

While the khans and their representatives exercised the tightest possible control over the actions of the princes of Suzdalia, paradoxically (and short-sightedly) they showed an astonishing tolerance where the Church was concerned. The reasons for this tolerance are beyond the scope of this book,[1] but it may prove helpful to consider briefly what forms this tolerance took and to discuss the results of the Tatars' benevolent attitude towards the Church.

Religious tolerance consisted by and large in the exemption of the Russian Church from the Tatar taxation system, the protection of Church property from would-be secularizers and the avoidance of deliberate persecution of the Church by the Tatars themselves.[2] The khans issued a series of charters (*yarlyki*) to the metropolitans, in which the precise terms of the privileges granted by the Tatars to the Church were laid down.[3] These documents, which were translated into Russian only when tax-collecting was entrusted to the Russians themselves,[4] were used by metropolitans, bishops

[1] Pashuto advances the theory that one of the aims of the Tatars in showing tolerance towards the Church was to oblige the Church to help them achieve political mastery over the princes, and that the clergy repaid their masters by toning down anti-Tatar tendencies in the literature of the day. (*See* Pashuto, *Ocherki*, pp. 275–6.)

[2] For examples of the Tatars' "protection" of the Church, *see* V. Milyutin, *O nedvizhimykh imushchestvakh*, pp. 36 sq.

[3] There are six extant genuine *yarlyki* (1267–1379). For an excellent textological study of their various redactions, *see* A. A. Zimin, "Kratkoe i prostrannoe sobraniya"; L. V. Cherepnin, *RFA*, vol. ii, pp. 53–9. The *yarlyki* are printed in *Pamyatniki russkogo prava*, vol. iii, pp. 465–70.

[4] *See* Zimin, op. cit., pp. 33–4.

and abbots as safeguards for their property, particularly in the sixteenth century when the Church's possessions were threatened not by the Tatars but by the state. So useful indeed did the *yarlyki* prove that at the end of the 1540's, at a time when the Church was very much on the defensive concerning her vast estates, an additional *yarlyk*, allegedly issued by Khan Uzbek to Metropolitan Petr, was forged, in which the Church was granted considerable privileges which the Tatar khans had never included in their charters.[1]

The results of the Tatars' tolerant attitude towards the Russian Church are not hard to perceive. Not only did the authority, prestige and political importance of the Church and the hierarchy increase at the expense of the unprivileged lay landowner and ruler, whose lands enjoyed no such indemnity and immunity and were open to devastation by Tatars and neighbours alike, but also the Church experienced an immense growth of wealth, of possessions both movable and immovable. Free from crippling taxation and secure in the knowledge that their estates were immune from outside interference, the abbots and bishops were able to attract agricultural labour to their lands and to increase their territory. At the same time monastic lands grew, thanks to the generosity of private landowners. In the age of depression following the Tatar invasions many a landowner turned to religion for spiritual and physical comfort, entered a monastery and bestowed his estates upon the abbot; while those who were unwilling to take so irrevocable a step could always grant their possessions to the monastery on condition that their souls be prayed for by the brethren in perpetuity—or as long as the grant lasted. Indeed, this religious urge to save one's soul by means of generous donations, an urge doubtless encouraged by the more acquisitive abbots, was responsible for a considerable flow of property from private to ecclesiastical hands.

This vast political and economic strengthening of the Church, which resulted directly and indirectly from the Tatars' policy of religious tolerance and from the economic conditions prevailing

---

[1] Some historians, taking Uzbek's charter to be genuine, have greatly exaggerated the privileges granted by the Tatars to the Russian Church in the thirteenth and fourteenth centuries. (*See*, for instance, A. V. Kartashev, *Ocherki*, vol. i, pp. 286–8; J. Blum, *Lord and Peasant*, p. 75.)

in north-east Russia after the Tatar invasion, had in its turn far-reaching consequences: it led ultimately to the centralization of the state, or at any rate was one of the most powerful factors in the unification of the state. A strong, rich and unified Church helped to break down political barriers, to neutralize separatist tendencies and to assist the centralizing aims of the grand princes. In the fourteenth century the abbots and bishops, not only of north-east Russia but of all Orthodox districts under the jurisdiction of the metropolitan, tended to show less allegiance and loyalty to a local prince than to the grand prince of Vladimir, who more often than not was working hand in glove with the metropolitan. And the stronger the power of the Church became, the more the secular authorities used it to further their own political ends. Thus, paradoxically, the Tatars, by strengthening and enriching the Church largely at the expense of the state, contributed to the centralization and unification of the state and so to the eventual overthrow of Tatar rule. Paradoxically, too, the state was eventually to suffer from the flow of land from private ownership to possession by the Church, which itself had been one of the consequences of Tatar rule and Tatar generosity. In the great age of land-hunger, the sixteenth century, when the state required the vast possessions of the Church to satisfy the needs of the new service nobility for *pomest'ya*, the grand princes were to find to their dismay that whereas it was reasonably easy to dispossess a layman, it was extremely difficult to lay hands on the latifundia of the Church. For the Church had surrounded her possessions with an aura of sanctity and her great polemicists had elaborated irrefutable theories, demonstrating the inviolability and inalienability of Church lands. Not the least of the weapons brandished by the defenders of Church possessions who were threatened by confiscation were the *yarlyki* themselves. For generations they remained living in the memory of the clergy, long after their practical use had disappeared. "Many of the impious khans," Metropolitan Makary reminded Ivan IV in 1550, "took nothing from the holy churches and monasteries, nor did they dare to move things immovable . . . but they gave their *yarlyki* to the holy metropolitans, forbidding anyone to offend or remove the land of the monasteries and the churches. . . ." After enumerating the various *yarlyki*, including the spurious charter of Uzbek, he concluded: "How much more is it befitting for you, O tsar, to show great zeal towards the holy churches and monasteries. Not only should you refrain from confiscating their lands; but you should grant them lands yourself!"[1]

Already in the last decade of the thirteenth century Moscow and Tver' were showing clear signs of political and economic superiority over all the other Suzdalian districts. While Andrey Aleksandrovich, the last "uncommitted" grand prince of Vladimir—that is to say, the last of the Vsevolodovichi to have no strong *otchina* behind him—was able to command the obedience and loyalty of the minor princes of what once had been the land of Rostov (Rostov, Yaroslavl', Uglich and Beloozero),[2] he was opposed by a powerful coalition consisting of Moscow, Tver' and Pereyaslavl'. There is no mention of any of the other principalities of Suzdalia in the struggle for ascendancy: Yur'ev, Starodub, Nizhny Novgorod, Suzdal', Galich, Dmitrov are barely mentioned in the chronicles at this period, and not one of them had the slightest claim to power. Pereyaslavl' was soon to become a temporary annexe of Moscow after the death of Grand Prince Dmitry's son Ivan without issue in 1302. Only the princes of Moscow and Tver' had sufficiently strong *otchiny* behind them to enable them to compete for supreme authority. How did these two principalities achieve such eminence? Why were they stronger than any of the other *otchiny* belonging to the descendants of Vsevolod III? To answer this question we must first of all examine the past history of Moscow and Tver' and trace their development and growth up to the end of the thirteenth century.

Moscow is first mentioned in the chronicles under the year 1147. From the brief account of a meeting between Yury Dolgoruky of Suzdal' and three princes of Chernigov,[3] it appears that Moscow was part of the principality of Rostov-Suzdal', a village or a small town on its western borders. As a nodal traffic point between

[1] *LRLD*, vol. v, section 3, pp. 129–36.
[2] *See* the list of princes who accompanied Andrey Aleksandrovich to the Horde in 1293 to complain of Dmitry Aleksandrovich (*PSRL*, x, pp. 168–9).
[3] *See PSRL*, ii, cols. 339–40.

Ryazan' and Chernigov in the south and Vladimir-on-the-Klyaz'ma in the north, the importance of Moscow grew rapidly during the second half of the twelfth century. It was fortified—that is to say, converted into a *gorod*, or stronghold—probably in the 1150's, as part, no doubt, of Yury Dolgoruky's extensive campaign of building strategic and mercantile centres in the southern and western areas of his principality.[1] At any rate we know that by 1177, when Gleb of Ryazan' burned Moscow to the ground, it was already provided with fortifications.[2]

When Vsevolod III died in 1212, Moscow presumably passed to his son and successor on the throne of Vladimir, Yury, as part of the district of Vladimir. During the inter-princely feuds which followed Vsevolod's death, the fourth eldest living son of Vsevolod, Vladimir, took refuge in Moscow after fleeing from his patrimony of Yur'ev, with which he was evidently dissatisfied. While he was there, he carried out an abortive campaign "with the Muscovites and with his army (*druzhinoyu*)" against the near-by stronghold of Dmitrov.[3] Eventually in 1213 he was dislodged from Moscow by Yury and sent off to the political backwater of Southern Pereyaslavl'. Moscow again became the possession of the grand prince. In January 1238, when the Tatars moving north after the sack of Ryazan' reached Moscow, they found it defended by an army. The *voevoda*, one Filip Nyan'ko, was killed and the youngest son of the grand prince, Vladimir, who was either ruling in Moscow or was in command of the local forces, was captured. The Tatars "slaughtered all the inhabitants, from old men to infants at the breast; and they set fire to the fortress and the holy churches, and they burned all the monasteries and villages."[4] Even allowing for a certain amount of epic exaggeration characteristic of the mediaeval Russian relation of disasters, it is clear that Moscow was by now a large town; it is significant that it was the first objective of the Tatars after Ryazan'. For an enemy advancing from the south Moscow was one of the keys to the whole of Suzdalia: without subduing Moscow, no enemy could move eastwards down the Klyaz'ma to Vladimir.

[1] *See* M. N. Tikhomirov, *Drevnyaya Moskva*, p. 15.
[2] *See* PSRL, i, col. 382: *"pozzhe gorod ves' i sela"*.
[3] *See Letopisets Pereyaslavlya Suzdal'skogo*, pp. 111–12.
[4] *PSRL*, i, cols. 460–1.

During the forty-five years following the Tatar invasions of
1237–8 almost nothing is known of Moscow. There are slender
indications that the town and district may have been given by
Grand Prince Svyatoslav Vsevolodovich to a nephew, Mikhail
Yaroslavich, when, in 1247 Svyatoslav, "distributed his nephews
among the towns, as their father Yaroslav had decreed".[1] Two
chronicles call Mikhail, who drove out his uncle from the throne
of Vladimir only to be killed fighting the Lithuanians shortly
afterwards, "Mikhail of Moscow".[2] Whether or not this provides
sufficient evidence to call Mikhail the "first appanage prince of
Moscow"[3] is relatively unimportant, for we know nothing of the
fate of Moscow during the thirty-three years following his death.
If he was in fact prince of Moscow, then we must assume that
the newly-created principality reverted as an escheat to the grand
prince on his death in 1248, for he left no heirs.

The first of the Vsevolodovichi who can incontestably be called
prince of Moscow was Aleksandr Nevsky's youngest son, Daniil.
It is not known when he was given Moscow as an *otchina*. Under
the year 1282 Daniil is mentioned in the chronicles as taking part
in the feudal war between his two elder brothers "together with
the Muscovites";[4] a much later source, the sixteenth-century
Stepennaya kniga, says that Daniil was given Moscow by his
father,[5] in other words, between 1261 when he was born and
1263 when Aleksandr Nevsky died. Yet another source, the
Suprasl'sky Chronicle, says that when Daniil died in 1303 he had
"ruled for eleven years".[6] Nor do we know how big the surrounding territory was. We can, however, guess from later evidence
that the original territory consisted of the basin of the upper
waters of the Moskva river between the influx of the Gzhel' in
the east and just west of the influx of the Ruza river in the west.

---

[1] *PSRL*, i, col. 471.

[2] *PSRL*, iv (i), p. 290; xv, col. 395.

[3] *See*, for example, A. V. Ekzemplyarsky, *VUK*, vol. ii, p. 273.

[4] *See PSRL*, xxv, p. 154. *Cf.* the sixteenth-century Nikon Chronicle which
calls him "Grand Prince Daniil of Moscow" (*PSRL*, x, p. 160).

[5] *See PSRL*, xxi, p. 296.

[6] *See PSRL*, xvii, p. 27. Tikhomirov thinks that "11" may be a scribe's
error for "21", in which case 1282–3 would be the date of his accession to the
"throne" of Moscow. (*See* Tikhomirov, *Drevnyaya Moskva*, p. 23.)

In the eastern and northern parts of the territory was the basin of the upper Klyaz'ma as far east as the influx of the Dubna river (*see* Map B).

Whether Daniil obtained the principality of Moscow in 1261–3, 1282–3 or 1293 is of relatively little importance to its history. What is important is the fact that the chronicle entries at the turn of the century show that the principality of Moscow had assumed a leading role in Suzdalian affairs and that the youngest son, whom Klyuchevsky has described as "deprived of rights and inheritance",[1] a kind of outlaw within the princely family, was now able to compete on equal terms with his brothers and cousins. Indeed, the Soviet historian M. N. Tikhomirov has described Daniil at the Congress of Vladimir in 1297 as standing "as it were at the head of the princely group struggling against [Grand Prince] Andrey Aleksandrovich".[2] This may be an exaggeration: the Trinity Chronicle does, it is true, mention him first amongst the anti-Andrey coalition ("on the other side stood Prince Daniil Aleksandrovich of Moscow and his cousin Mikhaylo Yaroslavich of Tver' and with them all the Pereyaslavlians to a man"),[3] but then the compiler of the pro-Moscow Trinity Chronicle would not have missed an opportunity to extol the progenitor of the house of Moscow. However, the events which followed the Congress of Vladimir show to what extent the other princes were now obliged to reckon with Daniil as one of the leading figures in the struggle for power.

The Congress of Vladimir had met to decide whom Pereyaslavl' belonged to, Grand Prince Andrey or Ivan Dmitrievich, who had "inherited" it from his father when the latter died in 1294. In spite of the presence of Tatar *posly* the congress almost ended in bloodshed. However, the bishops of Vladimir and Saray[4] intervened and an agreement was reached.[5] It was evidently decided that Pereyaslavl' was the possession of Ivan Dmitrievich, who immediately set off to the Horde to ratify his claim on the district, having requested Mikhail of Tver' to watch over his

---

[1] Klyuchevsky, *Sochineniya*, vol. ii, p. 15.
[2] Tikhomirov, *Drevnyaya Moskva*, p. 24.
[3] *TL*, p. 348.
[4] In 1261 the diocese of Saray was founded by Metropolitan Kirill.
[5] *See PSRL*, i, col. 484; xxv, p. 158; *TL*, pp. 347–8.

"patrimony" during his absence.[1] The grand prince had no intention of abiding by the decisions of the congress. He determined to seize Pereyaslavl' and then march on Moscow and Tver'. However, Daniil and Mikhail managed to prevent him from reaching Pereyaslavl' by blocking his path at Yur'ev-Pol'sky, half-way between Vladimir and Pereyaslavl'. Andrey was forced to give in and to acknowledge Ivan's right to Pereyaslavl'.

The question of Pereyaslavl' was by no means settled by the agreement of Yur'ev. In 1301 it was found necessary to hold another congress, this time in Dmitrov. The chronicles say little about the results of the congress: they merely mention a quarrel which had arisen between Ivan Dmitrievich and Mikhail. Again the prince of Moscow was present. His support for Ivan Dmitrievich of Pereyaslavl' was the deciding factor in the outcome of the congress. Opposed by the grand prince and Mikhail of Tver', Ivan Dmitrievich nevertheless managed to retain his hold over Pereyaslavl'. Neither the grand prince of Vladimir nor the prince of Tver' made any move to interfere in what was evidently looked on as a powerful alliance between Daniil and his nephew.[2]

Daniil's support of Ivan Dmitrievich was a shrewd political move: it ingratiated him both with the prince and with the inhabitants of Pereyaslavl'. Ivan died childless in 1302. The Trinity Chronicle says that "he gave his blessing to Prince Daniil of Moscow to rule in his place in Pereyaslavl', for he loved him more than all others."[3] Of course the information of the tendentiously pro-Moscow compiler of the Trinity Chronicle must be taken with a pinch of salt. The sober and factual Laurentian Chronicle makes no mention of any testamentary bequest;[4] and it is probable that Daniil was in fact obliged to seize Pereyaslavl' by force, as Andrey's *namestniki* had already installed

---

[1] See ibid. Cf. the Nikon Chronicle (*PSRL*, x, p. 171), according to which Ivan Dmitrievich entrusted Pereyaslavl' to Mikhail *and* Daniil.

[2] For the Congress of Dmitrov, see *PSRL*, i, cols. 485–6; *TL*, p. 349.

[3] *TL*, p. 350 (under 1303). Repeated in *PSRL*, xxv, p. 393 (under 1302). For further embroidery, see *PSRL*, x, p. 174. Note that in the Moscow *svod* of 1479 (*PSRL*, xxv) Pereyaslavl' is called Ivan Dmitrievich's *patrimony* (*otchina*).

[4] See *PSRL*, i, col. 486. Cf. the Ermolinsky Chronicle (*PSRL*, xxiii, p. 95) which states that "Ivan gave Pereyaslavl' to his uncle Danilo".

themselves there. Whatever the nature of Ivan's feelings towards his uncle and whatever means Daniil may have employed in order to take possession of Pereyaslavl', the inhabitants of the district showed no hesitation in opting for Yury Danilovich of Moscow, when Daniil himself died in 1303.[1] By diplomatic skill and by force of arms Daniil of Moscow had temporarily attached the immensely fertile and strategically important district of Pereyaslavl' to the *otchina* of Moscow.[2]

Of still greater, and more lasting, importance than the temporary annexation of Pereyaslavl' was the seizure of Kolomna and Mozhaysk. Kolomna, near the influx of the Moskva river into the Oka, as well as Serpukhov and the basins of the rivers Nara and Lopasnya, were probably incorporated into the territory of Moscow in 1301 or shortly afterwards, as a result of Daniil's successful campaign against Ryazan'. At the battle of Pereyaslavl'-Ryazansky (autumn 1301) Daniil defeated the Ryazanites, who appear to have been supported by Tatars, and captured Grand Prince Konstantin "by a certain cunning method".[3] In 1304 the district of Mozhaysk was seized from Smolensk by Daniil's sons.[4] The Soviet historian Cherepnin has described the results of this momentous increase in territory in the first four years of the fourteenth century as follows:

The annexation [of Kolomna, Pereyaslavl' and Mozhaysk] to the principality of Moscow increased its land almost threefold. No less important was the economic and strategic

[1] *See* below, p. 61, note 6.

[2] For the economic and strategic importance of Pereyaslavl', *see* Nasonov, *Mongoly i Rus'*, pp. 94–5; A. M. Sakharov, *Goroda SVR*, pp. 34 sq. M. N. Tikhomirov thinks that Daniil obtained Dmitrov at the same time as Pereyaslavl'. There is, however, no justification for his supposition. David Konstantinovich of Galich (d. 1280) is called by the chroniclers prince of Galich *and* Dmitrov, and there is no reason to believe that his brother Vasily, who ruled from 1280 to *c.* 1310, was not also prince of Dmitrov. At any rate he was succeeded by David's two sons, Fedor of Galich and Boris of Dmitrov. (*See* Tikhomirov, *Drevnyaya Moskva*, p. 24.)

[3] *See TL,* p. 350; *PSRL,* i, col. 486; xxiii, p. 95. *Cf.* x, p. 173. None of the chroniclers mention the annexation of Kolomna; it is simply referred to at a later date as a possession of the prince of Moscow. It is possible that the annexation of Kolomna was formally acknowledged in 1306. *See* below, p. 66.

[4] *See TL,* p. 351.

significance of the annexed districts. The river Moskva in all its length was now included in the principality of Moscow. Situated on its upper waters, Mozhaysk became the most important strongpoint on Moscow's western border. Possessing Moscow and Kolomna, the Moscow government was able to make use of the advantageous position of Moscow as a junction of the most important roads.[1]

Thus by 1304 the territory of the principality of Moscow had become a self-sufficient economic unit based on the whole length of the Moskva river together with all its tributaries; its southern borders included a considerable stretch of the Oka river, from Serpukhov to east of Kolomna, which afforded a certain measure of protection from Tatar incursions from the south and enabled Moscow to have free access to the northern areas of Ryazan'; and through the eastern portion of the principality flowed the waters of the upper Klyaz'ma, providing direct access to Vladimir. In political stature the prince of Moscow had grown immeasurably. He was able not only to command the respect of his brothers and cousins but even to fight and defeat the Tatars with impunity,[2] a feat which none of his successors dared to or were able to perform for three quarters of a century.

Of the early history of Tver' even less is known than of that of Moscow. While the chronicles give abundant information on the princes of Tver' during the second half of the thirteenth century, this information practically never concerns Tver' itself or the districts of Tver'. We know much about the activities of Yaroslav Yaroslavich and Mikhail Yaroslavich in Novgorod, Vladimir, Pereyaslavl' and the Horde; but we know next to nothing about how Tver' itself was ruled.

Tver' is first mentioned in the chronicles under the year 1209 when it was evidently used as a base for the expedition of the sons of Vsevolod III against Mstislav Mstislavich the Bold, who was occupying Torzhok.[3] It was evidently the extreme western outpost of the grand principality of Vladimir at the time. Whether

[1] Cherepnin, *Obrazovanie*, p. 460. *See* Map B.
[2] Viz. at the battle of Pereyaslavl'-Ryazansky in 1301.
[3] *See PSRL*, i, col. 435.

Tver' was a dependency of the grand prince himself during the first half of the thirteenth century or whether it was a *prigorod* of Pereyaslavl'-Zalessky[1] cannot be said for certain. In 1238 it was destroyed by the Tatars; the chronicles make no mention of the presence of a prince there.

The first known Vsevolodovich to rule in Tver' was the sixth son of Grand Prince Yaroslav Vsevolodovich, Yaroslav Yaroslavich, who from 1263 to 1271 was grand prince of Vladimir. When he was given Tver' is not known; it was probably in 1246, when Svyatoslav allocated the towns of Suzdalia to his nephews according to Yaroslav Vsevolodovich's will.[2]

As to the size of his principality, again nothing whatsoever is known. As, however, there is no information of any annexations made by its rulers during the entire history of Tver' as an independent state, it can be assumed that the boundaries were much the same in the mid-thirteenth century as they were in the fourteenth and fifteenth centuries (*see* Map B). The principality stretched on either side of the upper reaches of the Volga from just east of the Kalyazin monastery on the Volga and Kashin on the Kashinka river to Zubtsov and Opoki in the west. Tver' itself is situated at the confluence of the Tvertsa and Volga rivers—in other words at the junction of the main river route from Novgorod and the Volga. In the south the principality included the basin of the Shosha river and the most important tributary of the Shosha river, the Lama, at the source of which began the portage of the Ruza and the Moskva rivers; it also included most of the Dubna, all of the latter's tributary, the Sestra, and the upper waters of the Nerl' river, the river-route to Pereyaslavl'.

Almost the only information of importance concerning the principality during the reign of Yaroslav Yaroslavich is the establishment of an eparchy in Tver'. No details are available. All we know is that the first bishop was called Simeon, that he was connected with Polotsk[3] and that he buried Yaroslav in 1271.[4]

[1] In 1215 Yaroslav Vsevolodovich, who at the time was prince of Pereyaslavl', used Tver' to imprison two of his enemies in. (*See PSRL*, xxv, p. 110.)

[2] *See PSRL*, i, col. 471. There is no mention of Yaroslav Yaroslavich or Tver' under this date. He is first mentioned as "Yaroslav prince of Tver'" under the year 1254 when he fled to Ladoga. (*See* ibid., col. 473.)

[3] *See* E. Golubinsky, *IRTs*, vol. ii, part 2, p. 29.

[4] *See TL*, p. 331.

After Yaroslav's death his son Svyatoslav ruled Tver'. From the complete silence of the chroniclers we can only assume that his reign was a peaceful one. He died early in the 1280's and was succeeded by his only surviving brother Mikhail, the first in a long line of Tver''s great princes.

The frequent references to Mikhail Yaroslavich in the chronicles during the twenty years before his accession to the throne of Vladimir (1304) and the leading role which he played in the interprincely feuds of the eighties and nineties of the thirteenth century show beyond a doubt that Tver' had become one of the strongest of all the *otchiny* of Suzdalia, indeed the only *otchina* capable of competing with Moscow for leadership among the principalities of north-east Russia. So great indeed was Mikhail's authority that he was able to draw up a treaty with Novgorod, according to the terms of which the republic promised to assist him in case of attack by Grand Prince Andrey or the Tatars in return for Tverite assistance "should there be any offence to Novgorod".[1]

The bare outline of the political history of the two principalities in the second half of the thirteenth century does not of course satisfactorily answer the question: why did Moscow and Tver' achieve ascendancy over the other principalities? Why did not Suzdal', say, or Nizhny Novogorod or Rostov or Yaroslavl' emerge as the strongest state? Clearly the answer is not to be found in any of the facts given us by the chronicles. As has been seen, it was not just a question of genealogical superiority which helped Moscow or Tver'. True, the founder of the house of Tver' occupied the throne of Vladimir in his own right for eight years, during which time he showed a remarkable political activity in north-east Russia; but there are no indications that he used his authority to build up Tver', to strengthen her defences or to increase her territory. His recorded actions were the actions of a grand prince of Vladimir rather than of a prince of Tver'. Moscow, the *otchina* of the youngest son in the family, was not

---

[1] See GVNiP, Nos. 4–5, pp. 13–15. The treaty was probably concluded at the time of either the Congress of Dmitrov (1301) or the Congress of Vladimir (1296). Cherepnin, who summarizes the views of historians on the question of its dating, thinks it was drawn up just after the death of Dmitry Aleksandrovich (1293). (See Cherepnin, RFA, vol. i, pp. 267–8.)

ruled by a grand prince until 1317. Nor did the Church noticeably
lend its aid either to Tver' or to Moscow before the beginning of
the fourteenth century. The metropolitans of the thirteenth
century, as we have seen above, tended to support the grand
princes as grand princes and to help them maintain their authority
over their subjects rather than to bolster up the claims of any
individual principality to political leadership.

In order, then, to explain the phenomenon of the rise of Moscow and Tver' at the end of the thirteenth century, we must
look for clues elsewhere. Unfortunately, however, the available
sources are singularly unhelpful on questions of economic and
social history: there are barely any details of trade, few extant
treaties which mention the activities of merchants, tax-collectors
or customs officers and little reliable information on growth or
decrease in population in the period under consideration. Too
little is known of agricultural conditions—the availability of
labour, productivity, agricultural technique, etc.—during the
years following the Tatar invasions to enable us to compare conditions in the various districts of Suzdalia. The sources give too
few indications of land-ownership, colonizing activity, city crafts,
food prices, markets or inter-monastery trade for us to be able to
draw any useful conclusions concerning the economy of the lands
of Moscow and Tver', let alone the lesser principalities. Certain
conclusions, however, can be drawn from an investigation of the
road and river communications in the two districts and from a
consideration of the strategic advantages afforded by their
geographical situation.

Moscow, as has been pointed out by generations of historians,[1]
lies in the geographical and ethnographical centre of the densely
populated mesopotamian district between the Volga and Oka
rivers and in the centre of a convenient road and river transport
system. The main commercial and military artery was the Moskva
river, which crossed the larger, western, portion of the principality, flowing from west to east and dividing the coniferous forests
of the north from the belt of mixed forests in the south. The

[1] The most lucid exposition of Moscow's geographical situation is to be
found in Klyuchevsky's famous Lecture XXI (*Sochineniya*, vol. ii, pp. 8–13).
Cf. Tikhomirov, *Drevnyaya Moskva*; Cherepnin, *Obrazovanie*, pp. 456–7;
Sakharov, *Goroda SVR*, pp. 82 sq.

importance of the Moskva river as a thoroughfare for all types of traffic cannot be overstressed. By means of its various tributaries it connected the district of Moscow with all the surrounding principalities. To the south Moscow was connected with the Oka river by the Pakhra and the Nara rivers which were joined by a short portage.[1] As Tikhomirov has pointed out, throughout the early period of her history Moscow lay on the main route from Ryazan' to Vladimir; owing to impenetrable forests and marshes a more direct way between the two cities was impossible.[2] After the annexation of Kolomna at the beginning of the fourteenth century communications with the Oka and thence via the Volga to the Caspian were considerably simplified by the incorporation of the whole of the Moskva river into the principality of Moscow. Connection with the upper Volga was effected through the Ruza river, thence by portage to Volok Lamsky and along the Lama and Shosha rivers. As for the Klyaz'ma river, on which stood the capital Vladimir and which has been called "the most important trade route of the principality of Suzdalia",[3] its upper reaches ran through the eastern half of the principality and were connected with the Moskva river by the latter's two tributaries, the Istra and Yauza rivers. It is interesting to note that after the annexation of Kolomna the Yauza ceased to be used for regular river traffic—in the second half of the fourteenth century there were a number of dams and water-mills on the river and in its place the Muscovites began to use the Nerskaya river, which joins the Moskva north of Kolomna, and the southern tributary of the Klyaz'ma, the Ushna: between the two rivers a portage of not more than one kilometre was needed, as compared with the seven or eight kilometres of dry land between the Yauza and the Klyaz'ma.[4]

Moscow was provided not only with an excellent river network, which facilitated trade, but also with a natural defence system, which afforded protection on her three most vulnerable frontiers. On the east, some fifty to eighty kilometres from Moscow, was a dense forest zone which acted as a natural barrier against possible

[1] See *Podmoskov'e*, p. 30. Also *see* Map B.
[2] See Tikhomirov, *Drevnyaya Moskva*, p. 17.
[3] Tikhomirov, ibid., p. 15.
[4] See *Podmoskov'e*, pp. 28–30.

enemy attacks. Tikhomirov has pointed out that not only were
there no town-fortresses of any importance between Moscow and
Vladimir, but also there were no Tatar attacks on Moscow from
the east during the whole of the fourteenth and fifteenth centuries.[1] The western frontier was similarly protected by a belt of
dense forest and marshes to the west of Mozhaysk; and, again,
there was not one town of importance between Mozhaysk and
Vyaz'ma.[2] As for the south, after the annexation of Kolomna
Moscow acquired a natural frontier against the Tatars in the
shape of the Oka river.

The excellent trade routes running through the territory of
Moscow and the natural protection afforded by her frontiers had
far-reaching results. Moscow became not only a trading and
colonizing centre, but also a centre of attraction for the population
of more exposed outlying districts. The resulting increase in the
density of population led in its turn to a rise in the economy and
the creation of a more efficient and more numerous army.[3] Such
were the conditions essential for the emergence of a strong
principality.

The obvious economic advantage of the geographical position
of Tver' is that it lies on the Volga at the influx of the Tvertsa
river (see map B). Of all the trade routes from Novgorod to
mesopotamian Suzdalia and beyond—to the Caspian and the
East—by far the most convenient during the thirteenth and fourteenth centuries was the riverway up the Msta, thence by portage
to Vyshny Volochek and down the Tvertsa, through Novgorod's
gateway to the east, Torzhok, and thence as far as Tver'. From
Tver' there were two main routes to Moscow and the Oka river:
either by the Shosha and Lama rivers to Volok Lamsky and
thence via the Ruza to the Moskva; or by the more inconvenient
route along the Dubna–Sestra–Yakhroma rivers as far as the
portage to the upper Klyaz'ma, then by second portage to the
Moskva river.[4] As well as the main Msta–Tvertsa route Novgorod
also used the Msta–Medveditsa riverway to convey her merchants

---

[1] See M. N. Tikhomirov, Rossiya v XVI stoletii, pp. 106–7.
[2] See ibid., p. 106.
[3] See Cherepnin, Obrazovanie, pp. 456–7.
[4] See Zimin, "Novgorod i Volokolamsk," p. 107, note 40.

and goods to the Volga, a route which also passed through Tver' territory; while Bezhetsky Verkh, Novgorod's second "gateway" was linked to Kashin in the east of the distict of Tver' by the Kashinka river.[1] A glance at the map will show that Tver' was connected by her river network with numerous other Suzdalian centres—Uglich, Yaroslavl', Kostroma and Nizhny Novgorod on the Volga; Pereyaslavl'–Zalessky on the Western Nerl'; Vladimir via the Dubna and Klyaz'ma rivers; Dmitrov on the Yakhroma. Furthermore, there was easy access to Vyaz'ma and the northern districts of Smolensk along the Vazuza river, which joins the Volga near Zubtsov.

As far as natural defences are concerned, Tver' was in a less favourable position than Moscow. There were no great natural boundaries afforded by forests, marshes or rivers. Indeed, Tver' was singularly vulnerable to attack from any quarter, especially along her 100-kilometre frontier with Smolensk and Lithuania in the west and south-west. Yet the relative remoteness of her position from the southern frontiers of Suzdalia combined with the excellence of her communications naturally led to an influx of population, particularly in the period following the Tatar invasions,[2] just as Moscow's central position and immunity from attack attracted the inhabitants of the more vulnerable outlying areas.[3]

By 1304, at the beginning of the great struggle between Moscow and Tver', the first phase of which was to last for a quarter of a century, there was little to choose between the two principalities, politically, economically or geographically. There were at the time no obvious advantages which favoured one side, and no disadvantages which were to lead to the decline of the other. The superiority of Moscow's strategic position was to a large extent

[1] See Romanov, "Rodina Afanasiya Nikitina," p. 86.

[2] E.g. in 1293, just before the great Tatar invasion (*Dyudeneva rat'*), "the number of people who had fled to Tver' from other principalities and *volosti* had increased" (*TL*, p. 346).

[3] It should also be mentioned that culturally Tver' was one of the leading principalities at the beginning of the fourteenth century. Few cities could compete with her in architecture, art and literature. (*See* Sakharov, *Goroda SVR*, pp. 101 sq.; *Istoriya russkogo iskusstva*, vol. iii, pp. 20 sq.; O. I. Podobedova, *Miniatyury*, pp. 16 sq.)

counterbalanced by Tver''s control of the Volga, and particularly of the Tvertsa river. Both had leaders who had proved themselves, or were to prove themselves, as cunning, ruthless, resourceful and intelligent—all qualities essential for anyone engaged in the peculiarly savage cut-throat struggle for supremacy which was carried on throughout the first eighty years of the fourteenth century in north-east Russia. Neither principality was yet weakened by fragmentation: at the time of his accession Mikhail of Tver' had three infant children and no living brothers; Yury of Moscow had four younger brothers, none of whom ever appear to have been given what could be described as a patrimony or an appanage—they clearly assisted whoever was senior prince of Moscow and made no attempt to build up family nests for themselves in Zvenigorod, Kolomna or Mozhaysk. Neither principality can be said to have enjoyed any particular benefit from Church support, although the existence of a bishopric in Tver', while Moscow was merely part of the diocese of Vladimir, presumably gave Tver' a certain ecclesiastical seniority over Moscow and no doubt inclined Metropolitan Maksim to support Mikhail in the early stages of his struggle with Yury. Up to 1304 the Tatar khans had shown no disposition whatsoever to favour Tver' at the expense of Moscow, or vice versa. There is no evidence to show that the Tatars were aware of the rapidly growing strength of Moscow and Tver' or that, if they were, they took any steps to interfere with the process, either by strengthening or by weakening either side.

Only a bare outline of events is needed to show that the conflict between these two seemingly equal contestants for power soon became one-sided. Indeed, by 1328, after a quarter of a century of what almost amounted to internecine war between the two, it was clear to contemporaries that Tver' had lost any political and economic advantage she may have enjoyed in the past, and could now no longer be considered as a serious rival to Moscow by her neighbours. Why and how did Moscow gain the ascendancy not only over Tver' but over all the other principalities as well?

It has been common practice among historians writing on fourteenth-century history to catalogue the relevant factors which in their opinion led to the rise of Moscow—the superior

geographical position "at the hub of inner ways of communica-
tion",[1] the density of population in the basin of the Moskva river,
the support of the Church, the practice of direct succession from
father to son, the ability of the Muscovite princes to win and
exploit Tatar support, the policy of the princes of Moscow in
wooing the co-operation of the townsfolk, the preference of
Novgorod for the overlordship of Moscow to that of Tver', the
innate political shrewdness of Daniil's successors. All these factors
can be considered as perfectly valid causes of the rise of Moscow,
and all of them are to a certain extent interconnected and inter-
dependent. If, however, we are to explain the rise of Moscow as
anything more than a series of chance accidents which enabled
the Danilovichi—given the factors enumerated above—to
convert the minor patrimony of Moscow into the State of
Muscovy, we must try at least to establish some priority amongst
these factors, to bring some order into what looks like a jumble of
motives and reasons and to create what one historian has called a
"hierarchy of causes".[2] One of the aims of the following chapters
is to investigate stage by stage the process of the rise and growth
of Moscow up to the age of Dmitry Donskoy and to try to
produce some hierarchy among those causes which are ascertainable.

[1] Vernadsky, *Mongols*, p. 243.
[2] E. H. Carr, *What is History?*, p. 84.

2

The Struggle between Moscow and Tver', 1304–1328

[i] THE REIGN OF MIKHAIL OF TVER', 1304–1318

ON 27 July 1304 the grand prince of Vladimir, Andrey Aleksandrovich, died. The question of succession at once arose. Andrey's only son Boris had died the previous year; so too had his younger brother, Daniil of Moscow. According to the principle of accession to the grand-princely throne of Vladimir by seniority, the title of grand prince of Vladimir should have passed to his eldest cousin, Mikhail Yaroslavich of Tver', assuming that there were no surviving sons of Andrey of Suzdal'.[1] The observance of this practice of "horizontal succession" during the past century had been so regular that there can have been little doubt in the minds of the people of north-east Russia as to who was the rightful heir. So sure indeed were Andrey's boyars of the election of Mikhail that they anticipated the khan's decision and moved to Tver', where they took up residence and offered their services to the man they confidently believed would succeed their late master.[2] But they had reckoned without the princes of Moscow.

When he died in 1303, Daniil of Moscow had left five sons. The eldest of these, Yury, on hearing the news of the death of the grand prince, decided to contest Mikhail's right to the throne of Vladimir. There was no precedence for such a claim. Had Daniil survived Andrey he would have been next in the line of succession. But in accordance with the laws of seniority a nephew was automatically debarred from the title if his father predeceased the ruling grand prince. Unwritten laws and tradition, however, were not sufficient to guarantee the legitimate heir his throne.

[1] See below, p. 113, note 1. See also Appendix B, 2.
[2] See PSRL, xxv, p. 393.

Ultimately the final decision rested in the hands of the khan of the Golden Horde, without whose sanction and without whose plenipotentiary (*posol*) to assist at the enthronement in Vladimir no prince could assume titular seniority among his fellows. And so, when the death of Andrey became known, Mikhail and Yury lost no time in setting off for the Horde.[1] According to one source, Metropolitan Maksim, who four years earlier had transferred his see from Kiev to Vladimir, tried to stop Yury from opposing Mikhail. But Yury paid no heed.[2] It was, remarked the chronicler of Novgorod, the beginning of "the troubles in all the cities of Suzdal'".[3] The first phase in the civil war between the princes of Tver' and Moscow had begun.

Although Yury had no legal right to apply for the Tatar patent, Mikhail had good reason to respect and fear him as a military and political opponent. Not only had the princes of Moscow doubled the extent of their lands in the past five years by the seizure of Kolomna and Mozhaysk, but Yury had earlier entrenched himself in Pereyaslavl',[4] which, like Kostroma, was probably already considered part of the domain of the grand prince of Vladimir.[5] Furthermore he enjoyed the support of the people of Pereyaslavl',[6] who doubtless preferred the constant rule of a single dynasty to the impermanent shifting control of governors sent to rule them by whoever happened to be grand prince of Vladimir.

[1] See *PSRL*, iv (i), p. 252; xxv, p. 393; *NL*, p. 332: "They set off in dispute (*poidosha . . . vo spore*)." *Cf.* the corrupt and later version of the Voskresensky Chronicle: ". . . with speed (. . . *voskore*)". (*See PSRL*, vii, p. 184.)

[2] This occurs in one of the accounts of the murder of Mikhail at the Horde in 1318 (*see PSRL*, xxv, p. 161). The episode, however, may well have been the invention of Mikhail's hagiographer who is only too anxious to prove Mikhail's right to the title. According to this account, Yury was stopped by Maksim in Vladimir; but if he was travelling from Pereyaslavl', he would have taken the eastern Nerl' river and Vladimir would have been off his route. He was, in fact, ambushed "in Suzdal'". *See* below, p. 62. *See* also Podobedova, *Miniatyury*, pp. 20–2.

[3] *NL*, p. 92.

[4] *See* below, note 6.

[5] *See* above, p. 22.

[6] When Daniil's death was announced the inhabitants of Pereyaslavl' opted for Yury as their permanent prince (*Pereyaslavtsi yashasya za . . . Yur'ya*) and were unwilling to let him go to his father's funeral (*see PSRL*, xxiii, p. 96; xxv, p. 393; *TL*, p. 351).

Mikhail accordingly took steps to prevent his rival from reaching the khan. The Muscovite party, headed by Yury and including, probably, at least two of his brothers,[1] set off in the late summer of 1304 from Moscow or Pereyaslavl'. Near Suzdal' they were ambushed by the Tverites. They managed to escape, however, by another route and reached the Horde intact.[2] No mishaps befell Mikhail and his party.

In order to strengthen their respective claims to the throne and acting no doubt on the principle that possession is nine points of the law, both parties attempted to secure their lands outside their own principalities before appearing at the court of the khan. Yury, already in control of Pereyaslavl', tried to seize the other grand-princely district of Kostroma by sending his brother Boris there; with two thirds of what might be called the crown lands of Vladimir in his possession, he would be in a strong position at the Horde, or, if his mission to Saray failed, would be able to afford effective opposition to Mikhail on his return. Mikhail for his part made a determined effort to take control not only of Novgorod—by long-established custom the grand prince of Vladimir was also prince of Novgorod[3]—but also of Pereyaslavl'. Before leaving for the Horde he despatched his *namestniki* to Novgorod with instructions to take over the administration of the republic by force. Early in 1305 his armies marched on Pereyaslavl'.

All three attempts failed. Boris was seized by the Tverites— whether before or after he reached Kostroma is not known— and led off a captive to Tver';[4] the men of Novgorod refused to admit the would-be governors from Tver'[5] and took strenuous measures to prevent any possible further Tverite aggression. Remembering the ease with which any prince holding the key-town of Torzhok could effectively blockade Novgorod into

---

[1] Yury set out "with all his brothers" (*PSRL*, xxv, p. 393; *TL*, p. 352). These were probably Aleksandr and Afanasy. Boris was sent to Kostroma, probably before the main party set off, whereas Ivan, the youngest, remained i n Moscow.

[2] *See PSRL*, xxv, p. 393; *TL*, p. 352; *cf. PSRL*, xxiii, p. 96 (and also x, p. 174), where the place of ambush is given as *Kostroma*.

[3] *See above*, p. 32.

[4] *See PSRL*, xxiii, p. 96; xxv, p. 393; *TL*, p. 352.

[5] *See NL*, p. 92.

starvation and submission by cutting off the east–west flow of supplies along the Tvertsa river[1] and still suffering no doubt from the effects of the previous year's poor harvest and high food prices,[2] the Novgorodians hastened to strengthen the defences of their eastern outpost. They were only just in time; and when the expected army from Tver' arrived they were able to force a compromise. Both sides exchanged ambassadors and the formulation of a treaty was agreed upon. Drafts of a settlement based on previous treaties between Novgorod and Tver' were drawn up both by the Novgorodians and by the Tverites. It was decided, however, to await the arrival of the princes—or rather of the prince of Tver'—from the Golden Horde before the treaty be ratified.[3]

The Tverites were no more successful in their effort to seize Pereyaslavl'. Acting no doubt on previous instructions from Mikhail they attempted a raid on the town. The expedition was under command of Akinf, one of the leading boyars who had transferred their allegiance to Mikhail in the late summer of 1304. However, the arrival of the Tverite army was anticipated by Ivan Danilovich, who moved from Moscow to Pereyaslavl' before the attack took place. The Tverites were soundly defeated. Akinf was killed; his two sons managed to escape and fled back to Tver'. The men of Pereyaslavl', who fought side by side with the army from Moscow, once again showed their preference for a Muscovite leader.[4]

---

[1] *See*, for instance, *NL*, p. 322; *cf.* L. V. Danilova, *Ocherki*, p. 22, note 4.

[2] *See NL*, p. 91. *Cf.* Danilova, *Ocherki*, pp. 21–2.

[3] "They drew up a treaty (*dokonchasha*) before the arrival of the princes" (*NL*, p. 91). Cherepnin convincingly argues that the treaty document printed in *GVNiP*, No. 6, pp. 15–16, was the Tver' draft of the projected treaty; whereas Nos. 7 and 8 (pp. 16–19) were the Novgorod draft. Both drafts can be dated 1304 and are based on the thirteenth-century treaties between Yaroslav Yaroslavich of Tver' and Novgorod (*see* ibid., pp. 9 sq.). (*See* Cherepnin, *RFA*, vol. i, pp. 270–82.)

[4] *See PSRL*, xxiii, p. 96; xxv, p. 393; *TL*, p. 352 (misdated 1306); *cf.* the expanded account in *PSRL*, x, pp. 175–6. The battle of Pereyaslavl' probably took place in early 1305 or at the end of 1304. It is reported in the chronicles under the year 6812 (1 March 1304–28 February 1305) as the last event of the year. As Akinf left Gorodets on the Volga, where Grand Prince Andrey was buried, *after* 27 July 1304, it is not likely that he would have been ready to mount an expedition from Tver' much before the end of the year.

There is no information as to what took place at the Horde when the two princes met there in 1304–5; we do not know what their arguments consisted of or even whether they confronted each other in their quest for the title. One of the semi-hagiographical accounts of the murder of Mikhail in 1318 suggests that it was a question of cash;[1] indeed, it may well have been that at this stage the highest bidder won. At any rate Mikhail was granted the *yarlyk*. In 1305 he returned to Vladimir where he was put upon the throne.

Although Mikhail had won the initial advantage in his conflict with Yury of Moscow by acquiring the patent to the throne of Vladimir, he only realized the full extent of the problem which faced him and the difficulties which lay ahead when he returned to north-east Russia. He was confronted with the enmity of Moscow, the unwillingness of Peryaslavl' to submit to him and the aloofness, if not the open hostility, of Novgorod. To make matters worse, Boris of Moscow, kidnapped by the Tverites in the previous year, had evidently escaped and was now back in Moscow.[2] All that Mikhail held, apart from the principality of Tver' itself, was Vladimir and the districts of Kostroma and Nizhny Novgorod;[3] yet even in the latter two cities he had to contend with what appear to have been popular uprisings directed against the late grand prince's retainers, who had, it must be assumed, transferred their allegiance to Mikhail and had been acting in his name during his absence at the Horde.

He dealt with the various problems which faced him with determination and a certain degree of success. The uprising in Kostroma was evidently quelled with little difficulty—the chronicles make no mention of subsequent trouble there. On his way back from the Horde he stopped at Nizhny Novgorod and put to death those responsible for the murder of the late grand prince's boyars.[4] After his enthronement in Vladimir he marched

---

[1] See *PSRL*, v, pp. 207–8. This flowery account stresses Mikhail's right to the title and the deliberate attempt of the Tatars to stir up trouble between the princes. (*See* Cherepnin, *Obrazovanie*, p. 471.)

[2] This is clear from the fact that in 1306 Boris and Aleksandr defected from Moscow to Tver'. *See* below, p. 65.

[3] And presumably Gorodets on the Volga.

[4] The revolt of the common people (*chernye lyudi*) of Nizhny Novgorod

on Moscow and avenged himself of the death of Akinf and the failure of the Tver' expedition against Pereyaslavl' by defeating the Muscovites and settling for a temporary peace between the two principalities.[1] In the following year, 1306, he scored yet another victory, this time a diplomatic one, over his rival in Moscow. Whether as a result of his cautious policy towards Moscow or simply because of a quarrel among the Danilovichi, Boris and Aleksandr defected from Moscow to Tver'.[2] It proved, however, to be a hollow victory, for neither prince was of more than prestige value to Mikhail, and indeed neither remained long in Tver': Aleksandr died in the autumn of 1308, while Boris decided that Moscow was more to his liking than Tver' and managed to return to his family nest once more.[3]

Meanwhile the temporary peace between Tver' and Moscow enabled Yury to attend to the affairs of Ryazan'. Ever since 1301, when Daniil of Moscow had defeated the Ryazanites at the battle of Pereyaslavl'–Ryazansky,[4] Prince Konstantin Romanovich of Ryazan' had been held in virtual captivity in Moscow. The chronicles, unfortunately, barely mention the events of 1306–8 connected with Yury's dealings with Ryazan' but nevertheless

---

and Mikhail's revenge *on his way back* from the Horde is reported in the sixteenth-century Voskresensky Chronicle *after* Mikhail's march on Moscow and after the death of Metropolitan Maksim (16 December 1305). Mikhail, however, must have stopped in Nizhny Novgorod when he returned from the Horde *earlier* in 1305. Other chronicles (Novgorod Fourth, Sofiysky First, Ermolinsky and Moscow *svod* of 1479) say that Mikhail *Andreevich* (son of Grand Prince Andrey Yaroslavich) killed the *vechniki* (*PSRL*, iv (i), p. 253; v, p. 204; xxiii, p. 96; xxv, p. 393; *cf.* x, p. 176). It is not, however, known for certain if he was still alive at this date. His son Vasily Mikhaylovich died in 1309 (*PSRL*, x, p. 177).

[1] See *TL*, p. 352 (under 1306); *PSRL*, x, p. 176.

[2] See *PSRL*, xxiii, p. 96; xxv, p. 393; *TL*, p. 352 (under 1307).

[3] No details are known of Boris's *volte face*, but we find him fighting with Yury at the battle of Bortenevo in 1317. He was captured by Mikhail during the battle, taken once more to Tver' and later released by common agreement (*see PSRL*, xxiii, p. 98; xxv, p. 161; *NL*, p. 96; *TL*, p. 356). Boris died in 1320 and was buried in Vladimir (*see TL*, p. 356). For Aleksandr's death, *see TL*, p. 353.

[4] *See* above, p. 50.

C

give sufficient information to enable us to reconstruct them, albeit piecemeal.

In the spring or summer of 1306 Yury was in Ryazan',[1] negotiating, perhaps, the terms of the surrender of Kolomna or forcing the Ryazanites to accept them. After his return to Moscow in the autumn of 1306 a Tatar force led by one Tair appeared in north-east Russia. The chronicles make no mention of the scope, area or purpose of Tair's expedition, but it may be surmised that it was connected with Yury's visit to Ryazan' and that Tair was enforcing Yury's will in Ryazan' rather than operating in the confines of the grand principality of Vladimir.[2] It would seem that by now Yury had no further need for Konstantin Romanovich, who had originally been brought back to Moscow and held in reserve as a possible pro-Muscovite candidate for the grand principality of Ryazan';[3] or perhaps Konstantin had objected too strongly to Yury's activities in the district of Ryazan'. In any case Yury had him put to death in the winter of 1306.[4] His son Vasily, who went to the Horde to complain of his father's murder,[5] fared no better. In 1308 he was murdered in Saray, and in the same year yet another Tatar expedition ravaged Ryazan'.[6]

Whatever the reason for the murders of Konstantin and his

[1] See TL, p. 352, where under 1307 the entry "Prince Yury came to Moscow from Ryazan'" immediately precedes the entries concerning Tair's (autumn) expedition and the defection of Yury's brothers to Tver', both of which are recorded in the chronologically more reliable Ermolinsky Chronicle under 1306. (See PSRL, xxiii, p. 96. Cf. xxv, p. 393.)

[2] For Tair's expedition, see TL, p. 352; PSRL, xxiii, p. 96; xxv, p. 393. The Nikon Chronicle mentions it under 1305 (PSRL, x, p. 176).

[3] See PSRL, x, p. 173. Daniil had captured Konstantin "by a certain cunning method" and intended to conclude a pact with him and "let him go back to his patrimony, the grand principality of Ryazan'".

[4] See PSRL, xxiii, p. 96; xxv, p. 158; TL, p. 352 (dated 1307). Cf. PSRL, x, p. 176 (dated 1305 "during the fast of St. Philip", i.e. 15 November–24 December).

[5] This seems to be the most likely explanation of Vasily Konstantinovich's presence at the Horde. His death and the subsequent Tatar invasion of Ryazan' are only mentioned laconically in the Nikon Chronicle (PSRL, x, p. 176).

[6] Ilovaysky thinks that Vasily Konstantinovich's death was engineered by his cousins, the princes of Pronsk. (See D. Ilovaysky, IRK, p. 139.)

son, one fact emerges with clarity from the obscure account of Moscow–Ryazan' relations in the years 1306–8, namely that the Tatars, notwithstanding their evident co-operation with Konstantin at the battle of Pereyaslavl'–Ryazansky in 1301,[1] were now prepared to assist Yury of Moscow. For the first time in the conflict between Tver' and Moscow the Tatars were attempting to adjust the balance of power by supporting what appeared to them to be the weaker of the two principalities.

While the prince of Moscow settled his affairs with Ryazan', Mikhail of Tver' attempted to consolidate his position as grand prince of Vladimir. He had little success. Only in Novgorod did he manage—after considerable delay, it must be admitted—to establish his legal position. On 16 July 1307, two years after his return to Vladimir as grand prince, "he sat upon the throne in Novgorod"[2] and ratified the treaty which had been drafted three years before during his absence at the Horde.[3]

Elsewhere he met with failure: Pereyaslavl' remained in Muscovite hands; Yury of Moscow gained control of Nizhny

[1] "Prince Daniil killed many Tatars and captured Prince Konstantin of Ryazan'" (*TL*, p. 350; *PSRL*, xxiii, p. 93; xxv, p. 393). Vernadsky, on the strength of this evidence, has Konstantin "turn to the local Mongol *baskak* for protection". (*See* Vernadsky, *Mongols*, p. 193.)

[2] *PSRL*, iv(i), p. 253; xxiii, p. 97; xxv, p. 154; *NL*, p. 332. *Cf. NL*, p. 92 (Novgorod First Chronicle, *starshy izvod*), where the date is given as 1308, and *PSRL*, xv, p. 408 (Tver' Chronicle) where it is given as 1310. 1307 is the correct date: his enthronement took place "on Sunday, at the festival of the 630 holy fathers of the Council of Chalcedon" (i.e. 16 July). 16 July 1307 was in fact a Sunday. (*See* E. I. Kamentseva, *R. Khr.*, p. 46.)

[3] Evidently Novgorod was without *namestniki* from 1304 to 1307. Cherepnin thinks that Novgorod recognized the authority of Mikhail *before* 1307. He points out that under 1305 the Novgorod First Chronicle mentions the building of a church in Novgorod "during the rule of the Christ-loving Prince Mikhail" (NL, p. 92). (*See* Cherepnin, *RFA*, vol. i, p. 270.) Berezhkov, however, thinks that the chronicle entry is misplaced and should refer to 1308–9. (*See* N. G. Berezhkov, *Khronologiya*, p. 280.)
The treaty, the Novgorod and Tver' copies of which are printed in *GVNiP* (Nos. 9–10, pp. 19–22), was, in the opinion of Cherepnin, based on the Tverite treaty draft of 1304 (*GVNiP*, No. 6; *see* above, p. 63, note 3), which itself was based on previous treaties between Novgorod and Yaroslav Yaroslavich. (*See* Cherepnin, *RFA*, vol. i, pp. 280–2.) *Cf.* A. A. Zimin, "O khronologii", p. 309.

Novgorod;[1] and the Muscovites managed to hold their own when Mikhail marched against their capital in 1308.[2]

Most damaging in the long run, however, to Mikhail's chances of establishing the hegemony of Tver' was his failure to win the support of the Church, or rather the support of the head of the Church. Metropolitan Maksim, who during the short period of his residence in Vladimir had shown some predisposition towards Mikhail at the beginning of the latter's struggle with Yury of Moscow,[3] died in December 1305, and the question of who was to succeed him arose. Two candidates were sent to Constantinople for consecration—one from north-east Russia and one from south-west Russia. The candidate from Suzdalia, one Abbot Geronty, was evidently the nominee of Mikhail. According to the biased anti-Tverite biographies of his rival, Metropolitan Petr,[4] Geronty presumptuously assumed the dignity of metropolitan even before he left Vladimir and took with him on his journey to Constantinople not only the robes and vessels of the late metropolitan but also members of his staff in order the better to impress the patriarch and the emperor. The successful candidate, Abbot Petr, was despatched by Yury L'vovich, the prince of Galich, probably not as a successor to Metropolitan Maksim but as a replacement for the first metropolitan of Galich, Nifont, who had died at about the same time as Maksim.[5] Petr

---

[1] In 1311 Dmitry, Mikhail's son, planned to march against "Nizhny Novgorod and Prince Yury" (*see* below, p. 73). This would imply that Moscow had seized power in Nizhny Novgorod between 1304, when Grand Prince Andrey's boyars transferred their allegiance to Mikhail, and 1311. *Cf.*, however, Borzakovsky's views (V. S. Borzakovsky, *ITK*, p. 95).

[2] *See PSRL*, xxiii, p. 97; xxv, p. 159; *TL*, pp. 352–3. No reason is given for Mikhail's inconclusive expedition against Moscow. Its purpose may have been to take Pereyaslavl' from Yury by force.

[3] *See* above, p. 61, note 2. *Cf.* Presnyakov, *Obrazovanie*, p. 108.

[4] *See* Makary, *Istoriya*, vol. iv, pp. 312–16; *PSRL*, x, pp. 190–4; *PSRL*, xxi, pp. 321–32; V. O. Klyuchevsky, *drevnerusskie zhitiya svyatykh*, pp. 74, 82; V. A. Kuchkin, "Skazanie".

[5] For details, *see* below, pp. 125–6. Yury L'vovich, grandson of King Daniil of Galich and Volyn', succeeded in raising the bishopric of Galich to a metropolitan see in 1302 or 1303. (*See RIB*, vol. vi, Appendix, col. 126 (letter of King Casimir of Poland to Patriarch Philotheos, 1370); Kartashev, *Ocherki*, vol. i, pp. 297–8; K. Chodynicki, *Kościół prawosławny*, p. 5.) It is of course possible that Petr was sent as candidate for the metropolitan see of

arrived first in Constantinople—the boat in which Geronty crossed the Black Sea had lost its way—and was consecrated metropolitan, not of Galich, but of Kiev and all Rus'. The emperor and patriarch, having recently divided the Russian Church into two metropolitan sees by the appointment of Nifont to Galich, now reunited it in the person of Petr. In 1308 Petr arrived in Kiev. Early in the following year[1] he entered Vladimir, whither Maksim had transferred his see eight years before.

Frustrated in his plans to have his own candidate nominated, Mikhail accepted with bad grace the new spiritual head of his realm. But if the grand prince was prepared to tolerate the presence of Petr in Vladimir, the bishop of his own principality, Andrey, was not. The bishop of Tver' lost little time in stirring up trouble for the new metropolitan. Whether he objected to Petr as a politician or as a churchman we do not know. Unspecified accusations against him, clearly of an ecclesiastical nature, were sent by Andrey to the patriarch with a request that his activities be investigated at the highest level. There is, however, justification for suspecting that Andrey's behaviour was motivated largely by political considerations. Not only was he likely to have shared his prince's irritation at the failure of Geronty's mission (after all, Geronty was probably selected by the grand prince in consultation with Andrey), but we know that he himself was of Lithuanian origin[2] and may well have been an early advocate of what was later to be the typically Tverite policy of rapprochement with Lithuania and hostility towards the Golden Horde.[3] If this was the case, Petr's first recorded act on arrival in

---

Kiev and all Rus', which would include the diocese of Galich. Yury L'vovich, who was Mikhail's brother-in-law, evidently knew about Geronty's despatch. (*See* Presnyakov, *Obrazovanie*, p. 122; *cf.* Golubinsky, *IRTs*, vol. ii, book 1, pp. 101–5.)

[1] Between 1 March 1309 (beginning of the "March" year 6817) and 5 June when he appointed David archbishop of Novgorod. (*See* PSRL, xxv, p. 159.) *Cf.* PSRL, v, p. 204, where the year is given as 1308. *Cf.* also NL, p. 92; Berezhkov, *Khronologiya*, p. 280.

[2] He was the son of one Gerden', or Erden', a Lithuanian prince of Polotsk. (*See* PSRL, xvi, pp. 593, 601–2; xxv, p. 157; TL, p. 345.) It is interesting to note that the first bishop of Tver', Simeon, also came from Polotsk. (*See* V. T. Pashuto, *OLG*, p. 390, note 163.)

[3] *See* I. B. Grekov's somewhat exaggerated statement to the effect that

north-east Russia may well have aroused the suspicions of the bishop and prince of Tver', for in 1310 we find Petr actively interfering in the political life of the small western principality of Bryansk.

Unfortunately little or nothing is known of the history of Bryansk before the period under consideration except that it was incorporated into the principality of Smolensk, probably in the late thirteenth century when one Prince Roman, son of Gleb Rostislavich of Smolensk, ruled there.[1] His son Vasily took over the principality in the early years of the fourteenth century. As far as can be ascertained from the sparse information available, Vasily continued the policy of his father's predecessor and namesake, Roman of Bryansk and Chernigov—a policy of reliance on the support of, and submission to, the khan of the Golden Horde; perhaps too he even shared his hostility towards Lithuania,[2] although there is no evidence to confirm this. In 1309 he was driven out of his principality by his uncle, Svyatoslav Glebovich. He immediately proceeded to the Horde to complain to the khan.[3] Svyatoslav's rule in Bryansk was unpopular—perhaps because he was attempting a rapprochment with the old enemies of Bryansk, the Lithuanians—and the townsfolk rebelled. Meanwhile Vasily was leading a Tatar army north-west to oust his

---

"[Mikhail of Tver'] permanently maintained contact with the princes of Lithuania". The only evidence of this "permanent contact" is the fact that Bishop Andrey was a "direct relation of the princes of Lithuania". (*See* I. B. Grekov, *Ocherki*, p. 30.)

[1] *See* Baumgarten, *Généalogies*, vol. ii, pp. 97–8. *Cf.* Ekzemplyarsky, *VUK*, vol. ii, p. 81, note 255. Previous to this Bryansk was part of the principality of Chernigov. One Roman of Bryansk (patronymic unknown, but he should not be confused with Roman Glebovich), also known as prince of Chernigov, in 1263 married off his daughter Ol'ga to Vladimir Vasil'kovich of Volyn' (Yury of Galich's uncle) (*see* PSRL, ii, cols. 861–2) and in 1274 joined the expedition of Gleb of Smolensk and the princes of Turov, Pinsk, Lutsk and Vladimir-Volynsky, under Tatar command, to help Lev of Galich recover Dorogichin from Lithuania. (*See* ibid., cols. 871–4.) *Cf.* Baumgarten, op. cit., pp. 55–6; Pashuto, *Ocherki*, p. 294.

[2] Note that in 1263 Grand Prince Mendovg of Lithuania had attacked Bryansk. (*See* PSRL, ii, col. 860.) According to the "Genealogy of the Lithuanian grand princes" in the West-Russian chronicles, Bishop Andrey's father was first cousin of Mendovg. (*See* PSRL, xvi, pp. 593, 601–2.)

[3] *See* PSRL, x, p. 177.

usurper-uncle. The situation was serious enough to warrant the presence and the intervention of the metropolitan.[1] Petr urged Svyatoslav either to come to an agreement with his nephew and share the principality with him or to leave without fighting, but Syvatoslav refused to listen. He decided to resist the Tatars. The contest was uneven. Abandoned by the men of Bryansk, Svyatoslav was killed fighting. Vasily resumed control of the principality.[2]

We know nothing of the repercussions of Petr's activities in Bryansk. However much Mikhail of Tver' may have objected to his political interference in matters strictly outside the scope of his jurisdiction, he could not get rid of the metropolitan on any but ecclesiastical grounds. In late 1310 or early 1311, however, the patriarch's representative, who had been sent from Constantinople in answer to Bishop Andrey's complaints, arrived in north-east Russia. A Church congress was summoned and the assembled clerics and laity prepared to listen to and judge the conflict between the metropolitan and the bishop of Tver'.

Very little is known of the Council of Pereyaslavl'. Only the biographies of Petr mention it, and they give disappointingly few details of the proceedings. Apart from Petr and Andrey the only prelate present was Simeon of Rostov.[3] The grand prince was unable to attend—Petr's biographer explains his absence by saying that he was at the Golden Horde[4]—but his sons

---

[1] It is not known if Metropolitan Petr went to Bryansk solely in order to deal with the situation there. Borzakovsky in his monograph on the history of Tver' considers that Petr may have gone to Bryansk to meet the patriarch's representative who was to judge the conflict between him and the bishop of Tver'. (*See* Borzakovsky, *ITK*, p. 251.)

[2] Svyatoslav was killed in April 1310. Shortly after his victorious return Vasily marched with his Tatar allies against the neighbouring princeling of Karachev (between the Desna and the Upper Oka), one Svyatoslav Mstislavich, whom he killed. The aim of the expedition is not stated in the Nikon Chronicle (which alone mentions it)—it was probably to annexe Karachev to Bryansk. (*See PSRL*, iv (i), p. 254; x, pp. 177–8; xxiii, p. 97; xxv, p. 159; *TL*, pp. 353–4. *See* also P. V. Golubovsky, *ISZ*, pp. 310–11.)

[3] Probably a supporter of Andrey. He left his see shortly after the Council of 1311 (at the suggestion of the metropolitan?). (*See TL*, p. 354.)

[4] *See PSRL*, x, p. 192. No other source mentions Mikhail's visit to Saray in 1310 or 1311, and the evidence may be doubted. The Soviet historian Klibanov unjustifiably explains his absence by saying that he was "occupied with matters relating to the Golden Horde". (*See* A. I. Klibanov, *RD*, p. 101.)

Dmitry and Aleksandr were there, as well as "several other princes", including no doubt the princes of Moscow, in whose territory the council was being held.[1] The main accusation levelled against Petr was probably that of simony; at any rate this was the charge which Andrey later brought against the metropolitan in his subsequent complaints to the patriarch.[2] The proceedings were conducted with passion and at one stage nearly ended in blows. Petr offered to resign—an offer which, not unexpectedly, was turned down.

How the metropolitan conducted his case and how he succeeded in getting the council to reject the charges against him is not known.[3] But in the end he won the day and "dismissed with peace" those who had assembled to try him. In vain the bishop of Tver' attempted to renew his accusations; he sent off to the patriarch one Akindin, a monk, as a witness of Petr's ill-doings. And although the patriarch this time sent for Petr, requesting him to appear in person in Constantinople and to answer the charges brought by the bishop of Tver', nevertheless Petr once more managed to justify his actions and at length to rid himself of Andrey. In 1316, a year in which Mikhail was conveniently engrossed in the affairs of Novgorod, the see of Tver' was vacated. Andrey retired to a monastery, to be replaced by a nominee of the metropolitan.[4]

If the cool reception on arrival at the hands of the grand prince had not been enough to prejudice the metropolitan against Tver', the hostile attitude of the grand prince's bishop tipped the scale. As might be expected, Petr emerged from the Council of Pereya-

[1] I. B. Grekov, without mentioning his sources, states that Petr was defended by Yury of Moscow. (*See* Grekov, *Ocherki*, p. 36.)

[2] *See RIB*, vol. vi, No. 16, cols. 147–58.

[3] It may be that Petr himself accused Andrey of heresy. The question of heresy of an unspecified sort was undoubtedly raised at the Council; Klibanov is of the opinion that Andrey was involved and was counter-accused by Petr. (*See* Klibanov, *RD*, p. 104.)

[4] *See TL*, p. 353; *PSRL*, xxv, p. 160. For accounts of the Council of Pereyaslavl' and the subsequent events, *see PSRL*, x, p. 192; Makary, *Istoriya*, vol. iv, p. 314; *RIB*, vol. vi, cols. 147–58. (*See* also Presnyakov, *Obrazovanie*, pp. 122–4; Borzakovsky, *ITK*, pp. 96–7, 245–52; N. A. Kazakova and Ya. S. Lur'e, *AED*, pp. 44–5; Grekov, *Ocherki*, pp. 35–6; V. Sokol'sky, *Uchastie russkogo dukhovenstva*, pp. 45 sq.)

slavl' the staunch supporter of Moscow. In the same year (1311) he showed the princes of Tver' exactly where he stood in the conflict between the two principalities and just how effective his intervention in political matters could be. With Pereyaslavl' still in Muscovite hands, Mikhail could ill afford the loss of Nizhny Novgorod, which was now held by Yury of Moscow. Accordingly an expedition was mounted and placed under the nominal control of the twelve-year-old Dmitry, Mikhail's eldest son. The army reached Vladimir on its way east to Nizhny Novgorod. There it was stopped by the metropolitan, who, by withholding his blessing from Dmitry, prevented him from reaching his objective. Dmitry and the army waited for three weeks, hoping no doubt to persuade the metropolitan to change his mind and to sanction the campaign. But their efforts were in vain. The expedition was called off, and the army returned to Tver'.[1] It was one of the first recorded occasions on which the head of the Russian Church had exercised his right to veto a political undertaking of which he disapproved. Petr's action was symptomatic of the general anti-Tverite trend throughout north-east Russia.

Mikhail's failure to win the support of the metropolitan had far-reaching results. By alienating the head of the Church, the prince of Tver' incurred the enmity of other bishops as well—particularly those who enjoyed the confidence and support of Petr. Indeed it would not be an exaggeration to say that many of the political crises which Mikhai lhad to cope with during the last seven years of his reign were to some extent attributable to the influence and the authority of the metropolitan. At any rate, it is significant to note that the two districts which caused the grand prince most trouble were Novgorod and Rostov, the bishops of which, David and Prokhor, were both, if not the nominees, then at least the adherents of Metropolitan Petr.[2]

---

[1] See TL, p. 354; PSRL, xxiii, p. 97; xxv, p. 159.

[2] Archbishop David was elected by the Novgorodians after the retirement of Feoktist in 1307 and was consecrated by Petr in 1309. During the troubles of 1314 Mikhail's governors in Novgorod were arrested and held in the archbishop's palace. (See below, p. 75.)

Prokhor, the author of an oration in praise of Petr at the Council of Vladimir (1327) at which the latter was canonized, was appointed bishop of Rostov in 1311 in place of Simeon, who was perhaps a supporter of Andrey and who quit his see in the same year. (See Kuchkin, "Skazanie".)

Mikhail, it will be remembered, had established his authority
in Novgorod in 1307. For four years all was quiet, but the calm
was illusory. In the summer of 1311 a series of fires broke out in
the city. They were followed by looting.[1] The chronicles characteristically make no mention of the reasons for, or the results of,
these serious disturbances, nor do they say against whom they
were directed. But there can be little doubt that one of the causes
of popular dissatisfaction was the presence of the grand prince's
representatives in Novgorod. At any rate in the following year
Mikhail decided to punish the republic. After first removing his
governors and their retinues from Novgorod, he cut off the city's
supplies of grain from the east by blocking the Msta and Tvertsa
rivers. He then proceeded to occupy two of Novgorod's easternmost districts, Bezhetsky Verkh and Torzhok—the seizure of
which was virtually a prerequisite for the subjugation of Novgorod[2]—and waited for the Novgorodians to sue for peace. In

---

Information concerning Rostov is scarce in the chronicles, but it seems as
though the principality was a source of trouble to Mikhail. In early 1315
Yury of Moscow, travelling from Novgorod to Saray, made a detour to
visit Rostov (*PSRL*, iv (i), p. 256; v, p. 206; xxiii, p. 97; xxv, p. 160; the
Trinity Chronicle makes no mention of the visit). Later in the year, when
Mikhail arrived back from the Horde with his Tatar armies, Tatar represen-
tatives in Rostov "did much evil" (*PSRL*, i, col. 529; iv (i), p. 256). In 1316
Yury's brother-in-law, Vasily Konstantinovich of Rostov, arrived in Rostov
from the Horde with two Tatar officials (*posly*), who "did much evil to
Rostov" (*PSRL*, iv (i), p. 257; v, p. 206; xxv, p. 161. The Ermolinsky and
Trinity Chronicles make no mention of Vasily's arrival in Rostov).

[1] In the Novgorod First Chronicle (*starshy izvod*) a detailed description of
the fires and plundering is followed by "in that year (i.e. before 1 March 1312)
the office of *posadnik* was taken from Mikhail [Pavshinich] and given to
Semen Klimovich" (*NL*, p. 93). This is interpreted by Cherepnin as a result
of the "social disturbances" in Novgorod. (*See* Cherepnin, *Obrazovanie*,
p. 463.) V. L. Yanin, however, in his exhaustive study of *posadnichestvo* in
Novgorod, is of the opinion that this was merely a routine replacement of
one boyar-*posadnik* by another. The authority of the *posadnik* in the thirteenth
and fourteenth centuries was entirely independent of the grand prince or his
governors. Yanin postulates the existence (from the end of the thirteenth
century) of a council of five boyars, representatives of the five city districts
(*kontsy*), from whom one *posadnik* was elected annually. (*See* Yanin, *NP*,
p. 170; *cf. Sovetskaya arkheologiya*, No. 3, 1963, pp. 272-9 (review by A. A.
Zimin of Yanin's book).)

[2] E.g. in 1273 Vasily Yaroslavich of Kostroma occupied Torzhok while

the early spring of 1313 Archbishop David went to Tver' and concluded a truce with the grand prince. It was agreed that Mikhail be paid the sum of 1,500 silver *grivny*; the unpopular governors were sent back; and Novgorod once more came under Tverite control.[1]

As long as Mikhail remained in north-east Russia there was little the Novgorodians could or dared do but suffer his lieutenants in silence. The events of 1312 and 1313 had all too clearly demonstrated the strength of the grand prince and the determined nature of his reprisals. In 1313, however, the khan of the Golden Horde died, and Mikhail and Metropolitan Petr, together with all the "princes and bishops",[2] set off to Saray to pay their respects to the new khan, Uzbek, and to renew their patents. The metropolitan managed to return quickly, but Mikhail was held back in Saray for two years. Assured of his absence, the Novgorodians once more rose up in revolt against his governors. "In that year (1314) the men of Novgorod summoned a *veche* because they hated the *namestniki* of Prince Mikhail Yaroslavich of Tver', for they had suffered much offence and injury at their hands and they desired to expel them."[3] The popular discontent, aggravated no doubt by a current famine in the district of Novgorod, forced the city authorities to take drastic steps. An appeal was sent to Yury of Moscow, who immediately despatched one Prince Fedor of Rzheva to Novgorod. On his arrival the governors were arrested and confined in the archbishop's palace. Fedor of Rzheva then led an expedition against Tver'. For six weeks the armies of Novgorod and Tver' faced each other across the Volga at Gorodok (Staritsa), half-way between Rzheva and Tver'. At length, when the frosts came, a truce between Fedor and Mikhail's son Dmitry was concluded on terms wholly satisfactory to Novgorod.[4] Once again messages were sent to Moscow asking

---

his ally Svyatoslav Yaroslavich of Tver' sacked Volok Lamsky, Bezhetsky Verkh and Vologda prior to subjugating Novgorod. (*See PSRL*, xxv, p. 151. *Cf.* Zimin, "Novgorod i Volokolamsk", p. 106.)

[1] For the events in Novgorod in 1312 and early 1313, *see NL*, p. 94. For the approximate weight of a silver *grivna, see* below, p. 77, note 5.

[2] *PSRL*, x, p. 178.

[3] Ibid.

[4] Later treaties between Novgorod and Tver' mention the supersession

Yury personally to assume control of Novgorod. This time he agreed, and in early 1315 both he and his brother Afanasy arrived in Novgorod where they were solemnly enthroned. The people of Novgorod, say the chronicles, were delighted with their choice.[1]

Their joy was short-lived. In spite of the absence of Mikhail and the humiliation of his son, the Tverites were still able to blockade Novgorod effectively. During the early months of 1315 grain prices again rose both in Novgorod and Pskov; in the latter city there were civil disturbances; the looting which broke out was so serious that the Pskovite authorities executed fifty of the offenders.[2] Worse was to come. Mikhail had not spent two years at Uzbek's court for nothing, and in 1315, for the first time since his nomination as grand prince, he managed to gain the confidence and the support of the khan. He urged Uzbek not only to summon his rival, Yury of Moscow, to the Horde and thus remove him temporarily from the political arena while he, Mikhail, settled affairs within his realm, but also to supply him with an army to enable him to deal with his rebellious "subjects". The new khan, won over by the blandishments or the bribes of the grand prince, or perhaps alarmed at rumours of the growing strength of the princes of Moscow, complied with Mikhail's wishes. Neither the metropolitan nor his newly-appointed representative at Saray, Bishop Varsanofy, had been able to

---

and cancellation of an unspecified treaty "concluded at Gorodok on the Volga" (GVNiP, No. 11, p. 24, and No. 13, p. 26). Cherepnin (RFA, vol. i, pp. 286, 290) in his scholarly analysis of the early fourteenth-century Novgorod–Tver' treaties considers that this was the treaty concluded in 1314 between Fedor of Rzheva and Dmitry Mikhaylovich (as do Presnyakov, Obrazovanie, p. 125, note 3, and S. M. Solov'ev, Istoriya, book i, col. 905). The chronicles make no mention of Gorodok. They merely state that the two armies faced each other across the Volga.

[1] For the events of 1314–15, see PSRL, iv (i), pp. 255–6; v, pp. 205–6; x, p. 179; xxiii, p. 97; xxv, p. 160; NL, p. 94; TL, pp. 354–5. Cf. PSRL, xv, p. 408 (Tver' Chronicle), where it is stated that Yury, "having placed his brother Afanasy on the throne, set off for Moscow". None of the other chronicles mention Yury's departure for Moscow.

[2] See NL, p. 94; PL, ii, p. 88. The rise in grain prices, of course, may have been due to natural causes. The Pskov Chronicle mentions severe frosts.

prevail at the court of the khan or to argue the cause of the prince of Moscow.[1]

No sooner had Yury and Afanasy established themselves in Novgorod than Yury received a summons to proceed to the Golden Horde. He left in February or early March 1315, taking with him, according to some sources, a group of Novgorodians, perhaps to give evidence of the malpractices of the Tverite officials and of their misappropriation of funds which were owed to the khan.[2] In the autumn of the same year Grand Prince Mikhail arrived in north-east Russia accompanied by a Tatar army. He assembled an expeditionary force consisting of troops from all the "Lower lands". Afanasy and Fedor of Rzheva, on hearing the news, lost no time in raising an army and marching to the strategic outpost of Torzhok to defend the republic. They arrived there at the end of December 1315 and waited six weeks for the arrival of the grand prince.

In early February 1316 Mikhail Yaroslavich appeared with his combined army at Torzhok. On 10 February the two opposing forces clashed. The Novgorodians were soundly defeated, losing many of their senior boyars.[3] According to the chronicles of Tver', more than a thousand Novgorodians were killed and the outskirts of Torzhok were burned.[4]

Just how decisive and crushing was Mikhail's victory can best be judged by the immediate results. The grand prince refused to parley before the two leaders of the opposing army, Afanasy and Fedor, were handed over to him. When his request, which had been rejected the first time, was at length complied with, Mikhail dictated his terms: Novgorod was to pay a heavy indemnity;[5]

[1] In 1312 Petr removed Izmail from the see of Saray and replaced him with Varsanofy. No explanation is given in the chronicles. (See TL, p. 354.)

[2] See PSRL, iv (i), p. 256; v, p. 206; xxiii, p. 97; xxv, p. 160; TL, p. 355. Cf. the Novgorod First Chronicle (NL, p. 94), where there is no mention of Novgorodians accompanying Yury. The Tver' chronicles make no mention whatsoever of Yury's trip to the Horde.

[3] Including three of the five city representatives, Andrey Klimovich, Yury Mishinich and Mikhail Pavshinich. (See Yanin, NP, p. 169.)

[4] See PSRL, xv, col. 408; xv (i), col. 36.

[5] The Novgorod chronicles give the enormous sum of 50,000 grivny (NL, p. 95; PSRL, iv (i), p. 256); the Nikon Chronicle says 5,000 (PSRL, x, p. 179); the Ermolinsky Chronicle 500 (PSRL, xxiii, p. 98). It appears, however,

Afanasy of Moscow and the leading boyars were to be deported
to Tver' as hostages;[1] the fortifications of Torzhok were to be
dismantled;[2] and the Tverite *namestniki* were to return to Novgorod and to resume their duties there.[3]

Mikhail's overwhelming victory over Novgorod was not
sufficient to cow the republic into submission. Opposition to
Tverite control was as intense as it had been before the battle of
Torzhok. No sooner had Mikhail's governors arrived than the
Novgorodians secretly despatched a delegation to the Golden
Horde, no doubt to seek the support of Yury of Moscow, who
was then at the court of the khan, and to complain to Uzbek of the
behaviour of the grand prince. The delegation was caught on its
journey by the Tverites and sent to Tver'.[4] Again the city
rebelled. Pro-Tver' sympathizers were thrown into the Volkhov
river and the governors were expelled.[5] And again Mikhail
marched on Novgorod.

The second campaign of 1316, however, was a dismal failure.
Intending to attack Novgorod from the south (Torzhok, its
defences removed, no longer presented an obstacle), the Tver'

---

that the sum was reduced to 12,000 *grivny* at the treaty of 1317 (perhaps, then,
15,000 was the original sum demanded?). (*See* GVNiP, No. 11, p. 23;
Cherepnin, RFA, vol. i, p. 288.) A Novgorod silver *grivna* in the thirteenth
and fourteenth centuries weighed between 195 and 204·5 grammes. (*See*
E. I. Kamentseva and N. V. Ustyugov, *Russkaya metrologiya*, pp. 52–65.)

   [1] *See* NL, p. 95. No mention is made of the fate of Fedor of Rzheva.

   [2] *See* PSRL, xv, col. 408. *Cf.* x, p. 179: "He destroyed Torzhok."

   [3] *See* NL, p. 95. The treaty has not survived in manuscript. It is probably
the same *gramota novotorz'skaya* "which was drawn up in Torzhok", and
which is mentioned as superseded in the treaty of 1317 (GVNiP, No. 11,
p. 24), as well as the document "written in Torzhok in the presence of
Taitemer' (one of the Tatars who accompanied Mikhail from the Horde in
1315)" which is mentioned as superseded in the treaty between Yury,
Novgorod and Mikhail (ibid., No. 13, p. 26). According to the Nikon
Chronicle, Mikhail arbitrarily (*iz svoey ruki*) appointed two *posadniki*, Mikhail
Klementovich and Ivan Dmitrievich (PSRL, x, p. 179). The more reliable
Novgorod First Chronicle states that Semen Klimovich, who was one of the
five district representatives of Novgorod, became *posadnik* in 1316. (*See*
Yanin, NP, p. 169.)

   [4] *See* TL, p. 355; PSRL, xxv, p. 160. The Novgorod First Chronicle
makes no mention of the incident.

   [5] *See* NL, p. 95.

army got as far as the village of Ust'yany on the Lovat' river, just south of Lake Il'men'. It was clear to Mikhail that resistance would be stiff. A new system of fortifications (*ostrog*) had been built around Novgorod, and all the main provinces of Novgorod, as well as Pskov, had rallied round to defend the city. Mikhail gave the order to withdraw. Marching through unfamiliar territory and deliberately led astray by local guides, the unhappy army lost its way amidst the lakes and marshes. The exhausted soldiers burned or threw away their weapons and armour. Reduced to near-starvation, they chewed the leather of their belts and shin-guards. The cavalrymen returned home on foot having eaten their horses.[1]

The events which followed the battle and treaty of Torzhok in February 1316—the expulsion of Mikhail's governors from Novgorod, the summary justice dealt out to his sympathizers and the disastrous Tverite campaign, which was undertaken later in the year—by no means meant the liberation of Novgorod from Mikhail's control. True, the republic had rid itself of his *namestniki*, whose presence in the city symbolized the physical submission of Novgorod to Tver' and the overlordship of the grand prince. But Mikhail had two trump cards: supplies to Novgorod from the east were blocked,[2] and a number of Novgorod's senior citizens were being held as hostages in Tver'. These were intolerable conditions. Novgorod accordingly decided to reopen negotiations with the grand prince, and in January or February of 1317 Archbishop David was despatched to Tver' to start talks.[3] The purpose of his mission was to persuade Mikhail to release his hostages. According to the chronicle of Tver', he was successful. A treaty was concluded. Novgorod agreed to pay an indemnity of 12,000 *grivny* in lieu of the higher

---

[1] See *NL*, p. 95; *TL*, p. 355; *PSRL*, xv, cols. 408–9. The information that the Tverite army got lost because of the treacherous guides is, not surprisingly, only found in the Tver' chronicles.

[2] This is evident from the terms of the treaty of 1317. See below, p. 80.

[3] See *PSRL*, xv, cols. 408–9 (Tver' Chronicle), where David's mission is reported after Mikhail's unsuccessful campaign, under 6824 (1 March 1316 to 28 February 1317). Other chronicle accounts (originating in Novgorod and Moscow) say that David's mission took place *after* 28 February 1317 and that it was a failure ("the prince did not listen to him"). (See *NL*, p. 95; *PSRL*, v, p. 206; xxv, p. 161.)

sum agreed upon at the treaty of Torzhok in 1316;[1] this was to be paid in three instalments of 3,000 *grivny* (3,000 having already been paid) on 20 February, 6 March and 27 March.[2] As soon as the first instalment was paid Mikhail agreed to lift his economic blockade; the hostages would be freed and the previous treaties of Gorodok (1314) and Torzhok (1316) would be annulled on payment of the whole sum. All Novgorod land which had been occupied or illegally bought by Mikhail or his lieutenants was to revert to Novgorod. Prisoners of war held in Tver' were to be repatriated without ransom. Furthermore the grand prince agreed to undertake no aggressive action against Novgorod, Pskov or any of the dependent districts of Novgorod (*prigorody*), nor would he hamper Novgorodian merchants within his territories. Novgorod promised to take no reprisals against any of Mikhail's sympathizers.[3] Apart from these clauses, Novgorod

---

[1] *See* above, p. 77, note 5.

[2] "*Na sbor*" (i.e. *sobornoe voskresenie*, the first Sunday in Lent); "*na sredokrest'e*" (third Sunday in Lent); "*na verb'nitsyu*" (Palm Sunday). Easter in 1317 was on 3 April. (*See* Kamentseva, *R. Khr.*, Table 13.)

[3] The question of the dating of the treaty (*GVNiP*, No. 11, pp. 23–4) is a vexed one. Most serious pre-revolutionary scholars, including Borzakovsky and Presnyakov, considered it was concluded just after the battle of Torzhok (February 1316); immediately after the battle a temporary truce was arranged (*gramota novotorz'skaya*); this was converted into a treaty after both armies had returned home.

A. A. Zimin, the Soviet historian, also dates the treaty 1316, between 10 and 29 February, the first payment being due on 29 February, which was the first Sunday in Lent (Easter was on 11 April in 1316). He argues that "the contents of the treaty document clearly reflect the situation resulting from the military defeat of Novgorod"; but he says nothing of the superseded "treaty of Torzhok". (*See* Zimin, "O khronologii", pp. 309–12.) Cherepnin, on the other hand, dates the treaty early 1317, arguing, *inter alia*, that the clause in which Mikhail agrees to bear no ill will to Pskov and the other *prigorody* of Novgorod could only have meaning *after* the rallying of Pskov and the other Novgorod districts to the aid of Novgorod in 1316. (*See* Cherepnin, *RFA*, vol. i, pp. 282–90.)

I am inclined to accept Cherepnin's view, as I consider that the terms of the treaty are more applicable to the circumstances *following* the events of 1316 (Pskov's support of Novgorod, the retention of Novgorod boyars in Tver', etc.); and I conclude that the treaty was negotiated by Archbishop David shortly before 20 February 1317, the date of the payment of the first instalment. Thus I accept the evidence of the Tver' Chronicle (to the effect that David went to Tver' *before* 1 March 1317 and succeeded in concluding a

and Tver' were to revert to the terms of the treaty which had been ratified in 1307 when Mikhail was officially recognized as prince of Novgorod. In other words, Novgorod was once again to acknowledge the overlordship of the prince of Tver' and suffer the presence of his governors in the city.

Thus by February 1317 Mikhail had once again established his authority in Novgorod as grand prince. It was the last time he was to enjoy such power. The succeeding events of 1317, confused and confusingly reported by contemporary and later chroniclers, show that the strength of Tver', or any other principality for that matter, depended not so much on military superiority or political wisdom as on the degree of support enjoyed by the prince at the Golden Horde.

Soon after the treaty between Mikhail and Novgorod had been concluded, Yury of Moscow returned from the Golden Horde. He had not wasted his long stay at the khan's court. He arrived in north-east Russia with a Tatar wife (Konchaka, Khan Uzbek's sister), two Tatar officials (posly), Kavgady and Astrabyl, and a Tatar army. He also had obtained the patent for the grand-princely throne of Vladimir. On hearing the news, Mikhail, who had no reason to believe that he had been bereft of the title of grand prince in absentia, summoned the armies of the princes of Suzdalia and marched to meet his rival at Kostroma. For a long time the opposing armies faced each other on the banks of the Volga. At length parleys were initiated. Mikhail was told by Kavgady of the khan's decision. He had no alternative but to yield his title—and all his Suzdalian allies—to Yury, and to hasten back to Tver' where he proceeded to strengthen the fortifications in anticipation of a combined Muscovite-Tatar attack.[1]

---

treaty), rather than that of the other chronicles (to the effect that David went to Tver' *after* 1 March 1317 and failed to conclude a treaty). It is interesting to note that the treaty between Yury, Mikhail and Novgorod (dated early spring 1318) contains a reference to the supersession of *three* previous treaties: (i) that of Gorodok (1314); (ii) that "written in Torzhok in the presence of Taitemer'" (i.e. February 1316—*see* above, p. 77, note 5); and (iii) "the bishop's silver [document] (*vlad[ych]nya serebrenaya*)"—i.e. the treaty of February 1317. (*See GVNiP*, No. 13, p. 26.)

[1] The meeting of Mikhail and Yury at Kostroma and the yielding of the title are only mentioned in the Tver' chronicles. (*See PSRL*, xv, col. 409; xv (i), col. 37.)

While Mikhail saw to the defences of his capital, Yury of Moscow prepared to deliver the final crushing blow which was to subjugate or eliminate Tver'. He had every reason to be confident of success. He could count on the goodwill and considerable material support of the khan as well as the loyal co-operation of Novgorod, Pereyaslavl' and probably Rostov too. Furthermore, although he had no time to be officially placed upon the throne of Vladimir,[1] he was *de facto* grand prince and as such could dispose of the troops of the "Lower lands"—that is to say, the armies of the princes of Suzdalia, who owed military allegiance to the grand prince. He planned a joint attack on Tver': Novgorod was to attack from the north-west, from Torzhok; Yury, with the main army consisting of all the troops he could muster in Suzdalia as well as the Tatar force despatched by Uzbek, was to advance from Volok Lamsky, the Novgorod stronghold, from the south.

In the late summer or early autumn of 1317 the Novgorodians, whom Yury had alerted shortly after the confrontation of Kostroma,[2] set out for Torzhok. They spent six weeks in the frontier town attempting to achieve some sort of effective liaison with Yury, who at the time was collecting his forces and moving west. It was decided that at a given date both armies should attack Tver' simultaneously. The plan failed. Whether because of poor co-ordination or pure misunderstanding,[3] the Novgorodians set out from Torzhok too early. After preliminary skirmishing along the Novgorod-Tver' border had taken place, Mikhail

---

[1] In one of the accounts of Mikhail's murder, Mikhail went to Vladimir on his way to the Horde in 1318; it would appear, too, that the majority of his boyars were there. This would indicate that Mikhail, in fact, never relinquished Vladimir. (*See PSRL*, xxv, p. 162.)

[2] According to most sources, Yury sent a Tatar, one Telebuga (Tulabugha), to Novgorod. (*See NL*, p. 96; *PSRL*, iv (i), p. 257; v, p. 207; xxv, p. 161.) According to the Trinity Chronicle, however, Yury sent his brother Ivan to summon the Novgorodians. (*See TL*, pp. 355–6.)

[3] The most detailed, intelligible and reliable account of the movement of the Novgorodian army is given in the Tver' Chronicles (*PSRL*, xv, col. 409; xv (i), col. 37). The Novgorod First Chronicle, in which the account of the happenings of 1317 is quite independent of that found in the Trinity, Ermolinsky and Tver' Chronicles and just as contemporary, says that the Novgorodians "came to Torzhok and made a treaty with Prince Mikhail . . . for they did not know where Prince Yury was" (*NL*, p. 96).

marched from Tver' and soundly defeated the Novgorodians, who could hope for no assistance from Yury. Once again the Novgorodians were obliged to treat with Mikhail. They agreed—as no doubt they were forced to agree—that in the forthcoming struggle between Tver' and Moscow they would remain strictly neutral.[1]

Meanwhile Yury was approaching the lands of Tver' with his Russo-Tatar army. In October 1317[2] he entered the town of Klin in the southern districts of Tver' and began systematically to ravage the countryside. For five weeks his headquarters were only fifteen versts from Tver' itself. In an attempt to frighten Mikhail into submission, Kavgady, Uzbek's chief representative, who had accompanied Yury from the Golden Horde, sent his ambassadors to Tver'. But Mikhail refused to listen to his blandishments and threats. Thereupon Yury moved with his army to the Volga, intending to cross it and to overrun the northern section of the principality of Tver' as he had done the southern half.[3] At this juncture Mikhail decided to attack the invaders. The two armies met on 22 December 1317 at the village of Bortenevo near Tver'.[4] In spite of what must have been Yury's superiority in numbers[5] Mikhail won a decisive victory. Amongst the prisoners

[1] "They made a treaty with Prince Mikhail of Tver' to the effect that they would not intervene on either side (*kako ne v' stupatisya ni po odinom'*)." (*See NL*, p. 96.) A. A. Zimin considers that the copy of the treaty between Mikhail and Novgorod printed in *GVNiP* (No. 12, p. 24) was in fact the treaty agreed to at this stage. His arguments are quite unconvincing. (*See* Zimin, "O khronologii", pp. 311–12.) *Cf.* Cherepnin (*RFA*, vol. i, pp. 296–9) who considers it was a draft for the treaty of 1318.

[2] The Tver' chronicles say that he spent three months in the territory of Tver' before the battle of Bortenevo (22 December 1317). (*See PSRL*, xv, col. 410; xv (i), col. 37. *Cf.* x, p. 181.)

[3] *See PSRL*, xxv, p. 162.

[4] Cherepnin gives the location of Bortenevo as "forty versts from Tver' " (*Obrazovanie*, p. 467), which is the information given in most of the chronicle accounts. (*See*, for instance, *PSRL*, xxiii, p. 98.) According to Borzakovsky (*ITK*, note 467) Bortenevo is near the river Shosha, thirty-two versts from Staritsa (Gorodok).

[5] As well as Tatar and Moscow troops Yury had under him "all the Lower land", i.e. troops from Suzdalia, and perhaps from Ryazan' too. Mikhail had under his command only his own Tverite troops and "the men of Kashin". (*See PSRL*, xv, col. 410; xv (i), col. 37; *NL*, p. 95.)

were Yury's brother Boris and his wife Konchaka, who, rumour had it, was poisoned by her captors in Tver'.[1] Yury escaped with a handful of men and fled to Novgorod. As for the Tatars, it would appear that both Mikhail and Kavgady, who was in command of them, were anxious that they should not be involved in the battle. Mikhail, indeed, warned his men not to attack the Tatar force;[2] while Kavgady, realizing no doubt that not even Tatar support would save Yury from defeat, managed to avoid the battle by ordering his troops to withdraw in time.[3]

On the day after the battle Kavgady got in touch with Mikhail and entered Tver' with his Tatars. The situation was delicate. Kavgady was too powerful a figure to treat as the ally of a conquered enemy. He had not come to ask for peace—there was no question of Tver' taking up arms against the Tatars—he had come as the representative of Khan Uzbek to discuss the question of the title of grand prince of Vladimir. Who was now to be supreme amongst the Russian princes—the victorious Mikhail, who earlier in the year had relinquished the title, no doubt under Kavgady's pressure, or the vanquished Yury, who was still, in name at least, grand prince?

There are no details of Kavgady's talks with Mikhail.[4] All we know is that Mikhail behaved with circumspection and treated Kavgady with tact and respect. But judging from subsequent events we can guess that Kavgady's aim was to persuade Mikhail

[1] "Yury's princess ... died in Tver'; *some say* she was poisoned in Tver' ..." This comes from the composite account found in the sixteenth-century Nikon Chronicle. (*See PSRL*, x, p. 181.) The Trinity and Ermolinsky Chronicles both say she was poisoned; their information recurs in the Moscow *svod* of 1479. (*See TL*, p. 356; *PSRL*, xxiii, p. 98; xxv, p. 161.) The Tver' chronicles, as might be expected, make no mention of her death, while the pro-Moscow Sofiysky First Chronicle surprisingly denies the rumour (*PSRL*, v, p. 207).

[2] This information is found only in the Ermolinsky Chronicle account (*PSRL*, xxiii, p. 98), the "Tale of the murder of Mikhail" (*PSRL*, xxv, p. 162) and the Nikon Chronicle (*PSRL*, x, p. 181).

[3] *See PSRL*, xv, col. 410; xv (i), col. 38.

[4] According to the Ermolinsky Chronicle, Kavgady deceived Mikhail, telling him that the Tatars and Yury had attacked him without the khan's permission. This information also occurs in the "Tale of the murder of Mikhail" and in the Nikon Chronicle. It is found nowhere else. (*See PSRL*, xxiii, p. 98; xxv, p. 162; x, p. 181).

not to assume the title without reference to the khan, to make peace, temporarily at least, with Yury and to put off all decisions concerning the leadership of the Russian principalities until the matter could be discussed and decided at the court of the khan. There can be little doubt that his instructions were to withhold support from the stronger of the two princes—and Mikhail by his performance at Bortenevo had proved incontestably who was the more powerful militarily.

Early in 1318 the two rivals met once more on the Volga near a village called Sineevskoe. Yury appeared with "all Novgorod and Pskov"[1] as well as with Archbishop David. It is not known whether the object of his journey to the Volga was to fight or to parley. The "Tale of the murder of Mikhail of Tver'" and the Ermolinsky Chronicle state that "there was almost another battle", but that in the end both sides managed to reach an agreement.[2] The outcome of the meeting was a decision that both princes should go to the Horde where they could argue their cases before the khan. At the same time a treaty was negotiated by Yury between Mikhail and Novgorod, which dealt mainly with routine boundary questions, the return of illegally seized lands and the repatriation of prisoners of war. In the document Yury is named grand prince, Mikhail merely prince; no mention is made of Mikhail's rights as overlord in Novgorod.[3] He was no longer considered by the Tatars, the Muscovites or the

[1] *NL*, p. 96.

[2] *See PSRL*, xxiii, p. 98; **xxv**, p. 162; *cf*. x, p. 181. This, I think, indicates that Yury intended only to parley and not to fight. No other accounts mention the military side of the encounter. Besides, as Cherepnin has pointed out (*RFA*, vol. i, p. 294), it was unlikely that Yury would take the archbishop with him unless he was intending to negotiate. The representatives of Novgorod and Pskov were presumably taken by Yury because, firstly, they would strengthen his case and, secondly, the question of the patent concerned them vitally.

[3] *See GVNiP*, No. 13, pp. 25–6 (misdated winter 1318–19); Cherepnin, *RFA*, vol. i, pp. 290 sq.; Zimin, "O khronologii", p. 312.

According to the Novgorod First Chronicle Mikhail agreed to release "Yury's brother and princess (Konchaka or Boris's wife?)" (*NL*, p. 96). *Cf*. also *PSRL*, iv, p. 49, according to which Mikhail agreed to release Afanasy and the Novgorodians who had been held in Tver' as hostages since 1315.

Novgorodians as grand prince. The fact that he even agreed to meet Yury, to treat with the conquered Novgorodians and to go to the Horde speaks eloquently for Kavgady's grim persuasive powers.

In the early spring of 1318 Yury sent the Novgorodians and Pskovites home and returned to Moscow where, before setting off for the Horde, he consulted Kavgady on how best to conduct himself at the khan's court. Acting on his advice he gathered together "all the princes of the Lower lands, and [all] the boyars from the towns and from Novgorod"[1] and, accompanied by Kavgady, set off with them to the Horde. Yury's purpose in taking with him this impressive cavalcade of princes and boyars was presumably to lay before the khan overwhelming evidence of Mikhail's misgovernment and, doubtless, misappropriation of Tatar tribute, as well as to increase the total sum of money to be offered to the khan in bribes. Meanwhile Mikhail, still acting on the advice or orders of Kavgady, sent his younger son Konstantin ahead of him to the Horde. Before leaving himself he made one more attempt to settle matters with Yury. But Yury, now confident of his ultimate success in the struggle with Tver', killed his envoy and rejected his overtures.[2]

Mikhail made little haste to depart for the Horde.[3] His delay contributed to his undoing. Before he eventually arrived in September 1318, Kavgady and Yury, so the Tver' chronicles tell us, had already begun to lay their accusations before Uzbek.[4]

The formal trial took place at the end of the year. From the many and varied accounts of the proceedings it appears that three main charges were brought against Mikhail: he was accused firstly of withholding Tatar tribute; secondly of fighting against Kavgady; and thirdly of murdering Uzbek's sister. Mikhail denied the accusations. The first, and main, charge he attempted to refute with written evidence, denying that he had ever mis-

---

[1] *PSRL*, xxiii, p. 99; xxv, p. 162.

[2] *See PSRL*, xv, col. 410; xv (i), col. 38.

[3] In August, while Mikhail was in Vladimir, one Akhmyl was sent from the Horde instructing him to set off immediately. (*See PSRL*, xxv, p. 162.)

[4] *See PSRL*, xv, cols. 410–11; xv (i), col. 38.

appropriated moneys collected for the Tatar tribute.¹ He had not fought against the khan's representative—indeed he had "absolved him from battle" and treated him with respect. As for the third charge, that of being responsible for Konchaka's death, "he called upon God as a witness that it had never been in his thoughts to do such a thing."

The result of the trial was a foregone conclusion. Yury of Moscow and Kavgady had done their work well. Mikhail was sentenced to death. The chronicler of Tver' describes his execution (22 November 1318) simply, with an impressive absence of heroics and in a style reminiscent of the Primary Chronicle's version of the murder of Boris and Gleb:

Early on Wednesday the blessed Mikhail rose and told the priest to begin Matins and the Hours, and he listened with many tears and bitter sighing. And he bade him begin the office of the Holy Communion, and he himself sang from the books and prayed with emotion. And when he finished he sat down. And his son Konstantin and his attendants sat by him. . . . And one of his servants jumped into his tent and said: "O master, Kavgady and Yury are coming from the Horde to your tent." The blessed one, seeing them coming, said: "They are coming to kill me." And he quickly sent off his son to the khan's wife. Now Kavgady and Yury dismounted from their horses at the market-place near his tent. The murderers of the blessed one burst into his tent like wild beasts and merciless drinkers of blood. He stood there in perplexity; they seized him by the yoke [which had been attached to his neck], struck him heavily and hurled him against the tent so that the side broke. But he got up again. Then many seized him and threw him on the ground and kicked him with their feet. And one of the lawless murderers, by the name of Romanets, took out his

---

¹ According to a fifteenth-century account of his death (that found in *PSRL*, v, pp. 207–15, and xxv, pp. 161–6) Mikhail "spoke with much evidence, saying: 'How much treasure did I give to the khan and his princes!', for he had it all written down". Perhaps Mikhail's delay in coming to the Horde could be explained by his collection of "evidence". He must have known that withholding of money due to the khan would be the main charge against him.

great sword and struck the blessed one in the heart, on the right side, and twisting the blade around cut out his holy heart. And so he gave up his spirit to the hands of God.[1]

The varying accounts of the events of 1318, written either with a pro-Moscow or a pro-Tver' bias, make it hard to apportion blame for the murder of Mikhail. In some accounts the participation of Uzbek is so toned down as virtually to exonerate him, while Yury and Kavgady are portrayed as the forces of evil, working together for Mikhail's destruction.[2] In others, Uzbek's active role in stirring up trouble between the Russian princes is stressed, while Yury is shown more as a tool of the khan than as an active agent scheming for the downfall of his rival.[3] On the available contradictory and tendentious evidence all we can say is that Yury had every possible opportunity of influencing the khan and that it was entirely in his interest to do so and thus physically to have his rival removed. At the same time it must be borne in mind that at this juncture in Russo-Tatar relations no major political decision affecting the balance of power in Suzdalia could be taken without the approval of the khan and his advisers. Mikhail was eliminated because his removal fitted in with the overall Tatar policy of playing off one principality against another.

The events of 1317 and 1318 show more clearly than those of any year since Mikhail's accession just how powerless were the princes of north-east Russia to decide their own fate and to win supremacy by force of arms or economic pressure alone. In spite of, and because of, Tver''s obvious military superiority over Moscow, Mikhail was unable to retain the title of grand prince and the leadership which the title gave him over the other Russian princes. To a certain extent, of course, success at the Horde depended on the amount of wealth the individual prince was able to dispose of for the purpose of bribing the khan and his advisers;

---

[1] *PSRL*, xv, cols. 411–12.

[2] *See* the account in the Tver' chronicles, written, Cherepnin thinks, before the anti-Tatar uprising of 1327. The account betrays an anxiety on the part of the writer not to anger the khan unnecessarily. (*See* Cherepnin, *Obrazovanie*, pp. 469–70.)

[3] This is particularly the case with the florid description given in the Sofiysky First Chronicle (*PSRL*, v). (*See* Nasonov, *Mongoly i Rus'*, p. 88.)

at the same time his honesty and reliability as a tax-collector were taken into consideration, and no doubt they influenced the khan's choice to some degree. But it would be naïve to imagine that during the period under consideration the khans of the Golden Horde were motivated solely, or even largely, by greed. During the thirteenth century the Horde had been prepared by and large to allow the Russian princes to follow their own peculiar system of succession so long as no individual prince became unmanageably strong and no one district emerged superior in strength to the others—and this was largely guaranteed by the unparochial behaviour of most of the grand princes. But now two powers had emerged, both capable, if given the opportunity, of overrunning and subjecting all the other principalities of Suzdalia, and the Horde could not afford to allow either to achieve this supremacy. The only way of preventing it was consistently to uphold and strengthen the weaker of the two and actively to intervene with military support and political pressure. Indeed, when Moscow succeeded in gaining control of Novgorod in 1315, Uzbek came to the help of Tver'; and when Tver' defeated Moscow and Novgorod in the following year, Uzbek intervened on behalf of Moscow.[1]

When even military intervention and threats failed, drastic measures had to be taken. Such a drastic measure was the murder of Mikhail in 1318. He had shown himself to be too strong. In spite of Novgorod's determination to resist Tverite control and to espouse the cause of Moscow, he had managed somehow to retain his grip on the republic; in spite of opposition from the Church, he had achieved general recognition of his title among the princes of Suzdalia; and he had successfully resisted Yury in spite of Yury's Tatar backing. He had, therefore, to be removed. The charges which were formally levelled against him at the Horde in 1318 probably indicated little more than a conventional attempt to vest his trial with a semblance of justice. His real guilt in the eyes of the khan—for which he could hardly be arraigned—was that he had become too powerful. Perhaps, too, the Tatars, at a time when they were beginning to shown an active and aggressive

[1] Of course the persuasive powers of Yury and Mikhail should be taken into consideration as well. Both spent some time at the court of the khan before appearing in north-east Russia with Tatar armies.

interest in Lithuania,[1] suspected what may be described as the foreshadowing of Tver''s Western orientation: Mikhail's sister was married to King Yury of Galich; his eldest son was soon to be betrothed to a Lithuanian princess; and his bishop and adviser of the early years, Andrey, was the son of a Lithuanian prince—facts which Metropolitan Petr, who himself was a Galician by origin and who had first-hand knowledge of the delicate political situation in the border state of Bryansk, no doubt impressed upon Khan Uzbek during his visit to the Horde in 1313.

[ii] THE STRUGGLE FOR THE THRONE OF VLADIMIR, 1318–1328

Yury of Moscow reigned from 1318 to 1322 as grand prince of Vladimir. Very little is known about his rule. There are no extant treaties; the chronicles are reticent, to say the least of it; there is no information about the activities of the metropolitan; little or nothing is known about Muscovite control over the grand-princely territories of Vladimir, Pereyaslavl' and Kostroma;[2] no reasons are given for actions which seem to betoken violent changes of fortune or policy, such as Yury's sudden "flight" to Novgorod in 1321 or Uzbek's equally inexplicable decision to give the patent to Dmitry of Tver' in 1322. It is as though the subsequent chroniclers were anxious to expunge from the record all information which might be useful to the historian or which might further discolour the already tarnished reputation of the princes of Moscow.

One striking fact, however, emerges from the scattered recorded incidents of Yury's four years of reign: namely that the Tatars were more determined than ever before to control political affairs in north-east Russia. There is evidence of greatly increased Tatar activity and interference in Suzdalia: between 1320 and

---

[1] In 1315, for the first time since 1287, the Tatars invaded Lithuania and "caused great damage". (*See* Pashuto, *OLG*, p. 396.)

[2] Clearly Moscow held them all: Pereyaslavl' had not passed from Muscovite ownership since the beginning of Mikhail's reign; Yury was visited in Vladimir by a Tatar *posol* in 1320 (*see* PSRL, x, p. 187); and Yury's daughter was married in Kostroma (*see* PSRL, xv, col. 414).

1322 no less than four Tatar expeditions are recorded in the chronicles,[1] all of which caused much "evil" or "suffering". Yury was clearly under strict supervision from his masters at the Horde.

Yury's difficulties, however, were increased by the fact that he had to contend both with the latent hostility of the Tverites and with the rivalry of his youngest brother Ivan. It was the latter problem which proved the harder to deal with.

Ivan Danilovich had hitherto remained in the background. The chronicles, unaccountably, make no mention of his activities for fifteen years after the battle of Pereyaslavl' in 1305;[2] presumably he sat quietly in Pereyaslavl' during this period. In 1320 he set off to the Golden Horde. Why he went is not known. The purpose of his mission, however, may have been to pacify Uzbek and to forestall reprisals against Rostov, the inhabitants of which had in that same year expelled certain "evil Tatars".[3] Whatever the original purpose of his visit, there can be no doubt as to the way he employed his time at Uzbek's court and as to the result of his stay at Saray. In 1322 the future prince of Moscow and grand prince of Vladimir appeared in Suzdalia with Uzbek's special envoy, Akhmyl, who four years previously had been sent to hurry Mikhail of Tver' on his way to the Horde.[4] Although Akhmyl and his army took the customary and, as far as we know, totally unmotivated punitive measures and "did much beastliness throughout the Lower lands",[5] the real aim of his visit, and of

[1] 1320 in Rostov (*PSRL*, i, col. 530; iv (i), p. 258; v, p. 216; xxv, p. 166); 1320 in Vladimir (*PSRL*, x, p. 187); 1321 in Kashin (ibid.); 1322 in the "Lower lands" (*NL*, p. 96; *TL*, p. 357; *PSRL*, xxv, p. 167.)

[2] With the exception of the isolated, and dubious, mention of his mission to Novgorod in 1317. *See above*, p. 82, note 2.

[3] *See PSRL*, i, col. 530; iv (i), p. 258; and v, p. 216 (in all of which the expulsion of the Tatars from Rostov is mentioned, but not Ivan's trip to Saray); *TL*, p. 356 (where only Ivan's trip is mentioned); *PSRL*, xxv, p. 166 (where the two are combined).

The information contained in the Novgorod First Chronicle (*mladshy izvod*) to the effect that in 1320 Ivan joined Yury in a campaign against "Prince Ivan Rostislavich [*sic*]" of Ryazan' (*NL*, p. 338) can be rejected in favour of the more accurate and older *starshy izvod* of the same chronicle, according to which "Prince Yury invaded Ryazan' against Prince Ivan of Ryazan'" (*NL*, p. 96).

[4] *See above*, p. 86, note 3.

[5] *PSRL*, iv (i), p. 258; v, p. 216; xxiii, p. 101; xxv, p. 167; *TL*, p. 357. For

Ivan Danilovich's too, was to summon Yury to the Horde.[1] It looks as though Ivan had spent his two years at Saray ingratiating himself with the khan and working to bring about the downfall of his brother. Uzbek could have wished for nothing better: if one thing was more advantageous to the Tatars of the Golden Horde than two mutually hostile principalities in north-east Russia it was a split between the rulers of one of these principalities. We may be sure that Ivan received a sympathetic and encouraging hearing.

Although at the outset of Yury's reign as grand prince relations between Moscow and Tver' were strained, they soon improved. Yury returned to Moscow in the winter of 1318-19 bringing with him not only the corpse of his murdered cousin, but also Mikhail's son Konstantin and his boyars and servants who had accompanied him to the Horde in 1318; all of these Ivan held in Moscow as a pledge for the good behaviour of the three remaining sons of Mikhail—Dmitry, Aleksandr and Vasily. The first move to relax the tension between the two principalities was taken by Moscow. Metropolitan Petr's nominee and subsequent biographer, Bishop Prokhor of Rostov, went to Tver' in the summer of 1319 to conduct the negotiations. The Tverites were unable to bargain: the advantages—in the shape of the hostages—were all on Moscow's side. The widow and sons of Mikhail, urged on by the bishop of Tver', Varsanofy, yet another appointee of the pro-Muscovite metropolitan, decided to despatch Aleksandr, the second eldest brother, to Vladimir to come to terms with the grand prince.[2] On 29 June 1319 a treaty was concluded, the terms

---

some reason he "took" Yaroslavl', the prince of which, David Fedorovich, had just died. The capture and sack of Yaroslavl' was probably a reprisal for the anti-Tatar disturbances in neighbouring Rostov in 1320. *See* above, p. 91, note 3.

According to the Life of Tsarevich Petr of the Horde, Akhmyl, after sacking Yaroslavl', intended to march on Rostov. Bishop Prokhor fled, but was persuaded by Ignaty (Tsarevich Petr's great-grandson) to return and meet Akhmyl. Akhmyl, mollified by bribes and by Prokhor's healing of his son's eyes, left Rostov alone. (*See* Ekzemplyarsky, *VUK*, vol. ii, pp. 38-9.)

[1] *See PSRL*, xv, col. 414.

[2] According to the Chronicle of Tver' (*PSRL*, xv, col. 412) the initiative was taken by the bishop of Rostov; according to other sources (*PSRL*, v, p. 215; xxiii, p. 101; xxv, p. 166) the initiative was taken by Anna, Mikhail's

of which are not known, and Aleksandr was allowed to return to Tver' with his brother and with the body of his father. In the following year the agreement was sealed by the marriage of Konstantin to Yury's daughter Sofia in Kostroma.[1]

It may well be that the rapprochement between Tver' and Moscow was not to the liking of the khan. Even though Uzbek must by now have been aware of the ambitions of Ivan Danilovich, which, if properly exploited, were sufficient to cripple Moscow, nevertheless a state of antagonism between Yury and the princes of Tver' was preferable to one of friendship. Such considerations perhaps motivated the khan's actions in 1321. In the spring of that year one Gayanchar arrived in the Tverite town of Kashin ostensibly to collect overdue taxes.[2] He caused, the chronicler laconically states, "much distress in Kashin". But evidently Gayanchar's task was not only to harass the people of Kashin: it appeared that he, or at any rate some representative of the khan, instructed Yury of Moscow to march on Tver'. Barely a year after the dynastic alliance between the houses of Moscow and Tver' had been celebrated in Kostroma, Yury summoned all the available troops "from the Lower lands and Suzdal'" in Pereyaslavl' and proceeded north-west towards Kashin. Dmitry of Tver' and his brothers, meanwhile, set off with "the armies of Tver' and Kashin" to meet Yury. The two forces met on the Volga. Thanks to the mediation of the bishop of Tver' a battle was avoided and a treaty was drawn up. Dmitry agreed not to attempt to become grand prince and to hand over to Yury the sum of 2,000 silver rubles, evidently the Tatar tribue which Kashin, or perhaps the whole principality of Tver', owed to the Tatars.[3]

widow, and her sons, who were anxious only to recover Mikhail's corpse; this was grudgingly granted by Yury.

The Tver' Chronicle talks of "Prokhor bishop of Rostov and Yaroslav of Starodub" (*Prokhor episkop Rostovski i Yaroslav Starodubsky*). As there was no known Prince Yaroslav of Starodub (and certainly no bishop of that name —Yaroslav is not a Christian name), this is clearly an error for "bishop of Rostov, Yaroslavl' and Starodub". Cherepnin mistakenly thinks there were two bishops involved—of Rostov and of Yaroslavl'. (*See Obrazovanie*, p. 473.)

[1] See PSRL, xv, col. 414; xv (i), col. 41.
[2] He was assisted by a "Jewish money-lender". (*See PSRL*, xv, col. 414; xv (i), col. 41.)
[3] See NL, p. 96; PSRL, iv (i), p. 258; v, p. 216; x, pp. 187–8; xv, col. 414;

Whether or not the Tatars were behind the clash between Moscow and Tver' in 1321, the results can only have been highly gratifying to the khan. In spite of the dynastic links between the two families and in spite of the promises made by Dmitry not to contend for the grand principality, in the following year Dmitry Mikhaylovich went to the Horde, probably to complain of the fiscal misdeeds of the grand prince, and certainly to urge the khan to give him the patent. The old rivalry was still there. Still more satisfying from the Tatar point of view was the fact that directly after the meeting on the Volga Yury decamped with all the cash he had collected from Dmitry and betook himself to Novgorod where he was to stay almost continuously for the next four years. By his action he had outlawed himself, voluntarily or involuntarily, and he had given Dmitry the pretext for complaint. The Tatars, it is true, lost the 2,000 rubles which Yury should have paid them. But the most powerful prince in north-east Russia had discredited himself and, as it were, removed himself from the political scene.

It is hard to explain Yury's act. The chroniclers of Tver' leave no doubt as to what he did: "In that winter (1321, after the treaty with Dmitry) Prince Yury, having taken the tribute money from the Mikhaylovichi [which he had received] according to the treaty, did not go to meet the khan's envoy (i.e. to hand it over), but went with the money to Novgorod."[1] At first sight it looks like an act of open defiance. But was it so in fact? Might not Yury's departure to Novgorod be explained by the fact that he was called there on urgent business and had no opportunity of handing over the tribute money to the representative of the khan? It is interesting to note that the chronicles of Moscow and Novgorod make no mention of his refusal "to meet the khan's

---

xv (i), col. 41; xxiii, p. 101; xxv, p. 166. In the Tver' and Nikon Chronicles, ex-Bishop Andrey, who retired in 1316, is named as the mediator. Presnyakov thinks that Andrey negotiated the treaty and that the pro-Moscow Varsanofy may have left Tver' during the crisis. (*See* Presnyakov, *Obrazovanie*, p. 134, note 2.) The silver rubles here referred to were probably Novgorod rubles equal to *grivny* in value (*see* above, p. 77, note 5.) A Muscovite ruble was equal to half a Novgorod ruble in value. (*See* Kamentseva and Ustyugov, *Russkaya metrologiya*, p. 60.)

[1] *PSRL*, xv, col. 414; xv (i), col. 41.

envoy";[1] it should be remembered that it was, after all, in the interest of the Tverites to discredit Yury and to give Dmitry Mikhaylovich some pretext, however feeble, for breaking his oath and "seeking the grand principality".

That Yury was urgently needed in Novgorod there can be little doubt. Not only do the Novgorod chronicles specifically state that he was "summoned",[2] but also the military requirements in the north made it imperative that Novgorod should have a prince of the widest possible military and diplomatic experience to conduct her affairs. During the last third of the thirteenth century and the first twenty years of the fourteenth there had been an almost uninterrupted state of war between Novgorod on the one hand and Norway and Sweden on the other.[3] Indeed, between 1311 and 1320 there were no less than five recorded acts of war between Novgorod and the "Germans" (i.e. the Swedes and Norwegians),[4] mostly clashes between the outpost town of Korela on the west coast of Lake Ladoga and the Swedish stronghold of Vyborg (Viipuri) over the disputed Finnish border territories. Furthermore an experienced military commander was required by the Novgorodians to help them wage their wars and increase their empire in the north, in the lands beyond the Volga. Yury was the last Russian grand prince ever to lead the forces of free Novgorod or to conduct her diplomacy. So important were his activities there that the Russian chronicles contain little else but news of Novgorod during the years 1323 and 1324.

Yury arrived in Novgorod probably at the end of 1321 or at the beginning of 1322. One chronicle[5] mentions a quarrel between

---

[1] The only other chronicle to mention the fact is the Nikon Chronicle (*PSRL*, x, p. 138), which, according to Nasonov, used as one of its sources the 1425 Kashin redaction of the Tver' chronicles. (*See* Nasonov, "Letopisnye pamyatniki", section 4.)

[2] "*pozvan novgorodtsi*" (*NL*, p. 96).

[3] *See* I. P. Shaskol'sky, "Dogovory Novgoroda s Norvegiey," p. 46.

[4] Viz. 1311, Prince Dmitry Romanovich's (of Bryansk?) campaign into Finland (*NL*, p. 93); 1313, clash between Swedes and town of Ladoga (ibid., p. 94); 1314, revolt of Korela (ibid., p. 94); 1318, Novgorod's invasion of Finland (ibid., p. 95); 1320, piratical raid on Norway by Luka and Ignat Molygin—the first recorded *ushkuynik* raid: *see* V. N. Bernadsky, *Novgorod*, p. 39; *PSRL*, iv (i), p. 258.

[5] *See PSRL*, x, p. 188.

Yury and Novgorod, which was patched up early in 1322; the Novgorod chronicles are careful to omit any reference to it. Once an agreement had been reached with the leaders of the republic, Yury set about Novgorod's military affairs in earnest. His first act was to have the siege artillery of Novgorod put into working order.[1] The guns were soon to be needed. In the spring of 1322 the Swedes attacked Korela. Yury led a Novgorod army north and defeated them.[2] He then set off west to retaliate by attacking the Swedish stronghold of Vyborg. The expedition was a failure—Yury was unable to capture the town and left after bombarding it with six guns for a month.[3]

While Yury was occupied with the affairs of Novgorod, Dmitry of Tver' set off to try his luck at the Golden Horde. His mission was entirely successful. Uzbek gave him the patent and a "powerful envoy" to seat him upon the throne. He returned to northeast Russia as grand prince in the autumn or winter of 1322.[4] The end of Yury's political career, however, was marked not so much by Dmitry's success at the Horde as by his own brother's re-emergence on the political scene. At about the same time as Dmitry left Suzdalia for the Horde, Ivan arrived with Akhmyl, whose task it was both to punish Rostov and Yaroslavl' for the anti-Tatar revolt of 1320 and to summon Yury to the presence of the khan.[5]

On returning from his Finnish expedition, Yury was greeted with the news that Uzbek demanded his presence in Saray and that Dmitry of Tver' was either in the process of succeeding him or had already done so. There was little he could do but comply with the khan's instructions. Resistance was out of the question, especially in view of the fact that his brother Ivan, with full

---

[1] See NL, p. 96.

[2] See NL, p. 96; PSRL, x, p. 188.

[3] See NL, p. 96.

[4] He left just before or after Yury's Finnish expedition. (See PSRL, x, p. 188 (before); xv, col. 414, and NL p. 96 (after).) Budovnits states that he "accused Yury of keeping back the money due to the khan". (See Budovnits, "Otrazhenie", p. 87.) Cf. Nasonov, Mongoly i Rus', p. 90.

[5] Most of the chronicles mention Akhmyl's arrival immediately after Dmitry's departure (PSRL, iv (i), p. 258; v, p. 216; xv, col. 414; xxiii, p. 101). Cf., however, the Trinity and Nikon Chronicles (TL, p. 357; PSRL, x, p. 188).

Tatar backing, was probably in control of Moscow by now.[1] All he could hope to do was to argue his case, declare his innocence and attempt to bribe the khan. With a party of representatives from Novgorod, whom he begged to accompany him, he set off eastwards towards the "Lower lands".[2] With him he took his "treasury (*kazna*)"—all his cash and valuables—intending, no doubt, either to prove his innocence with regard to any charges Dmitry might have made concerning misappropriation of Tatar tribute or to pay his way back to the good favours of the khan. The Tverites were waiting for him. Dmitry's brother Aleksandr caught Yury in the area of Rzheva, west of Tver',[3] captured his boyars and relieved him of all his possessions. Yury managed to escape to Pskov.[4]

With few or no men, no money and no possessions the fugitive prince can hardly have been a welcome visitor in Pskov. Yet Pskov, that home of so many lost causes, received him well, "with honour and wholeheartedly",[5] says the local chronicler. What advantage the Pskovites hoped to gain by harbouring an outlaw, it is hard to say. The best they can have wished for was that Yury would persuade the Novgorodians to lend military assistance in their struggle with the Livonian Order—indeed they may well have extracted a promise of future help from Yury in exchange for which he was to be allowed to remain unmolested in Pskov until his fate was decided.[6]

Yury arrived in Pskov in the autumn of 1322. His arrival preceded the most intensive and determined series of attacks

[1] Both his other brothers, Boris and Afanasy, were dead: the former died in 1320, the latter (in Novgorod) in 1322.

[2] See NL, p. 96.

[3] "*Na Urdome*". There is a river Urdoma in the Yaroslavl' district and a village of Urdom near Rzheva. Presumably the latter is meant here. (*See* Ekzemplyarsky, *VUK*, vol. i, p. 69, note 180.)

[4] See NL, pp. 96-7; PSRL, iv (i), p. 258; v, p. 216; x, p. 188; xv, col. 414.

[5] PL, ii, pp. 22, 89.

[6] After mentioning an attack by the Teutonic Order on Pskov in March 1323 the Pskov chronicler adds bitterly: "but Yury and the Novgorodians did not help". Later in the year the Pskovites while under heavy attack from the Livonians sent messenger after messenger to "Grand Prince Yury and to Novgorod"—it was in vain, and the chronicler again repeats: "but Grand Prince Yury and the Novgorodians did not help". (*See* ibid., pp. 89-90.)

D

that the Livonian Order had carried out against Pskov for a long time. Since the end of the thirteenth century when the great Lithuanian-born hero of Pskov, Prince Dovmont, had inflicted his final decisive defeat on the Livonians and forced them to withdraw, there had been a state of peace between the two neighbours. It was as though Yury's presence in Pskov acted as a signal for the Germans to recommence their offensive. At first it amounted to little more than a few isolated acts of aggression, but it was enough to make the Pskovites take decisive action. Unable to rely on their own resources or on aid from Novgorod, they sent to Lithuania for help. On 3 February 1323 "Prince David", the *voevoda* of Grodno, turned up and took over the defences of Pskov.[1]

It was hardly surprising that Novgorod was not prepared to help her sister-state. While the Pskovites were requesting Lithuania to help them in their struggle against the Germans, the Novgorodians were discussing terms for a defensive and offensive pact with the Livonians against Lithuania. Indeed, six days before David's arrival in Pskov, the *Komturs* of Wenden and Dünemunde signed a treaty with "Bishop David, *Posadnik* Varfolomey, *Tysyatsky* Avram and all the people of Novgorod", in which both sides agreed to help each other against the Lithuanians and to sign no peace with them without mutual consultation; furthermore, should Pskov ally herself to Lithuania, then both Novgorod and Livonia were to assist each other in case of Pskovite aggression and to continue the struggle until Pskov was again subjected to Novgorod (*"het se den Novgarderen underdanich werden"*).[2]

The Novgorodians made no effort to abide by the terms of the treaty. Throughout the spring and summer of 1323 Pskov and

[1] See PL, ii, pp. 22, 89. *Cf*. Pashuto, OLG, p. 393; H. Paszkiewicz, *Jagiellonowie*, pp. 340–1.

[2] For the German text of the treaty, *see* GVNiP, No. 37, pp. 65–7.

Pashuto considers that the treaty of 1323 was the result of the Novgorod *boyarstvo*'s alarm at the invitation of Prince David to Pskov and that it was "directed against the Lithuanian prince in Pskov". This is clearly a misunderstanding, as the treaty was signed *before* David of Grodno arrived in Pskov. The "prince" mentioned in the only surviving (German) copy of the treaty must refer to Yury—indeed, he is twice referred to as the prince of *Novgorod* (*"de Novgarden koning"*, *"der Novgardere koning"*). (*See* ibid., pp. 65, 66; Pashuto, OLG, p. 393.)

Livonia were at war. As soon as Prince David arrived in February, he led his army and the Pskovites across the Narova river and ravaged the northern territories of the Order as far as the port of Revel' (Tallinn). Twice the Germans retaliated—in March they invaded, but withdrew after a few days, and in May they returned with a large army to besiege Pskov. On both occasions the Pskovites appealed in vain to Novgorod and to Yury for help. They were saved from disaster by the reappearance of Prince David and his Lithuanian army. He succeeded in driving the Germans out of the land of Pskov and forcing the Order to accept terms favourable to the Pskovites.[1]

As soon as it became known that Pskov had summoned, and, in February 1323, received, Lithuanian help, and that consequently, according to the treaty with Livonia, Novgorod and Pskov were technically in a state of war, Novgorod was obliged to request Yury to leave Pskov immediately. There were two good reasons for this. Firstly, Yury, whom the Novgorodians still considered grand prince of Vladimir in spite of Dmitry of Tver''s appointment by Uzbek, could only prove an embarrassment if he remained in Pskov, which was now overtly allied with Lithuania.[2] Secondly, and more important, Novgorod needed a general of experience, even though he had no army of his own, to conduct her affairs in the north and the north-east. Yury, for his part, was only too anxious to leave Pskov: he had no means of persuading the Pskovites to drop their dangerous alliance with Lithuania which might well be exploited by Yury's enemy, Dmitry of Tver', himself married to the daughter of the grand prince of Lithuania.[3] Furthermore, Dmitry of Tver' might well demand his extradition from Pskov.

Yury left Pskov for Novgorod a few days after the arrival of David and his Lithuanian army[4]. With a single-mindedness

[1] See PL, ii, pp. 22–3, 89–90. There is no extant copy of the treaty.

[2] It is interesting to note that Novgorod and Lithuania were virtually at war with each other during 1323 and 1324. In 1323 the Lithuanians attacked the Lovat' river district; in 1324 (after Yury's departure) they attacked Velikie Luki. On both occasions they were driven off by the Novgorodians. (See NL, p. 97.)

[3] Dmitry married Maria, daughter of Grand Prince Gedimin, in 1320. (See PSRL, xv, cols. 413–14.)

[4] According to the Pskov Chronicle, Yury was still in Pskov when David

strange in one so recently engaged in the unseemly inter-princely struggle for power in Suzdalia, he devoted himself to Novgorod's Scandinavian affairs. He was eminently successful. A large expedition was sent to the northern province of Norway, Haalogaland, where the castle of Bjarka (Bjarkøy) was captured and burned.[1] More important, Yury occupied himself with securing the river Neva, which provided Novgorod with her most valuable exit to the sea. The importance of the Neva to Novgorod's trade and defence in the thirteenth and fourteenth centuries cannot be overstressed. In 1300 the Swedes made determined efforts to control the Neva: a large expedition was sent to establish a base on the river and thus block Novgorod's maritime trade with the west. For a year the Swedish fort of Landskrona (*Venets Zemli* in the Russian chronicles) dominated the Neva. How well Novgorod appreciated the danger can be seen from the account of her trade discussion with Lübeck early in 1301, in which Grand Prince Andrey, as prince of Novgorod, talks of the king of Sweden taking "from us and from you the route along the Neva (*den wech . . . na der Nu*)" and mentions the hope that the fortress of Landskrona would be destroyed.[2] In fact Landskrona was destroyed and burned in the same year (1301) by Andrey,[3] who acted with the same decisiveness as his father had displayed in defeating Folkung Birger on the Neva in the battle of 1240. But although the Swedes no longer had a base on Novgorod territory, they were still able to sail unhampered up the Neva into Lake Ladoga.[4] Yury's great contribution to the security of Novgorod was his founding in 1323 of the key fortress of Orekhov, Oreshek or Orekhovets,[5] as it is variously called in the

---

arrived on 3 February 1323 (*see PL*, ii, p. 22). The Novgorod First Chronicle mentions as its last entry under 6830 (i.e. 1 March 1322 to 28 February 1323) that "the Novgorodians summoned Yury [from Pskov] according to the treaty". (*NL*, p. 97.) Yury left Pskov between 3 and 28 February 1323.

[1] *See* Shaskol'sky, "Dogovory Novgoroda s Norvegiey", p. 46. Bjarka was the residence of the regent Erling Vidkunsson and evidently an administrative centre. (*See* F. N. Stagg, *North Norway*, 1952, pp. 33, 64–5.)

[2] *See GVNiP*, No. 33, pp. 62–3.

[3] *See NL*, p. 91.

[4] As witness the attack on the town of Ladoga by the Swedes in 1313.

[5] Later named Shlissel'burg, the "key fortress", by Peter I.

sources, at the influx of the Neva into Lake Ladoga. It meant the end of Swedish incursions up the Neva. It also meant the temporary end of hostilities between Novgorod and Sweden, for shortly after the completion of the stronghold ambassadors from King Magnus Ericsson of Sweden arrived at Oreshek to conclude a "permanent peace" with Yury and the representatives of Novgorod. The treaty of Orekhov (12 August 1323), which defined the frontiers between the possessions of Novgorod and Finland to the mutual satisfaction of both, was long to remain binding.[1] Three years later a similar treaty was concluded with Norway.[2]

Yury's work for Novgorod was not yet over. He was to perform one further service to the republic. In 1324 he set off with an army to the Zavoloch'e district in the basin of the Northern Dvina river. The objective of the expedition was the town of Ustyug in the extreme north-eastern corner of the principality of Rostov. In the previous year a party of Novgorodians, who were proceeding on some unspecified but probably predatory or mercantile mission to the Yugra district east of the Pechora river, had been captured by the men of Ustyug.[3] Yury took the town by storm. He then sent back the army to Novgorod and set off eastwards to the district of Perm'. From there he travelled south along the Kama and Volga rivers to the Golden Horde.[4]

The dramatic and important events which followed Yury's Ustyug campaign are briefly and unsatisfactorily described by the sources. All we know is that Yury went to the Horde and that he was killed there by Dmitry of Tver' on 21 November 1325. A few of the chronicles add that Dmitry killed him "without the permission of the khan",[5] and the Nikon Chronicle, embroidering on the text of the earlier Muscovite compilations, explains

---

[1] See GVNiP, No. 38, pp. 67–8; NL, p. 97.

[2] See GVNiP, No. 39, pp. 69–70.

[3] See PL, ii, p. 97.

[4] After the capture of Ustyug the "princes of Ustyug" concluded a treaty with Yury "according to the ancient customs" (NL, p. 97). A considerable time must have elapsed between Yury's capture of Ustyug and his departure for the Horde as he only arrived there in November 1325. The capture of Ustyug may have taken place in the early spring of 1325.

[5] E.g. NL, p. 97; PSRL, xxiii, p. 102; xxv, p. 167. The Tver' and Trinity Chronicles merely say that Yury was killed at the Horde without explaining by whom. (See PSRL, xv, col. 415; xv (i), col. 42; TL, p. 357.)

that he "relied on the favours of the khan".[1] There is no explanation as to why Yury suddenly decided to journey to the Horde or
as to how Dmitry of Tver' learned of his decision.[2] Did Yury
take any Novgorodians with him? Was he summoned by the
khan? Where was his brother Ivan at the time? These and other
questions cannot be answered owing to the singular reticence of
the chroniclers, who, as is so often the case, appear to be deliberately concealing information. All that can be said is that Dmitry's
murder of Yury was probably an act of private revenge and that in
committing it he entirely miscalculated the mood of the khan.

Yury's corpse was brought back to Moscow where, on 3
February 1326, it was buried by all the bishops of the Russian
Church headed by the faithful Metropolitan Petr.[3] There could
have been no greater demonstration of the Church's loyalty to
Moscow. Some years before, when the corpse of Yury's own
victim, Mikhail of Tver', was brought back to north-east Russia,
only one bishop, Varsanofy of Tver', had been present at the
burial.

Dmitry Mikhaylovich was arrested immediately after the
murder, but he was not executed for his crime until nearly a year
later (15 August 1326). Again the chroniclers are singularly
unhelpful: we are not told why Uzbek waited for a year before
punishing Dmitry, or indeed why he punished him at all. True,

---

[1] *PSRL*, x, p. 189.

[2] Evidently after Yury left Novgorod for Ustyug in 1324 Dmitry took up
residence in Novgorod as grand prince of Vladimir and prince of Novgorod.
This is clear from Novgorod's treaty with Aleksandr Mikhaylovich of Tver'
(1327), in which the previous princes of Novgorod are listed as: Yaroslav
(Yaroslavich), Vasily (Yaroslavich), Dmitry (Aleksandrovich), Mikhail
(Yaroslavich), Yury (Danilovich) and *Dmitry* (Mikhaylovich). (*See GVNiP*,
p. 27.) Dmitry would, then, have heard of Yury's plans from the Novgorodians who were sent back after the treaty of Ustyug.

[3] *See NL*, p. 97. Present were: (i) Metropolitan Petr; (ii) Archbishop
Moisey of Novgorod, who had just been consecrated by Metropolitan Petr
as David's successor; (iii) Bishop Prokhor of Rostov; (iv) Bishop Varsanofy
of Tver'; (v) Bishop Grigory of Ryazan'. There was probably no incumbent
of the see of Suzdal' at the time (*see* P. M. Stroev, *Spiski*, col. 653). The
bishop of Saray (Varsanofy) was not present. Stroev considers he may have
been the bishop of Tver' as well (*see* ibid., col. 441; *cf.* Grekov, *Ocherki*, p. 36),
although Varsanofy of Saray is mentioned as alive two years after Varsanofy
of Tver''s death (*see* Stroev, *Spiski*, col. 1033).

the compiler of the Nikon Chronicle, indulging in his usual practice of supplying motives for bare facts, tells us that the khan held Dmitry "in great disgrace (*opala*) until he could make up his mind what to do with him", and that he eventually had him killed because "he was extremely angry with all the princes of Tver' and called them rebels (*kramol'niki*) and enemies and hostile to him".[1] But such an explanation is neither satisfactory nor illuminating. Certainly the khan's action in executing Dmitry might be explained by pique at Dmitry's arbitrary behaviour.[2] But the reasons for the delay of nearly a year before Dmitry was killed must be sought elsewhere.

It might be argued that in executing Dmitry Uzbek was once again playing off one principality against another, attempting to strengthen one prince at the expense of his rival. Had Ivan of Moscow been granted the patent to the grand-princely throne then and there this might have been Uzbek's purpose. But in fact Uzbek appointed Dmitry's brother Aleksandr to take his place. It was not, then, just a question of adjusting the balance of power between Tver' and Moscow, or at any rate this was not the primary purpose of the khan. Rather we must look to Dmitry Mikhaylovich's Western connections.

It is perhaps still too early to talk of a formal alliance between Lithuania and Tver', but there were already unmistakable indications of a Lithuanian orientation in Tverite foreign policy. Grand Prince Mikhail, it will be remembered, was the brother-in-law of Yury I of Galich, who had strong ties with Lithuania and Poland; his adviser, Bishop Andrey, was of Lithuanian origin. Dmitry himself was married to the daughter of Grand Prince Gedimin of Lithuania. Tver''s Lithuanian orientation, however, is more strikingly demonstrated by the treaty between Lithuania and Novgorod which was drawn up in 1326 while Dmitry's *namestniki* were presumably still in control of the republic[3] and

[1] *PSRL*, x, pp. 189, 190.

[2] The chronicles stress that it was an act of private revenge. Cherepnin, however, thinks that Yury's murder had Uzbek's silent approval—Yury had ceased to be the khan's faithful servant (*see* Cherepnin, *Obrazovanie*, p. 475). Nasonov, on the other hand, thinks that it was done without Uzbek's approval (*see* Nasonov, *Mongoly i Rus'*, p. 90, note 8).

[3] Dmitry, during his reign as grand prince of Vladimir, had ruled in Novgorod. (*See* above, p. 102, note 2). There is no reason to suppose that

which marked a complete reversal of Novgorod's previous policy of aggression towards Lithuania, a policy in all probability inspired by the princes of Moscow.

Unfortunately very little is known about the treaty or its conditions. All we know is that in the spring of 1326 a delegation consisting of "the brother of Gedimin, Voin, prince of Polotsk, and Prince Vasily of Minsk and Fedor Svyatoslavich" arrived in Novgorod and made a treaty with Novgorod and the Livonian Order.[1] At a time when the state of Lithuania was expanding to the south and east at the expense of the old western and north-western principalities which had formerly come under the influence of Kiev, any such move of rapprochement with Tver' or Novgorod could only have been regarded with misgivings by the Tatar khan; indeed, it is interesting to note that Uzbek himself, soon after the murder of Yury, despatched a Tatar expedition to ravage Lithuania.[2]

While it may be easy to find some credible explanation for Uzbek's execution of Dmitry, the same cannot be said for his appointment of Aleksandr of Tver' to the grand principality. If

---

Novgorod shook off Tverite control from 1324, when Yury left, to 1327, when Aleksandr of Tver' signed a treaty with Novgorod.

[1] See NL., p. 98. Cf. PSRL, x, p. 190, where the delegation is described as "the brothers of . . . Gedimin: Voina, Prince Vasily of Polotsk, Prince Fedor Rostislavich of Minsk". The treaty was evidently concluded between 11 March and 30 March 1326, as it is sandwiched between events which took place on those dates (see PSRL, xxv, p. 167).

Lyubavsky thinks that Fedor Svyatoslavich was prince of Kiev and a subject of Gedimin. Pashuto sees in him the son of Svyatoslav Mikhaylovich of Mozhaysk and prince of Dorogobuzh and Vyaz'ma. (See M. K. Lyubavsky, Ocherk, pp. 22–3; Pashuto, OLG, p. 392.) It seems more likely that he was the son of Svyatoslav Glebovich of Bryansk, who was killed in 1310 (see above, pp. 70–1 sq.).

[2] See PSRL, x, p. 189. In the previous year Gedimin had received Tatar envoys in his capital, Vil'na. (See Pashuto, OLG, p. 396, note 223.)

In some of the versions of the historical song, "Shchelkan Dudentevich", which in all probability refers to the uprising in Tver' of 1327, Shchelkan is described as being absent in Lithuania collecting tribute during Khan Uzbek's distribution of Russian cities to his "brothers-in-law (shur'ya)". (See Istoricheskie pesni, pp. 76–7, 84.) He may well have been in charge of the expedition to Lithuania in 1325. For a very different view of the song, however, see A. A. Zimin, "Pesnya o Shchelkane".

Dmitry was suspected of Lithuanian leanings, why should Aleksandr have escaped suspicion? True, Aleksandr had been tested for Tatar loyalty during the year his brother was held prisoner at the Horde—Uzbek had sent him to north-east Russia with troops and "Tatar creditors", "and the Lower lands suffered grievously." [1] By 15 August 1326, the day of his brother's death, he was back at the Horde. After Dmitry's execution he was given the patent to the grand-princely throne in spite of what the compiler of the Nikon Chronicle calls Uzbek's "anger with all the princes of Tver' ". [2] Perhaps Uzbek's real aim was to give Aleksandr sufficient rope to hang himself, to put him in a position in which there was no alternative but to compromise himself and thus bring about the destruction of Tver'. It should be borne in mind that during Dmitry's year of imprisonment at Saray, Ivan Danilovich is reported as having visited Uzbek. [3] The prince of Moscow was hardly likely either to counsel, or to acquiesce in, the granting of the *yarlyk* to his rival unless he were likely ultimately to benefit from it or unless he were assured of the future support of the khan. If such indeed were the hopes of Ivan they were fully justified by the events of the succeeding years.

The events of 1327—the uprising in Tver', the slaughter of the Tatars and the resulting sack of Tver'—are related in the chronicles in a variety of versions: some are contemporary, some are of a later period; some represent the interests of Tver', some those of Moscow or Novgorod. And all contain greater or lesser elements of bias. [4]

---

[1] *NL*, p. 97; *PSRL*, iv (i), p. 260. The later Muscovite *svody* changed "Lower lands" to "the land of Tver' ". (*See PSRL*, v, p. 217; xxv, p. 167.) The Trinity Chronicle makes no mention of Aleksandr's mission.

[2] *PSRL*, x, p. 190. "Although he was angry with them he gave the grand principality after Grand Prince Dmitry's death to his brother Aleksandr."

[3] *See PSRL*, x, p. 190, which gives merely his departure and return (at the same time as Aleksandr's). Although this is not mentioned in any other source, there seems no reason to suspect the Nikon Chronicle this time—the facts are stated with complete absence of padding.

[4] There were originally clearly two basic accounts of the events of 1327, both independent of each other. The first, Tverite, account, in which Aleksandr is portrayed in a passive, guiltless role and which in structure, wording and fact is strikingly different from all other versions, is found only in the Rogozhsky and Tver' Chronicles (*PSRL*, xv (i) and xv; *cf. Predislovie letopistsa knyazheniya Tferskago blagovernykh velikikh knyazey Tfer'skikh: PSRL,*

Divesting the facts of their tendentious interpretations and interpolations by the different chroniclers, we have the following bare summary of events. In 1327, after Aleksandr Mikhaylovich had assumed authority as grand prince, Uzbek sent his cousin, one Chol-Khan (Shchelkan or Shevkal in most versions) to Tver' with a Tatar force. After the Tverites had been subjected to considerable persecution they rose up in revolt and massacred Chol-Khan, his troops and all the Tatar merchants in the town.[1]

---

xv, cols. 465–6). The accounts found in the Novgorod First and Fourth Chronicles, the Sofiysky First Chronicle, the Ermolinsky Chronicle and the Moscow *svod* of 1479 clearly have a common source different from that of the Tverite version. The earliest version is that of the Novgorod First Chronicle (relatively untendentious as far as Aleksandr and Ivan are concerned and containing only information likely to interest Novgorodian readers); the Novgorod Fourth Chronicle gives a muddled and biased (anti-Tatar and anti-Tver') rendering of the events of 1327 and includes, misplaced *before* the uprising in Tver', an account of the aftermath and Tatar retaliation which is the same as that found in the Novgorod First Chronicle. The account found in the Sofiysky First Chronicle (*PSRL*, v, pp. 217–18) is close to that of the Novgorod Fourth Chronicle. The version of the Moscow *svod* of 1479 is similar in tone to that of the Novgorod Fourth and Sofiysky First Chronicles, although Ivan of Moscow's responsibility for the Tatar reprisals is considerably toned down ("Grand Prince Ioann *and* Prince Aleksandr Vasil'evich of Suzdal' went against Tver' *on the khan's orders*", etc.). The similarly biased Ermolinsky Chronicle version is a clumsy contraction either of the Moscow *svod* of 1479 or, more likely, of a *source* of the Moscow *svod*. (For evidence of contraction by the Ermolinsky Chronicle rather than enlargement by the Moscow *svod*, see the phrase "[*Shcholkan*] *obrete vremya, yako sobrashasya vsi vo grad*. Uvedashe zhe se *knyaz' Aleksandr i sozva Tverichi…*" *PSRL*, xxiii, p. 102. *Cf. PSRL*, xxv, p. 168.) Note that both the Ermolinsky and the Moscow *svod* versions contain certain details and information not found in either of the Novgorod Chronicle accounts or the Sofiysky First Chronicle account. It would therefore appear that both used a common source different from that used by the compiler of the Novgorod Fourth and Sofiysky First Chronicles. For a detailed examination of the sources, *see* J. L. I. Fennell, "The Tver' Uprising of 1327".

[1] According to the Novgorod First Chronicle the "*khopyl'sky*" merchants were slain ("*i torgovtsi gost' khopyl'skyi iseche*"; *NL*, p. 98); this is repeated in the accounts found in the Novgorod Fourth Chronicle and the Moscow *svod* of 1479. The author of the Ermolinsky Chronicle account, evidently not understanding the term "*khopyl'sky*", changed it to "Polish (*pol'skikh*)"; *cf.* the L'vov Chronicle, which is very close to the Ermolinsky Chronicle, where "from Polotsk" is found—"*polottskie*". (*PSRL*, xx, p. 178.)

Who exactly these *khopyl'sky* merchants were is hard to say. In the Tver'–

The revolt probably spread to other towns as well.[1] Ivan of Moscow, according to most reports,[2] set off immediately to the Horde and returned with a powerful punitive force commanded by five *temniki* (captains of 10,000 men). Tver', Kashin and Torzhok (and probably many other towns) were sacked. Novgorod, where Ivan had prudently established his governors before setting off to the Horde, was spared; the Novgorodians, who had presumably shown signs of disaffection under Aleksandr's governors, managed to bribe the Tatars to leave the republic untouched. The prince of Ryazan', Ivan Yaroslavich, was put to death. The only districts which the Tatars showed no inclination to touch were, not surprisingly, those of Moscow: "Our Lord, the Saviour," sanctimoniously remarked the compiler of the Trinity Chronicle, "protected our pious prince Ivan Danilovich and for his sake [saved] the town of Moscow and all his patrimony from the . . . Tatars."[3] Aleksandr Mikhaylovich fled to Pskov. Novgorod, in spite of the treaty concluded earlier in the year with Tver',[4] refused to offer him asylum. His brothers hid in Ladoga in the north of Novgorod's territory until it was safe for them to

---

Novgorod treaty of 1317 they are mentioned as having taken the third instalment of 3,000 *grivny* (*see* above, p. 80): "*a tret'ii 3000 poyasha khopyli k sobe*" (*GVNiP*, No. 11). It is also known that there was a *khopyl'sky ryad* (merchants' street) in Novgorod in the fourteenth century (*see* ibid., p. 167). Vasmer calls them "merchants from Central Asia" (*see* M. Vasmer, *REW*, vol. 3, p. 260). Both Professor Pritsak of Harvard University and Professor Karl Menges of Columbia University, whom I consulted on this question, think that *khopyl'* may be of Volga–Bulgar origin: the *khopyl'skie gosti* were probably merchants from the district of Bolgary on the Volga.

[1] The Novgorod First Chronicle says that Aleksandr "slaughtered many Tatars in Tver' and in other towns" (*NL*, p. 98). Kashin and Torzhok (the latter probably held by Aleksandr's *namestniki*) were perhaps affected—they were later punished along with Tver'.

[2] Only the cautious Rogozhsky Chronicle of Tver' makes no mention of Ivan's role in the events of 1327. Cherepnin (*Obrazovanie*, p. 481) considers that the Rogozhsky Chronicle version was compiled at the court of the Tver' princes shortly after Ivan I received the patent and while Tver' was trying to recover from the effects of the Tatar reprisals. This would explain the evident desire not to antagonize either Ivan or the Tatars unduly. (*See PSRL*, xv (i), cols. 42–4.)

[3] *TL*, p. 359. *Cf. PSRL*, xv (i), col. 44.

[4] *See GVNiP*, No. 14, pp. 26–8; Cherepnin, *RFA*, vol. i, pp. 299–305.

return to their shattered principality.[1] Tver''s supremacy was ended. She was not to recover from the blow of 1327 sufficiently to be able to resist Moscow again for forty years.

From an examination of the sources which describe the events of 1327 it is fairly simple to deduce *what* probably happened. It is harder, however, to discover *why* the events described took place. Certain of the more extravagant interpretations of the chronicles must be rejected. It is, for instance, most unlikely that Chol-Khan's plan was to kill Aleksandr Mikhaylovich, to sit upon the throne of Tver' himself, to place Tatars on other Russian thrones and to convert the Russians to Islam.[2] It is also unlikely that Aleksandr was moved by thoughts of revenge alone to attack the Tatars in full battle array[3] and thus risk the eventual destruction of his principality. Nor is it likely that Ivan Danilovich and the principality of Moscow were saved from Tatar ravages solely by the loving mercies of the Saviour.[4] As for Uzbek's motives in sending Chol-Khan to Tver', the author of the narrative of events given in the Tver' Chronicles probably came closest to the truth when he described the behaviour of the Tatars in Tver'. On arrival in Tver', Chol-Khan drove Aleksandr from his palace and began to persecute the local population: "He raised up a great persecution against the Christians by force, plunder, murder and abuse." Aleksandr, far from rushing to arms and heroically avenging his father and brother, as he is portrayed as doing by later sources, wisely urged the Tverites to have patience. "The townsfolk . . . complained many times to the grand prince, asking him to defend them; but seeing the wrath of his people and being unable to protect them, he bade them be patient." Eventually the patience of the people of Tver' was strained to breaking point: a petty insignificant incident—the Tatars seized a

---

[1] For an analysis of the various accounts of the events of 1327, *see* Fennell, "The Tver' Uprising of 1327"; Cherepnin, *Obrazovanie*, pp. 475–97; *cf.* A. A. Zimin, "Narodnye dvizheniya," p. 64.

On the question of the relevance of the so-called "historical song about Shchelkan" to the events of 1327, *see* Ya. S. Lur'e, "Rol' Tveri", pp. 102–9; Zimin, "Pesnya o Shchelkane"; N. N. Voronin, "Pesnya o Shchelkane". *Cf.* the commentary of B. N. Putilov on the song in *Istoricheskie pesni*, pp. 631–2.

[2] *See PSRL*, iv (i), pp. 260–1; xxv, p. 168. *Cf.* xxiii, p. 102.

[3] *See* ibid.

[4] *See PSRL*, xv (i), col. 44; *TL*, p. 359.

certain deacon's "fat young mare" while he was watering it in the Volga—was enough to spark off an uprising; a *veche* was hurriedly assembled and the Tverites proceeded to massacre every Tatar they could lay hands on.[1]

From this skilful and very vivid account it is clear that the Tatars behaved with extreme provocation; indeed it would seem that the entire object of their occupation of Tver' (and of other towns too where Tver' officials were in control) was deliberately to provoke the population until an unpardonable act of aggression was committed against the occupation forces. If indeed, as suggested above, Uzbek appointed Aleksandr grand prince in order to destroy him and his principality, such an act of deliberate provocation on the part of Chol-Khan would be entirely in keeping with the khan's intentions and mentality.

Ivan's behaviour could not be disguised even by the most sycophantic attempts at concealment and whitewashing. Clearly he was in the wings the whole time, waiting patiently for an opportunity to denounce his cousin to the khan. As soon as he heard of the massacres of the Tatars in Tver' he set off to the Horde. Confident of receiving the *yarlyk*, he sent his governors to Novgorod before he left. He returned not with the title but with a punitive Tatar army, with which he proceeded to lay waste the districts of Tver' and, no doubt, any others which had shown sympathy for the rule of Aleksandr.

So ended the first phase of the struggle between Tver' and Moscow, a phase from which Moscow emerged victorious. Once again we may put the question: why was Moscow victorious? From a consideration of the first years of the conflict it is impossible to talk of Moscow's geographically superior position— indeed, as has been shown, Tver' with her control of the Volga was geographically in a far stronger strategic and economic position, especially as regards her relations with Novgorod. Nor can we yet talk of the influence of the personality of the princes or of their determination and strength of character: one cannot ascribe any more single-mindedness or political wisdom, at this stage, to a Yury or an Ivan than to a Mikhail or an Aleksandr. Nor yet can one talk of Moscow's genealogical advantages over

[1] See PSRL, xv (i), cols. 42–3.

Tver'. Indeed, the only factors which can be taken into consideration are the will of the khan and, though still in a relatively embryonic stage, the support of the Church.

It must be repeated again that a prince was strong only if the khan wanted him to be strong and was only as strong as the khan allowed him to be. Assuming that a Tatar policy existed and assuming that this policy was to keep north-east Russia in a permanent state of weakness, we can see why the Tatars from 1304 to 1327 almost consistently supported Moscow. Again and again Tver' had shown her military superiority over Moscow, over Novgorod and once even over the combined forces of Moscow and "all the land of Suzdal'" (at the battle of Bortenevo in 1317). But yet another reason for the khan's support of Moscow is to be found in Tver''s Lithuanian orientation, which during the first phase of the conflict was just beginning to manifest itself. As for the Church's preference for Moscow, a preference born, it would seem, of a concatenation of pure accidents, one can at this stage only see its most elementary manifestations. In the later periods, as the power of the Horde gradually receded and the Russian principalities acquired more and more independence from their suzerain, both Lithuanian support for Moscow's enemies and the Church's support for Moscow became steadily more noticeable.

3

The Age of Ivan Kalita

WHEN IVAN of Moscow departed post-haste to the Horde in the autumn of 1327 to inform Uzbek of the crimes committed against the Tatars in Tver', he no doubt expected to return home as grand prince. He was disappointed. Uzbek sent him back not with the *yarlyk* but with a vast Tatar punitive army, 50,000 strong,[1] and with instructions to punish Tver' by razing her cities to the ground and bringing back her prince to the khan. Together with the prince of Suzdal', Aleksandr Vasil'evich, Ivan set about his task. Whether Aleksandr Vasil'evich joined Ivan because he had been told to by the khan or whether he attached himself to the Tatars out of sheer self-preservation we do not know: at least there is nothing to show that the principality of Suzdal' was harmed by the Tatars in 1327. However well Ivan, Aleksandr Vasil'evich and Fedorchuk, the Tatar commander-in-chief, did their job in destroying the principality of Tver', they failed in the other part of their mission—Aleksandr Mikhaylovich fled to Pskov when Tver' was attacked and Ivan was unable to find him, let alone bring him back to the khan.[2]

Most of the chronicles state as their first entry for the year 1328 that "Grand Prince Ivan Danilovich sat upon the grand principality", in other words was officially given the supreme title, and that a period of "great peace" followed. Some chroniclers elaborate on this theme and say that the peace lasted for forty years and meant the cessation of Tatar incursions.[3] The Novgorod

[1] The numbers are not stated, but at any rate the army contained five *temniki*, commanders of 10,000 men. (*See* above, p. 107.)

[2] The sources make no mention of Fedorchuk's army attacking Pskov; it is probable therefore that Aleksandr Mikhaylovich hid in Pskov (as did his brothers in Ladoga) and that Ivan simply did not know where he was.

[3] See TL, p. 359; PSRL, iv (i), p. 262; v, p. 218; xv (i), col. 44; xv, col. 417; xxiii, p. 102; xxv, p. 168.

First Chronicle, however, says nothing of Ivan's enthronement. It begins its entries for 1328 with the information (contained later in the year in other chronicles) that Ivan, together with his nephew Konstantin Mikhaylovich of Tver' (whom no doubt he had extracted from his hiding-place in Ladoga) and an ambassador sent by the Novgorodians, set off to the Golden Horde where they were told by Uzbek "to seek Prince Aleksandr [Mikhaylovich]".[1]

The fact that the Novgorod First Chronicle is silent about Ivan's enthronement is not, of course, sufficient evidence to allow us to deny the validity of the statements found in the other chronicles. However, in one of a series of short articles preceding the text of the Novgorod First Chronicle (*Komissionny spisok*) entitled "And these are the princes of Rus'", the following entry occurs immediately after a brief mention of the Tatar punitive expedition of 1327 ("Fedorchuk's campaign"): "and after Turlak's army[2] the princes went to the Horde, and Uzbek shared the principality between them. To Prince Ivan Danilovich he gave Novgorod and Kostroma, half the principality; to the prince of Suzdal', Aleksandr Vasil'evich, he gave Vladimir and the Volga district (i.e. Nizhny Novgorod and Gorodets) and he (Aleksandr) ruled for two and a half years." There follows a short anecdote describing how Aleksandr removed the bell of the cathedral of Vladimir, took it to Suzdal' but returned it because it refused to ring and because he realized that "he had offended the Mother of God". After Aleksandr of Suzdal''s death (1331) "Grand Prince Ivan Danilovich went to the Horde, and the khan granted him the grand principality over all the land of Rus'."[3] In other words, between 1328 and 1331 the grand principality was divided between Aleksandr Vasil'evich of Suzdal', who ruled the eastern portion including the symbolic capital city of Vladimir and who was

[1] See *NL*, pp. 98, 341. The compiler of the Nikon Chronicle, baffled no doubt by contradictory evidence, tries to simplify matters by stating that on this occasion Uzbek gave Ivan the title of grand prince of Vladimir and Konstantin Mikhaylovich that of grand prince of Tver'. (*See PSRL*, x, p. 195.)

[2] Turlak, or Turalyk, was one of the *temniki* in Fedorchuk's army. (*See PSRL*, xxv, p. 168.)

[3] *NL*, p. 469. For the question of the date of Aleksandr's death, *see* below, p. 119, note 2.

presumably given the title of grand prince, and Ivan Danilovich, who was granted control over Novgorod and Kostroma. Pereyaslavl', it appears, still remained in Muscovite hands. There is no reason to doubt this information. It is factually and convincingly reported, and it is unlikely that the popular episode of the bell of Vladimir was invented to add verisimilitude to a piece of tendentious falsification. There was nothing exceptional or even unexpected in Uzbek's decision. The splitting up of the grand principality between two princes was not without precedent—in 1249 Ivan's grandfather, Aleksandr Nevsky, had been granted "Kiev and all the Russian land", while Aleksandr Vasil'evich's great-grandfather, Andrey, "sat upon the throne of Vladimir". Besides, there is every reason why Uzbek should have split the grand principality at this particular juncture. Now that Tver' was eliminated, temporarily at least, as a power to be reckoned with, it was too dangerous to leave the prince of Moscow in supreme control. A new rival had to be found. And of all the surviving dynasties among the Vsevolodovichi the house of Suzdal' was the strongest, in that, thanks to the paucity of the descendants of its founder Andrey Yaroslavich, the original principality had not been split up. There were only two greatgrandsons of Andrey, Aleksandr and Konstantin. The other surviving dynasties which might have had a claim to the title—the houses of Rostov, Uglich, Beloozero, Yaroslavl', Yur'ev, Starodub, Galich and Dmitrov—had long lost all semblance of power and all interest in the question of succession to the grandprincely throne. The two descendants of Grand Prince Andrey, however, still ruled the principality of Suzdal' which had been granted to their great-grandfather in 1256 on his return from exile in Sweden; and if they did not at this time actually hold the lands of Nizhny Novgorod and Gorodets, which had constituted Andrey's original patrimony, they probably laid claim to them as a family possession.[1] In Uzbek's eyes the house of Suzdal' seemed a suitable replacement for the house of Tver' as a counterbalance to the principality of Moscow. It must also be remembered that Ivan had clearly failed in his mission of 1327

---

[1] See Presnyakov, *Obrazovanie*, p. 261; *cf.* Ekzemplyarsky, *VUK*, vol. ii, pp. 390–8. In 1311 Nizhny Novgorod was in the hands of Yury of Moscow. (*See* above, p. 73.)

when he had been sent not only to destroy Tver' but also to deliver Aleksandr Mikhaylovich to the Horde: the refusal to grant him the full title in 1328 can indeed be looked upon as a sign of Uzbek's dissatisfaction with his servant.

It may well be asked why the Muscovite and Tver' chroniclers should have been at such pains to conceal the truth and to represent Ivan as supreme ruler three years before he obtained the patent. The answer is not hard to find. The chronicle accounts in question were composed or edited either at the court of the prince of Moscow or at the palace of the metropolitan, who by now had transferred his see to Moscow.[1] It is therefore not surprising to find Ivan I glorified as the great statesman to whose political wisdom north-east Russia owed so long a period of peace and freedom from Tatar invasions. Nor is it surprising to find Ivan's more dubious acts of political expediency glossed over by his panegyrists. If there was little edifying in the picture of a prince scurrying about the Russian lands to fulfil the behests of the khan, there was still less that was likely to appeal to posterity in the portrayal of a descendant of Aleksandr Nevsky obliged to share the realm with a descendant of the prince who had been forced to flee to Sweden—and denied the right to call himself grand prince. The whole business of the occupation of the throne of Vladimir by the prince of Suzdal', even though it only lasted three years, was best forgotten. Besides, the recording of such information might be used at a later date by unscrupulous descendants of Aleksandr of Suzdal' wishing to claim their right to the supreme title.

Having failed to deliver the scapegoat for the rebellion of Tver' at his first attempt notwithstanding the assistance of 50,000 Tatar troops, at his second Ivan appeared determined to succeed. He set about his task with vigour as though the very question of the title of grand prince depended on the success of his mission. He used every weapon at his disposal. And when physical means failed he had recourse to spiritual pressure. The sorry events of 1329—hardly a creditable page in the history of Muscovy— were described with gusto and in detail by most of the chroniclers; only those of Tver', afraid no doubt to hurt the feelings of the princes of Moscow, barely mentioned the story of the expulsion

[1] See M. D. Priselkov, IRL, pp. 122 sq.; Budovnits, "Otrazhenie", p. 80.

of their ex-prince from Pskov, a story from which the only person to emerge with a semblance of dignity was Aleksandr Mikhaylovich himself.[1] The first attempt to extradite Aleksandr was made in the summer of 1328. On their return from the Horde, Ivan of Moscow, Konstantin of Tver' and the Novgorodians sent ambassadors to Aleksandr "ordering him to go to the Horde". In spite of the impressive nature of the delegations—Novgorod sent her archbishop, Moisey, and her current *tysyatsky*—and the forcefulness of their persuasion, Aleksandr refused to move from Pskov.[2] Recent family history had taught him that a summons

[1] The following groups of sources describe the events of 1328–9:
i. The Pskov First, Second and Third Chronicles (*PL* i, pp. 16–17; ii, pp. 23, 90–2), all of which derive from a common Pskovite prototype. The original account was clearly written in Pskov at the time of the event, and the versions found in the Pskov chronicles, though not without later epic embroidery, are obviously close to it. All of the first episode (the first embassy to Aleksandr) is omitted: the story begins with the concentration of forces in Novgorod in March 1329. The tone of the Pskov versions is entirely sympathetic to Aleksandr, cautiously non-committal where Ivan of Moscow is concerned (although the devil is made to "inspire the Russian princes to seek out Aleksandr") and aggressively anti-Tatar ("accursed Uzbek").
ii. The Novgorod First Chronicle (*NL*, pp. 98–9, 341–2). Short, laconic and quite independent of the Pskov version which its author either did not know or preferred to ignore.
iii. The Novgorod Fourth and the Sofiysky First Chronicles (*PSRL*. iv (i), pp. 262–3; v, p. 218). A flowery, composite account, based mainly on i. and ii. and similar in tone to i. The Sofiysky First Chronicle, however, omits the devil as the inspirer of the Russian princes.
iv. The Ermolinsky Chronicle and the Moscow *svod* of 1479 (*PSRL*, xxiii, p. 103; xxv, pp. 169–70). Close to i., ii. and iii.; the tone is entirely sympathetic to Ivan of Moscow, and the diabolical motivation of i. and iii. is carefully omitted. It is possible that both derived not only from the common source of iii. (itself fed by i. and ii.), but also from another source not known to iii. (note the phrase "*tverdo/krepko yashasya po/za . . .*" found only in iv.).
[2] *See NL*, pp. 98, 341; *PSRL*, iv (i), p. 262; v. p. 218; xxiii, p. 103; xxv, p. 169. The Trinity, Rogozhsky and Tver' Chronicles make no mention of the mission, just as they are silent on the events of 1329.
From the chronological arrangement of entries under 1328 in the Ermolinsky Chronicle and the Moscow *svod* of 1479, it would appear that Ivan, Konstantin and the Novgorodians returned from the Horde in the early summer and sent their ambassadors to Pskov before 7 September.

to Saray was as good as a death sentence. The example of his father and brother was sufficient to implant in him the profoundest mistrust of the khan, especially a khan who employed the services of the insidious and subservient prince of Moscow. It was clear that Uzbek would not be satisfied with such a report of failure on the part of Ivan. Indeed one source says that he sent his ambassadors to all the Russian princes, ordering them "to arrest Prince Aleksandr Mikhaylovich of Tver' and to send him to the Horde".[1] Whether this is true or not cannot be ascertained (the source is the composite sixteenth-century Nikon Chronicle), but at any rate on 26 March 1329 an imposing array of princes and their armies converged in Novgorod: "Grand Prince Ivan Danilovich . . . the princes of Tver', Konstantin and Vasily Mikhaylovich, Prince Aleksandr of Suzdal' and many other princes of Rus'."[2] Soon after their arrival the recently appointed successor of Metropolitan Petr, the Greek Feognost (Theognostos), turned up in Novgorod, sent for no doubt by Ivan as an additional weapon to be used against the recalcitrant fugitive in Pskov.

It proved no easy task to dislodge Aleksandr of Tver'. The Pskovites, on granting Aleksandr sanctuary in 1327 and appointing him prince of Pskov, had signed an agreement with him in which they swore "not to hand him over to the Russian princes".[3] The first step was to attempt once again peacefully to persuade him to surrender. A joint Muscovite–Novgorodian delegation with a stiffening of troops[4] urged him to go to the Horde of his own accord. His refusal would mean the destruction of Pskov by the Tatars, said the ambassadors. At first Aleksandr agreed to make the sacrifice "for all the Christian people"; but he was persuaded

[1] *PSRL*, x, p. 201.

[2] *NL*, p. 98; *cf.* the Pskov chronicler's account (Pskov Third Chronicle): "The devil inspired the Russian princes to seek out Prince Aleksandr at the order of . . . Uzbek. And they raised up the whole of the Russian land and they came to Novgorod. And they raised up the Novgorodians and all the land of Novgorod from Beloozero [*sic*] and from Zavoloch'e (the land of the Northern Dvina) and from Karelia." *PL*, ii, pp. 90–1 (*cf. PL*, i, Pskov First Chronicle, where Karelia is omitted).

[3] *PL*, ii, p. 23 (Pskov Second Chronicle).

[4] According to the Pskov First and Third Chronicles (but not the others), Ivan sent with his representative Luka Protas'ev a *druzhina*, or detachment of troops.

by the singularly magnanimous Pskovites not to leave. "Go not to the Horde", they said. "Should anything happen to you we will all die together with you."[1] While the Christian humility and self-sacrifice of Aleksandr and the altruism of the Pskovites probably represent little more than literary embellishments dear to hagiographers and compilers of chronicle narratives the aim of which was to arouse sympathy for the hero, it is clear that the threat was formally delivered and that the challenge was accepted by Aleksandr and the Pskovites. It is hard to conceive of any possible motive behind the Pskovites' show of bravado except the assurance of Lithuanian support.

It was perhaps this latter consideration which made Ivan show some caution in his dealings with Pskov.[2] He moved his army—the troops of all the princes of the Lower lands as well as the Novgorodians—to the town of Opochka some hundred miles south of Pskov on the Velikaya river. The purpose of the move was more to scare the Pskovites into submission by a show of force than to attempt to take Pskov by storm. Indeed, according to nearly all versions of the incident, Ivan decided against a direct attack, realizing that Pskov was impregnable. Rather than turn back and be forced once again to admit his failure to his suzerain he brought his most effective weapon into action. He asked the newly-appointed metropolitan to help. Feognost turned out to be amenable to persuasion. He fulminated an anathema against both Aleksandr and all the Pskovites: the fugitive and those who had given him sanctuary were excommunicated.

Where force and threats of force failed, the power of the Church prevailed. Neither Aleksandr nor the Pskovites could tolerate such an edict. "O my brothers and friends," Aleksandr is alleged to have said to the Pskovites, "let not this curse and excommunication be upon you because of me. I shall leave your city, and your oath to me and my oath to you shall no longer be

---

[1] See PL, i, pp. 16–17; ii, p. 91; PSRL, iv (i), pp. 262–3; v, p. 218; xxiii, p. 103; xxv, p. 169 (where the Pskov episodes are misplaced under the year 1330; cf. the Voskresensky Chronicle, PSRL, vii, p. 201).

[2] Ivan's caution is well illustrated by the Pskov account of the peace negotiations, in which the movement of Ivan's army to Opochka is described as having taken three weeks "because [Ivan] did not wish to anger the Pskovites". (See PL, i, p. 17; ii, p. 91.)

valid."[1] After extracting a promise from the Pskovites that his wife would be cared for and not surrendered to the Muscovites,[2] he left Pskov and fled to Lithuania. That he intended to be absent only for a short time is evident from the fact that he left his wife behind. Indeed, he returned eighteen months later[3] and remained for ten years in Pskov as prince. The Pskovites informed Ivan and the metropolitan of Aleksandr's departure. Grudgingly Ivan concluded a treaty with Pskov; the metropolitan lifted the ban and Archbishop Moisey gave his blessing to the inhabitants of the second largest city in his diocese.[4]

How much truth there is in the story of Aleksandr's forced departure from Pskov cannot be reliably ascertained. It seems, however, most likely that it was the show of force and the metropolitan's action which compelled Aleksandr to leave and that the relations between the prince of Tver' and the republic of Pskov were as cordial as the Pskovite chroniclers make them out to be. From the whole episode two salient features emerge. First, there is evidence of the strong ties linking the Tverite princely family and the grand principality of Lithuania; Pskov, too, is shown again as a centre of Lithuanian influence. Secondly, the attempts to remove Aleksandr from his stronghold and the comparative ease with which the metropolitan accomplished what guns and troops were unable to achieve show just how powerful a weapon the support of the Church was and how effectively it could be used in inter-princely conflicts.

[1] *PL*, i, p. 17; ii, p. 91. *Cf. PSRL*, iv (i), p. 263; v, p. 218; xxiii, p. 103; xxv, p. 169.

[2] This is only found in the Pskov Chronicle accounts.

[3] *See PSRL*, xxv, p. 170.

[4] The two versions of the Novgorod First Chronicle differ considerably from the versions mentioned above. They make no mention of the early attempts of Archbishop Moisey and the Novgorodians to persuade Pskov to surrender Aleksandr. Feognost's excommunication of Pskov is mentioned only in one of the versions (*mladshy izvod*) and is shown to be ineffective: in the older version (*starshy izvod*) it is not even mentioned. The Pskovites got rid of Aleksandr ("*vyprovadisha ot sebe*") only when "Prince Ivan and all the princes and the Novgorodians marched on Pskov". (*See NL*, pp. 98–9, 342.)

The Novgorodian version was probably designed to salve Novgorodian pride—after all, their army and their archbishop had clearly failed in the first place. It was evidently written immediately after the event and probably

Although historians tend to describe the results of the Pskov incident as a triumph for Ivan and the principality of Moscow,[1] it must be pointed out that only the fact that Ivan could rely on the support of the Church and could rally the princes of the Lower lands and the republic of Novgorod can be described as a political success. The operation itself miscarried. Once again Ivan had failed to deliver the recalcitrant prince of Tver' to the Horde. His zeal was not rewarded. He had to wait for another two years before he received the *yarlyk*.

After the fiasco of Pskov there was little that Ivan could do but wait for his co-ruler, the prince of Suzdal', to compromise himself or to die. Aleksandr of Tver' was irretrievably out of reach in Lithuania, and, empty-handed, Ivan could hardly expect an enthusiastic welcome at the Golden Horde. He had not long to wait. At the end of 1331 Aleksandr Vasil'evich of Suzdal', grand prince of Vladimir, died.[2] Ivan set off to the Horde immediately, accompanied by the eldest brother of Aleksandr of Tver', Konstantin. Early in 1332 he returned as grand prince. He was installed on the throne by a Tatar named Albuga (Albugha?).[3]

Ivan's reign as grand prince lasted for nine years. Notwithstanding the later, pro-Muscovite, chronicler's claim that Ivan's assumption of the title ushered in an age of calm and peace unprecedented since the Tatar invasion—"There was great peace

before Moisey's "voluntary" retirement in 1330. It has nothing in common with the Pskov versions.

[1] *See*, for instance, Cherepnin, *Obrazovanie*, p. 500.

[2] 1332 is the usually accepted date of Aleksandr Vasil'evich's death, as the majority of the chronicles give it as such, viz. *PSRL*, iv (i), p. 265; v, p. 220; xxiii, p. 104; xxv, p. 170; *cf.* the Trinity Chronicle (p. 361), where the date is given as 1333. The date 1331, which is given in the Tver' chronicles, however (*PSRL*, xv, col. 417; xv (i), col. 46), is probably correct for the following reasons: (i) the article ("These are the princes of Rus'") which mentions the sharing of the *yarlyk* (*NL*, p. 469) says that Aleksandr of Suzdal' ruled for two and a half years ("*pol'tret'ya godu*")—i.e. from 1328 until 1330 or 1331, but not 1332; (ii) Ivan went to the Horde *at the end of 1331* (after 8 December 1331), (*see PSRL*, iv (i), p. 265; v, pp. 219–20; xxiii, p. 104; xxv, p. 170); he did not, and could not, go to the Horde later, in 1332 or 1333; he married for the second time in 1332 (*PSRL*, xv (i), cols. 46–7) and was fully occupied in Novgorod (*NL*, pp. 344–6).

[3] *See NL*, p. 469.

for forty years"[1]—the disappointingly scant available evidence shows that it was a period of tension, confusion, instability and growing danger from the West.

From the meagre, seemingly haphazard and at times tendentiously pruned or re-edited information contained in the various chronicle accounts of the reign it is hard to extract a logically constructed narrative of events, let alone to create a single-minded statesman out of Ivan. Nevertheless out of the chaos certain patterns emerge, and if it is difficult to find in Ivan's behaviour evidence of little more than a crude opportunism dictated by circumstances, there are somewhat clearer indications of a deliberate Tatar policy and signs of a new, calculated *Drang nach Osten* in the neighbouring state of Lithuania.

Whatever sources we examine—chronicle accounts flavoured by pro-Moscow, pro-Tver' or pro-Novgorod sympathies, or even so dispassionate a document as Ivan's will—we cannot be mistaken in one thing: Ivan was if anything still more dependent on the Golden Horde than his predecessors had been. The control of the khan over the Russian principalities never relaxed during his rule. From 1332 to 1339 Ivan made at least four trips to Saray: he despatched his children there with a copy of his will; he received instructions from Uzbek and carried them out or attempted to carry them out; he collected or attempted to collect Tatar tribute in Novgorod; he led his army against Smolensk in 1339 "at the behest of the khan". How many other actions of his were also "at the behest of the khan" we do not know. It is, therefore, difficult to talk of a conscious policy of the grand prince of Moscow and Vladimir. We must rather consider firstly what the khan of the Golden Horde was attempting to do and secondly what benefits for the principality of Moscow—or for all the north-east Russian lands—his vassal was trying to extract from his precarious circumstances.

There can be little doubt that Tatar policy towards north-east Russia changed with the accession of Ivan Danilovich to the throne of Vladimir. Whereas in the past there appears to have been a conscious attempt on the part of the khans to play off one Russian prince against another and to prevent one prince from becoming all-powerful at the expense of his rivals by supporting

[1] *TL*, p. 359.

the latter at the crucial moment, now Uzbek was content to leave
the authority in the hands of Ivan alone. It might, of course, be
argued that the restitution of Aleksandr of Tver' to his patrimony
in 1338—with Tatar troops, be it noted—was evidence of Uzbek's
desire temporarily to curb the power of Moscow. But the speed
with which Uzbek seemingly changed his mind and the remarkable similarity with the provocatory tactics employed by the
Tatars in 1327 lead one to suspect that Uzbek had no intention
whatsoever of allowing his old proven adversary to acquire
military or political strength at the expense of Moscow or any
other principality. In any case the restoration of Aleksandr was an
isolated example of Tatar interference in inter-princely affairs:
on no other occasion did the Horde supply military aid to anyone
who might be remotely considered as a potential rival to the prince
of Moscow. Ivan may have enjoyed little or no freedom of
political action, his conduct of government may have been
dictated to him by his master, but at least he was allowed to
manage his domestic affairs unhampered by Tatar-supported
rivals.

What was the cause of this change of attitude in Tatar policy?
It cannot be sought in the absence of a suitable candidate, for
when Aleksandr of Suzdal' died his brother Konstantin took over
his principality and indeed ruled it with efficiency and imagination
for nearly a quarter of a century. Konstantin was a worthy successor to his brother. Yet Uzbek made no move to strengthen his
authority or to set him up in any form of opposition to Ivan.
There are two more cogent reasons which would satisfactorily
explain Uzbek's attitude to the prince of Moscow. Firstly Ivan
proved, as we have seen, an ideal servant. His willingness to
carry out the khan's commands had been amply demonstrated
before he received the *yarlyk*; his repeated trips to Saray made him
persona grata at Uzbek's court. Furthermore, his sister-in-law,
Konchaka, murdered, so rumour had it, by the Tverites in 1317,
had been the sister of the khan. Yet the malleability of the prince
of Moscow and his readiness to comply with the wishes of the
Tatars merely made him a suitable, probably the most suitable,
candidate for the throne of Vladimir and cannot wholly explain
Uzbek's readiness to relax control over the struggle for power
among the descendants of Vsevolod III. To find a more satis-

factory explanation of Tatar policy we must look once again to the Lithuanian question.

Ever since the middle of the thirteenth century Lithuania had been expanding to the east and the south at the expense of ethnically Russian lands. So-called Black Rus'—the lands watered by the Upper Neman river—was annexed and ruled by Mendovg (Mindaugas). By the end of the twenties of the fourteenth century the principalities of Polotsk, Vitebsk and most of Minsk had been firmly incorporated into Lithuania. But the grand principality was bordered in the east and the south-east by virtually uncommitted districts, most of which were under the direct suzerainty of the khan of the Golden Horde. Such were the lands of Smolensk, Turov-Pinsk, Chernigov-Seversky (including Bryansk), all principalities which in the eleventh and twelfth centuries had been subject to, or were in some form dependent on, the grand prince of Kiev. To the south lay the two principalities of Volyn' and Galich, which from 1325, after the extinction of the male descendants of King Daniil, were ruled, independently of Lithuania or Poland, by Prince Bolesław of Mazovia (known as Bolesław–Yury II). On most of these territories Lithuania under the patient and intelligent rule of Grand Prince Gedimin was gradually and, it seems, peacefully encroaching. A lack of precise information prevents us from knowing to what extent they came under his control during his reign from 1316 to 1341; but it would appear that at any rate Smolensk, Chernigov and Kiev, which was ruled probably by his brother Fedor, [1] owed him allegiance, shared perhaps with the khan. Indeed, they may well have been as much part of his state as were Polotsk, Vitebsk and Minsk. Bolesław-Yury of Volyn' and Galich managed to keep his northern and western neighbours at bay throughout his reign of fifteen years, but it was only a temporary respite for the south-west Russian

[1] A Prince Fedor ruled in Kiev in 1331—possibly with a Tatar *baskak* in attendance. (*See NL*, p. 344.)

From certain Greek fragments of memoranda found in the Vatican and connected with Metropolitan Feognost it appears that Gedimin had a brother named Fedor (presumably his baptismal name). (*See* M. D. Priselkov and M. R. Vasmer, "Otryvki", p. 58.)

Turov-Pinsk may have been under control of the rulers of Volyn' and Galich during most of the first forty years of the fourteenth century.

principalities, which at his death in 1340 were instantly and irrevocably annexed by Lithuania and Poland.

Gedimin's feelers stretched still farther afield. To the north-east his influence was making itself felt in Novgorod, Pskov and Tver': one has only to remember the Lithuanian embassy to Novgorod in 1326,[1] the military assistance so willingly supplied by David of Grodno to Pskov in 1323,[2] and the strong links which tied Tver' to Lithuania. To the south of Muscovy too there were indications, albeit faint ones, of the spread of Lithuanian influence—a prince of Novosil' in the Upper Oka district (perhaps a vassal of Gedimin?) was put to death in the Horde in 1326 at the same time as Gedimin's son-in-law Dmitry Mikhaylovich of Tver' was killed;[3] and a prince of Murom, Yaroslav, evidently had connections with the metropolitan of Lithuania, for in 1330 a member of Metropolitan Feognost's entourage (or perhaps Feognost himself) recorded the fact that the prince of Murom owed the late metropolitan the sum of fifteen *grivny*.[4] While on the basis of this slender evidence it would be an exaggeration to talk of a Lithuanian threat to, or blockade of, Muscovy from the south-east,[5] nevertheless it is hard to ignore or deny the far-reaching influence of the grand prince of Lithuania during the twenties and the thirties of the fourteenth century.

[1] *See* above, p. 104.

[2] *See* above, pp. 98–9. In his treaty with the Livonian Order of 2 October 1323 Gedimin mentions the "Pskovites and all the Ruthenians subjected to us" to whose advantage the treaty was concluded. (*See* B. Ya. Ramm, *Papstvo i Rus'*, p. 198.)

[3] *See* TL, p. 358. This is the only mention of Aleksandr of Novosil', presumably a descendant of Mikhail of Chernigov. A later prince of Novosil', Ivan, was married to Gedimin's grand-daughter. (*See* Baumgarten, *Généalogies*, vol. i, p. 89.)

[4] *See* Priselkov and Vasmer, "Otryvki", p. 50. For the evidence that the dead metropolitan was probably Feofil of Lithuania, *see* below, p. 130. The same fragments, published by Priselkov and Vasmer, also mention one "Andrey in Kozel'sk" (again in the Upper Oka district) who "held fifteen *grivny* of the metropolitan" (ibid., p. 58). It is interesting to note that on 23 July 1339, three months before the murder of Mikhail Aleksandrovich and his son Fedor at the Horde, "Prince Andrey Mstislavich of Kozel'sk was murdered by his nephew" (*TL*, p. 363). No reasons are given for the murder; nor is anything more known about Andrey.

[5] *See* Paszkiewicz, *Jagiellonowie*, pp. 331–2.

It has often been pointed out by historians that Gedimin's policy as regards his Russian-speaking neighbours was one of infiltration, of peaceful insinuation into lands which, because of their unfortunate geographical position, could rely on no military support from the stronger principalities in the north-east, were economically depressed as a result of the Mongol invasions and were more or less subservient to the khan of the Golden Horde. Neither Moscow nor Tver' nor any other north-eastern principality had the time, strength or opportunity to interfere in what was later to be considered as the true inheritance of the princes of Vladimir and the objective of the later princes of Moscow—the territories which had formed the pre-Mongol Kievan state. And it is doubtful whether the Tatar authorities, whose task of policing these depressed areas was clearly a relatively simple and profitable one, would have permitted such intrusion. One must assume that the Russian population of these districts welcomed, or at any rate offered no resistance to, the peaceful conquerors from Lithuania, who could offer their "subjects" some degree of protection against unpredictable Tatar interference. How the actual annexation was effected we do not know. All that is known is that relatives of the grand prince of Lithuania, usually after baptism, took over the districts as prince or governor.

There was, however, another method of securing the allegiance of the uncommitted principalities of what came later to be known as White Russia and the Ukraine, namely that of attempting to unite them ecclesiastically. Ever since Mendovg's renunciation of Catholicism in 1260 the grand princes of Lithuania had remained stubbornly pagan. Yet Gedimin, while ready to treat with the Curia and to express his willingness to accept Catholicism if only to achieve diplomatic support against the aggressive Teutonic and Livonian knights, was at the same time prepared to negotiate with Constantinople in order to further his plans of peaceful conquest. The rulers of south-west Rus' were equally concerned with the preservation of their autonomy by means of an independent Church hierarchy; while the princes of Moscow and Tver', as has been pointed out above, realized only too well the importance of maintaining the support of the Church. All three interested parties sought to exploit the hierarchy in order to win control of, or in some cases to retain their hold on, the old lands of Kiev. The princes of Volyn' and Galich and the grand prince of Lithuania attempted to gain their ends by establishing separate metropolitan sees for their domains; the princes of Moscow aimed at securing the subordination of all the Orthodox subjects in the ethnically Russian lands to the metropolitan of Kiev and All Rus', who in view of the transfer of the see from Kiev to Vladimir by Maksim at the turn of the century and in view of the marked preference shown by Maksim's successors for Moscow over all other Russian cities had virtually become metropolitan of Vladimir and Moscow and All Rus'.

The first attempt to establish a metropolitan diocese independent of Kiev occurred at the beginning of the fourteenth century in Volyn' and Galich. As has been mentioned above,[1] thanks to the initiative and the efforts of the son and grandson of Daniil of Galich—Lev I and Yury I—the bishopric of Galich was raised to the status of a metropolitan see. The first metropolitan was Nifont. His diocese, called by the Greeks the metropolis of Little Rus' (ἡ μητρόπολις τῆς μικρᾶς 'Ρωσιάς)[2] contained five bishoprics, four of which formed an integral part of the two principalities of Volyn' and Galich (Vladimir in Volyn', Peremyshl', Lutsk and Kholm), while the fifth, Turov, lay outside the traditional territory of Volyn' but was probably subject to Yury I at the time.[3]

The fate of the metropolitan diocese of Galich is obscure. All we know is that the first four incumbents were named Nifont, Petr, Gavriil and Fedor—so, at least, said King Casimir of Poland in 1370 in a letter to the patriarch of Constantinople, in which he attempted to establish by precedent the rights of Galich to the dignity of a metropolitan see.[4] It would appear that Nifont died at about the same time as Metropolitan Maksim of Kiev in 1305, for on the death of the latter Yury of Volyn' and Galich sent off his own candidate, Petr, to Constantinople for consecration as

---

[1] See p. 68.

[2] See RIB, vol. vi, Appendix, cols. 15–16, note.

[3] See ibid. The most universally accepted date of the founding of the metropolitan see of Galich is 1303: see Y. Fijałek, "Średniowieczne biskupstwa", p. 493; Paszkiewicz, Jagiellonowie, pp. 317–18; Chodynicki, Kościół prawosławny, p. 5. Cf. A. V. Solov'ev, "Velikaya, Malaya i Belaya Rus'", p. 28, note 27.

[4] See RIB, vol. vi, Appendix, p. 126.

metropolitan of Galich. Petr was appointed metropolitan of Kiev
and All Rus' in preference to the candidate sent by Grand Prince
Mikhail of Tver',[1] and evidently Galich was reduced to a bishopric, although it is possible that Metropolitan Petr held the
titles of metropolitan of Kiev and All Rus' and metropolitan of
Galich conjointly.[2] There can be little doubt that whatever the
outcome of Petr's trip to Constantinople and however he fulfilled
and interpreted his role as metropolitan of Kiev and All Rus',
Yury I of Volyn' and Galich was disillusioned—sufficiently disillusioned to turn to Pope Clement V and to initiate talks with the
Curia on the possibility of union with the Catholic Church.[3]
As for the third incumbent, Gavriil, nothing whatever is known
about him: the sources, both Russian and Greek, are silent. He was
probably bishop of Galich before 1328; perhaps whoever was
ruler of Volyn' and Galich at the time managed to get him nominated metropolitan.[4] Of Fedor more is known. In May 1328 he was
consecrated bishop of Galich by the newly-elected metropolitan
of Kiev and All Rus', Feognost, in the presence of the five bishops
of the diocese which originally formed the metropolitan see of
Little Rus'.[5] It looks as though his consecration was a deliberate
demonstration of the dependency of the six "Little Russian"
bishoprics on the see of Kiev-Vladimir-Moscow. It is indeed
significant that one of the very first recorded acts of Feognost

[1] See above, pp. 68–9.
[2] See, however, the views of Fijałek, who considers that there were two
Petrs: one the metropolitan of Kiev, the other the metropolitan of Galich.
(See Fijałek, "Średniowieczne biskupstwa," p. 498.)
[3] An embassy was sent to Pope Clement some time before 1309. (See
Paszkiewicz, Jagiellonowie, p. 317, note 5.)
[4] All that is known of the south-western diocese during the period 1305–28
is that one of the bishops, Feodosy of Lutsk, was present at Metropolitan
Petr's funeral in Moscow in December 1326 (see TL, p. 358, and other
chronicles). This may be indicative of the closure of the metropolitan see
of Galich by 1326; on the other hand, Feodosy may simply have been an
emissary of the new prince of south-west Rus', Bolesław-Yury II, sent to
Ivan of Moscow. (See Paszkiewicz, Jagiellonowie, p. 321.)
[5] Mark of Peremyshl', Grigory of Kholm, Feodosy of Lutsk, Stefan of
Turov and Afanasy of Vladimir. (See V. Vasil'evsky, "Zapisi", p, 450.) The
information concerning this consecration and others mentioned below is
found in the same fourteenth-century Greek collection which contained the
"fragments" discovered in the Vatican. (See above, p. 122, note 1.)

after his own consecration in Constantinople as metropolitan of Kiev took place in south-west Rus' and was linked, if not with the abolition of the independent see of Galich, then at least with the declaration of its subjection to his jurisdiction.

The importance of the see of Volyn' and Galich to the metropolitan of Kiev and the determination of the local prince, Bolesław-Yury II, acting perhaps in concert with Gedimin of Lithuania,[1] to make the see independent are amply illustrated by subsequent events. After completing his business in south-west Rus'—presumably he visited each of the six dioceses—Feognost went north. In March 1329 he was in Novgorod where he politically assisted Ivan of Moscow by excommunicating Aleksandr of Tver' and the Pskovites.[2] In October of the same year we find him consecrating the new bishop of Rostov in the presence of Bishops Fedor of Galich and Grigory of Ryazan'.[3] The Greek source which mentions this and other consecrations performed by Feognost, a source perhaps compiled by Feognost himself, unfortunately does not say where the ceremonies took place. Only the date and the names of the bishops present are given. In spite of the fact that one of the accounts of the excommunication of Pskov in 1329, the version of the Ermolinsky Chronicle and the Moscow *svod* of 1479, states that after Ivan had concluded a truce with Pskov "Feognost set off for the land of Volyn'",[4] the metropolitan undoubtedly remained in Suzdalia until March 1330, when once again he consecrated two bishops, Daniil of Suzdal' and Fedor of Tver', this time in the presence of the bishops of Rostov, Saray and Ryazan' (but not Fedor of Galich), and probably in Vladimir on the Klyaz'ma.[5] From this

---

[1] Bolesław-Yury married Gedimin's daughter in 1331. See Długosz, *HP*, col. 1022.

[2] *See* above, p. 117.

[3] *See* Vasil'evsky, "Zapisi", p. 450.

[4] *See PSRL*, xxiii, p. 103; xxv, p. 170. This is not mentioned in any other of the early chronicle accounts.

[5] *See* Vasil'evsky, "Zapisi", p, 452. Judging from the participants it seems most probable that these two consecrations took place in Vladimir on the Klyaz'ma, notwithstanding the evidence of the Nikon Chronicle, according to which Fedor was consecrated in Vladimir *in Volyn'* (*see PSRL*, x, p. 203). The Tver' Rogozhsky Chronicle also mentions his appointment, but says nothing of the place. (*See PSRL*, xv (i), col. 45.)

evidence it would appear either that Feognost took the bishop of Galich with him on his journey from south-west Rus' to Suzdalia in 1328, perhaps in order to make sure of his obedience for the time being, or that Fedor joined Feognost after the excommunication of Pskov in 1329 in order to discuss with him further the question of the future of the see of Galich. Whatever the case, Fedor parted company with Feognost some time between October 1329 and March 1330. Contrary to the wishes of the metropolitan of Kiev he proceeded to Constantinople where once again the bishopric of Galich was raised to the dignity of a metropolis. In April 1331, according to the records of the patriarchal see, we find the metropolitan of Galich attending a synod in Constantinople presided over by the oecumenical patriarch.[1]

If we assume that the patriarchal records are an unimpeachable source, there can be little doubt that Bolesław-Yury and his prelate had won a considerable diplomatic victory over Feognost of Kiev. The independent metropolitan see of Galich and Volyn' had been re-established. But they had reckoned without the authority and tenacity of Feognost. In a remarkably short time Fedor was back in south-west Rus'. On 25 August 1331 we find him once again present at a consecration, that of Archbishop Vasily of Novgorod, performed by Feognost in Vladimir in Volyn', and once again we find him styled merely bishop of Galich.[2] Evidently Feognost, who had been in Volyn' since September 1330, took drastic steps to bring the rebellious bishop of Galich to heel. In 1332, after completing his eparchal business in Volyn', Feognost returned to Constantinople where doubtless he confirmed the closure of the troublesome metropolitan

---

[1] See *APC*, vol. i, p. 164. Fedor is not mentioned by name; but the metropolitan of Galich is listed as ninth among twelve prelates present at the synod. He is given the title of ὑπερτίμος ("most honourable") which would imply that his rank was metropolitan (τοῦ Γαλίτζης καὶ ὑπερτίμου). (*See* V. Grumel, "Titulature de métropolites byzantins".)

[2] See Vasil'evsky, "Zapisi", p. 452. Present at Vasily's consecration were Bishops Afanasy of Vladimir, Fedor of Galich, Grigory of Kholm and Mark of Peremyshl'. The Russian sources all add Grigory of Polotsk, perhaps confusing him with the bishop of Kholm whom they call Ivan (there was a Bishop Ioann of Smolensk in the years 1330 and 1335). (*See NL*, p. 343; *PSRL*, iv (i), p. 264; x, p. 205.)

diocese.[1] For at least thirteen years no more attempts were made to resuscitate the independent see of Galich.[2]

The real danger to the unity of the Russian Church under the metropolitan of Kiev and the greatest threat to the independence of the uncommitted Russian lands lay in the establishment of a separate metropolitan see of Lithuania. The first metropolitan was appointed between the years 1315 and 1317, probably shortly after Gedimin's accession in 1316.[3] Remarkably little is known of him, his activities or the dimensions of his eparchy. His seat was in Novgorodok (Nowogródek) in Black Rus'.[4] Under his jurisdiction were undoubtedly the lands of Black Rus', most probably the principality of Polotsk and perhaps even the districts of Chernigov-Seversky (including Bryansk), Kiev and Smolensk.[5] In January 1327, significantly enough at the time of the appointment of Feognost to the vacant see of Kiev, the metropolitan of Lithuania was in Constantinople; he is mentioned (but not by name) as participating in a synod.[6] Two years later, in April 1329, he was again (or still?) in Constantinople: this time we are told his name, Feofil (Theophilus).[7] What he was doing in Constantinople

---

[1] In April 1332 he consecrated Pavel bishop of Chernigov, probably in Vladimir or Galich (Vasil'evsky, "Zapisi", p. 451); in 1333 he arrived back in north-east Rus' from Constantinople and the Golden Horde. (See NL, p. 346; PSRL, iv (i), p. 265.)

[2] Bishop Fedor of Galich is mentioned again in September 1335. (See Vasil'evsky, "Zapisi", p. 452.)

[3] Under Patriach John XIII (1315–20). The first mention of a Lithuanian metropolitan (unnamed) occurs in the Greek sources under the date August 1317 (see APC, vol. i, p. 72; Paszkiewicz, Jagiellonowie, p. 322). Some scholars think that the see was founded in 1299–1300. (See Fijałek, "Średniowieczne biskupstwa", pp. 513 sq.; Chodynicki, Kościół prawosławny, pp. 11–12.)

[4] See Paszkiewicz, Jagiellonowie, p. 325.

[5] It is possible that the bishop of Turov attempted to transfer his see to the metropolitan of Lithuania after May 1328 (the last time he is mentioned in Feognost's list of bishops). We know that Gedimin left Pinsk, which included Turov, to his son Narimunt, but it is not known when Lithuania formally annexed the territory. It is interesting to note that among the "fragments" of Feognost, written probably in 1330 while he was in south-west Rus', the following is found: "Canon 21 of the Council of Antioch: a bishop shall not be transferred from one eparchy to another." (See Priselkov and Vasmer, "Otryvki", p. 56.)

[6] See APC, vol. i, p. 143.

[7] See ibid., p. 147. Cf. Pashuto, OLG, p. 390, where he is misnamed Filofey.

apart from attending synods we do not know, but it would be surprising if his presence there was not connected with the confirmation of the independence of his see, or with the struggle for its existence in face of opposition from Feognost.

Shortly after his last-mentioned appearance in Constantinople Metropolitan Feofil died. Feognost, who, it will be remembered, was still in Vladimir on the Klyaz'ma as late as March 1330, left for Volyn' on hearing the news of his death. By September he was already in Vladimir Volynsky attending to the affairs of the late metropolitan[1] and, no doubt, transferring the Lithuanian Orthodox dioceses to his own eparchy of Kiev. No more is heard of the independent see of Lithuania during Feognost's lifetime. Once again the metropolitan of Kiev had succeeded in closing a rival see.

Baulked in his efforts to win control over the West Russian Orthodox lands by peacefully establishing independent church authorities, Gedimin attempted to interfere in the ecclesiastical affairs of the republic of Pskov, or rather in the affairs of the newly appointed archbishop of Novgorod. Shortly after the latter's consecration in Vladimir Volynsky (25 August 1331) ambassadors arrived at the residence of Metropolitan Feognost. They had been sent by Aleksandr Mikhaylovich of Tver', who had just returned to Pskov after his enforced exile in Lithuania, by Gedimin and by "all the Lithuanian princes". With them they brought one Arseny, "wishing to appoint him bishop of Pskov".[2]

On the face of it this was a strange request to make of the metropolitan, who two years previously had anathematized and excommunicated the rebellious republic for harbouring Aleksandr of Tver'. Pskov was, and always had been, directly under

[1] This information is contained in the "Fragments" of Feognost (see above, p. 122, note 1). The dead metropolitan is not mentioned by name, but there can be little doubt that it was Feofil and not Petr or the last metropolitan of Galich. According to the "Fragments", which contain the only mention of the dead metropolitan and Feognost's activities in Volyn', one "Prince Dmitry" had seized thirty-four horses belonging to the late metropolitan as well as a gold cross of his (Priselkov and Vasmer, "Otryvki", p. 58). This was evidently Lyubart-Dmitry, Gedimin's son, who was probably ruling in Black Rus' at the time and who was later prince of Volyn' and Galich.

[2] NL, p. 343; PSRL, iv (i), p. 264; xxiii, p. 104; xxv, p. 170.

the jurisdiction of the archbishop of Novgorod. The creation of a bishopric of Pskov would imply the severance of ecclesiastical and political ties between the two republics. The new diocese would come immediately under the metropolitan of Kiev and All Rus'; and this would mean a drastic curtailment of the diocese and the income of the archbishop. Neither Aleksandr Mikhaylovich, nor Gedimin, nor the Lithuanian princes, amongst whom no doubt figured the disgruntled Lyubart-Dimitry of Black Rus', could have expected that the emissaries would receive a sympathetic hearing from Feognost alone. What, then, is the explanation for this seemingly naïve request? To answer this question we must consider the events which befell Archbishop-elect Vasily earlier in the year.

In the last week of March 1331 two envoys from the metropolitan arrived in Novgorod to summon the archbishop-elect, who had been chosen earlier in the year by the Novgorodians,[1] to Volyn' for his consecration. For some reason Vasily postponed his departure for three months; according to the local chronicles he was occupied with the building of stone defences in Novgorod. On 24 June he set off accompanied by two boyars.[2] While crossing Lithuanian territory, probably the district of Polotsk, the party was attacked and captured by Gedimin's men. Under duress they agreed to grant Gedimin's son, Narimunt, patrimonial rights to certain Novgorod *prigorody* in the north— "Ladoga, Orekhovets, Korela, the land of Karelia and half the town of Kopor'e". Only after they had satisfied the demands of the Lithuanians were they allowed to proceed to Vladimir.[3] Between August 25, the date of Vasily's consecration, and 1 September, the date of his departure from Vladimir, the envoys from "Aleksandr, Gedimin and all the Lithuanian princes" presented themselves at Feognost's court.

Now it seems not unlikely that these two episodes—the

---

[1] His predecessor, Moisey, had quit the see "of his own accord" in the spring of 1330. (See NL, p. 342.)

[2] See NL, p. 343.

[3] See PSRL, iv (i), pp. 263–4; xxiii, p. 103; xxv, p. 170. The Novgorod First Chronicle significantly makes no mention of Gedimin's assault and merely states that Vasily's party arrived in Vladimir "thanks to the providence of God and the assistance of the Holy Spirit" (NL, p. 343).

"attack" on Vasily and the Pskov-Lithuanian mission to Feognost
—were connected. In both cases Grand Prince Gedimin is mentioned by name as the prime motivator on the Lithuanian side.
Furthermore the very fact that the Novgorod chronicler—most
probably a member of the archbishop's entourage—chose later
to expunge from the records any mention of Gedimin's attack
on the archbishop-elect and the conditions wrung from them
indicates that the archbishop and his advisers preferred to forget
the whole business, or wanted posterity to forget it. It may then
be possible that the demands made upon the archbishop-elect's
party were not only political but also ecclesiastical, and that
Vasily was forced to agree to the establishment of a bishopric in
Pskov. In view of subsequent events, and particularly in view of
the archbishop's readiness to forget the traditional anti-Tverite
animosity of the republic, it may even be within the bounds of
possibility that no force was used by Gedimin or his agents and
that no coercion was necessary to persuade Vasily to accept
Narimunt. It would not be hard to explain away the chronicler's
falsification of facts by his desire to reinterpret what might later
be construed as treachery on the part of the archbishop-elect.[1]

If in fact the question of the Pskov diocese was raised by
Gedimin or his representatives at the meeting with Vasily in
June or July 1331, then we must assume that the purpose of the

---

[1] The original account of Gedimin's "attack" on the Novgorodians was
clearly written by a member of the archbishop's party and was probably
included in the first draft of the Novgorod First Chronicle; from there the
episode found its way at a later date into the Novgorod Fourth Chronicle
compilation (PSRL, iv (i), pp. 263–4), but not, significantly, into the pro-
Moscow Sofiysky First Chronicle compilation. It is interesting to note that
the Sinodal'ny copy of the Novgorod First Chronicle (i.e. the oldest
recension) breaks off at the arrival of the metropolitan's envoys in Novgorod
"to summon [Vasily] to his consecration"—in other words *just before* the
description of the episode in Lithuania. The continuation—both the hand-
writing and the ink are different—merely mentions Vasily's consecration in
Volyn' (*see NL*, p. 99). The later recension, which from the account of the
years 1331 to 1353 inclusive was clearly written at Archbishop Vasily's court
or at his command, deliberately omits the entire story (*see* above, p. 131,
note 3). That the story was originally included in the Novgorod First
Chronicle is shown by the fact that when Narimunt eventually arrives in
Novgorod the same terminology is used by the Novgorod First Chronicle.
(*See* below, p. 143.)

exercise was to present the metropolitan with a *fait accompli* in the shape of an archbishop-elect who was willing, or who had agreed against his will, to acquiesce in the establishment of a separate bishopric. But they patently miscalculated the mood of the metropolitan. Feognost had no hesitation in rejecting the envoys' pleas. It was decided to punish the Pskovites, so the Novgorod chronicler self-righteously remarks, for their "haughtiness", for "setting Novgorod at nought" and for breaking their oath to Novgorod by receiving back Aleksandr of Tver' "from Lithuanian hands". The Pskovite and Lithuanian envoys were sent back "abashed".[1]

As was to be expected, Gedimin was displeased with the failure of his plan. There was little he could do to punish Feognost; any reprisals against the metropolitan of Kiev and All Rus' might have an adverse effect on the uncommitted principalities which were now under Feognost's ecclesiastical jurisdiction. But action could be, and was, taken against Vasily, whom he doubtless held responsible to a large extent for the failure of the negotiations on Pskov. When it became known that the new archbishop of Novgorod intended to return home via Kiev, thus giving Lithuanian territory as wide a berth as possible ("because they feared Lithuania"), Gedimin despatched 300 men to arrest him and his party. Vasily, however, was warned in time by messenger from Feognost, avoided the town of Kiev where Prince Fedor (probably Gedimin's brother[2]) was ruling, and arrived in the neighbourhood of Chernigov. There Prince Fedor, assisted by a local Tatar *baskak* and a small detachment of troops, caught up with them. The Novgorodians, however, managed to resist, to pay their way out and to escape back to Novgorod via Bryansk and Torzhok. They arrived home on 8 December 1331. Again it is interesting to note that the Novgorod chronicler excludes all mention of Lithuanian aggression directed against the archbishop: there is no word of Vasily's fear of Lithuania, of the 300 men sent by Gedimin to arrest Vasily or of any warning given by Feognost. Only the "brigandry" of Fedor of Kiev outside Chernigov is described.[3] It is as though the chronicler was

---

[1] *NL*, p. 343; *PSRL*, iv (i), p. 264.
[2] *See* above, p. 122.
[3] *See PSRL*, iv (i), p. 264; xxv, p. 170. *Cf. NL*, p. 344.

anxious to remove from the records all traces of Vasily's dealings with Gedimin, friendly or hostile.

Thus by the end of 1331 Feognost's victory in the struggle with Lithuania, Tver' and south-west Rus' for ecclesiastical control over the Russian lands can be said to be complete. He had closed the metropolitan sees of Galich and Lithuania and had presumably brought under his control all the Orthodox dioceses which had formerly been under the jurisdiction of the metropolitan of Kiev. He had lent his aid to the secular authorities and had assisted the prince of Moscow to remove his rival from Pskov; and he had frustrated Gedimin's plans for an independent bishopric of Pskov. It may, of course, be questioned whether Feognost was acting primarily as a Greek in the interests of the oecumenical patriarch or whether he identified himself wholeheartedly with the political aspirations of Moscow. But whatever the true motives for his actions, it cannot be denied that he proved the staunch and effective friend of Ivan of Moscow and a thorn in the flesh of Gedimin of Lithuania. The latter's territorial expansion was seriously hampered by the determination of the metropolitan to allow no diminution of his authority.[1] As will be seen later, it is likely that Feognost enjoyed a certain amount of support, if not protection, from the khan of the Golden Horde during the reign of Ivan I.

Frustrated in his ecclesiastical policy by the machinations of the metropolitan, Gedimin began to interfere more actively in the affairs of his neighbour, Ivan of Moscow. Of all the districts under the direct control of Ivan as grand prince of Vladimir, Gedimin could only consider three possible terrains for the furthering of Lithuanian interests: Tver', Novgorod and Pskov. Of these Tver' was, at the beginning of the thirties, the most unlikely to yield favourable results. Although Aleksandr, the head of the Tverite princely family, was a firm ally of Gedimin, he was nevertheless in exile and remote from the affairs of his principality. His two surviving brothers, Konstantin and Vasily, were committed to the cause of Moscow. Indeed Konstantin, who had married Ivan's niece Sofia in 1320, appears to have enjoyed little or no independence from Moscow since the

[1] Cf. the views of S. B. Veselovsky in *Feodal'noe zemlevladenie*, pp. 333–4.

uprising in Tver' of 1327; after first fleeing with his brother
Vasily to the Novgorod town of Ladoga when Ivan appeared
with his Tatar punitive force in 1328, he later followed Ivan
obediently to the Horde, participated in the semi-military campaign against his own brother Aleksandr in Pskov, and once
more accompanied Ivan to the Horde in 1331 when the prince of
Moscow went to receive the *yarlyk*. Since 1328 or 1329 he had
ruled Tver' quietly and unobtrusively, but as the vassal of Ivan.
Vasily, who had also accompanied Ivan on his Pskov campaign
in 1329, probably ruled Kashin,[1] the eastern portion of the
principality of Tver'. There can be little doubt that he too was as
faithful a servant of Ivan as was his brother Konstantin; it is
interesting to note that in 1330 he allied himself with the family
of the princes of Bryansk by marrying Elena Ivanovna,[2] the
niece both of Vasily Romanovich of Bryansk, whose cause had
been so strongly supported by Metropolitan Petr and the Tatars
in 1309,[3] and of Dmitry Romanovich, who, liberally assisted by
Tatar troops, attacked his cousin Ivan Aleksandrovich, the
Lithuania-oriented ruler of Smolensk, three months later.[4]

There remained Novgorod and Pskov. Of these two Pskov
presented Gedimin with no difficulty. The close links of the
smaller republic with Lithuania during the twenties of the
fourteenth century have been mentioned above. There is no
reason to suppose that Aleksandr's forced departure from Pskov
in 1329 had inclined the Pskovites in any way to pro-Moscow
sentiments or that the homage paid by the Pskovite ambassadors
to Ivan after the prince had left had any degree of sincerity or was
any more than a temporary admission of the need to bow down to
circumstances—indeed, the fact that Aleksandr returned to Pskov
in 1331 from Lithuania and was welcomed by the Pskovites

---

[1] At any rate his descendants were appanage princes of Kashin. *See*
Appendix B, 5, p. 328.

[2] *See* Baumgarten, *Généalogies*, vol. ii, p. 101; V. N. Tatishchev, *Istoriya*,
vol. 5, p. 85.

[3] *See* above, pp. 70–1.

[4] *See PSRL*, xv (i), col. 47; *cf. PSRL*, x, p. 206. It may well be that Feognost
himself married them. Some time between March and September 1330 he
probably passed through Bryansk on his way from Vladimir on the Klyaz'ma
to Vladimir in Volyn'.

shows just how slender were the ties by which Pskov had been bound to Moscow at the treaty of Opochka in 1329.[1]

Novgorod, however, presented a very different picture. Throughout most of the first thirty years of the fourteenth century the Novgorodians had shown undeniable, indeed quite undisguised, sympathy for Moscow and antipathy for Tver'. The prince of Tver', whenever he happened to be grand prince of Vladimir and thus *ipso facto* ruler of Novgorod, had invariably encountered opposition from within the republic; popular uprisings—incited, one must assume, by interested factions among the ruling classes—had forced Tverite governors to leave the city; Muscovite princes—or Moscow-oriented princes—had found refuge in Novgorod, just as Aleksandr of Tver' had found refuge in Pskov; Novgorod troops had shown little hesitation in fighting the Tverites when urged to do so by the Muscovites or the Tatars. All of this, of course, as has been pointed out above, is largely to be explained by the control which the princes of Tver' could exercise over the import of food supplies into Novgorod from the east. But another explanation may also be found in the influence and the political affiliations of the leading member of the republic—the archbishop.

The role of the archbishop in Novgorod affairs during this period cannot be overstressed. He was the representative of the people of Novgorod (indeed he was elected by them), just as the prince of Moscow was the representative of the people of Moscow; he was the chief spokesman for Novgorodian interests in most dealings with outside states; he was the chief negotiator at treaties which concerned the interests of Novgorod. His position amongst the Russian clergy was undisputed: not only was his diocese the largest by many times, but he was also the senior prelate after the metropolitan. There can be little doubt too that he was the chief formulator of Novgorod's internal and external policy. The explanation for the pro-Moscow orientation of Novgorod during much of the first three decades of the fourteenth century must therefore also be sought in the political leanings of her archbishops. David (1309–25) had little love for Tver': throughout his episcopate there was a constant state of friction between Novgorod and Tver', whereas relations with

[1] *See* above, p. 118.

Moscow were uniformly friendly. Nor must it be forgotten that an overt act of hostility towards Tver' was committed in 1314 by the archbishop, or with his approval, when Prince Mikhail's governors were locked up in David's palace in Novgorod.[1] As for David's successor Moisey, during the first portion of his episcopate (1325–30)—he retired from the see in 1330, but was reinstated on Archbishop Vasily's death in 1352 and continued as archbishop until 1359—his deeds can only be construed as pro-Muscovite: having been consecrated by Metropolitan Petr in Moscow, he attended the burial of Yury Danilovich of Moscow who had been murdered by Dmitry of Tver'; in 1327 he refused sanctuary to Aleksandr Mikhaylovich, who begged the Novgorodians to allow him to take refuge there after the massacre of the Tatars in Tver';[2] and after Aleksandr's flight to Pskov Archbishop Moisey was twice the leading member of delegations—together with the representatives of Ivan of Moscow—which were sent to Pskov to persuade Aleksandr to give himself up.[3]

If we look back, then, on Novgorod's record for the past quarter-century and if we consider the state of affairs within Novgorod immediately following the Pskov episode of 1329— Novgorod was occupied by Ivan I's governors and the archbishop patently supported Moscow—it would appear that the situation was far from favourable for Lithuania. In 1330, however, an event took place which, it seems, profoundly influenced

---

[1] See above, p. 75.
[2] See NL, p. 98—the only source to mention Aleksandr's request for sanctuary in Novgorod.
[3] See above, pp. 115, 116.
Rybakov is of the opinion that Moisey "almost always emerges as the opponent of Moscow and the adherent of Lithuania". He bases his claim largely on chronological coincidence: i.e. his election coincided with the fall of Yury of Moscow, while his "removal" "coincided with the arrival in Novgorod of Ivan Kalita and Metropolitan Feognost" (this is wrong). (See B. A. Rybakov, Remeslo drevney Rusi, p. 771.) Archbishop Vasily's foreign policy, on the other hand, "presents a complete contrast". He was "the representative of the tiers-état, of the interests of the 'black people', of the Novgorod posad" (ibid., pp. 772, 774). Kazakova, to a certain extent, shares Rybakov's views on the political leanings of Moisey and Vasily (see Kazakova and Lur'e, AED, pp. 35–9). Cf. the views of Klibanov (Moisey—"the bitter enemy of Moscow": RD, p. 139) and Cherepnin, Obrazovanie, pp. 501–2, (See also A. D. Sedel'nikov, "Vasilij Kalika", pp. 224 sq.)

Novgorod's relationships with her western and eastern neighbours for the next decade. Archbishop Moisey retired. Whether he retired of his own free will as the chronicler of Novgorod indicates or whether he was forced to do so by opponents of his policy we cannot say for certain. The very wording of the chronicle text, however, suggests that his withdrawal from public affairs was strongly opposed by his supporters, who sought to retain him as the head of the administration, and that his final decision was followed by eight months of hesitation, if not indeed of conflict between opposing factions within the republic. "Archbishop Moisey", runs the text, "took the supreme tonsure (*skhima*) of his own will (*po svoey voli*) and the Novgorodians . . . entreated him to sit upon his throne again, but he did not listen to them. . . . And the Novgorodians took much consultation (*mnogo gadavshe*) and were without a bishop for about eight months."[1]

If we assume that Moisey was, like his predecessor, politically inclined towards Moscow (at any rate during his first term of office), and if we assume that there was already in Novgorod a strong faction which favoured a Western orientation in Novgorodian policy, then it is not surprising to find in Moisey's replacement a candidate of the "anti-Moscow", "pro-Lithuanian" party. There is nothing in the circumstances of Vasily's election or in what we know of his background and origins to help us: he was "a good and humble man who had been a priest at Ss. Kuz'ma and Dem'yan in the Kholop'ya Street".[2] But the events of the years following his election and consecration show so marked a change in Novgorod's attitude towards Moscow and Lithuania that unless we can dissociate the archbishop from Novgorodian politics and deny his influence as a policy-maker, it would be hard to see in him anything but an opponent of Moscow.

He returned to Novgorod from his eventful journey to Volyn' on 8 December 1331. If Ivan I was not himself in the city at the time of his arrival, his governors certainly were.[3] It was a delicate

[1] *NL*, p. 99.

[2] Ibid. Rybakov considers that the Kuz'madem'yanskaya church was the patronal church of the corporation of smiths in Novgorod—hence Vasily's connection with the *posad*. (*See* Rybakov, *Remeslo drevney Rusi*, p. 767.)

[3] The Novgorod First Chronicle states that he returned *pri knyazi Ivane*

situation. Having agreed to hand over to Narimunt fortresses, towns and districts in the northern border districts of Novgorod territory—areas of great strategic importance in the struggle with Sweden for the Finnish marches—the archbishop and his advisers had virtually agreed to a defensive alliance with Lithuania and to a breach with Moscow. The coexistence of a son of Gedimin and a governor of Ivan in Novgorod itself, or even in Novgorod territory, was unthinkable.

Clearly nothing could be done to change the existing order—to exchange Muscovite control for Lithuanian protection—while Ivan was still in the republic or even in his own capital. But Novgorod was used to violent upheavals and knew by experience that a change of authority could best be effected when the current grand prince was absent from the city, or, better still, from north-east Russia. The opportunity arose at the end of 1331 when on the death of Aleksandr Vasil'evich of Suzdal' Ivan hastened to the Horde to obtain his right to the whole of the grand principality.[1] After his departure disturbances broke out in Novgorod. As is unfortunately so often the case the local Novgorod chronicler is laconic and cryptic in the extreme in describing what happened: "Disturbers of the peace set to work (v'stasha kramolnitsi)," he says; ". . . they plundered the house of Semen Sudokov and the lands of his brother Ksenofont."[2] However, he inserts between these two items the important information to the effect that the office of *posadnik* "was taken from Fedor Akhmyl and given to Zakhary Mikhaylovich". That this was no standard annual change of office but that it was linked with the disturbances can be seen from the context itself. Its importance lies in the fact that Fedor Akhmyl was the *posadnik* who accompanied Archbishop Moisey and the Muscovite embassy to Pskov in 1329 to persuade Aleksandr of Tver' to depart to the Horde,[3] and may therefore be

---

(*NL*, p. 344), which could mean "in the presence of Ivan" or "during the rule of Ivan [in Novgorod]". It is interesting to note that Vasily spent nearly a month in Torzhok before returning to Novgorod.

[1] For the question of the dating of the death of Aleksandr Vasil'evich and the departure of Ivan, *see* above, p. 119, note 2.

[2] *NL*, p. 99, Cherepnin thinks that the Sudokovs may have been supporters of Ivan I. (*See* Cherepnin, *Obrazovanie*, p. 503.)

[3] *See* Pskov First and Third Chronicles (*PL*, i, p. 16; ii, p. 91), the only sources to mention Fedor by name. Yanin considers that the change of

considered to have been a supporter of the pro-Moscow faction.

Of course the disturbances may have had social and economic causes: we know that 1332 was a year of great drought and famine, in the eastern principalities at any rate,[1] and this may well have affected Novgorod. But it looks as though the *kramol'niki* were rather activated by political motives: it is not unlikely that gangs of professional rioters could be hired to implement in the most practical way the policy of this or that faction within the city, just as was the practice in the fifteenth century. At any rate the disturbances, or whatever unrecorded events occurred in Novgorod during the first half of 1332, were looked upon by Ivan when he returned from the Horde as "treason (*izmena*)"[2] on the part of Novgorod. As soon as he arrived back in north-east Rus' Ivan let his extreme displeasure be felt in Novgorod by demanding what were evidently new imposts or fines ("trans-Kama silver") and by occupying the Novgorod border towns of Torzhok and Bezhetsky Verkh, which amounted to a formal declaration of intended hostilities.[3]

---

posadniki in 1332 (at the end of the year another change took place) reflects a conflict between the two halves of the city—the Trade Side (*Torgovaya storona*) and the Cathedral Side (*Sofiyskaya storona*). (*See* Yanin, *NP*, p. 186. *See* also N. A. Rozhkov, "Politicheskie partii", pp. 275–6.)

[1] *See TL*, p. 361; *PSRL*, v, p. 220; xv, col. 418; xv (i), col. 46; xxiii, p. 104; xxv, p. 170. No mention of the drought is made in the Novgorod chronicles, which may mean that it did not spread so far west. Famine in the east, however, would clearly affect Novgorod's food supplies.

[2] According to the Novgorod First Chronicle (later recension) Ivan punished Novgorod "contrary to his oath (*cheres tselovanie*)". In the continuation of the Synodal copy (earlier recension) the words "contrary to his oath" were evidently deleted and replaced by "for the treason of Novgorod (*za novgorodskuyu izmenu*)". *See NL*, pp. 344, 99. Neither phrase is found in any of the other chronicles.

[3] Cherepnin considers that the "disturbances" in Novgorod were caused both by the famine and by Ivan's demands of "trans-Kama silver" ("a tax levied on Novgorod possessions beyond the Kama river and partially used for the building of fortifications"). (*See Obrazovanie*, p. 503.) From the sequence of events in the chronicles, however, it is obvious that the "rebellion" took place *before* Ivan arrived and demanded the "trans-Kama silver".

Connected with the demand for "trans-Kama silver" is the entry in the Vychegodsko-Vymsky Chronicle under 6841 (1333): "Grand Prince Ivan Dmitrievich became angry with the men of Ustyug and the Novgorodians for not paying black tribute (*chornyy vykhod*) to the khan on behalf of Vychegda

It was indeed war—not over Novgorod's refusal to pay the money demanded by Ivan, as some historians have suggested,[1] but because Ivan (and the khan, we must assume) could not tolerate Novgorod's *volte face*: by now the grand prince was aware of the rioting in Novgorod, which had resulted in the removal of one of his supporters from the office of *posadnik* and in demonstrative attacks on others. He was probably aware too of the agreement made between the archbishop-elect and Gedimin of Lithuania in 1331; and perhaps he even suspected that Archbishop Moisey's retreat was not as voluntary as official church circles in Novgorod made it out to be. He seemed determined to teach the "treacherous" city a lesson. On 6 January 1333 he entered Torzhok with an army consisting of detachments sent by "all the princes of the Lower lands" as well as troops from Ryazan'. After removing his governors from the city—the ruling prince's habitual action on opening hostilities against Novgorod—he proceeded to "ravage the district of Novgorod . . . until the first Sunday in Lent" (February 7).[2]

---

and Pechera (i.e. the districts in the Vychegda and Pechora river basins), and they gave Ivan Vychegda and Pechera for tribute (i.e. they gave him the right to collect taxes from them), and from that time the prince of Moscow began to collect tribute from the people of Perm'" (*Vychegodsko-Vymskaya letopis'*, p. 257). In other words Ivan's agents became responsible for collecting Tatar tribute from the two Novgorod colonies Vychegda and Pechora, which the chronicler lumps together under the term "people of Perm' (*permskie lyudi*)". A. L. Khoroshkevich is clearly at fault when she interprets this as evidence of the political submission of the Komi-Perm' district to Moscow ("from 1333 onwards the Komi area was permanently subjected to Moscow"—A. L. Khoroshkevich, *Torgovlya Velikogo Novgoroda*, p. 51). According to all Novgorod treaties from 1264 to 1371, in which Novgorod's possessions are stated, Perm' and Pechora always figure in the list of districts following the words: "and these are the *volosti* of Novgorod". (*See GVNiP*, pp. 9, 11, 12, 15, 17, 20, 22, 27, 29.)

[1] *See*, for instance, Presnyakov, *Obrazovanie*, p. 143; Borzakovsky, *ITK*, p. 127; Solov'ev, *Istoriya*, vol. i, col. 923.

[2] *NL*, pp. 99, 345. Berezhkov considers that the occupation of Torzhok and Bezhetsky Verkh mentioned under 1332 and the entry into Torzhok in January 1333 refer to one and the same event (*see* Berezhkov, *Khronologiya*, pp. 284, 294–5). It seems to me more likely that Ivan first sent detachments to occupy Torzhok and Bezhetsky Verkh in 1332, as soon as he learned of Novgorod's treachery. He then collected an army with which to punish Novgorod.

There was nothing the Novgorodians could do to resist or ward off the depredations of the grand prince; the agreement of 1331 between Archbishop Vasily and Gedimin had not yet been implemented and Novgorod was without any form of military protection except for her own inadequate army. Ivan's demonstrative show of force precipitated events. Two embassies, the first led by Lavrenty, archimandrite of the Yur'ev monastery, the second by Archbishop Vasily, were sent to Ivan to ask for a temporary peace and to urge him to evacuate the districts which his troops had occupied; the archbishop offered him a gift of five hundred rubles. But their overtures were not listened to. Ivan refused to treat with the republic or to withdraw his army. There was no alternative for Novgorod but to turn to Lithuania.

As soon as Archbishop Vasily returned from the second fruitless mission to Ivan he went to Pskov. It was the first time an archbishop of Novgorod had set foot in this part of his diocese for seven years. He was received by the Pskovites "with great honour". While he was there he christened the son of Prince Aleksandr of Tver'.[1] This was an act of open defiance. Aleksandr, who had returned to Pskov some two years earlier from Lithuania, was still under the metropolitan's ban of excommunication and was little more than an outlaw living in Pskov and enjoying full Lithuanian support. Vasily could hardly have demonstrated more clearly his disloyalty towards the metropolitan, who at the time was out of the country,[2] or his and Novgorod's leaning towards Lithuania.

If any doubts still lingered in Ivan's mind as to the treachery of Novgorod, they were soon dispelled: in October 1333 Prince Narimunt, the son of Grand Prince Gedimin of Lithuania, arrived in Novgorod escorted by two boyars who had been sent to fetch him. He was received "with honour", he was given the northern districts which had been promised him two years before[3]

---

[1] See NL, p. 345; cf. PSRL, iv (i), p. 265; v, p. 220; xxiii, p. 104.

[2] See NL, p. 346; PSRL, iv (i), p. 265. He arrived back in Moscow from Constantinople and the Golden Horde probably at the end of 1333 or the beginning of 1334. His return is the last entry under 6841 in the Novgorod First Chronicle.

[3] See above, p. 131.

—and was given them on a full patrimonial basis[1]—and he signed
a treaty with Novgorod, pledging total support to the republic.[2]
The breach with Moscow was complete.

It amounted to a total reversal of Novgorod's policy. Ever
since the beginning of the "great troubles" at the turn of the
century Novgorod had resolutely turned her back on Lithuania.
Only on one previous occasion, in 1326, had some form of an
agreement been reached between Novgorod and Lithuania, and
that was during the rule of a prince of Tver'.[3] Now by acquiesc-
ing in the presence of Aleksandr of Tver' in Pskov and by accepting her first Lithuanian prince as mercenary defender of the
republic (ostensibly against her northern neighbours), Novgorod
was for the first time throwing in her lot wholeheartedly with the
West.

It also amounted to a considerable triumph for Gedimin of
Lithuania. The vast lands of Novgorod and Pskov could now be
said to lie within his sphere of influence as much as, say, Smolensk,
or Kiev, or the Upper Oka principalities. If his plan to expand
territorially by establishing independent ecclesiastical authorities
had had to be shelved for the time being, the spread of his influence to the two republics, which the princes of Suzdalia had
since the early thirteenth century looked upon as a western
adjunct to their lands and as allies if not vassals of the grand
prince of Vladimir, was now beginning to make itself noticed.
His success with Archbishop Vasily consoled him for his failure
with Metropolitan Feognost. Of course Gedimin's achievement
must not be exaggerated. This was no annexation, comparable,

[1] "*V otchinu i v dedinu i ego detem*" (*NL*, p. 346): the formula is repeated
from the original account of the agreement between Vasily and Gedimin
of 1331 (*PSRL*, iv (i), pp. 263–4) which was deliberately omitted in the
Novgorod First Chronicle. (*See* above, p. 132, note 1.)

[2] "*Tselova krest k velikomu Novugradu za odin chelovek*" (*NL*, p. 346). Note
that in all the chronicle accounts of the year 1333, except for the Novgorod
First and Fourth Chronicles, Vasily's visit to Pskov and Narimunt's arrival
in Novgorod are related *before* Ivan's march on Torzhok. The sequence of
events was probably deliberately altered in these basically pro-Moscow
chronicles (viz. Sofiysky I, Ermolinsky and Moscow *svod* of 1479) in order
to justify Ivan's reprisals on Novgorod. The sequence given in the Novgorod
chronicles, however, must be accepted for obvious chronological reasons.

[3] *See* above, p. 104.

say, with the annexation of Polotsk or Black Rus', which were now an integral part of the domains of the grand prince of Lithuania. But it paved the way for future Lithuanian interference in north-west Russian territories, it undermined the solidarity of Novgorod's ruling classes with Moscow and, above all, it laid the foundations for a pro-Lithuanian party amongst the Novgorod *boyarstvo* and merchants.[1] The constant inter-faction conflicts of the fifteenth century can be said to date back to 1333, or rather to 1331.

It may well be asked how Novgorod, still technically at war with Moscow, and with some of her territory occupied by a hostile Muscovite–Suzdalian army, found the impetus and the opportunity to take so decisive a step. In the past Novgorod had usually wriggled out of such situations by paying a huge fine, by submitting to the will of whoever emerged victorious in the east and held the key town of Torzhok, and by agreeing to accept the victor's lieutenants. The answer to this question may well be that Ivan I at this particular juncture did not present the same military threat to Novgorod as had the princes of Tver' in the past. One notes, indeed, a certain hesitancy in his behaviour, perhaps a lack of confidence both in himself and in the support he could count on from the Horde. The city of Novgorod was not attacked, nor do her armies appear to have been defeated in the field or even challenged. There is no mention of the traditional cutting off of grain supplies. Indeed the contemporary Muscovite chronicler passes over the entire story of the Torzhok campaign, the Novgorod peace overtures, the resumption of relations with Pskov and the arrival of Narimunt in complete silence. As far as the Moscow records are concerned there might never have been a breach of the peace with Novgorod; clearly in the eyes of the Muscovite chronicler the defection of Novgorod did not redound to the credit of either the grand prince or the metropolitan. Furthermore it is recorded that in the same year a Lithuanian princess, one Aigusta, perhaps a grand-daughter of Gedimin,[2] was brought to Moscow as a bride for the seventeen-year-old Semen, the grand prince's eldest son—a sign, perhaps of Ivan's sense of insecurity and his unwillingness to break off irrevocably

[1] *See* Presnyakov, *Obrazovanie*, p. 142.
[2] *See* TL, pp. 361–2; Paszkiewicz, *Jagiellonowie*, p. 345.

relations with Lithuania.[1] If we add to these considerations the fact that Archbishop Vasily offered Ivan the somewhat derisory sum of only five hundred rubles as an inducement to call off his troops and vacate the lands which he had occupied, it will be seen that Novgorod did not take the threat of Muscovite reprisals as seriously as she had done those of Tver' in the past.

There was, however, one further fact which facilitated Novgorod's decision and smoothed Gedimin's path—the absence of both the metropolitan and the grand prince from the country at the time. Feognost had left Volyn' some time in the summer of 1332; he spent approximately a year on his journey to and from Constantinople and Saray.[2] As for the grand prince, he was summoned to the Horde towards the end of 1333. The Tver' Chronicle, the only source to mention his departure, laconically remarks: "That winter Saray came to fetch Grand Prince Ivan, and they set off together for the Horde."[3]

1333 was the year in which Lithuanian expansion eastwards during the reign of Ivan I reached its peak. It is precisely this threat— the threat of a new and powerful East European state gradually and peacefully encroaching on the lands of the khan and the prince of Vladimir—which helps to explain the dramatic change in Tatar policy towards north-east Russia during the fourth decade of the fourteenth century. As was discussed above, Uzbek at the beginning of Ivan I's reign desisted from his previous policy of playing off one Suzdalian prince against another and was content to allow the prince of Moscow to enjoy undisputed supremacy amongst his cousins. This, it must be repeated, was not only because Ivan Danilovich proved a willing and intelligent agent of the khan or because the arrangement suited the fiscal interests of the Horde, though to be sure these factors were taken into consideration at Saray. It was because of the new danger in

---

[1] Such is the view of Presnyakov (*Obrazovanie*, p. 144, note 1).

[2] When he returned in 1333 is not known, but according to the Trinity Chronicle, which is often weak chronologically, he consecrated a church in Moscow on 20 September 1333 (*see TL*, p. 361). This may have been in 1334.

[3] *PSRL*, xv (i), col. 47. According to the Nikon Chronicle (*PSRL*, x, d. 206), the Tatar envoy's name was Saranchuk.

the West. The Tatar administration was perfectly aware of the rapid expansion of Lithuanian influence and above all of the appeal of Gedimin's peaceful penetration amongst the uncommitted principalities. It was no simple task for the khan to combat such methods: there was no physical "enemy" to dislodge—only a metropolitan, perhaps, or a bishop, or a relative of Gedimin, who in all probability was more of a help than a hindrance in the administration of the territory; there was little point in sending expeditions to ravage the still impoverished districts of Seversk or Podolia. The only way for the khan to put a stop to Lithuanian expansion was to pit the prince of Moscow against the prince of Vil'na. In other words the khan was prepared for the time being to neglect the problems involved in adjusting the balance of power between the Vsevolodovichi and to switch from the limited local field of Suzdalian affairs to international politics. Ivan was allowed to conduct his own business unhindered by local rivals and to gain certain benefits for Moscow at the expense of his neighbours so that he might provide a safeguard against excessive Lithuanian growth. Playing off Tver' or Suzdal' against Moscow might have been sound policy in the past; but now it had become evident that only a strong Moscow could satisfactorily combat a strong Lithuania.

It is only by bearing in mind the khan's growing preoccupation with Lithuania and by realizing that it was this very preoccupation which conditioned his attitude towards the principalities of north-east Russia that we can understand something of the highly complex sequence of events which followed the crisis of 1333. As usual the available sources present a confused and often sadly fragmentary picture. At first glance the main protagonists appear to act with a remarkable inconsistency, changing their policies, it seems, at random. Of course much is lost as a result of the reluctance of the local chroniclers to report objectively or even to report at all, and motives for actions, when supplied, tend merely to confuse the issue. However, by carefully analysing the sources, by watching out for parochial bias and by bearing in mind the ultimate objective of Tatar policy, we can discern a certain degree of consistency of action, a certain pattern of events conditioned not only by chance but also by purpose.

Uzbek was faced with two problems which had to be solved if

the balance of power in north-eastern Europe was to be adjusted
satisfactorily from a Tatar point of view. Firstly, Novgorod had
to be removed from the Lithuanian sphere of influence; secondly,
Pskov had to be brought back into the orbit of the prince of
Vladimir. Both these problems were of course also the problems
of Ivan of Moscow and Metropolitan Feognost: the energies of
both of them were largely directed towards these two objectives
during the last six years of the thirteen-thirties.

Of the two, Novgorod presented the more immediate problem.
It was a delicate situation calling for tact rather than brute force;
and it is noteworthy that both interested parties, Gedimin and
Ivan, approached the problem with a hesitancy that almost
amounted to indecision. Lithuanian aid to the republic was highly
ineffective: neither Gedimin nor his son Narimunt appear to have
objected to or physically to have resisted Ivan's reaffirmation of
his authority in Novgorod. The only sign of Lithuanian irritation
was a raid on the district of Torzhok in 1335. At the same time
Ivan eschewed the aggressiveness of his predecessors, refrained
from seizing the key border towns of Torzhok and Bezhetsky
Verkh and preferred to use diplomatic methods. Even when re-
established in power he used no threats or violence to persuade
the Novgorodians to take up arms against Pskov. Indeed the
peaceful and friendly nature of his discussions with the Novgorodians is stressed by the local chronicler.[1]

The first steps in the attempt to effect a reconciliation between
Novgorod and Moscow were taken early in 1334 by the metropolitan. Feognost, who had arrived back in north-east Russia
from Constantinople and Saray in the previous year, summoned
Archbishop Vasily to his seat in Vladimir on the Klyaz'ma.
Ostensibly the purpose of Vasily's visit was to assist at the
consecration of the new bishop of Saray which took place in
June 1334. But in fact there can be little doubt that Vasily was
summoned to Vladimir to discuss the political situation and more
specifically to prepare the ground for a peaceful solution of the
crisis.[2] The mediation of the metropolitan was successful. As

[1] See NL, p. 346. Much of the caution shown by both sides may of course
be ascribed to the dynastic marriage between Semen of Moscow and Aigusta
of Lithuania.

[2] It is also the view of Paszkiewicz that Feognost acted as a go-between.

soon as Ivan arrived back in Moscow from the Horde, whither undoubtedly he had been called to discuss the question of Novgorod's disaffection and Aleksandr's continued presence in Pskov, a Novgorod delegation was sent to him. There are no available details of the nature of their discussions or of the terms of the agreement reached. But at any rate we know that an agreement was reached. The delegation was received "with love".[1] "Grand Prince Ivan bestowed his favour upon his patrimony Novgorod the Great [and] forgave them their hostility."[2] In February 1335 he entered Novgorod and once again was recognized as prince of Novgorod. The short-lived alliance with Lithuania was over; Narimunt quit the lands newly bestowed on him;[3] and the pro-Lithuanian faction in Novgorod was temporarily subdued.

These, however, were not the only concessions made by Novgorod. It seems likely that either at the time of Vasily's talks with Feognost or during the Novgorod delegation's discussions with Ivan, some ecclesiastical concessions were made as well. At any rate there are indications that steps were taken to rehabilitate the former archbishop, the pro-Muscovite Moisey. He was brought out of his "retirement" in 1335 and was permitted to carry out the public function of laying the foundation stones of two churches. In the Novgorod First Chronicle he is even called "Archbishop (vladyko) Moisey" and is mentioned side by side with Archbishop Vasily.[4] It was probably at this time too, and almost certainly as a result of Ivan's resumption of control in Novgorod, that Archimandrite Lavrenty, the head of the senior Novgorod monastery, the Yur'ev monastery, was removed from his post, just as Moisey had been five years earlier, and replaced by one Iosif ("Esif"). The head of the Yur'ev monastery, the "archimand-

---

(See Paszkiewicz, Jagiellonowie, p. 346. Cf. Ekzemplyarsky, VUK, vol. i, p. 75.) Vasily's visit to Vladimir is mentioned in NL, p. 346; PSRL, iv (i), p. 266; and x, p. 206. For his presence at the consecration of Afanasy of Saray in June 1334, see Vasil'evsky, "Zapisi", p. 451.

[1] NL, p. 346.

[2] PSRL, xxv, p. 171.

[3] He left behind, however, his son Aleksandr in Orekhov. (See below, p. 155.)

[4] See NL, pp. 346, 347.

rite of Novgorod" as he is often called in the sources, occupied a position in the Novgorod church hierarchy second only to that of the archbishop. His office was elective—he was chosen, probably for a limited period only, by the *veche*—and consisted not merely in administering the Yur'ev monastery, but also in heading a council of the abbots of the major Novgorod monasteries, which met independently of the archbishop. He was, in other words, the representative of the black clergy in the government of the republic, and as such responsible for the vast wealth of the richest Novgorodian monasteries.[1] It was therefore of importance to Ivan that the archimandrite should be a man politically well-disposed towards him. Now very little information on Lavrenty is available, but there is just enough to make us suspect that his sympathies were pro-Lithuanian. As has been mentioned above,[2] he was the leader of the first, unsuccessful, Novgorod delegation to Ivan I after the latter's occupation of Torzhok in 1333. Immediately after his mission he is reported as fortifying the Yur'ev monastery as if in expectation of an attack.[3] Four years later, after his "retirement", he is known to have stirred up the populace against his pro-Muscovite successor.[4]

It must not be imagined that Vasily's agreement with Ivan and the latter's formal accession to the "throne" of Novgorod in February 1335 meant that all opposition to Moscow within the city was extinguished. It was not. The events of the twelve months following Ivan's entry into Novgorod show just how active and alive were the pro-Lithuanian elements. Ivan's first recorded act on arrival was to organize a campaign against Pskov. He planned to attack Pskov with "the Novgorodians and all the Lower land", in other words with troops from all the districts formally under his command. His purpose was once again to try to dislodge Aleksandr from his stronghold and to hand him over to the khan. The Novgorodians, however, in spite of the

[1] *See* V. L. Yanin, "Iz istorii vysshikh gosudarstvennykh dolzhnostey v Novgorode", pp. 123 sq.

[2] *See* above, p. 142.

[3] Note that this information is given only in the additional entries to the Synodal copy of the Novgorod First Chronicle (*NL*, p. 100). In the *Komissionny* copy of the First Chronicle (which can be considered as the official continuation of the Synodal copy) this information is missing.

[4] *See* below, p. 153.

amicable nature of their discussions with Ivan, refused to co-
operate. Ivan was obliged to cancel the expedition. All he could
do was persuade the Novgorodians to break off peaceful relations
with Pskov.[1]

Novgorod's refusal to take part in the campaign against Pskov
and against the prince of Tver', whose son Archbishop Vasily
had only recently baptized, was not the only manifestation of dissatisfaction with what must have appeared to many as a political
volte face on the part of the archbishop. In the summer of 1335
the Lithuanians decided to repay the Novgorodians for breaking
the treaty and obliging Narimunt to leave. They attacked the
district of Torzhok. Ivan riposted by burning the two fortress-
towns of Osechen and Ryasna "and many other fortresses as
well".[2] No mention is made in any of the sources of Novgorodian
participation in the defence of their territory. Evidently the
citizens of Novgorod preferred to maintain neutrality where
Lithuania and Pskov were concerned.

Frustrated by Novgorod's refusal to co-operate either in the
projected invasion of Pskov territory or in the retaliatory in-
cursion into Lithuanian-controlled land, Ivan once again attempted to win his ends by diplomacy. On his return to Moscow
in the summer of 1335 he requested that a delegation from the
republic visit him. The archbishop, the current *posadnik* and
tysyatsky, and a group of senior boyars went to Moscow. They
were treated with respect and flattery. Unfortunately the only
chronicler to mention the mission merely states that Archbishop
Vasily "saw much great honour" in Moscow and is silent on the
negotiations and on any agreement which may have been reached.[3]

Whatever was the result of the talks in Moscow, the delegation's
visit appears to have led to serious disturbances in Novgorod in
the winter of 1335. The republic indeed was on the brink of civil
war. Both "Sides" of the city—i.e. the Trade, or eastern, Side, and

---

[1] *See NL,* p. 346.

[2] *NL,* p. 347; *PSRL,* iv (i), p. 266; v. p. 220; xxiii, p. 104. Both Osechen
and Ryasna were in the semi-autonomous principality of Rzheva (bordering
the principalities of Smolensk, of which it was once a part, and Tver' and
the lands of Novgorod). Osechen was on the Volga near the influx of the
river Itomlya, Ryasna—thirty kilometres to the north-east. (*See* M. K.
Lyubavsky, *Obrazovanie,* p. 82 and map.)

[3] *See NL,* p. 347; *cf. PSRL,* iv (i), p. 266.

the Cathedral, or western Side—took up arms against each other.
"Owing to the inspiration of the devil this side and that side rose
up in arms against each other on either bank of the Volkhov."[1]
In fact the disturbances came to nothing. Probably the archbishop
intervened and pacified the two "sides". At any rate "God
protected Novgorod, and they came together in amity."[2] The
fact that the Novgorodian chronicler does not causally link up the
archbishop's mission with the uprising of 1335 should not lead us
to think that there was no connection between the two or that this
was in any way a "protest by the broad masses of the population
of the *posad*", an "anti-feudal rebellion".[3] As was the case in the
riots of 1331–2, there may have been economic factors which
aggravated the temper of the commonalty—1335 was probably a
year of drought, to judge from the number of widespread fires
which broke out[4]—but there can be little doubt that the civil
disturbances of the winter of 1335–6 were primarily a reflection
of the deep rift between the two political factions within the
republic. The fact that the balance between the two appears to
have been maintained would indicate that the strength of the two
parties was roughly equal.

Whatever concessions Ivan managed to extract from the
Novgorod delegation in the summer of 1335 he can hardly have
been satisfied with the state of affairs on his western borders.
Although he retained his governors in the city—there is no
mention of their withdrawal until 1339—his control over
Novgorod was shaky and unpredictable. The northern districts
bordering on Swedish-Finnish territory were held by representatives of Prince Narimunt and in all probability their garrisons
were manned by the latter's troops. The situation in the city itself
was dangerous. By issuing a charter to the Yur'ev monastery
which granted the monks certain legal and fiscal privileges connected with their land holdings in the Novgorod district of
Volok Lamsky (sandwiched between Muscovite and Tverite
possessions), Ivan evidently hoped to make sure, in case of war,
of the support of the abbot, Archimandrite Iosif, to strengthen

---

[1] *NL*, p. 347.   [2] Ibid.

[3] Cherepnin, *Obrazovanie*, p. 505. The chronicler makes *no* mention of the
social status of the participants.

[4] In Moscow, Vologda, Vitebsk and Yur'ev (Derpt). (*See NL*, p. 346.)

Moscow's position in Volok and to increase the dependence of the
population of Volok on the Moscow-appointed governors, who
shared the administrative control of the district with Novgorod.[1]

In spite of the unresolved conflict and the mutually hostile
factions in Novgorod, Ivan's governors managed to maintain
the peace throughout 1336, during which year the grand prince
was absent at the Golden Horde. No untoward incidents are
reported in the chronicles. But the calm was illusory. At the
beginning of 1337, shortly after Ivan's return from the Horde,
there was yet another popular uprising in Novgorod. This time
the object of the mob's anger was Archimandrite Iosif, who, as
has been mentioned above, was probably appointed abbot of the
Yur'ev monastery at the instigation of Ivan when the latter
formally took over control of Novgorod in 1335. "Incited by the
devil," so runs the official account of the episode, "the common
people (*prostaya chad'*) rose up against Archimandrite Esif; and
they held a *veche* and locked up Esif in the church of St. Nicholas;
and the disturbers of the peace (*koromolnitsi*) sat around the
church for a night and a day watching over him."[2]

Nothing is known of the causes or the immediate outcome of
this seemingly trivial uprising. On the face of it it might simply
be a case of an outburst of anti-clerical feeling amongst the
population, or the manifestation, say, of the displeasure of the
peasants on the monastic estates.[3] There is, however, one clue
which would indicate that the disturbances were directly linked
with the political situation. In the unofficial additional entries
attached to the end of the Synodal copy (older recension) of the

[1] The charter is printed in *GVNiP*, p. 143. It is undated, but it was probably issued between 1335 (the date of the first appointment of Iosif, who is
mentioned by name in it) and 1337, when Ivan declared war on Novgorod.
Cherepnin considers that it was issued "when Ivan was already planning his
expedition to Zavoloch'e" (i.e. 1337). (*See* Cherepnin, *RFA*, vol. ii, p. 117;
cf. Danilova, *Ocherki*, pp. 55–6.)
Volok Lamsky, though belonging to Novgorod, was governed jointly
by the *volosteli* of both Novgorod and whoever was grand prince and/or
prince of Novgorod. (*See* Zimin, "Novgorod i Volokolamsk", pp. 104 sq.)
[2] *NL*, p. 347.
[3] Cherepnin argues unconvincingly that the uprising was connected with
Ivan's charter to the Yur'ev monastery. (*See Obrazovanie*, p. 505.)

Novgorod First Chronicle, which breaks off in the middle of the narration of the events of 1330,[1] after the words "rose up against Archimandrite Esif" we find "on the advice of the old archimandrite Lavrenty".[2] These words, which were censored in the official version of the chronicle, indicate that the rabble was roused by the deposed archimandrite against his pro-Muscovite successor. It is significant too that Iosif took refuge in the church of St. Nicholas in the Yaroslav Palace (*Yaroslavov dvor*), the administrative centre of Novgorod and probably the residence of Ivan's governors. The chronicler himself, if not an eyewitness, then at least a contemporary and probably a member of Archbishop Vasily's entourage, could not forbear to express his sympathy for Lavrenty by adding the ironical rider, in which he subtly adapted the words of Solomon: "Whoso diggeth a pit *for another* shall fall therein."[3]

That Ivan and his governors interpreted the uprising in Novgorod as an act of hostility there can be little doubt. At any rate war was declared on Novgorod and an expedition was sent, not against the city of Novgorod this time, but against her possessions in the Northern Dvina district. It was a dismal failure, so the official chronicler of Novgorod points out, not without malicious pleasure: the Muscovite army was "put to shame by the strength of the Cross".[4] Of course Ivan may have been, and probably was, acting on instructions received at the Horde; or his expedition may have been planned to raise money in order to satisfy Tatar demands.[5] But the primary cause of action, whether this action was dictated by Uzbek or was spontaneous, must surely be sought in Novgorod's intractability, in the strength of her pro-Lithuanian faction—amply demonstrated by the disturbances of 1335 and early 1337—and in her refusal to co-operate against

[1] *See* above, p. 132, note 1. The narrative breaks off just before the description of Vasily's eventful journey to Volyn'.

[2] *NL*, p. 100.

[3] *NL*, pp. 100, 347. *Cf.* Prov. xxvi. 27. Note that the quotation is included in the "official version" (*komissionny spisok*). Although the latter omits mention of Lavrenty's part in the "uprising", it is tinged with distinct anti-Moscow feeling in the description of Ivan's subsequent campaign against Novgorod. (*See NL*, pp. 347–8.)

[4] *NL*, p. 348. (*See* S. V. Rozhdestvensky, "Dvinskie boyare", pp. 62–3.)

[5] Such is Presnyakov's view. (*See Obrazovanie*, p. 145.)

Aleksandr of Tver'. In other words the fruitless northern campaign was conceived both as a show of strength and as an act of reprisal against Lithuania, or rather against those people in Novgorod who supported Lithuania.

Needless to say the breach of the peace and the Dvina campaign of 1337 did little or nothing to help Ivan and Uzbek achieve their main objective—the removal of Novgorod from the orbit of Lithuanian influence. Ivan, it is true, managed to keep his governors in the city and to have some say in Novgorod's affairs.[1] But the situation was dangerous and the grand prince could not consider himself or his representatives securely in control of Novgorod. Significantly, the pro-Muscovite Iosif was removed and replaced by the rightful archimandrite, Lavrenty,[2] a sure indication of the strength of the pro-Lithuanian faction and the unpopularity of the Muscovites within the republic.

Strangely enough the Novgorodians were persuaded eventually to seek a reconciliation with Moscow not by anything that Ivan did or did not do, but rather by the inactivity—the sheer lethargy, it seems—of the Lithuanians. Instead of exploiting an explosive situation within the city, instead of helping Novgorod to defend her northern frontier against the Swedes, Gedimin of Lithuania chose to abstain from Novgorod affairs at the very moment when he might have succeeded in gaining a firm grip on Novgorod and Pskov. For a year and a half—from mid-1337 to the end of 1338—there was trouble in the north, and in precisely those towns and districts which had earlier been handed over to Narimunt and which now contained presumably his commanders or some of his troops. Korela, Orekhov, Ladoga, Kopor'e, Novgorod's northern outposts, her defence line against Swedish attacks from Finnish territory, all are mentioned during

---

[1] In May 1338 one Philipp, the grand prince's representative ("*van des groten koninges weghene Phillipe*"), as well as his *namestnik* in Novgorod, one Feliks ("*mesenick Felyce*"), were part of a delegation of Novgorodians which concluded a treaty with the Germans in Derpt (Dorpat) concerning certain matters of dispute. (*See GVNiP*, No. 40, pp. 71–2; L. K. Goetz, *DRHV*, pp. 174–8.)

[2] This is not specifically mentioned in the sources, but under 1338 it is stated that "Archimandrite Lavrenty of St. George (i.e. the Yur'ev monastery) died, and Esif was appointed [archimandrite]." *NL*, p. 349. *Cf.* Stroev, *Spiski*, p. 45.

this period as scenes of local warfare against the Swedes. The Swedes invade, the Novgorodians drive them back and the Novgorodians alone conduct peace-talks with the Swedes. There is no mention of any help whatsoever being received from the Lithuanians—indeed Narimunt's total neglect of his "patrimonial" possessions is emphasized by the Novgorod chronicler. Again and again the Novgorodians sent messengers asking him to come to their aid, but to no avail. He even removed his son (Aleksandr) from Orekhov where he commanded the local garrison.[1] Twice in the description of clashes between Novgorod's most vulnerable outpost, Korela, and the Swedes, there are dull hints of treachery[2] (perhaps on the part of the Lithuanian garrison?).

Was this strange unwillingness on Gedimin's part to follow through what had been so successfully begun indicative of a change of policy vis-à-vis Novgorod, a temporary renunciation of his plans for expansion to the north-east, a realization that the time for the active encroachment on Moscow's territory had not yet come? Unfortunately we cannot answer these questions owing to lack of sufficient evidence. Given the known facts, however, the only rational explanation of Gedimin's negative attitude towards Novgorod is to be found in Lithuania's military commitments elsewhere. We know that in 1338, perhaps in 1337 as well, Lithuania was engaged in war with the German Knights, a war about which we have no details; all we know is that as a result of it the Order was obliged to conclude a trade agreement with Lithuania in November 1338, the terms of which were largely favourable to the latter.[3] Probably the principality of Polotsk was involved in the conflict, for at the same time as Gedimin was drawing up his treaty with the Order, the missing defender of Novgorod's northern frontier, Narimunt, was concluding on behalf of Polotsk an agreement on weights and measures with Riga.[4] We can only assume that after his forced departure from

---

[1] For details of the Novgorod–Swedish war of 1337–8, see NL, pp. 348–9; PSRL, iv (i), pp. 266–7; v, 220–1. Peace was eventually signed in the winter of 1338–9.

[2] See PSRL, v, p. 220 and NL, p. 348.

[3] For details of the treaty, see I. Tikhomirov, "Torgovye snosheniya", pp. 234–6; Pashuto, OLG, p. 281; Goetz, DRHV, pp. 336–8.

[4] See Pashuto, OLG, p. 281; Goetz, DRHV, pp. 336–8.

Novgorod in 1334 Narimunt had been helping his uncle Voin to defend Lithuania's easternmost dependent principality, Polotsk.[1] As well as conducting a war with the Germans, the Lithuanians were also obliged to defend themselves against the Tatars in 1338. Again, no details are available. Only the Nikon Chronicle laconically remarks that "in that year (1338) the Tatars waged war on Lithuania".[2]

Unable to rely on any physical support from the West, the Novgorodians appear to have reconciled themselves to the overlordship of the prince of Moscow. As soon as Ivan returned to north-east Rus' from the Horde in 1339 they despatched an embassy to him, certainly to hand over their share of the Tatar tribute, and probably to seek some sort of agreement and understanding.[3] It was not, of course, technically speaking, a peace mission; Ivan, it must be repeated, had not removed his *namestniki* from Novgorod as a result of the Dvina campaign of 1337, even though the latter had amounted to a virtual declaration of war; indeed, before setting off on his last trip to the Horde in 1339 he had sent his youngest son, the twelve-year-old Andrey, to Novgorod as a symbolical expression of his continued authority over the republic.[4] But it was a demonstration of Novgorod's desire for peace with Ivan.

As so many previous attempts to find a peaceful solution to the problem of viable relations between Novgorod and Moscow had failed, so too did this. Motivated perhaps by greed, but more probably acting simply on the orders of the khan, Ivan accepted the tribute brought by the Novgorodian ambassadors and then sent his own envoys to Novgorod demanding yet another payment of tribute. "Give me", he is reported to have said, "the khan's request, that which the khan has demanded of me."[5]

---

[1] Voin, Gedimin's brother, evidently ruled in Polotsk from 1326 (*see* above, p. 104) to 1342. (*See* V. E. Danilevich, *Ocherk istorii Polotskoy zemli*, pp. 155–7.)

[2] *PSRL*, x, p. 208.

[3] *See NL*, p. 350; *PSRL*, v, p. 221; xxiii, p. 105; xxv, p. 172. From the Novgorod First Chronicle and the Sofiysky First Chronicle it would seem that the Novgorodians sent two embassies to Ivan in 1339, the first on an unspecified mission, the second to hand over the tribute. *Cf.*, however, the versions of the Ermolinsky Chronicle and the Moscow *svod* 1479.

[4] *See TL*, p. 362.   [5] *NL*, p. 350.

The Novgorodians refused, saying that this was an unprecedented demand, entirely out of keeping with the contracts signed between Ivan and Novgorod.[1] Their refusal to pay led once more to a breach of the peace. At the end of 1339 or the beginning of 1340 Ivan for the last time removed his governors from the city.[2] Before he had time, however, to apply economic pressure on Novgorod or militarily to force the republic to accept his demands, he was dead. Novogorod was left in much the same state of political suspension as she had been at the beginning of Ivan's reign. The problem which Ivan had set himself seven years before—of confirming once and for all his own authority in Novgorod and removing Novgorod from the Lithuanian sphere of influence—had not been solved. True, Narimunt's brief tutelage of the republic had turned out to be a dismal failure and Gedimin had seemingly let slip a golden opportunity to assert his authority; true, the archbishop was to all appearances slightly more amenable to persuasion from Moscow. But none the less, there were no signs of any diminution of the influence of the pro-Lithuanian faction in Novgorod, there were no signs that Moscow's rule had become any more acceptable to the inhabitants of Novgorod. Indeed, Novgorod had nothing to thank Ivan of Moscow for—he had not even helped her wage her successfully-concluded war with Sweden in 1337-9—nor had Ivan in any way been able to provide an attractive alternative to Lithuanian protection.

If Ivan and Uzbek failed in this the first of their two objectives, in the second—the return of Pskov to the orbit of the grand prince of Vladimir and Moscow—they can be said to have gone some way towards achieving their aim. Although Pskov at the end of the thirties was not, as far as we can tell, directly under Muscovite political control, at least the main hurdle in Ivan's path had been removed; Aleksandr of Tver' had been extracted from Pskov and physically destroyed; and Pskov had broken her ties with Novgorod.

To what extent pure chance entered into the pattern of events culminating in the destruction of Aleksandr of Tver' we cannot of

[1] See ibid.
[2] See NL, pp. 350-1.

course say. If, however, we assume that these particular events happened largely because Uzbek and Ivan wanted them to happen, or rather planned that they should happen, and if we consider that they happened in accordance with what we can assume to have been Uzbek's overall policy towards north-east Russia, then we can try to interpret them as part of a conscious pattern without having recourse to determinism or to the inexplicability of chance coincidences. Once again, before we try to analyse the events leading to Aleksandr's death it must be stressed that Uzbek's main aim was not the strengthening of Tver' at the expense of Moscow, nor the playing off of one Suzdalian principality against another, but the creation of a relatively powerful and unified north-east Russian state capable of putting a stop to Lithuanian expansion or aggression eastwards.

In 1336 Aleksandr Mikhaylovich of Tver' had been ruling in Pskov for four or five years after his return from Lithuania. Nothing is known of this rule: the sources make no references to any act of open hostility between Pskov and Moscow or between Pskov and the German Knights during this time. In fact the safety of Pskov on both these fronts was guaranteed, firstly, by the refusal of the pro-Lithuanian faction in Novgorod to permit Ivan to attack Pskov (or at any rate their refusal to join Ivan's anti-Pskov coalition of princes); and secondly by Aleksandr's presence in Pskov, which resulted, no doubt, in a considerable stiffening of Pskovite military resources by means of Lithuanian forces.

When Aleksandr had returned to Pskov from Lithuania in 1331 or 1332, he had returned with the ultimate aim of recovering his own principality of Tver', if not the grand principality of Vladimir as well. He could scarcely have been satisfied with his life in Pskov as the defender of a border state against possible German or Muscovite attacks, as little more than a glorified mercenary who had to rely on the shaky support of Gedimin for any foreign venture he might plan to undertake. Small wonder then that by the middle of the thirties he began to show signs of restlessness. In 1334 or early 1335 he sent his son Fedor to the Horde, probably in order to investigate the situation and to sound the ground for a possible reconciliation between himself and the khan. In 1335 Fedor returned not to Pskov but to Tver' together with a Tatar official (*posol*), one Abdul (*Avdul*).[1]

Why Fedor returned to Tver' instead of Pskov we do not know. At any rate he stayed there for at least a year, informing his father in Pskov of his arrival. In the winter of 1336 Aleksandr Mikhaylovich took the unprecedented step of visiting his own principality of Tver'. The chronicles merely state that he went there and brought his son back to Pskov, implying that the aim of his journey was to fetch Fedor.[2] Historians have suggested other purposes—to make his peace with his brother Konstantin,[3] who, to judge from the scant information available, was quietly ruling Tver' under the careful supervision of his wife's uncle, Ivan of Moscow,[4] or merely "to find out the attitude of the local boyars, servants and townsfolk towards him".[5] A more likely explanation is that he went to find out from Abdul and his son what Uzbek had had to say about his projected return to Tver'. It is worth noting that in the same year Ivan of Moscow made a hurried trip to the Horde, the purpose of which was almost certainly to bring back instructions to Aleksandr, or some form of inducement with which to persuade him to visit Saray.[6]

The persuasions of Ivan and the assurances of Abdul convinced Aleksandr that it would be safe for him to travel to the Horde and that the khan was prepared to discuss his reinstatement as prince of Tver'. As a precautionary measure, however, he decided to get in touch with Metropolitan Feognost. It was "for the sake of his blessing and his prayers", says the Tverite chronicler, that Aleksandr sent his boyars to the metropolitan, and because he had no wish to risk the disinheritance of his children in Tver' by remaining until his death in Pskov.[7] A more likely explanation is that Aleksandr sought a guarantee of his safety from the Church,

---

[1] See PSRL, xv (i), col. 47. That he was accompanied by Abdul is only mentioned in the Nikon Chronicle (*see* PSRL, x, p. 207).

[2] See PSRL, xv (i), col. 47; xv, col. 418.

[3] See Paszkiewicz, *Jagiellonowie*, p. 348.

[4] See PSRL, xv, col. 417 (under 6837—1329).

[5] Cherepnin, *Obrazovanie*, p. 505.

[6] See NL, p. 347; TL, p. 362. In the Tver' Rogozhsky Chronicle Ivan's return from the Horde is mentioned before Aleksandr's trip to Tver' (*see* PSRL, xv (i), col. 47).

[7] See PSRL, xv (i), cols. 47-8; xv, col. 418.

or at any rate a safe conduct for all the principalities though which he had to pass.¹ At last, in 1337, armed with the "blessing of the metropolitan and all the bishops",² he set off with his boyars and servants to the Horde.

Aleksandr's decision to quit Pskov and to attempt to reinstate himself in Tver' caused no small consternation in Novgorod. 1337, it will be remembered, was the year of Ivan's declaration of war on the republic and his fruitless invasion of the Northern Dvina district. The Novgorodians, who two years previously had staunchly defended Pskov and her prince by refusing to sanction Ivan's projected campaign against Pskov, now looked askance at what no doubt seemed to them a reversal of Aleksandr's previous policy of friendship with the West and hostility towards the Tatars, a betrayal of the mutual trust between Aleksandr and Novgorod, which had been confirmed by Archbishop Vasily's baptism of Aleksandr's son in 1333.³ Just before Aleksandr left for the Horde in 1337 the archbishop of Novgorod visited Pskov, ostensibly to pay the second largest city of his diocese a routine ecclesiastical visit (*na pod'ezd*), but in fact to try to urge the prince not to undertake his trip to Saray. But Aleksandr had made up his mind. He rejected the archbishop's advice and warning. The Novgorod chronicler, unwilling to compromise Archbishop Vasily, whose position as a statesman attempting to preserve the independence of Novgorod by diplomatically tacking between Lithuania and Moscow was hazardous and delicate, merely states that the Pskovites "refused judgment" (in other words, refused to permit Vasily to carry out his functions as judge) and that the archbishop left "having anathematized Pskov".⁴

At the Horde Aleksandr Mikhaylovich was granted what he had been led to suppose he would be granted—full pardon for his earlier transgressions (the massacre of the Tatars in 1327 and the refusal to hand himself over to Ivan) and the right to return to Tver' as its prince. The conversation between Aleksandr and the khan as reported by the Tver' chronicler is clearly fictitious and

¹ For a somewhat different view of the purposes of Aleksandr's mission to Feognost, *see* Presnyakov, *Obrazovanie*, p. 155, note 2.
² *PSRL*, xv (i), col. 48.
³ *See* above, p. 142.
⁴ *See NL*, p. 348; *PSRL*, iv (i), p. 266.

has little connection with reality: Aleksandr allegedly states his willingness to die for any sins he may have committed against the khan, while the latter says that he is prepared to forgive him because he has at last made the journey to Saray.[1] All that need concern us is the fact that Uzbek conferred upon Aleksandr the patent for Tver'.[2]

Few historians have failed to express surprise at Uzbek's decision to reinstate the miscreant Aleksandr in Tver' and most serious ones have sought to explain his action by the desire once again to set up Tver' against Ivan whom they picture as having become too powerful for Uzbek's liking. Cherepnin, for example, one of the leading Soviet experts on the fourteenth century, baldly states that "the Horde was scared by the swift rise of the principality of Moscow" and adds that the khan may have been dissatisfied with Ivan's method of collecting Tatar tribute.[3] But no historians have yet remarked on the striking similarity between the events of 1338 and those of 1326.

Twelve years before, after the execution of his brother Dmitry, Aleksandr Mikhaylovich had been given the patent to the grand-princely throne of Vladimir by Uzbek in spite of Uzbek's professed "anger with all the princes of Tver'".[4] It was suggested above that the purpose of Uzbek's seemingly paradoxical behaviour had been to force Aleksandr into a compromising situation and thus give the Tatars legitimate excuse to destroy Tver'.

[1] See PSRL, xv (i), col. 48.

[2] The Nikon Chronicle, which expands the Rogozhsky version with quite superfluous and typical verbiage, makes Uzbek grant Aleksandr "the *grand* principality of Tver'"; it seems unlikely that the principality was raised in status at this time to that of grand principality. (See PSRL, x, pp. 207–8.) According to the Rogozhsky Chronicle it appears that Aleksandr went to the Horde a *second* time in 1338 (see PSRL, xv (i), col. 48). This is unlikely, although Cherepnin finds it credible (see Cherepnin, *Obrazovanie*, p. 506). It is more likely that Aleksandr left for the Horde in 1337 (see NL and PL, ii, p. 92), spent some time there and returned in the summer of 1338.

[3] See Cherepnin, *Obrazovanie*, p. 506. He does, however, go on to say that "perhaps the khan was also guided by the wish to remove Aleksandr from the sphere of influence of the grand principality of Lithuania". Cf. the views of Presnyakov who considered that "the return of Aleksandr Mikhaylovich to the princely throne of Tver' was an undoubted political defeat for Ivan." (Presnyakov, *Obrazovanie*, p. 155.) Cf. Paszkiewicz, *Jagiellonowie*, p. 348.

[4] See above, p. 105.

F

It was also pointed out that Ivan of Moscow had visited the Horde during the year preceding Aleksandr's nomination and that in all probability he had acquiesced in the temporary grant of the *yarlyk* to his rival.

Much the same happened in 1338. Uzbek, in granting Aleksandr the right to the title of prince of Tver', was not setting him up in rivalry to Ivan in order to diminish the power of the prince of Moscow, which was in any case at its lowest ebb at this particular juncture. Nor can it be considered probable that Aleksandr's return to Tver' clashed with Ivan's interests or that his relations with the Horde were initiated without Ivan's knowledge.[1] True, the Trinity Chronicle states that Aleksandr, when he set off from Pskov to the Horde, "did not conclude a treaty with the grand prince",[2] but this does not imply either that Ivan was unaware of his intention to plead his cause at Saray or that he was against his projected visit to the khan. The situation closely resembled that of 1326. Aleksandr was permitted to return to Tver' in order that he might discredit himself in the eyes of the Tverites—and indeed of any other Russians who might witness his predicament—and thus ultimately bring about his own destruction. And Ivan of Moscow is known to have visited Uzbek on the eve of the latter's decision to summon Aleksandr. As will be seen below, the method used by Uzbek to discredit and fatally compromise Aleksandr bears a remarkable similarity to that used in 1327.

It might well be asked why Uzbek and Ivan resorted to such devious means in order to remove Aleksandr Mikhaylovich. Why not simply execute him at the time of his first visit to the Horde? The answer to this question is to be found in the evident concern felt by Uzbek, and possibly Ivan, for the reactions of the other interested parties. The brusqueness of an immediate execution would have undoubtedly still more antagonized Novgorod, Pskov and Lithuania, to say nothing of possible sympathizers among the semi-vassals of Ivan I, such as the princes or Beloozero and Yaroslavl'. At the same time, such swift and arbitrary justice, even though it in fact differed little from the eventual "punishment" meted out by Uzbek to Aleksandr, would unnecessarily

[1] Such is Presnyakov's view. (*See* Presnyakov, *Obrazovanie*, p. 155.)
[2] *TL*, p. 362.

have aroused the passions of the Tverites. On the other hand the majority of the people of Tver' would not be sorry to see their prince removed *after* a bout of destructive aggressiveness by the Tatars, whose appearance in Tver' was irrevocably linked in their minds with the return of Aleksandr; nor would the neighbouring districts fail to benefit from the example of Tver' suffering as the result of the reinstatement of a recalcitrant ruler.

As for the reasons for the energy and ingenuity displayed by Uzbek and Ivan in their attempt to liquidate Aleksandr Mikhaylovich, again it must be emphasized that he was dangerous in their eyes because of his Lithuanian connections and because he represented an extension of Gedimin's power eastward and the encroachment of Lithuanian influence on to Russian soil. His connections with Gedimin were undisguised and were known to all. A prince who ruled in Pskov with Lithuanian backing and who had sympathizers in many of the north-eastern Russian lands was not to be tolerated at any cost.

Aleksandr Mikhaylovich arrived back in Tver' from the Horde in the autumn of 1338. Most of the chronicles say nothing of the circumstances of his return—they merely state that he had been given permission by the khan to resume his activities as prince of Tver' and that he had sent for his wife and children from Pskov.[1] The Rogozhsky Chronicle of Tver', however, adds that he was accompanied by Kindyk and Abdul,[2] "powerful envoys", as they are called. The subsequent narrative in the chronicle, though laconic in the extreme, leaves no doubt at to what happened as a result of the arrival of Kindyk and Abdul and their detachments. "It was in autumn and the population (*khristianom*) suffered greatly. And many boyars departed to Grand Prince Ivan in Moscow."[3] Some historians have attempted to explain this transfer of allegiance by the dissatisfaction resulting from Aleksandr Mikhaylovich's introduction of new elements into the ranks of the Tverite nobility: he is alleged to have brought with him to

[1] *See NL*, p. 349; *PSRL*, iv (i), p. 267; v, p. 221; xxiii, p. 105; xxv, p. 171.
[2] *See PSRL*, xv (i), col. 48. The names of the two envoys are also repeated in the Trinity Chronicle. (*See TL*, p. 362.)
[3] *PSRL*, xv (i), col. 48. This passage is *not* found in the Trinity Chronicle.

Tver' two boyars of German stock and others of his followers from Pskov.[1] However, there is no need to go so far afield for a satisfactory explanation of the defection of the Tverites. We have only to compare the events of 1338 with those of 1327 to see that here again we have a case of deliberate Tatar provocation. The behaviour of Kindyk and Abdul—the latter was well acquainted with conditions in Tver': he had accompanied Prince Fedor from the Horde in 1335[2]—was probably little different from that of Chol-Khan. They were not in Tver' to keep the peace or to assist Aleksandr rule his patrimony; they were there to provoke unrest and dissatisfaction with the prince. Not for nothing did the author of the story of Aleksandr's execution, found in the Tver' chronicles, put the following words into the mouth of Aleksandr while he was debating whether to obey Uzbek's final summons to the Horde: "If I do not go the people will suffer great distress."[3] By their presence in Tver' and by what can only be explained as their provocative behaviour Uzbek's agents succeeded in making Aleksandr's tenure of the principality impossible.

Aleksandr Mikhaylovich was executed in the Horde in 1339. The most substantial account of his summons and journey to Saray and of his execution there is contained in the Tver' chronicles.[4] According to these Aleksandr sent his son Fedor with Abdul to the Horde in the winter of 1338–9. At the same time Ivan I set off to the khan. As a result of certain accusations made by unspecified "lawless people" who were inspired by "that all-cunning wicked counsellor the devil", Uzbek despatched one Istorchey to Tver' in order to fetch Aleksandr, "not with fury but with calm".[5] In the spring of 1339 Istorchey arrived in Tver'

[1] See Ekzemplyarsky, *VUK*, vol. i, p. 77, note 201; Paszkiewicz, *Jagiellonowie*, p. 351; *cf.* Presnyakov, *Obrazovanie*, p. 158, note 2.

[2] See *PSRL*, x, p. 207.   [3] *PSRL*, xv (i), col. 49.

[4] See *PSRL*, xv (i), cols. 49–51; xv, cols. 418–21. In the latter account (the Tver' Chronicle) the beginning is missing; otherwise the two are more or less the same.

[5] *PSRL*, xv (i), cols. 48–9. After the words "Ivan went to the Horde" the following is found: "and being unable to tolerate this (what? perhaps a sentence has been omitted here), the devil . . . entered amongst lawless people [and] taught them to slander Prince Aleksandr, and he (the devil) filled the ears of the lawless khan with bitter-worded flatteries." (*PSRL*, xv (i), col. 48.) "Lawless people" clearly refers to the Tatars (*bezzakonny* being a

and informed Aleksandr that the khan was willing to let him bring back his son from the Horde. Aleksandr, however, though realizing the deceit behind Istorchey's words, decided to go and to sacrifice himself for the good of the people. "If I go," he mused, "I shall lose my life; if I do not go, the people will suffer great misfortunes." He arrived at the Horde towards the end of September. After a month's delay, during which time Aleksandr was told, now that the khan would grant him the grand principality, now that he would be killed,[1] he was put to death with his son Fedor in the presence of one Tovluby (Toghlubay) on 28 October 1339. Their bodies were brought back to Tver' where they were buried. On the way there they were met by Metropolitan Feognost in Vladimir and by Konstantin and Vasily of Tver' (as well as the bishops of Tver' and Rostov) in Pereyaslavl'.

The Tver' account is remarkable on several scores. In the first place it is striking for its unpolitical nature. Just as Yury of Moscow and Uzbek were virtually exculpated by the Tver' account of the execution of Aleksandr's father in 1318, so too is the blame virtually lifted from Ivan and Uzbek here. Although Ivan is shown as going to the Horde at the same time as Fedor in the winter of 1338–9, no attempt is made to connect his presence at the khan's court with the summoning of Aleksandr: indeed, as has been shown above,[2] the chronicler is at pains not to implicate the grand prince; and no mention is made of the subsequent journey of his three sons to the Horde.

At the same time the guilt for Aleksandr's murder is carefully removed from Uzbek; he sends for Aleksandr only after he has been given *false* information by his advisers. Indeed the only evil character in the tale is the devil himself. As in the Tver' account of the murder of Mikhail Yaroslavich, there is very little information to show why Aleksandr was put to death. There is no mention of a trial, no mention of the khan's motives (except that evil advisers had urged him to summon Aleksandr from Tver').

---

habitual epithet for them); hence it would seem as though the chronicler was anxious not to accuse Ivan of advising the khan to summon Aleksandr.

[1] Cherepnin sees in the delay of one month a period of deliberation between pro-Tver' and pro-Moscow elements of the Tatar *vel'mozhi*. (*See* Cherepnin, *Obrazovanie*, p. 508.)

[2] *See* above, p. 164, note 5.

Again there is a striking similarity between the portrayal of Aleksandr as the passive martyr willing to die "for the Christian race"[1] and his father who "accepted the blessed passion . . . for the numerous Christian race".[2] Clearly, then, the account was written, as Cherepnin suggests, by someone in Tverite ecclesiastical circles, and probably not long after the event.[3] Indeed the fact that it deliberately absolves both Ivan and Uzbek from any blame for the execution of the prince might indicate that it was composed before their deaths (in 1340 and 1341 respectively).

The other accounts of the episode found in the Novgorod First and Trinity Chronicles and in various other chronicles and *svody* which derive from these[4] are entirely different in content and spirit. Although shorter, they contain considerably more factual details. For instance: at the time of Aleksandr's summons Ivan I and his two sons Semen and Ivan were both at the Horde;[5] Aleksandr was sent for "on the advice [of the grand prince]";[6] not only was Aleksandr sent for, but also princes Vasily Davidovich of Yaroslavl', Roman ("Romanchyuk") Mikhaylovich of Beloozero "and all the princes".[7] According to the Novgorod First Chronicle, Vasily of Yaroslavl' showed such resistance to the summons that Ivan of Moscow was obliged to send a detachment of 500 men to arrest him and deliver him to the Horde by force.[8] The Trinity Chronicle adds the interesting information that Ivan, who had returned to Moscow earlier in year the "favoured by God and the khan", sent his three sons, Semen, Ivan and Andrey, to the Horde in the early autumn of 1339.[9]

In these accounts of the summons and execution of Aleksandr all the poetic trimmings of the Tver' versions are absent. There are none of the lyrical, semi-hagiographical traits found in the

[1] *PSRL*, xv (i), col. 50 ("*za rod khristianesk*").

[2] *PSRL*, xv (i), col. 41 ("*za mnogiy rod khristian'skyy*").

[3] *See* Cherepnin, *Obrazovanie*, p. 508. As in the case of the Tverite account of Shchelkanovshchina, however, some embellishments may have been added by a later redactor, probably in the mid-fifteenth century. (*See* Fennell, "The Tver' Uprising of 1327".)

[4] *See NL*, pp. 349–50; *TL*, pp. 362–3; *cf. PSRL*, v, pp. 221–2; xxiii, p. 105; xxv, p. 172.

[5] *See TL*, p. 362.   [6] *See NL*, p. 349 ("*ego zhe dumoyu*").

[7] *See NL*, p. 349; *TL*, p. 363.   [8] *See NL*, p. 350.

[9] Between 23 July and 28 October. (*See TL*, pp. 362, 363.)

Rogozhsky and Tver' Chronicles, nor is any attempt made to endow Aleksandr with martyr-like qualities. His death is represented in the two main non-Tverite contemporary accounts precisely as one would expect it to be represented. The anti-Moscow Novgorodian First Chronicle (anti-Moscow, that is to say, at this particular moment) distributes blame equally between Ivan I ("On his advice . . . he (Uzbek) sent Tatars summoning Aleksandr . . . to the Horde")[1] and Uzbek ("Khan Uzbek summoned him with deceit intending to kill him . . . and he listened to the deceitful words of the pagan one and came and [with his son] was killed").[2] The pro-Moscow Trinity Chronicle, whose editor understandably had no love or respect for Aleksandr of Tver',[3] records the execution in a matter-of-fact tone, as though there were no need to seek justification for it. No attempt is made to stress the pathos of the event or to provide a villain. Uzbek and the Tatars are simply not mentioned: the identity of the executioners is left to the reader to guess. Ivan and his sons are entirely exonerated. Not only is no mention made of Ivan's "counsel" to the khan, allegedly the cause of the latter's summoning of Aleksandr, but the first half of the entry under the year 1339 seems to contain a deliberate contrast between Ivan's dealings with the khan and Aleksandr's: "In that year," runs the second phrase of the 1339 entry, "Grand Prince Ivan returned from the Horde to Rus', to his patrimony, favoured by God and the khan. And in that year Prince Aleksandr of Tver' went to the Horde." The contrast in the sentence describing the murder and the return of the Muscovite princes is still more striking: "On 28 October . . . Prince Aleksandr Mikhaylovich of Tver' and his son Prince Fedor were killed at the Horde and their bodies were cut to pieces; but Prince Semen and his two brothers were sent back to Rus' with love, and they arrived in Rus' from the Horde favoured by God and the khan."[4] The chronicler is, it seems, anxious to stress the divine nature of Ivan I's dealings with the

[1] *NL*, p. 349. [2] *NL*, p. 350.

[3] In the Trinity Chronicle the massacre of the Tatars in Tver' (1327) is not mentioned, nor is the attempt of Ivan I to extract Aleksandr from Pskov. Aleksandr's visit to the Horde in 1338 is portrayed almost as though it was an offence against the grand prince: "[he] went to the Horde, but not having concluded a treaty with the grand prince . . ." (*TL*, p. 362).

[4] *TL*, pp. 362, 363.

Tatars: the princes of Tver', one is led to believe, only got what was their due.

What, then, can be concluded from these three, at times contradictory and biased, accounts of the elimination of Aleksandr of Tver' and his eldest son? We can piece together the bare facts: Aleksandr was ordered to go to the Horde with his son and was executed there. It seems likely that there was no formal trial and that no accusations were brought against Aleksandr: one would have expected the sources, whatever their bias, to report on this aspect of the episode, as they had done in the case of the murder of Mikhail Yaroslavich in 1318. We know why both Uzbek and Ivan required the removal of Aleksandr. We know how the circumstances in Tver' were arranged—the return of the prince accompanied by Tatar emissaries and their detachments, the provocative behaviour of the occupants, perhaps even incidents similar to those which took place in 1327 and which led to the eventual massacre of the Tatars—to facilitate and justify the removal of Aleksandr. It only remains to enquire how the Tatars managed to persuade Aleksandr to go to the Horde and to sacrifice himself for his principality.

The Tverite chronicler, of course, is anxious to have his readers believe that Uzbek attempted to summon Aleksandr by guile ("not with fury but with calm") and by promising him the fulfilment of his desires: this is perhaps in order to stress Aleksandr's wisdom and prescience in seeing through the deceit of his executioners.[1] It would seem, however, more likely that straightforward threats were used—Uzbek and Ivan can hardly have been so naïve as to believe that blandishments and promises would hoodwink a man with Aleksandr's experience of Tatar methods and interprincely politics. Perhaps the most logical explanation of Abdul's departure to the Horde with Fedor in the winter of 1338–9— an event entirely unexplained in the Tver' Chronicles—is that Abdul had been instructed to bring back Aleksandr after the disturbances in Tver' had taken place, but that Aleksandr, strengthened in the knowledge that he could rely on outside support (Yaroslavl' and Beloozero), had refused and had agreed on some sort of a compromise. This would then explain the reason for

---

[1] His hesitation is stressed in the following words: "knowing and yet not knowing their godless guile" (*PSRL*, xv (i), col. 49).

Ivan's hasty journey to the Horde, his advice to Uzbek on what methods to use in order to persuade Aleksandr to present himself at Saray and his insistence on the need to summon other intractable princes as well so that they might witness and learn from the khan's method of dealing with those who pursued a policy contrary to his own. Once again it must be pointed out that it is unlikely that Ivan journeyed to the Horde in order to persuade Uzbek to get rid of his "rival"; he was consulted on the best methods of dealing with a prince whom both he and the khan had long decided to destroy.

If further evidence is required to show that plain threats were used to urge Aleksandr to leave Tver' and that he was offered the bare alternative of handing himself over to the khan or seeing his principality sacked once more by the Tatars, it is only necessary to remember the utterances put into Aleksandr's mouth by the Tverite chronicler: "If I go I shall lose my life; if I do not go the people will suffer great misfortunes,"[1] and the chronicler's insistence on his "dying for the Christian race". Furthermore we must bear in mind the words uttered by Aleksandr when on the eve of his departure to the Horde he learned of the illness of his brother Konstantin, who had ruled Tver' during his absence from 1329 until 1338: "This is the preceptor (*nastavnik*) of our fatherland, by means of whom our people found strength after the war" (i.e. after the invasion of Fedorchuk).[2] It was Aleksandr's final realization of defeat, his recognition of the sad fact that Tver' could only enjoy security by accepting a compromise and by acknowledging for the time being the hegemony of the grand prince of Moscow.

The execution of Aleksandr Mikhaylovich in 1339 marked the end of an age for Tver', the end of a thirty-five-year struggle with Moscow for supremacy and the beginning of the fragmentation of the principality of Tver' into a number of lesser districts—*udely*.[3] The rule of Tver' passed once more into the hands of the seemingly docile Konstantin, husband of a Muscovite princess. Ivan Kalita removed the bell from the Cathedral of the Saviour in

[1] *PSRL*, xv (i), col. 49.
[2] Ibid.
[3] *See* Presnyakov, *Obrazovanie*, pp. 191 sq.; and below, pp. 225 sq.

Tver' and brought it to Moscow.[1] Few acts could have illustrated more symbolically the temporary suppression of Tver''s independence and claim to supremacy. If Uzbek had not succeeded in bringing back Pskov into the orbit of the grand prince of Vladimir, he had at least removed from the political scene the most powerful ally of Gedimin in north-east Russia.

It must not be imagined that all Tatar methods of dealing with the danger of a growing Lithuania were as indirect and devious as those described above. Direct methods were indeed applied more than once during the reign of Ivan I. Apart from refusing to support any other rival Suzdalian principality and thus indirectly building up Moscow as the main bulkhead of opposition against Lithuanian eastward expansion, the Tatars also undertook direct military action against Lithuania and in particular against the Lithuanian-controlled principality of Smolensk.

During the thirties of the fourteenth century there were three instances of Tatar intervention in the affairs of Lithuania. On one occasion, in 1338, there is only the evidence of the sixteenth-century Nikon Chronicle to the effect that in that year the Tatars waged war on Lithuania.[2] No other details are known. More information, however, is available on the other two instances of military intervention in Lithuanian affairs—the clash between Bryansk and Smolensk in 1333 and the Russo-Tatar invasion of the district of Smolensk in 1339.

In 1309–10, it will be remembered, Metropolitan Petr had intervened in the quarrel between Svyatoslav Glebovich, who had usurped the throne of Bryansk, and his nephew Vasily Romanovich, who immediately sought aid from the Tatars. He intervened, as was to be expected, on the side of the latter.[3] Very little is known of the history of Smolensk or Bryansk during the second and third decades of the fourteenth century; Smolensk was presumably ruled during most of this period by Ivan Aleksandrovich, son of Grand Prince Aleksandr Glebovich of

---

[1] See PSRL, x, p. 211; xv (i), col. 52.
[2] See PSRL, x, p. 208. In 1337 Tatars and Russians from south-west Russia (Tartari cum Rutheni) attacked Lublin in Poland. (See I. P. Filevich, Bor'ba Pol'shi i Litvy-Rusi, p. 50; Nasonov, Mongoly i Rus', p. 112, note 1.)
[3] See above, pp. 70–1.

Smolensk,[1] who died in 1313. There is no reason to believe that the relations between Ivan Aleksandrovich and Gedimin of Lithuania were anything but the most friendly; indeed we may assume that Ivan, who in a treaty between Smolensk and the Germans in 1340 designated Gedimin as "my elder brother",[2] ruled Smolensk if not as a vassal of the grand prince of Lithuania then at least in some form of political dependency on him.[3] Furthermore, there was little chance of Smolensk not being dependent on Lithuania in view of the fact that, as Presnyakov has pointed out, most of Smolensk's trade routes were in Lithuanian hands anyhow.[4] As for Bryansk, it seems to have enjoyed a certain degree of independence. Certainly there is no evidence of any form of dependency on Lithuania throughout this period. It seems most likely that Bryansk remained in Moscow's sphere of influence, ruled by the aggressive Vasily Romanovich until 1314[5] and then by his brothers Ivan (until the end of the 1320's?) and Dmitry (last mentioned in 1341) (see Appendix B, 7, p. 330).

The first Tatar invasion of Smolensk took place in the winter of 1333. Only the Tver' Rogozhsky Chronicle and the later Nikon Chronicle mention the event. According to the former, Prince Dmitry Romanovich of Bryansk, whose niece had married the pro-Muscovite Vasily Mikhaylovich of Kashin in 1330[6] and whose daughter was to marry the future Ivan II of Moscow in 1341,[7] attacked Smolensk "with the Tatars Kalontay and Chiricha and many voevody".[8] The fighting was evidently fierce. However, the invasion was a failure, perhaps because Smolensk was defended by the Lithuanians, and Dmitry and his Tatars were obliged to come to terms with Ivan of Smolensk.[9] Of great interest is the timing of the invasion: the winter of 1333 was a period of crisis for Ivan of Moscow and of triumph for

[1] See PSRL, x, p. 178. Cf. Presnyakov, Obrazovanie, p. 160, note 1.
[2] SGGiD, vol. ii, No. 8, pp. 10–11.
[3] See Golubovsky, ISZ, pp. 316–17.
[4] See Presnyakov, Obrazovanie, p. 161; cf. Lyubavsky, Ocherk, pp. 29–30.
[5] He died in 1314. (See PSRL, x, p. 179; xv, col. 408; xv (i), col. 36.)
[6] See PSRL, x, p. 203; xv, col. 417.
[7] See TL, p. 365; PSRL, xv (i), col. 54.
[8] In Golubovsky's opinion the reason for the attack was Smolensk's evident wish to annexe Bryansk. (See Golubovsky, ISZ, p. 314.)
[9] See PSRL, xv (i), col. 47; x, p. 206.

Gedimin of Lithuania. Narimunt was installed in Novgorod's northern *prigorody*; Archbishop Vasily of Novgorod had demonstrated his pro-Lithuanian sympathies by baptizing Aleksandr Mikhaylovich's son in Pskov; and Ivan I had been obliged to renounce his claims on Novgorod. The Tatar-Bryansk attack on Smolensk was no doubt intended as a warning to Gedimin.

The campaign of 1333 ended in failure for the pro-Muscovite Dmitry and probably resulted in his temporary removal from Bryansk and in the political alignment of Bryansk with Lithuania and Smolensk.[1] Six years later the Tatars undertook a far more serious invasion of the land of Smolensk, which seems to have had as its main aims the capture of Smolensk, the isolation of the principality from Lithuania and the reduction of its prince once more to the status of fully-dependent vassal of the Tatars; in addition to these objectives the invasion was clearly planned to serve as a demonstration of Russo-Tatar military strength and solidarity and as a threat to Gedimin.

The official account of the campaign, which originated in Moscow and which was repeated almost without variation in the Tver' chronicles and in most later compilations,[2] indicates two things clearly. Firstly, the initiative for the expedition came from Saray. "In that winter (1339–40) there came from the Horde an envoy (*posol*) by the name of Tovluby whom the khan sent to

[1] Dmitry was replaced by Gleb Svyatoslavich, probably the son of the pro-Lithuanian anti-Muscovite Svyatoslav Glebovich, who in 1310, after refusing to be influenced by the pressure of Metropolitan Petr, was killed and replaced by his nephew Vasily Romanovich, Dmitry's brother (*see* above, pp. 70–1 sq.). When Gleb replaced Dmitry is not known, but it was probably soon after the attack on Smolensk of 1333 (there is no mention of troops from Bryansk taking part in the Tatar-Muscovite campaign of 1339 against Smolensk). In December 1340 Gleb was murdered after what was evidently a popular uprising. He was supplanted by Dmitry. (*See* below, pp. 202 sq., Appendix B, 7.)

[2] The basic account is contained in the Trinity Chronicle (*TL*, p. 363, under 1339) and in the two Tver' chronicles (also under 1339) (*PSRL*, xv, col. 421; xv (i) cols. 51–2). *Cf. PSRL*, iv (i), p. 270; v, p. 222; x, p. 211; xxv, p. 172, in all of which it is dated 1340. The Ermolinsky Chronicle account is a strongly condensed version of what is found in the Trinity or Tver' Chronicles (*see PSRL*, xxiii, p. 105). *Cf.* also the Ustyuzhsky Chronicle (*UL*, p. 51) for a much shortened account.

wage war against the town of Smolensk."[1] The account goes on to describe how first he was joined by the prince of Ryazan' and how the combined Tatar and Ryazan' force marched from Pereyaslavl'-Ryazansky to Smolensk. "The grand prince Ivan Danilovich", it is then stated, "sent his army too, together with Tovluby, at the command of the khan."[2] Secondly, the expedition was on a very large scale, certainly by comparison with previous ventures of this nature. The chronicle names all the Great-Russian districts which contributed troops to the joint force— Ryazan', Moscow, Suzdal', Rostov, Yur'ev. As well as these, two minor Smolensk princes, Ivan of Drutsk and Fedor of Fominskoe,[3] turned traitor and joined the invading armies. The Nikon Chronicle adds that a detachment of "Mordvinian princes and Mordvinians"—Ryazan''s eastern neighbours—also took part on the side of the invaders.[4]

The campaign was as much a failure as the Bryansk-Tatar affair of 1333. Of course the Moscow chronicler is careful to say nothing that might be interpreted as derogatory to the allied forces; but still, from his account it is clear that Tovluby's army, although it suffered few losses, failed singularly in its mission: "Having stood a few days by Smolensk the army turned and went away without having taken the city. And the whole Russian army was protected by the mercy of God and was in no way harmed."[5] The only damage reported was the traditional ravaging of enemy territory during the withdrawal.[6] Although the available sources make no mention of resistance on the part of the prince of Smolensk, it can only be assumed that Gedimin took

[1] TL, p. 363. Cf. Paszkiewicz, Jagiellonowie, p. 352: he considers that the initiative came from Moscow.

[2] TL, p. 363.

[3] For Fedor of Fominskoe, see A. I. Kopanev, "O 'kuplyakh' Ivana Kality", pp. 27 sq. Cf. N. Astrov's curious article "Udel'ny knyaz' Fedor Yur'evich Fominsky". Astrov most improbably identifies him with Fedor Rzhevsky (see above, p. 75). Fominskoe is near the influx of the Vazuza river into the Volga between Zubtsov and Rzheva: in other words, on the north-eastern boundaries of the district of Smolensk. Drutsk is on the river Drut', in the principality of Vitebsk.

[4] See PSRL, x, p. 211.

[5] TL, p. 363. Cf. PSRL, xxv, p. 172: "[they] retreated, having achieved nothing."

[6] See UL, p. 51.

swift and effective action to defend his "younger brother" and that it was largely Lithuanian troops that warded off the Russo-Tatar invasion.

Before we attempt to assess the achievements and the short-comings of Ivan Kalita as ruler of Moscow and grand prince of Vladimir, several questions must be asked concerning his relations with the rulers of neighbouring principalities and con-cerning his land policy. Did Ivan, as grand prince of Vladimir, exercise more or less authority over the other princes of Suzdalia, the descendants of Vsevolod III, or over his still more distant cousins, the descendants of Svyatoslav Yaroslavich or Mstislav Vladimirovich, than his predecessors had done? And as prince of Moscow did he increase the size of the territory which could be said to belong incontrovertibly to him and his sons, and was he able to assure for himself and his descendants the reputation of the leader of the Russian lands, the national defender of the Russian territories against external enemies?

First of all we must consider—as much as the scant sources permit it—the relations between Ivan Danilovich and the princes of the neighbouring north-eastern Russian principalities. These latter fall into two categories. There were the peripheral districts which since the eleventh or twelfth centuries had belonged to specific branches of the princely family: Ryazan', Murom and Pronsk, which had remained in the family of the youngest son of Svyatoslav II, Yaroslav of Murom, ever since early in the twelfth century; other principalities in this category, the patri-monies of various descendants of Yaroslav the Wise, had either lost all economic and political significance, such as Chernigov and Southern Pereyaslavl', or had become entirely independent states, such as Volyn' and (Western) Galich, or had been more or less absorbed by Lithuania, or had fallen into her sphere of influence (Polotsk, Turov, Minsk, Smolensk, and others). Secondly, there were the lands of Suzdalia proper—all the principalities which had been left by Vsevolod III to his sons and grandsons—Rostov, Yur'ev, Starodub, Suzdal', Tver', (North-ern) Galich, Dmitrov and Moscow.[1]

[1] Pereyaslavl'-Zalessky, Kostroma and Vladimir, as has been pointed out above, were not hereditary principalities: they appear to have be-

What control, if any, did Ivan I as grand prince of Vladimir exercise over these lands? Of the first category of principalities, we can only talk with any degree of certainty of Ryazan' (including the appanage principality of Pronsk).[1] Of the remainder of those in the first category, apart from those that had achieved complete autonomy or had been annexed by Lithuania, too little is known to enable us to discuss their relationship, if ever there was any relationship, with Moscow.[2]

With most of their territory lying south of the Oka, the great natural boundary which so often protected the Suzdalians from attacks from the south, the Ryazanites were virtually defenceless against the Tatars, as defenceless as the land of Kiev and its eastern neighbour Pereyaslavl'. In the early fourteenth century Moscow was not prepared actively to meddle in the affairs of Ryazan' without the permission or the support of the Tatars. And although there is some slight indication of ties between Murom and the metropolitan of Lithuania,[3] it is unlikely that Gedimin or his predecessors were able to do more than maintain contact with the princes of Ryazan'. Ryazan', indeed, suffered throughout the first forty years of the fourteenth century from almost complete political and military isolation. And yet it would appear that some sort of compact existed between the princes of Ryazan' and those of Moscow. As has been pointed out above,[4] in the first decade of the fourteenth century Ryazan' was clearly under Muscovite influence. Practically nothing is known of Moscow-Ryazan' relations during the next thirty years, certainly not enough to allow us to form any valid judgment concerning the degree of Ryazan''s dependence on Moscow. It may well be that in the treaty which followed Yury Danilovich's campaign against Ivan Yaroslavich of Ryazan' in 1320[5] it was stipulated that Ryazan' was to aid the prince of Moscow when told to by the

---

longed by right to whoever held the title of grand prince of Vladimir.

[1] Nothing whatever is known of the history of Murom from the mid-thirteenth century to the mid-fourteenth century.

[2] Only Bryansk, ruled by princes of the Smolensk dynasty, appears to have enjoyed some degree of alliance with Moscow during the first forty years of the fourteenth century. What exactly the relations consisted of is not known.

[3] See above, p. 123.   [4] See above, pp. 65 sq.

[5] See above, p. 91, note 3.

latter, and it is possible that Ivan Yaroslavich's murder at the Horde in 1327 was a punishment for his refusal to take part in the joint Russo-Tatar punitive campaign against Tver'.[1] In 1333 we know that unspecified Ryazan' princes obediently joined Ivan I's coalition of Suzdalian princes in the occupation of Torzhok and the operations against Novgorod;[2] and again in 1339 Ivan Ivanovich Korotopol of Ryazan' is mentioned as first in the list of Russian princes who formed the bulk of Tovluby's expeditionary force against Smolensk.[3] Yet this evident alignment of Ryazan' on the side of Moscow was probably dictated not so much by the terms of any treaty between Moscow and Ryazan' as by the demands of the Tatars themselves. There was no question of Ryazan' being lowered to the semi-dependent status of a Suzdalian principality; this is evident from the fact that the prince of Ryazan' still collected the *vykhod* at the end of the 1330's and was responsible for handing it over to the Tatars and not to the grand prince of Vladimir.[4] In other words Ryazan' was no more a vassal of the grand prince of Vladimir at the end of Ivan I's reign than she had been at the beginning of the century; indeed, Presnyakov sees in Ivan Korotopol's reign signs of "significant and increasing independence of the principality of Ryazan' in relation to the Great-Russian grand-princely centre"; he even considers it possible that Ivan Korotopol first began to use the title of Grand Prince of Ryazan'.[5]

As for the districts of the second category—those principalities which had originally formed the "patrimony" of Vsevolod III and had been distributed by the grand prince as family possessions

[1] After describing how the Novgorodians managed to buy off the Tatars with two thousand silver rubles, the Novgorod chronicler continues: "and at that time (. . . *zhe togda*) the Tatars killed Ivan, prince of Ryazan'"; see NL, p. 98.

[2] See NL, p. 99. Note that this information, found in the *additional* entries to the *starshy izvod* of the Novgorod First Chronicle, is not found in the *mladshy izvod*.

[3] See above, pp. 172 sq.

[4] See the account of Tovluby's campaign against Smolensk: Aleksandr Mikhaylovich of Pronsk is described as setting off to the Horde with the tribute when he was caught by his cousin Korotopol of Ryazan' and put to death. (See TL, p. 363.)

[5] See Presnyakov, *Obrazovanie*, p. 231.

among his descendants, the so-called "Lower lands", as they were known to the chroniclers—there is slightly more evidence to help us determine the relationship between them and Ivan I as grand prince of Vladimir. But the evidence is largely indirect: reports of military action by "all the princes of Suzdal'" under the orders of the grand prince, indications of the grand prince's right to purchase land in their territories, hints of Muscovite administration in princely patrimonies, dynastic marriages. No copies of treaties between the grand prince and the local princes have survived. We can still only guess at the conditions which bound the princes of Suzdal' to their senior brother, the grand prince, in the early fourteenth century, just as we are obliged to guess at the relationship between prince and grand prince throughout the preceding three centuries.

Of all the Suzdalian territories, excluding Tver' and Moscow, most is known of the senior principality—Rostov—during the reign of Ivan I. Originally Rostov had been by far the largest of the lands distributed by Vsevolod III to his sons. Stretching from Beloozero in the north-west and Ustyng in the north-east to Rostov in the south and including both Yaroslavl' and Uglich on the Volga, the entire district had been handed down by Vsevolod to his eldest son Konstantin in 1211. Throughout the thirteenth and early fourteenth centuries a certain amount of fragmentation of the territory took place—the northern district of Beloozero broke off and became a separate patrimony under the grandson of Konstantin Vsevolodovich, Gleb Vasil'kovich; Yaroslavl', through lack of male heirs, passed, via a great-granddaughter of Konstantin, to a branch of the princes of Smolensk; while Uglich, though it enjoyed a certain degree of independence from Rostov at the beginning of the fourteenth century, probably reverted to the prince of Rostov by the beginning of Ivan I's reign. According to later genealogical books Rostov itself was split into two halves in 1328 between the sons of Vasily Konstantinovich, Fedor and Konstantin, on the occasion of the latter's marriage to Ivan I's daughter Maria. However, Fedor died in 1331, and Konstantin remained on the throne of Rostov, apparently sole ruler of Rostov and Uglich and seemingly the obedient vassal of his father-in-law.[1] Apart from the fact that Konstantin showed no

[1] See Appendix B, 3.

signs of disobedience to Ivan I—or at any rate no disobedience that was recorded—and indeed, like the prince of Ryazan', answered the summons of the grand prince in 1333 and 1339, there is also the later evidence of the biographer of St. Sergy of Radonezh, who portrays Rostov under Ivan I as little more than a province of Moscow, suffering under Muscovite boyars and subjected to an oppressive Moscow-appointed governor.[1]

Of the other Suzdalian lands none shows quite the same degree of submissiveness as Rostov; but then even less is known about them. Of the majority the most we can say is that there is no record of any overt opposition to Ivan Kalita: the princes of Yur'ev-Pol'sky, Starodub, Galich and Dmitrov,[2] all direct descendants of Vsevolod III, ruled their lands quietly and, with one exception (Fedor Ivanovich of Starodub, who was executed at the Horde in 1330 for unspecified reasons)[3] in evident harmony with both khan and grand prince; all presumably joined in Ivan I's occupation of Torzhok in 1333;[4] and Ivan Yaroslavich of Yur'ev-Pol'sky marched with Tovluby against Smolensk in 1339, "sent by Grand Prince Ivan Danilovich".[5] All, we must assume, with the possible exception of Fedor of Starodub, regularly handed over their share of the Tatar tribute to the grand prince for transmission to the Horde.

[1] See PSRL, xi, pp. 128–9: Life of Sergy Radonezhsky by Epifany the Wise. (See Klyuchevsky, Zhitiya svyatykh, p. 107.) Of course, too much credence should not be given to Epifany's descriptions of Rostov under Ivan I. As Nasonov rightly points out, "the author of the Life of Sergy evidently somewhat modernizes the event he describes". (See Nasonov, Mongoly i Rus', p. 109.)

[2] The principality of Dmitrov was probably reunited with that of Galich (from which it had been temporarily separated at the death of David Konstantinovich in 1280) in 1334 when Boris Davidovich of Dmitrov died heirless at the Horde (see PSRL, xv (i), col. 47—no mention of foul play). Nasonov puts forward the ingenious, and plausible, view that Dmitrov was handed over to Prince Ivan of Drutsk, the minor Vitebsk princeling who defected in or before 1339 and took part in Tovluby's expedition against Smolensk (see above, p. 173). He bases his theory on information contained in Grand Prince Semen's will to the effect that Semen bought "a village in Dmitrov . . . from Ivan of Drutsk" (DDG, p. 14). (See Nasonov, Mongoly i Rus', p. 105, note 3.)

[3] See PSRL, x, p. 203; xv (i), col. 45.

[4] "Prince Ivan came to Torzhok with all the princes of the Lower lands" (NL, pp. 99, 345).

[5] See TL, p. 363.

As for the principality of Suzdal' itself, there is practically no information concerning the first ten years of the rule of Konstantin Vasil'evich who took over the district on the death of his brother Grand Prince Aleksandr in 1331. There is some slight evidence to show that the "Volga district" (Povolzh'e), that is to say the lands of Nizhny Novgorod and Gorodets, part of the territory of his brother, were taken from Konstantin Vasil'evich, who had every right to consider them his own,[1] and were included in the grand-princely lands of Ivan I, i.e. districts such as Vladimir, Pereyaslavl'-Zalessky and Kostroma, which had no patrimonial prince, but which were at the disposal of the grand prince only as long as he occupied the throne of Vladimir. The evidence is that Ivan I's eldest son was in Nizhny Novgorod at the time of his father's funeral;[2] a year later Konstantin was given the title of grand prince of Nizhny Novgorod and Gorodets (in other words he was reinstated in his father's old patrimonial estate);[3] while in 1343 Grand Prince Semen of Moscow attempted in vain to persuade the khan to grant him the right to rule Nizhny Novgorod.[4] Otherwise all we know is that Konstantin Vasil'-evich, like his cousins in the other "Lower" principalities, took part in Tovluby's campaign of 1339 and presumably in Ivan's expedition against Torzhok in 1333.

The only two princes to show any sign of resistance to Ivan I were Vasily Davidovich of Yaroslavl' and Roman Mikhaylovich of Beloozero, both rulers of districts which had broken off and separated from the principality of Rostov in the thirteenth century.

---

[1] See above, p. 113. [2] See PSRL, x, p. 211; xv (i), col. 53; TL, p. 364.

[3] See PSRL, xv (i), col. 54. Nizhny Novgorod was the original patrimony of Grand Prince Andrey Yaroslavich, Aleksandr Nevsky's brother. (See above, p. 29.)

[4] See PSRL, xv (i), col. 55. There is also the additional information that Konstantin Vasil'evich at his death in 1355 "had ruled fifteen years" (PSRL, x, p. 228; xv (i), col. 64; TL, p. 374). Note that Presnyakov is sceptical about the reliability of the Nikon Chronicle's evidence (the Rogozhsky Chronicle, PSRL, xv (i), was not known to him) and considers that Semen was not necessarily ruling in Nizhny Novgorod in 1340: he may have been there en route to the Horde. (See Presnyakov, Obrazovanie, p. 262, note 1.) Nasonov, however, is convinced that Nizhny Novgorod and Gorodets formed part of the grand principality of Vladimir during Ivan I's reign. (See Nasonov, Mongoly i Rus', pp. 96–8.) Cherepnin (Obrazovanie, p. 531) is of the same opinion.

Little is known of the form their resistance took, but both appear to have been partisans of Aleksandr Mikhaylovich of Tver' in 1339. According to the Novgorod First Chronicle, at the time of the summoning of Aleksandr to the Horde in 1339 "at the advice of the grand prince", Vasily Davidovich of Yaroslavl' was also sent for, while the Trinity Chronicle adds to his name that of "Romanchyuk (diminutive of Roman) of Beloozero".[1] There can be little doubt that both Vasily and Roman were summoned to the khan in order that they might be dealt with at the same time as Aleksandr of Tver'; indeed it would not be unreasonable to assume that they, and perhaps others too,[2] formed an anti-Moscow bloc in support of Aleksandr and Gedimin. Vasily of Yaroslavl' even showed signs of physical opposition to Ivan, who "sent 500 men against him to arrest him, but he fought free from them"— information which significantly enough was only reported in the anti-Moscow Novgorod First Chronicle and carefully excised from the official Moscow versions of the events of 1339.[3]

What precisely happened to these two rebel princes at the Horde is not known; indeed, it is not even certain that they ever reached Saray—the chroniclers merely state that they *set off* for the Horde. But it is interesting to note that Ivan I, in his anxiety no doubt to avoid the spread of a threatening anti-Moscow coalition among those princes who should have owed him allegiance, concluded dynastic marriages with the houses of Yaroslavl' and Beloozero, and, in both cases, probably soon after the crisis of 1339. Vasily Davidovich's son Vasily was

[1] See *NL*, pp. 349–50; *TL*, p. 363.

[2] The Novgorod First Chronicle rather vaguely adds to "the Tatars summoned Aleksandr and Vasily Davidovich of Yaroslavl'" the words: "*and all the princes*".

[3] Apart from the Novgorod First Chronicle (*NL*, p. 350), the information of Ivan's attempted capture of Vasily is only mentioned in the Sofiysky First Chronicle (*PSRL*, v, p. 221), which repeats the version of the Novgorod First Chronicle, making it, however, quite clear that Vasily went *with* Aleksandr. Compare the Novgorod First Chronicle version: ". . . the khan sent for [Aleksandr], and he set off to the Horde, and Vasily of Yaroslavl' [went], against whom Ivan sent 500 men . . ." and the Sofiysky First Chronicle version: ". . . and he set off, and with him [went] Prince Vasily Davidovich of Yaroslavl', against whom Ivan . . . sent 500 men . . ." Note that neither the Trinity nor the Ermolinsky Chronicle nor the Moscow *svod* of 1479 mentions Ivan's attempt to arrest Vasily.

married to Ivan's daughter Anastasia, while Roman Mikhaylovich's son Fedor was married to another daughter of the grand prince, Fedos'ya (Theodosia).[1] These matrimonial alliances evidently outweighed the dislike or mistrust felt by the supporters of Aleksandr Mikhaylovich for Ivan I—or perhaps the murder of the princes of Tver' proved an awesome and instructive enough example. At any rate there is little evidence to show that the princes of Yaroslavl' and Beloozero, or any other princes for that matter, were willing or able to offer any more effective resistance to Ivan. It was only on Ivan's death a few months later that the old animosity towards Moscow seems to have broken out again. Vasily of Yaroslavl' was one of three dissident princes who went to the Horde to dispute the transfer of the *yarlyk* to Ivan I's son Semen.[2] Roman of Beloozero, however, remained loyal to Moscow.

Before any conclusion can be reached concerning the nature of the relationship between Ivan I and those north-east Russian

[1] *See* Kopanev, "O 'kuplyakh' Ivana Kality", in which the author examines the genealogical book of the Monastyrev princes. According to this, "one sister of the grand prince [Semen Ivanovich], Nastas'ya, was married to Prince Vasily of Yaroslavl', while the other was married to Prince Fedor of Beloozero" (ibid., p. 27). Kopanev has convincingly shown that the "Vasily of Yaroslavl'" was Vasily *Vasil'evich* and not his father Vasily Davidovich. The latter was married to one Evdokia, usually described by historians as the daughter of Ivan I solely on the strength of the Novgorod First Chronicle: ". . . Vasily of Yaroslavl', against whom Prince Ivan, *his father-in-law (test')*, sent 500 men . . ." (*NL*, p. 350). Kopanev argues that in this case the Novgorod chronicler was either prejudiced or ignorant and points out that no other sources mention V. D. Yaroslavsky's marriage to a daughter of the grand prince. Cherepnin only accepts half of Kopanev's arguments: he agrees that Fedos'ya Ivanovna was married to Fedor of Beloozero, but still thinks that Evdokia was a daughter of Ivan I, and patently misstates Kopanev's case. (*See* Cherepnin, *Obrazovanie*, p. 509, and p. 509, note 3.)

[2] In one of the entries attached to the sixteenth-century Voskresensky Chronicle dated 6849 (1341) the following words are found: "After his (Ivan I's) death the Russian princes quarrelled (*soproshasya*) concerning the grand principality: Prince Konstantin Mikhaylovich of Tver', Prince Vasily Davidovich of Yaroslavl' and Prince Konstantin Vasil'evich of Suzdal'; and they went to the Horde concerning the grand principality" (*PSRL*, vii, p. 237). Kopanev mentions this in his article, but, misreading a footnote of Ekzemplyarsky, gives a wrong reference (*Russkaya letopis' po Nikonovu spisku*, vol. iii, pp. 172–3).

districts which had not been annexed by Moscow, the burning question of Ivan's so-called "purchases" must be considered. In the second will of Ivan I's grandson, Grand Prince Dmitry Donskoy, drawn up in 1389, the following bequests are made: "I bestow upon my son Prince Yury my grandfather's purchase (*kupleyu*), (Northern) Galich and all districts[1] . . . And I bestow upon my son Prince Andrey my grandfather's purchase, Beloozero and all districts. And I bestow upon my son Prince Petr my grandfather's purchase, Uglich Field and all that is dependent upon it for taxation purposes."[2] Now these "purchases", or perhaps annexations—the word *kuplya*, as Platonov has pointed out, has also the meaning of "joining together"[3]—are not mentioned in the wills and treaties of Ivan I or his sons Semen and Ivan II. How then are we to interpret Dmitry Donskoy's references to Ivan I's "acquisition" of the three principalities of Galich, Beloozero and Uglich?

This problem has perplexed numerous historians and none has produced a satisfactory explanation. It has been suggested that the three principalities were bought by Ivan I and attached not to the land of Moscow—i.e. not to the patrimony proper of the Danilovichi—but to the grand-princely territory, while the princes of these districts were left with certain proprietary rights to them. Another theory is that the three princes concerned sold their lands and their independence to Moscow on the condition that they be allowed to remain there with certain (unspecified) rights. A third view is that Ivan I never in fact bought the lands in question, but that they were seized by Dmitry Donskoy, who then called them his "grandfather's purchases" in order to lend some legal justification to an unjustifiable action.[4]

Two Soviet historians, who have recently tackled the problem, have come to somewhat different conclusions, while admitting that there is too little information to say what exactly was the nature of these "purchases". According to the findings of one,

---

[1] I.e. not just the city but the whole principality.   [2] *DDG*, p. 34.
[3] *See* Kopanev, "O 'kuplyakh' Ivana Kality", p. 37, note 1.
[4] Broadly speaking these are the views of Karamzin, Solov'ev, Klyuchevsky, Chicherin, Sergeevich, Lyubavsky, Presnyakov and Nasonov. For a summary and criticism of these views, *see* Kopanev, op. cit., pp. 24–5; Cherepnin, *RFA*, vol. i, pp. 17–18.

"there is no basis for denying the possibility of agreements concluded by Kalita",[1] the best example of which he sees in a compact probably drawn up between Ivan I and Prince Fedor Romanovich of Beloozero on the occasion of the latter's wedding to the former's daughter, which he dates 1339–40. "The marriage of the grand prince's daughter to the prince of a weak *udel* meant the still greater submission of the latter. The *udel* was subjected to Moscow. . . . This was probably what was half a century later called 'the purchase' of Ivan Kalita."[2] The second historian to deal with the question, Cherepnin, is equally convinced that the "purchases" took place and that Ivan I in fact mentioned them in a third draft of his will which has not survived.[3] This third draft he took or sent to the Horde in 1339 in the hope of getting the khan to ratify his vast acquisitions—a hope which, he thinks, was frustrated by the princes of the lands in question.[4] Although his plan was never in fact sanctioned by the khan, Ivan nevertheless came to an agreement with the princes of the purchased lands, whereby "Galich, Beloozero and Uglich were transferred to Kalita as sovereign owner; the princes of Galich, Beloozero and Uglich, however, retained some right of ownership and control over these lands" by analogy with the practice of certain ecclesiastical institutions which left vendors the right to live on their old lands, though depriving them of the actual right of possession.[5]

Unfortunately very little is known about the history of the three principalities during the fifty years following Kalita's death; and what little is known tends to contradict most of the theories mentioned above. We know, for instance, that Galich had a prince and that in 1363 Dmitry Donskoy "drove Dmitry of Galich out of Galich";[6] we also know that there were independent princes of Beloozero up to and possibly after 1380; furthermore, in 1363 Ivan Fedorovich of Beloozero was in active opposition to Dmitry of Moscow.[7] Uglich, as has been pointed out above,[8] reverted to Rostov at the beginning of Ivan I's reign as an escheat

[1] *See* Kopanev, op. cit., p. 25.   [2] Ibid., p. 37.
[3] Two drafts have survived and are printed in *DDG*.
[4] *See* Cherepnin, *RFA*, vol. i, pp. 17 sq.
[5] *See* Cherepnin, *Obrazovanie*, pp. 510–11.   [6] *TL*, p. 379.
[7] *See* ibid.; *PSRL*, xi, p. 2.   [8] *See* above, p. 177.

and nothing is known of its further fate until 1389.[1] It is clear, therefore, that if in fact Ivan I did buy or annex the three principalities, he allowed the princes of two of them to continue ruling, and their sons appear to have enjoyed the same privileges. Once again we must regretfully come to the conclusion that there is insufficient evidence to show that Ivan I effectively altered the relationship between himself and the principalities of Galich, Beloozero and Uglich or made them in any way dependent on himself either as prince of Moscow or as grand prince of Vladimir. Cherepnin's and Kopanev's theories of "conditional ownership" cannot be accepted unreservedly in view of the silence of the sources—particularly the wills and treaties of Semen and Ivan II. On the other hand the theory of Sergeevich and Nasonov, according to which the three principalities were not annexed by Ivan I but seized by Dmitry Donskoy and later called "purchases" to justify their seizure, is to a large extent invalidated, so thinks Kopanev, by the fact that Starodub, which was also seized by Dmitry Donskoy in 1363, was not included among the "purchases" of Ivan I.[2]

Shortage of evidence and the contradictory nature of what little evidence there is prevents us, then, from building any extravagant theories as to the meaning of Ivan Kalita's "purchases" or from prematurely making him a "gatherer of the Russian lands". All that we can do is hint at the possibility of some sort of financial agreement between Ivan and the three districts, resulting perhaps in some form of temporary conditional vassalage—an agreement which in all probability was repudiated by the princes of Galich, Beloozero and Rostov[3] as soon as Ivan I died in 1340. The only landed estates which Ivan is

---

[1] In 1363 Dmitry Donskoy drove Prince Konstantin Vasil'evich of Rostov out of Rostov (see TL, p. 379; PSRL, xi, p. 2). This might imply the annexation of Uglich.

[2] See Kopanev, op. cit., p. 25. It should be pointed out, however, that Starodub is not mentioned at all in Dmitry Donskoy's will, nor in any subsequent grand prince's will. Presumably the princes of Starodub were allowed to remain in and administer their patrimony as subjects of the grand prince, their territory not being at his disposal for distribution amongst members of his family.

[3] Assuming, that is, that Uglich was by then part of the principality of Rostov.

known to have bought outside the boundaries of the principality of Moscow are mentioned in the second copy of his will: two in Novgorod, one in Vladimir, two in Yur'ev, two in Kostroma, one in Rostov and three in Pereyaslavl';[1] these were left to his sons and widow, with the exception of the land in Rostov which was granted on precarious tenure to one Boris Vorkov,[2] and the three estates in Pereyaslavl' which were bestowed on a monastery. There is unfortunately no possibility of gauging the size of these districts—all are referred to by the term *selo*, which could be taken to mean a village or all the land centred on a small town or village. But it is interesting to note that, with the exception of the two estates in Yur'ev and the one in Rostov, all the lands purchased were either in Novgorodian or purely grand-princely territory and did not form part of the patrimonies of the Suzdalian princes —in other words, in the case of the estates in Vladimir, Pereyaslavl' and Kostroma, he bought from landowners whose immediate suzerain was the grand prince himself.

To sum up Ivan's relations with the rulers of the neighbouring principalities, it can be said that remarkably little seems to have changed since the beginning of his reign. Between Ivan and the princes of Ryazan' there was, as before, some form of military understanding whereby Ryazan' forces came to the aid of Moscow when told to; the *de jure* equality of the prince (or grand prince) of Ryazan' and the grand prince of Vladimir in the eyes of the khan of the Golden Horde is illustrated by the fact that the collection and delivery of Tatar tribute was carried out by the local princes of Ryazan' and Pronsk (and Murom?) quite independently of Vladimir. As for the princes of the "Lower lands", again there is no striking evidence of change. There was the same obedience shown to the grand prince in military matters as had been shown to Ivan's predecessors on the grand-princely throne whatever their provenance. If there were more signs of

[1] See *DDG*, p. 10.

[2] "As for the estate of Bogorodichskoe which I bought in Rostov, I have given it to Boris Vorkov; should he serve any son of mine, the estate is his; should he not serve my children, the estate will be taken away." As to whether the estate in question was a *pomest'e* or a *votchina*, see N. P. Pavlov-Sil'vansky, *Feodalizm v drevney Rusi*, p. 109; Veselovsky, *Feodal'noe zemle-vladenie*, pp. 299–301; Cherepnin, *RFA*, vol. i, pp. 18–19.

submissiveness in Rostov than there had been before, there were at the same time indications of open rebellion elsewhere and of an attempt by at least two princes to form a coalition with the anti-Moscow prince of Tver'. Perhaps at the end of Ivan's reign an agreement of sorts was reached concerning the political status of the rulers of the three territories of Galich, Beloozero and Uglich—but nothing was to come of it in the subsequent reigns and the princes concerned were quick to shake off any dependence on Moscow into which Ivan's financial or matrimonial transactions may have led them. As for the question of the territorial expansion of the Muscovite principality, Ivan I, so frequently misnamed by historians the "gatherer of the Russian lands",[1] was able to do little or nothing to enlarge the territory at the disposal of the prince of Moscow. All the "wise and thrifty"[2] Kalita could show for his acquisitive efforts was a handful of estates scattered throughout the districts of which he and his children were the overall suzerains anyway.

One of the hardest tasks in assessing the achievements of Ivan I is to determine to what extent the guaranteeing of the succession to the grand-princely throne of Vladimir for his sons and grand-sons—in other words for the house of Moscow—can be ascribed to the effort and policy of Ivan himself. From a purely Muscovite point of view, the assurance of the *yarlyk* for Semen, if it was the work of Ivan, was undoubtedly his greatest and most far-reaching achievement. Of course, it must not be assumed that Ivan converted the right to the grand principality into an unassailable Muscovite prerogative. The time had not yet come when a prince of Moscow could describe the throne of Vladimir as his patrimony. Yet that the foundations for this guarantee had been laid during the rule of Ivan I there can be no doubt.

We can assume that the establishment of a single strong principality in the north-east Russian lands was in keeping with Uzbek's policy of checking Lithuanian expansion eastward. It has been pointed out many times above that ever since Lithuanian

<hr>

[1] The term *s'bratel' Ruskoy zemli* appears to have been first used by the biographer of Dmitry Donskoy, writing either at the end of the fourteenth or at the beginning of the fifteenth century. (*See PSRL*, iv, p. 349.)

[2] Vernadsky, *Mongols*, p. 201.

growth had begun to assume alarming proportions the Tatars were prepared to keep the north-east Russian principalities relatively unified under one strong prince This had succeeded the old practice of ensuring Suzdalian weakness by playing off one prince against another. It would, then, be reasonable to expect a perpetuation of this policy on the part of the Tatars by the granting of the *yarlyk* to Ivan's children. Nevertheless some credit must go to Ivan for his persuasive powers: after all it was he who convinced the khan that a strong Moscow was to the advantage of the Tatars and that a Muscovite prince was most likely to carry out his wishes faithfully. His frequent journeyings to the Horde bear witness to the assiduity of his attentions. But an even better indication of his desire and ability to convince the khan of the suitability of his heirs for the throne of Vladimir is to be found in his will.

If we consider that the old order of accession by seniority to the grand-princely throne was still effective at the end of the 1330's, or rather that the tradition was still alive in the minds of the north-east Russian princes, then it will be clear that Ivan had no right to expect his eldest son to succeed him: no eliminating process had yet taken place whereby only the Danilo-vichi, the princes of the house of Moscow, could consider themselves eligible for the title. An eliminating process had, of course, taken place nearly a century before, confining the *yarlyk* to the descendants of Yaroslav Vsevolodovich and excluding, by some unwritten law, the heirs of his brothers Konstantin and Svyato-slav, that is to say the houses of Rostov and Yur'ev.[1] The families of the three eldest children of Yaroslav—Aleksandr Nevsky, Andrey of Suzdal' and Yaroslav of Tver'—had shared the *yarlyk* between them ever since the last quarter of the thirteenth century.[2] According to the centuries-old law of succession, the title should have passed on the death of Ivan I (Yaroslav's great-grandson) to the next eldest of the remaining great-grandsons.

[1] The descendants of Vsevolod's youngest son, Ivan—the princes of Starodub—were presumably considered *izgoi*, "orphaned princes" or out-casts, as Ivan died before he could accede to the throne of Vladimir.

[2] The descendants of Konstantin Yaroslavich—the princes of Dmitrov and Galich—were disqualified, as their father had predeceased his brothers. Grand Prince Vasily, the youngest son of Yaroslav, had died heirless.

Of these there were only two: Konstantin and Vasily Mikhay-lovichi of Tver'. Konstantin of Tver', therefore, as the elder of the two, had the right to claim the grand-princely throne on Ivan I's death. Another possible candidate, though a generation removed, was Konstantin Vasil'evich of Suzdal', by virtue of the fact that his brother Aleksandr had held the *yarlyk* from 1328 to 1331. Ivan, therefore, had to contend with three strong rivals for the grand-princely title, two princes of Tver' and one prince of Suzdal': indeed, in view of the fact that the Danilovichi were technically speaking *izgoi* themselves and should have been debarred from succession because of Daniil's early death,[1] all three of his rivals had legally more right to the throne of Vladimir than his own sons had.

Ivan drew up his will in early 1339 or late 1338, just before setting off to the Horde with his two eldest sons for the last time.[2] Two copies of the will have survived, both written at the same time and, with the exception of the list of estates purchased by Ivan[3] which is only found in the second copy, more or less identical. Thus, the first extant testament of any grand prince of Vladimir (or of Kiev for that matter) contains instructions for the division of the possessions of the grand prince among his children and wife. It is the will of Ivan as prince of Moscow and not grand prince of Vladimir: in other words, he is distributing only purely Muscovite possessions—districts which belonged to him as prince of Moscow. It makes no mention of the *yarlyk*, the title of grand prince, the territories dependent on the grand prin-cipality (Vladimir, Pereyaslavl' and Kostroma), nor is anything said of Novgorod.[4]

The three sons of Ivan are given approximately equal shares: Semen is given the districts of Mozhaysk and Kolomna, Ivan that of Zvenigorod, and Andrey those of Serpukhov and Lopasnya. Ivan's wife and daughters are granted a number of estates in the

[1] He predeceased his brother, Grand Prince Andrey, by one year.

[2] On the question of the dating of the will, *see* Cherepnin, *RFA*, vol. i, pp. 12 sq. In the light of Cherepnin's convincing arguments no other dating seems to me admissible.

[3] *See* above, p. 185. The two copies are printed in *DDG*, pp. 7–8, 9–11.

[4] With the exception of course of the scattered estates which Ivan had bought in these districts.

central Moscow district, as well as certain taxation privileges. No mention is made of the town and province of Moscow except for the somewhat vague statement: "I leave my patrimony of Moscow to my sons." As well as territorial dispositions Ivan also left instructions for the distribution of fiscal benefits and private possessions (clothing, jewellery, horses) amongst his dependants.

By comparison with subsequent inter-princely treaties and, to a certain extent, grand-princely wills, Ivan's testament is particularly striking in several respects. Firstly, the division of property among the three sons is remarkably even. No one son receives a preponderant amount of land, and Semen, the eldest, is not given the advantage over his brothers in the shape of the largest share; secondly, there is very little attempt in the will to stress the political seniority of Semen over his brothers: there is merely a clause enjoining Semen to look after the rest of the family: "I entrust to you, my son Semen, your younger brothers and my princess. You will care for them in God's name."[1] Finally, there is a sense of impermanence and even a certain vagueness about the provisions of the will; it is, as it were, a purely temporary arrangement, an *ad hoc* share-up of the available territory. No mention is made of permanent ownership, of patrimonial, hereditary grants. Indeed change is envisaged. Should the frontiers of Muscovy expand or decrease according to the fluctuations of Tatar policy, then the heirs of Kalita must be prepared to adapt their holdings to the situation: "If, for my sins," runs a clause, "the Tatars should seek any of your districts (*volosti*) and if they should be taken from you, then you, my sons and my princess, are to share out the [remaining] districts between you in order to replace that which is lost."[2] It is as though Ivan I was anxious to emphasize the complete equality of the three brothers, the common nature of their inheritance, and, above all, their joint collective administration: "As for the 'numbered people',[3] these my sons are to administer jointly (*sobcha*) . . ."[4]

What was the purpose of this seemingly deliberate vagueness

---

[1] *DDG*, pp. 8, 10.   [2] Ibid.

[3] The *chislennye lyudi*, or *chislyaki*, were, according to Cherepnin, that part of the population "liable to tribute destined mainly for Tatar needs". (*See* Cherepnin, *RFA*, vol. i, p. 19.)

[4] *DDG*, pp. 8, 10.

on the part of the grand prince? Why did Ivan make no effort legally to assure for his sons any right of ownership over the districts left them or, and this is the important point, to guarantee and bolster up the seniority of his eldest son? Two explanations are possible. Firstly, in Muscovite Rus' a testament was very different from a treaty. There was no question of oath-taking; there were no clauses which had the same legally binding effect as the solemn mention of Cross-kissing in the inter-princely treaties. The prince in his will was merely giving his sons an indication of his wishes: any vagueness, it was understood, could be corrected by a treaty. The father's *ryad* was merely the basis for the sons' *dokonchanie*.

The second reason for the vagueness of Ivan's will and the apparent unwillingness to assure Semen of a firm position is to be found in what Cherepnin calls Ivan's "desire to ensure the grand-princely dignity for his descendants".[1] By demonstrating the unity of the Moscow princely family, of whom Semen was merely *primus inter pares*, and by stressing the equality of the three heirs, all of whom would be equally responsible for administering the state and collecting and delivering Tatar tribute, Ivan hoped to convince the khan of the suitability of his sons for the *yarlyk*. In other words, the will was conceived as a witness to the readiness of the house of Moscow to continue Kalita's policy of obedience and subservience to Tatar wishes. And indeed, as Cherepnin has convincingly shown,[2] it was largely with this in mind that Ivan wrote his will in 1338 or 1339 and took it with him and his two sons to the Horde for ratification. The despatch of all three sons to Saray later in 1339 was surely connected also with the will: no doubt some form of agreement between Uzbek and the future grand princes of Vladimir was reached. By asking the khan to approve of his testamental dispositions, which after all were no concern of Uzbek's, Ivan was virtually asking for a guarantee that the *yarlyk* would stay in his family. It was perhaps no coincidence that the khan appended his seal to the will and a few months later, when Ivan died, unhesitatingly appointed Semen grand prince of Vladimir.

After examining in some detail the events of the 1330's in north-

[1] Cherepnin, *RFA*, vol. i, p. 19.   [2] *See* ibid., p. 16.

east Russia and after considering the problems which faced
the khan and his method of solving them, we are in a better
position to evaluate Ivan Kalita's role in the shaping of events, his
contribution to the creation of the Muscovite state, and the significance of his reign in the history of north-east Russia.

The personal role of Ivan as a formulator of policy and the
scope of his influence on the growth of the principality of
Moscow have been unduly exaggerated by many modern historians. He is portrayed as the first great statesman among the
descendants of Daniil, as the victor in the struggle with Tver',
as the centre of a federation of princes, as the first "gatherer of the
Russian lands" and as the true strengthener of the power of the
principality of Moscow.[1] Much of his reputation is due to the
extravagant praise of contemporaries. The compiler of the pro-
Moscow Trinity Chronicle, it will be remembered, inserted under
the year 1328 the celebrated eulogy of his reign in which the great
"peace" lasting forty years and the cessation of Tatar raids are
attributed to him.[2] The same praise is meted out to him by two
Moscow scribes in an entry made in a Gospel in 1339: not only
did a "great calm" result from his reign, but also he is lauded for
his good rule, for the establishment of law and order in the
country and for the provision of a certain measure of social
security.[3]

It will perhaps help to restore the balance if we consider briefly
what might be termed the achievements of Kalita's reign as well
as the failures. On the credit side first and foremost must be
placed the continuing support of the Church for the prince of
Moscow. It is true that the ground had been prepared by Yury,
who was quick to take advantage of Metropolitan Petr's quarrel
with Mikhail of Tver'; but it was Ivan who did most to bind the
metropolitan to Moscow. It was he, it appears, who persuaded
Petr to choose Moscow as his place of burial: four and a half
months before his death Metropolitan Petr together with Ivan

---

[1] *See*, for instance, the views of Solov'ev (*Istoriya Rossii*, book i, col. 930);
Klyuchevsky (*Sochineniya*, vol. ii, pp. 22, 37); Cherepnin (*Obrazovanie*, p. 512).
[2] *See* above, p. 111.
[3] *See* I. Sreznevsky, "*Svedeniya i zametki*", pp. 145–8; Cherepnin, *Obrazovanie*, pp. 513–15. Cherepnin points out that the Gospel entry of 1339 was
almost certainly dictated by Ivan himself.

Danilovich laid the foundation stone of the Uspensky Cathedral, in which the metropolitan "with his own hands built a stone grave for himself in the wall".[1] And it was probably largely due to his influence that Metropolitan Petr was persuaded to reside in Moscow during much of his life in the north-east.[2]

As for Petr's successor, Feognost, it would be hard to imagine a churchman more dedicated to the cause of Moscow at the time and more suited to serve the interests of her prince. As has been amply demonstrated above, most of the metropolitan's recorded actions directly or indirectly benefited Ivan Kalita: indeed Feognost's church policy in the West can be said largely to have thwarted the expansionist schemes of Gedimin of Lithuania. Whether Feognost was in fact acting primarily in the interests and on the instructions of the oecumenical patriarch, or whether his actions were dictated primarily by a desire to assist Moscow in the inter-princely and international conflicts of the day, we do not know. But whatever his motives, the results of his actions speak for themselves; and much of the credit for acquiring the Church's invaluable political support must go to the prince of Moscow himself. Indeed we know that Ivan Kalita was the first north-east Russian prince with sufficient foresight to endow the metropolitan see with extensive estates, thus rendering the incumbent morally, if not physically, indebted to the ruler. So large did the estates become that Feognost's successor Aleksey was obliged to draw up a contract with the prince of Moscow which defined his exact rights and his political obligations *vis-à-vis* the grand prince and which virtually converted the metropolitan's possessions into what a modern historian has called "a semi-independent vassal principality".[3]

The second great and lasting achievement of Ivan I was the

---

[1] *TL*, p. 358.

[2] *See*, for instance, the words of the sixteenth-century Nikon Chronicle: "the blessed Petr saw him (Ivan) shining in Orthodoxy, adorned with every kind of good deed, generous to the poor and respectful of the holy churches of God and their servitors. . . . And the divine bishop loved him dearly and began to live in that city more than all other places" (*PSRL*, xi, p. 193). The official residence was not transferred from Vladimir to Moscow either by Petr or by Feognost, but by Aleksey. (*See* Veselovsky, *Feodal'noe zemle-vladenie*, pp. 334–5.)

[3] *See* ibid., pp. 333–6.

securing of the patent to the grand-princely throne for his sons, indeed for the house of Moscow—an achievement which was to lead to the virtual exclusion of all other houses from the succession, and the establishment of the descendants of Daniil of Moscow as the recognized ruling dynasty in north-east Russia. That this establishment of the house of Moscow as the sole repository of grand-princely authority was achieved largely thanks to the efforts of Ivan I there can be no doubt. It was brought about not so much by strengthening the position of Moscow, by enlarging its territory or political authority over the other principalities, or by increasing its military efficiency. It was brought about to a certain extent by improving the fiscal potentialities of the prince and to a large extent by convincing the khan of the reliability of the Danilovichi. As has been shown above, Ivan achieved his ends by patiently ingratiating himself with the khan, by regularly collecting and delivering the tribute and above all by getting the khan to approve of the terms of his will.

Besides these two major achievements, what little is known of Ivan's exploits at home and abroad seems insignificant. There are indications that during his reign, and perhaps at his initiative, steps were taken to codify existing Byzantine and old Russian legal monuments:[1] a chronicle note mentions that Ivan "rid the Russian land of thieves and brigands".[2] The only successful independent military venture against external enemies appears to have been a small retaliatory raid on the Lithuanian strongholds of Osechen and Ryasna in 1335.[3] The only other foreign venture on record, the campaign against Smolensk in 1339, was basically a Tatar enterprise. To the list of his achievements might be added the purchase of certain scattered districts which are mentioned in his will, and, perhaps, the conclusion of some sort of financial agreement with the princes of Galich, Beloozero and Uglich.[4] But it must also be pointed out that, apart from these imprecise territorial acquisitions, the territory of the principality of Moscow was in no way increased: the boundaries were the same in 1339 as they had been thirty-six years earlier.

Against the achievements of Ivan's reign we must set the failures. It was largely in the sphere of his relations with the other

[1] See Cherepnin, *Obrazovanie*, pp. 516–17.   [2] *NL*, p. 465.
[3] See above, p. 150.   [4] See above, pp. 182–4.

territories of north-east Russia and their rulers that Ivan's policy was unsuccessful. In the early years of his reign he failed in his attempt to arrest Aleksandr of Tver' and to deliver him to the Horde—and the Pskov fiasco of 1329 cost him the supreme title for nearly three years. In Novgorod he was quite unable to maintain his authority or to keep in check the dangerous rebellious elements, and even though for part of his reign his governors were present in the city, their control was precarious. The Novgorodians no longer stood in awe of the grand prince of Vladimir, who by tradition was titular ruler of the city, and were able to shrug off his authority with an impunity and insouciance which would have been unthinkable in the days of the grand princes from Tver': they were able to baulk his plans for an invasion of Pskov by simply refusing to take part; their troops in the north were able to crush his retaliatory invasion of the Dvina district with ease; and their envoys had no hesitation in refusing his demands for additional Tatar tribute in 1339. Furthermore, a dangerous pro-Lithuanian party had sprung up in the republic during Ivan's reign, or at any rate had first begun to make its presence felt during the 1330's. By the end of his reign he was just as far from solving the problem of Novgorod as he had been at the beginning. As for Pskov, although Aleksandr of Tver' was successfully persuaded to quit the city and return to Tver' and although as a result of this a welcome breach between Pskov and Novgorod occurred in 1337, there is no evidence whatsoever to show that Pskov was in any way more amenable to Muscovite authority at the end of Ivan's reign than she had been at the beginning. Lithuanian influence in the two republics was presumably as strong in 1339 as it had been earlier in Ivan's reign; and the fact that they were both saved from becoming Lithuanian provinces was due to the apparent lethargy of Gedimin and to his unwillingness to exploit success, rather than to any efforts of Ivan. As far as the still technically independent Suzdalian principalities are concerned, there is no evidence to show that Ivan, as grand prince of Vladimir, was able to command their unanimous obedience and respect. Indeed, we have seen that there are strong indications of an anti-Moscow bloc among the northern princes, sympathizers no doubt of the prince of Tver', and that Ivan was obliged to conclude matrimonial alliances with the rebelling princes.

Finally, it must be repeated that in order to get the known circumstances of Ivan's reign into correct perspective it is essential constantly to bear two things in mind. Firstly, events were influenced not so much by the determination of the grand prince as by the decisions of the khan. In attempting to assign causes to the major events of the period 1328–40, we cannot give first priority to the will and what we must assume to have been the policy of Ivan. In other words, things did not happen principally because Ivan and his advisers wanted them to happen or decreed that they should happen: they happened largely because the khan's policy was what it was. Thus, for instance, Aleksandr of Tver' was eliminated not because he was the enemy of Ivan or even because Ivan advised the khan to remove him, but first and foremost because he was the ally of Gedimin and as such—in Uzbek's eyes at any rate—a potentially dangerous element amongst the north-east Russian principalities. Ivan was the servant of the khan, the executor of his orders. He did what he was told to do—except in purely domestic affairs—and extricated what he could for himself and his principality from circumstances dictated by the will of the khan.

The second point to bear in mind is the fact that Uzbek's policy towards north-east Russia changed radically at the beginning of Ivan's reign as grand prince. Whereas during the first three decades of the fourteenth century the policy of the khan was directed towards keeping Suzdalia relatively weak by supporting now the prince of Moscow, now the prince of Tver', now the prince of Suzdal', during the thirties no inter-princely rivalries were encouraged by the Tatars. Moscow alone was allowed to grow strong in order to provide an effective barrier to Lithuanian expansion. For the first time the Tatars had become aware of the growing power of the grand prince of Lithuania, and for the first time Lithuania had begun to play a major role in the history of north-east Russia.

4
The Period of Transition, 1340–1359

IVAN KALITA died on 31 March 1340. He was succeeded as grand prince of Vladimir by his two eldest sons, Semen the Proud, as he was known (1340–53) and Ivan II (1353–9). The twenty years which followed his death were remarkable for the continuity of trends which had become noticeable already in the 1330's. The policy of the two major protagonists in the struggle for supremacy in north-eastern Europe—the rulers of Lithuania and Moscow—showed little change. Ol'gerd of Lithuania carried on his father's policy of attempted expansion eastwards by means of ecclesiastical and lay penetration into the uncommitted and committed lands on his north-eastern frontiers; Semen, and Ivan II (at any rate in the latter part of his reign), remained the faithful and obedient servants of the khan, attempting no resistance to Tatar rule and prepared to carry out their master's commands uncomplainingly. The attitude of the Tatars to their subjects, though adapting itself to circumstances, was by and large similar to that of the preceding period. The prince of Moscow, while able, virtually unopposed, to maintain his nominal control over all the "Lower lands", was unable to increase significantly the territory of his principality or in any noticeable way to consolidate his position as grand prince. The Church continued to afford strong support to the ruler of Moscow and to exercise a powerful influence in inter-princely and international politics.

If a simple explanation were needed for this striking continuity of policy, it could of course be found in the fact that Jani-Beg, Semen and Ol'gerd, the three successors of the three rulers who died in 1340 and 1341, appear to have learned much from their fathers and to have consciously preserved their policies. It should also be remembered that the metropolitan of Kiev and All Rus', Feognost, survived the years 1340 and 1341, which saw so many deaths among the rulers of eastern Europe,[1] and acted as it were as a bond with the past both in Suzdalia and in the Orthodox districts of Lithuania.

In spite, however, of the overall similarity in trends between the age of Ivan I and the two decades after his death there were some striking new tendencies noticeable in the general political set-up in north-east Rus'. Firstly, Suzdal' and Nizhny Novgorod began to emerge in the 1340's and the 1350's as a power capable of supplanting Tver' and rivalling Moscow in the race for hegemony over the other districts. Secondly, the period following Ivan's death is marked by the fragmentation of Tver', the division of the district into appanages proper and the resulting internecine war, ably fanned by Moscow and the Horde, between branches of the Tverite princely family. Thirdly, there are signs of the emergence of an opposition party within the principality of Moscow itself and of a serious divergence of opinion among the Muscovite boyars on questions of foreign policy—the beginning of the dichotomy between what might be called the "conservative" and "progressive" groups among the advisers of the prince and perhaps too among other layers of society. And fourthly, there is evidence of an entirely new system of territorial distribution within the Muscovite princely family—the *"udel'ny"* or "appanage" system. Indeed the so-called "appanage period", a term loosely and inaccurately employed by historians to cover the thirteenth and fourteenth centuries, can be said to start from the post-Kalita age.

The years 1340–59 were a period of transition, maturation and preparation. During the reign of Semen and, to a certain extent, during that of Ivan II the ground was prepared for the first "gathering of the Russian lands" under Ivan II's son Dmitry Donskoy and for the latter's conversion of the principality of Moscow into the grand principality of Moscow, Vladimir and All Rus'. In the following pages an attempt will be made to examine various aspects of the history of this transition period with the purpose of discovering how exactly the ground was being prepared, or was preparing itself, for the drastic and decisive changes which took place during the reign of Dmitry Donskoy.

[1] Bolesław-Yury II of Volyn' and Galich also died in 1340.

[i] THE HORDE AND NORTH-EAST RUSSIA

The most striking similarity between the attitude of Uzbek towards his subject Russian *ulusy* and that of his son and successor Jani-Beg is to be found in their appreciation of, and reaction to, Lithuania's *Drang nach Osten*. Both realized the dangers of Lithuanian growth and both took an active interest in Moscow-Lithuanian relations. Just as Uzbek's policy of maintaining a relatively strong principality of Moscow was governed by the apprehensiveness aroused by Lithuanian expansion, so too was Jani-Beg prepared to countenance the handing-over of power from one prince of Moscow to another, a process which broke all the traditional laws of succession, but which had been sanctioned by Ivan I's shrewd presentation of his will. And he was prepared to continue supporting Moscow not only because Semen was just as malleable and subservient as his father had been, but also because Ol'gerd was proving just as energetic and just as dangerous as *his* father. The more Ol'gerd tampered with the affairs of his eastern neighbours, the more inclined was the khan to support Semen when it came to intervening directly in the relations between Lithuania and Moscow.

Jani-Beg's attitude to Lithuania and Moscow-Lithuanian relations is most vividly illustrated by the events of 1348. In that year Ol'gerd sent his brother Koriad-Mikhail, prince of Nowogródek and Black Rus' since 1329,[1] to Khan Jani-Beg at the Horde. The purpose of his mission was to ask the khan for military assistance. One version of the incident, found in the Tver' Rogozhsky Chronicle and the Trinity Chronicle, probably the earliest and most reliable account, says nothing about whom Ol'gerd required assistance against; it merely states that "Ol'gerd . . . asked the khan for an army to help him."[2] A second, probably later, account, found in the Moscow *svod* of 1479 and the

---

[1] Koriad was the fifth eldest son of Gedimin. In 1329 he was prince of Nowogródek (Novgorodok). (*See* Pashuto, *OLG*, p. 322.) At the death of Gedimin he was left Black Rus' less Slonim (*see PSRL*, xvii, col. 71); he presumably continued to reside in his capital of Nowogródek. Mikhail was evidently his baptismal name. The Russian sources talk of Koriad (or Korol'yad) and Mikhail as if they were two people.

[2] *PSRL*, xv (i), col. 58; *TL*, p. 369.

Ermolinsky Chronicle, says that help was required "against Grand Prince Semen".[1] Which of these two is correct is hard to say: "against Grand Prince Semen" may well have been added by a later copyist in order to intensify the dramatic situation, and Ol'gerd's original request was probably for military assistance against the Livonians, or for a general military alliance with the Tatars.[2] Whatever the substance of the original request, the reaction of Semen, when he heard about the presence of a Lithuanian mission in Saray, was immediate. After taking counsel with his brothers and boyars, he sent an embassy to Saray headed by one Fedor Glebovich.[3] The envoys complained to the khan that "Ol'gerd and his brothers had laid waste the khan's *ulus* and the grand prince's patrimony."[4] One account, that found in the Ermolinsky Chronicle, even makes the Muscovite ambassadors complain that Ol'gerd was at that very moment engaged in making war on Jani-Beg's lands "and insulting the grand prince".[5] The khan needed little persuading. The entire Lithuanian delegation, including a detachment of troops which had accompanied it, was despatched under Tatar escort to Moscow and handed over in custody to Semen.[6] In the following year Ol'gerd was obliged to pay Semen a large sum of money to

[1] *PSRL*, xxiii, p. 109; xxv, p. 177.

[2] This is borne out by Semen's subsequent complaints to the khan to the effect that Ol'gerd had been, or was, attacking Semen's districts—in other words, Semen warned Jani-Beg that the *real* purpose of Ol'gerd's mission was to make war on Semen. Hrushevsky considers that Ol'gerd's aim was to achieve an alliance against Poland (*see* M. Hrushevsky, *IUR*, vol. iv, p. 33, note 3). *Cf.* H. Paszkiewicz (*Polityka*, p. 119, note 2), who considers that the alliance was against Semen. Vernadsky, without offering any evidence, states: "Olgerd ... sent his brother Koriat to warn the khan of the imminent danger to the interests of both the Golden Horde and Lithuania in the growth of the Moscow state. Ol'gerd proposed to the khan a Mongol–Lithuanian alliance against Moscow." (*Mongols*, p. 206.)

[3] *See TL*, p. 369; *PSRL*, xv (i), col. 58; xxiii, p. 109; xxv, p. 177. *Cf.* the very abbreviated account in the Novgorod Fourth Chronicle where Fedor Glebovich is called "prince" (*PSRL*, iv (i), p. 279; *cf.* x, p. 219). In a margin is added, in a later hand, "of Rostov". There were, however, no Fedor Gleboviches in the Rostov dynasty. He may have been the same Prince Fedor Glebovich who in 1354 seized Murom and whose origins are quite unknown. (*See TL*, p. 374; *PSRL*, xxv, pp. 179–80.)

[4] *TL*, p. 369; *PSRL*, xxv, p. 177.   [5] *PSRL*, xxiii, p. 109.

[6] The two basic accounts of the incident, one found in the Rogozhsky and

release his brother and the remainder of the Lithuanian delega-
tion.¹ A treaty was concluded, no doubt on terms highly
satisfactory to Moscow.

Whatever the reasons for Ol'gerd's attempted alliance with the
Tatars, the achievements of Muscovite diplomacy in 1348 and
1349 were little short of a triumph for the grand prince of
Vladimir. More important still, the ease with which the Muscovite
diplomats managed to persuade the khan to hand over an entire
embassy—an embassy which was seeking the friendship of the
Tatars—shows only too well just how predisposed the khan was
to favour Moscow. Despite the relative failure of Ol'gerd's
initial military ventures on his eastern borders, Jani-Beg was no
more inclined than had been Uzbek to contribute to any
strengthening of Lithuanian power at the expense of Moscow;
indeed, his action shows that he was still prepared to lend the
whole weight of his support to Moscow in the growing conflict
between the successors of Gedimin and Ivan I.

It must not, however, be imagined that Jani-Beg and his
advisers were prepared to oppose Lithuania in the context of
any international conflict or that they were blind to the intense
struggle which was going on between Lithuania and Poland
for the old lands of south-west Russia and to the incessant wars
between Lithuania and the Teutonic Knights. Indeed, between
1350 and 1352 some sort of an alliance was struck up between
Ol'gerd and Jani-Beg, and in the spring of 1352 Tatars actively
aided Ol'gerd by raiding Podolia and Galich, both of which were
at that time in Polish hands.² But this military alliance, it must

---

Trinity Chronicles (under 1348) and the other in the Ermolinsky Chronicle
and the Moscow *svod* of 1479 (under 1349), are similar in most details and
both clearly have a common source or sources. The Novgorod First
Chronicle is silent; the Novgorod Fourth Chronicle contains only a truncated
account of the affair which is unintelligible without the lengthier descriptions.
It is interesting to note that while the Ermolinsky Chronicle account, as in
many other cases, appears to be little more than a shortened form of the
1479 *svod*, nevertheless the different wording of the Muscovites' complaint
to Jani-Beg indicates that the compiler was abbreviating not the *svod* itself,
but the *source* of the *svod*.

¹ See *TL*, p. 370; *PSRL*, xv (i), col. 59; xxiii, p. 109; xxv, p. 177.

² "Tartari . . . ab Olgerdo . . . donis et promissionibus variis illecti, terram
Podoliae Regno Poloniae subiectam . . . vastarunt" (Długosz, *HP*, col. 1096).

be stressed, had nothing to do with the Moscow-Lithuanian conflict: it occurred during one of the rare periods when Moscow and Vil'na were at peace and may well have been engineered by Semen himself.[1] Furthermore the alliance was not directed against Moscow but against Poland, and the purpose of it was to prevent further eastward encroachment of the Polish armies. In 1349 King Casimir of Poland had invaded and succeeded in occupying a large part of what had been the territory of the old principality of Volyn'. The two sons of Gedimin, Keystut and Lyubart, had lost considerable portions of their districts, while still further south, in Podolia, the sons of the hapless Koriad were probably subjected to Poland.[2] The Tatars were fully aware of Casimir's actions and intentions—their ambassadors had visited the king in that same year[3]—and it was precisely to check the growing power of Poland that in 1350, much to the consternation of the king, they formed an alliance with Lithuania.[4] The alliance was short-lived. It lasted only as long as Semen and Ol'gerd were not at war with each other. And when in the autumn of 1352 Poland and Lithuania made peace, it ceased to have any meaning. Indeed three years later, when Casimir once more invaded Lithuanian territory, it was the Poles who, thanks to Casimir's diplomacy, now enjoyed Tatar military support.[5]

If further evidence is needed to show that the Tatars intended to support Moscow in the conflict with Lithuania during the forties and fifties of the fourteenth century, we have only to consider the ease with which Semen managed to gain political

[1] Peace between Semen and Ol'gerd was concluded in early 1349 and sealed by two dynastic marriages: Lyubart Gediminovich of Volyn' married Semen's niece Agafa Konstantinovna of Rostov, while Ol'gerd married Semen's sister-in-law Yuliania Aleksandrovna of Tver' (both in 1349; *see* TL, p. 370; *PSRL*, xv (i), col. 59). In 1350 Semen and his two brothers went to the Horde probably in order to negotiate the Lithuanian-Tatar settlement, although the sources merely state that he went there and returned in the same year. (*See* TL, p. 371; *PSRL*, x, pp. 221–2; xxv, p. 177 (under 1351).

[2] For details, *see* Paszkiewicz, *Polityka*, pp. 117–20; *Jagiellonowie*, p. 383.

[3] "Anno Domini 1349 nuncii Thartarorum venerunt ad regem Poloniae" (*MPH*, ii, p. 885).

[4] Casimir complained to the pope in the winter of 1350–1 of the Tatar "confederacio cum Litwanis". (*See* Paszkiewicz, *Jagiellonowie*, p. 384, note 1.)

[5] *See* Paszkiewicz, *Jagiellonowie*, p. 397.

control over the vast lands of Smolensk and Bryansk, the political affiliation of which was of extreme economic and prestige value to the rulers of both Lithuania and Moscow. It was not that Semen was able to annexe either district or to impose his lieutenants on them; but by careful diplomatic manoeuvring and by impressive sabre-rattling he was able to ensure that both were politically aligned with Moscow rather than with Lithuania by the end of his reign.

As has been mentioned above, Bryansk, ruled by the brothers Vasily, Ivan and Dmitry Romanovichi, had been in the political sphere of influence of Moscow from 1310 to some time shortly after 1333. The abortive Tatar-Bryansk campaign against Smolensk in 1333 had led to the temporary removal of Dmitry, the youngest of the three pro-Muscovite brothers, and the probable realignment of Bryansk with Smolensk and Lithuania.[1] The new ruler of Bryansk, about whom lamentably little is known, was Gleb Svyatoslavich.[2] He was presumably the son of Svyatoslav Glebovich, who in 1309-10 had refused to listen to the advice and cajolery of Metropolitan Petr and had been killed while trying to defend his city against his nephew Vasily and the Tatars.[3] What his policy was we do not know, but it seems not improbable that he was orientated towards Lithuania, as had been his father. At any rate we know that no troops from Bryansk took part in the Russo-Tatar campaign against Smolensk in 1339, and the circumstances of his murder were strangely reminiscent of those of his father's death twenty years previously. In 1340 the population of Bryansk rose in rebellion against their new prince. Again, the account of the incident found in the chronicles mentions no reason for the uprising; it merely states that the people of Bryansk "assembled in a *veche* and slew Prince Gleb Svyatoslavich on 6 December [1340]".[4] However, the fact that the Tver' Rogozhsky Chronicle calls the men of Bryansk "evil rebels (*zlye koromolnitsi*)" while the Tver' Chronicle *svod* calls them "accursed Bryanskites (*klyatii Bryantsy*)"[5] might indicate that the dissatisfied

---

[1] *See* above, p. 170, note 1.

[2] The only known facts concern his murder in 1340.

[3] *See* above, pp. 70-1.

[4] *TL*, p. 364; *PSRL*, xv (i), col. 53. In other chronicle versions (viz. the Novgorod First and Fourth Chronicles, the Sofiysky First Chronicle and the Moscow *svod* of 1479) no mention is made of a *veche*.

[5] The only other chronicle to contain an opprobrious description of the

populace were pro-Muscovite or pro-Tatar in their sympathies and were rebelling against Gleb because of his pro-Lithuanian tendencies, just as thirty years earlier the townsfolk had rebelled against his father. Still more significant is the fact that Metropolitan Feognost himself was present at the uprising of Bryansk in 1340. His role is hard to assess: he is merely described as being unable to quieten the rebellious population or to prevent them murdering the prince, who had evidently sought sanctuary with the metropolitan in the church of St. Nicholas.[1] The most plausible explanation of his presence in Bryansk is that he was attempting to do what his predecessor Petr had done thirty years before—persuade the prince not to resist the Tatars and to turn his back on Lithuania.

Whether Gleb's murder was merely the result of the spontaneous indignation of the mob or whether it was engineered by Muscovite agents we cannot say for sure. But one thing is certain: the disturbances of December 1340 ended in a way which could only have been satisfactory to Semen and the khan. The pro-Muscovite Dmitry Romanovich was once more installed on the throne of Bryansk. As a demonstration of his political sympathies he married off his daughter to Semen's fifteen-year-old brother Ivan (the future Ivan II) in the winter of 1341-2.[2] For

---

Bryanskites is the Trinity Chronicle: this is probably explainable by the proximity of the texts of the Rogozhsky and Trinity Chronicles and is not likely to reflect the political views of the compiler of the Trinity Chronicle. It may of course simply express the disapproval of the compiler for any "*koromol'niki*" whatever their political leanings: indeed, both the Moscow *svod* of 1479 and the Trinity Chronicle condemn the Bryanskites for their behaviour in 1309-10 and call them *koromol'niki*.

[1] Or so it would appear from the account found in the Novgorod First Chronicle: "At that time the metropolitan was there (in Bryansk) and he was not able to quieten [the rebellious Bryanskites], but he came out of the church of St. Nicholas" (*NL*, p. 353; repeated in *PSRL*, iv (i), p. 268). The Moscow *svod* account, which clearly derives from the Novgorod version and not from the Tver' or Trinity versions (these make no mention of the church of St. Nicholas), attempts to clarify matters by changing the word-order: ". . . the Bryanskites killed Prince Gleb Svyatoslavich, coming out of the church of St. Nicholas. For at that time Metropolitan Feognost was in Bryansk and was unable to quieten them." From this version it is not clear who was leaving the church.

[2] See *TL*, p. 365; *PSRL*, xv (i), col. 54; xxiii, p. 106; xxv, p. 173.

sixteen years after the coup of 1340 all was quiet in Bryansk. The town and district were evidently in the sphere of influence of Moscow and the Tatars during this period. It was only in 1356 or early 1357 that Lithuania at last regained control of Bryansk after yet another rebellion, this time undoubtedly inspired by Lithuanian agents, which reversed the results of the uprising of 1340.[1] For nearly a century and a half Bryansk was to remain in Lithuanian hands.

The principality of Smolensk presented Semen with a tougher proposition altogether. It was farther from Moscow. It was closer to the strongly-held Lithuanian district of Vitebsk. It enjoyed natural defences in the shape of forests and marshes. It was a territory which Ol'gerd and his brothers had every intention of maintaining in a state of benevolent neutrality, if not of incorporating into the grand principality of Lithuania. As has been mentioned above,[2] during the twenties and thirties of the fourteenth century Ivan Aleksandrovich, the senior member of the house of Smolensk, had ruled the district and had ruled it in some form of political dependence on the grand prince of Lithuania. After the failure of the Tatar attack on Smolensk in 1333 and the fiasco of the combined Russo-Tatar invasion of 1339, Ivan Aleksandrovich remained even more decisively within the Lithuanian sphere of influence: in 1340, it will be remembered, he called Gedimin his "elder brother" in a treaty with the Livonian Order.[3]

During the first twelve years of Semen's reign there is little information on Smolensk in any of the sources. But there can be no doubt that the political affiliations of Ivan Aleksandrovich did not change during this period and that the land of Smolensk, though perhaps not all its rulers, owed some form of allegiance to the sons of Gedimin. Indeed in the great battle on the river Strava in 1348 we find troops from Smolensk fighting side by

[1] In 1356 Ol'gerd attacked Smolensk where one "Prince Vasily of Smolensk" was ruling. This was probably the son of one of the former Bryansk princes, Ivan or Dmitry Romanovichi, who had succeeded the latter some time after 1341. Vasily went to the Horde, obtained from the khan the right to rule Bryansk, and returned as ruler. However, he died shortly afterwards, and after a rebellion Ol'gerd had little difficulty in reasserting his control over the principality. (*See* PSRL, x, p. 228; xv (i), col. 65.)

[2] *See* above, p. 170 sq.   [3] *See* above, p. 171.

side with Ol'gerd's Ruthenian subjects from Vladimir in Volyn', Berest'e on the Bug, Vitebsk and Polotsk,[1] a sure indication that Ivan Aleksandrovich's relationship with Grand Prince Ol'gerd was little different from that of the latter's brothers and nephews who ruled the lands of the old Kievan State, now part of the grand principality of Lithuania. While there is no evidence to support Presnyakov's claim that "during the 1340's Smolensk troops [took part] in the wars of Ol'gerd against the Livonian Order",[2] nevertheless it is unlikely that their participation in the campaign of 1348 was an isolated occasion and that no service ties bound Ivan of Smolensk to Ol'gerd.

In spite of Ivan Aleksandrovich's evident loyalty towards Ol'gerd, there were sure signs of disaffection amongst the junior members of his family. By 1339 the minor princes of Drutsk and Fominskoe had defected to Moscow.[3] The pro-Lithuanian Gleb Svyatoslavich of Bryansk had been murdered in 1340 and replaced by the pro-Muscovite Dmitry Romanovich.[4] In the early years of Semen's reign yet another princeling of the house of Smolensk transferred his allegiance to the grand prince of Vladimir—Fedor Svyatoslavich of Dorogobuzh and Vyaz'ma. Unfortunately very little is known about Fedor Svyatoslavich: we do not know for certain when or why he deserted, whose son he was and how large his principality was. It seems, however, likely that he defected at about the same time as the Bryansk upheavals of 1340-1,[5] that he was the brother of Gleb Svyato-

---

[1] The Ruthenian–Lithuanian army under Ol'gerd was returning from a raid on the lands of the Order when it was caught deep in Lithuanian territory on the river Strava (near Kovno) by the Germans, who inflicted a crushing defeat on Ol'gerd.

For the various German sources which mention the composition of the Lithuanian forces (Hoeneke's Rhymed Chronicle, Hermann of Wartburg's Livonian Chronicle and Wigand of Marburg's Chronicle), *see* Paszkiewicz, *Jagiellonowie*, p. 376, note 2. Nearly all the Russian chronicles mention the battle, but they give no details of the participants.

[2] Presnyakov, *Obrazovanie*, p. 160, note 1. Presnyakov's information is based solely on the known fact of Smolensk participation in the Strava battle.

[3] *See* above, p. 173.   [4] *See* above, pp. 202–3.

[5] All that is known is that in 1345 his daughter married Semen and that he was placed in Volok Lamsky, which Semen granted him "as a patrimony" (*v votchinu*) after his defection. (*See* Kopanev, "O 'kuplyakh' Ivana Kality", p.

slavich of Bryansk[1] and that his principality, on the upper reaches of the Dnepr and its tributary the Vyaz'ma, bordered Moscow's westermost district of Mozhaysk. Although Fedor's defection did not lead to the annexation of his former principality by Moscow and although the marriage of his daughter to Semen of Moscow in 1345 turned out to be a conspicuous failure,[2] nevertheless Fedor's change of allegiance meant a further weakening of the house of Smolensk and may be construed as a sign of a split within the principality, the formation of two mutually opposed factions—pro-Moscow and pro-Lithuania. It was yet another diplomatic victory for Semen of Moscow.

During the first twelve years of his reign Semen was content to leave Smolensk alone and not to interfere actively with his immediate neighbour. For much of the time he was too engrossed with affairs at home to be able to raise an expedition. Besides, experience was showing that bribery, intimidation or persuasion was just as effective a means of gaining political control over a semi-independent state as was military interference. The terms of the hollow peace dictated by Semen to Ol'gerd in 1349[3] no doubt obliged Ol'gerd to respect the neutrality and independence of Smolensk. Semen, however, can scarcely have placed himself under a similar obligation, or, if he did, he can have had little intention of abiding by such terms. Three years later he dramatically broke the peace by mounting an invasion of Smolensk.

One may well ask why Semen should have chosen this particular moment to attempt the seizure of Smolensk by force. Lithuania

---

27.) Paszkiewicz thinks that he was driven out of his principality by Smolensk and Lithuania. (*See* Paszkiewicz, *Jagiellonowie*, p. 369.) In addition to Volok, Fedor Svyatoslavich may also have been granted part of the district of Torusa, which the minor service princes of Torusa had evidently given to Ivan I or Semen. (*See* below, p. 223.)

[1] *See* above, p. 104. He was probably the same Fedor Svyatoslavich who was on Voin Gediminovich's delegation to Novgorod in 1326 (*see* ibid.).

[2] In 1346 Semen sent Princess Evpraksia back to her father who married her off to the earlier defector, Prince Fedor of Fominskoe. According to a later Genealogical Book, the cause of Semen's dissatisfaction with his bride was her frigidity: "As soon as she lay with the grand prince she seemed like a corpse to him." (*See* Astrov, "Udel'ny knyaz' Fedor Yur'evich Fominsky", pp. 65–6.)

[3] *See* above, p. 201, note 1.

and Moscow were at peace. Ol'gerd and his relatives had not been showing any signs of aggressiveness on their eastern border since the conclusion of the treaty of 1349. The Tatars, who had signed a pact with the Lithuanians in 1350 or 1351, were during the year of the invasion actually helping Lithuania by attacking Polish-held Podolia and Galich.[1] There is nothing in the available sources to show that Semen had received any encouraging information from his agents or allies in Smolensk territory. Why then did Semen choose to launch his expedition in 1352? The answer is to be found in the extraordinary preoccupation of the Lithuanians with other fronts at the time. In 1349, 1350 and 1351 bitter fighting had been going on between Poland and Lithuania in and for the the old principalities of south-west Rus'. After Lithuania's efforts to recapture Volyn' in 1350 the Poles had attacked again in 1351 and taken Lyubart of Volyn', Ol'gerd's brother, prisoner. In the late summer of 1351 the Poles and the Hungarians had invaded Podlyash'e, the Lithuanian frontier district north of Volyn'. In March 1352 Polish and Hungarian forces again invaded Volyn' and besieged Yury Narimuntovich in Bel'z.[2] Of still greater importance is the fact that in February 1352, on the eve of the planned invasion of Smolensk by Semen,[3] Ol'gerd and Keystut, assisted by troops from Smolensk, carried out a large-scale invasion of Semigalia.[4] Thus, at the time when Semen planned to attack the district of Smolensk, Lithuanian troops were heavily engaged in the west and in the north; furthermore, the defences of Smolensk were considerably weakened by the absence of part, if not all, of Ivan Aleksandrovich's troops.

[1] See above, p. 200.   [2] See Paszkiewicz, *Polityka*, pp. 130–1.

[3] No exact date is given in the Russian sources for Semen's expedition, but all sources give 6860 (i.e. *after* 1 March 1352) as the year.

[4] See J. Voigt, *Geschichte Preussens*, vol. v, pp. 93–6; Paszkiewicz, *Jagiellonowie*, pp. 386, note 3, 394. Wigand mentions the "king of Smolensk" (*rex de Smalentz*) taking part in the battle of Labiau and adds that he was the "son of [Keystut's] brother". See *Scriptores rerum Prussicarum,* vol. ii, p. 518. It may therefore be possible that Ol'gerd placed one of his sons in command of the army from Smolensk, but it seems unlikely that he replaced Ivan Aleksandrovich as prince of Smolensk. Golubovsky doubts whether Smolensk troops took part, from the mention of "Patriky of Smolensk" in the sources. Patriky was a son of Narimunt and had no connection with Smolensk. (*See* Golubovsky, *ISZ*, p. 317, note 3.)

Semen's expedition is reported drily and succinctly in the Russian chronicles. He set off "in great force"—the chronicler uses a well-worn cliché to denote a major operation[1]—together with his brothers Ivan and Andrey and "all the princes". When they arrived in Vyshgorod, half-way between Vereya and Borovsk on the Protva river, they were met by envoys from Ol'gerd who sued for peace. Semen parleyed with the Lithuanians and came to an agreement with them. There is no indication as to what the terms were; but evidently the ambassadors were satisfied, for Semen "paid heed to the word of Ol'gerd, made peace and dismissed the envoys with peace". Semen had no intention of honouring the agreement. He moved west, or south-west, towards the Ugra river, still "intending to march on Smolensk". His movements were being carefully watched, for when he reached the Ugra he was approached by yet another delegation, this time from Smolensk itself. They knew that Semen had no thought of abiding by the terms of the treaty of Vyshgorod. They pleaded with him for a week; their pleas met with more success than those of the representatives of Ol'gerd. Semen cancelled the operation. He dismissed his army and returned to Moscow. Again there is no indication of the nature of the conditions agreed to. All we know is that Semen "sent his envoys from there to Smolensk, and they made peace".[2]

It had turned out to be quite unnecessary for Semen to attempt the capture of Smolensk by force. It would be naïve to assume that he was bought off by the envoys from Smolensk or that he dissolved the only major expeditionary force of his reign as a result of an amicable agreement with the enemy, an agreement according to which the latter would maintain a state of strict neutrality between Moscow and Lithuania. The parleys on the Ugra certainly led to the partial subjugation of Smolensk to Moscow. No doubt the internal troubles of the thirties and the

---

[1] "*v sile tyazhtse i velitse*".

[2] The Smolensk campaign is reported in nearly all the Russian chronicles except the Novgorod First Chronicle. All accounts are much the same and clearly have a common source. The version found in the Trinity and Rogozhsky Chronicles is slightly larger than that of the Ermolinsky Chronicle and the Moscow *svod* of 1479 and contains the additional information that Ivan and Andrey participated. (*See TL*, p. 372; *PSRL*, xv (i), cols. 60–1; xxiii, p. 110; xxv, p. 178.)

forties, exemplified by the defections of the various junior
members of the princely family of Smolensk, had eased Semen's
task. Indeed, as has been suggested above, it would not be hard
to envisage the existence, prior to 1352, of two factions, pro-
Moscow and pro-Vil'na, within the principality, much the same
as in contemporary Novgorod.

Of course it is impossible to judge just what this "subjugation"
meant. It was not an annexation, as Mozhaysk or Kolomna had
been earlier in the century. There was no question of Smolensk
being ruled by a member of the grand-princely family or accepting
Muscovite lieutenants and administrators, just as during the
previous thirty years there had been no question of Gedimin and
Ol'gerd imposing a member of their family on Smolensk as
local ruler. It seems more likely that the pro-Lithuanian Ivan
Aleksandrovich was merely removed (or he may have fled to
Lithuania) and replaced by a pro-Moscow member of his family.
The obvious candidate was Vasily of Bryansk. Indeed, when
Ol'gerd attacked Smolensk and Bryansk in 1356 in an effort to
win back the principality to his own sphere of influence, he came
up against one "Prince Vasily of Smolensk", who fled to the
Horde and whose son was taken prisoner by the Lithuanians.
It seems therefore likely that the pro-Muscovite Dmitry Romanovich, who had been reinstated on the throne of Bryansk at the end
of 1340 or the beginning of 1341, died some time in the 1340's
and was replaced by either his son or nephew Vasily,[1] who in his
turn became ruler of Smolensk and Bryansk in 1352.

The extension of Semen's authority over the whole of the
former principality of Smolensk was a triumph for Moscow. It
was a serious, though temporary, check to Ol'gerd's eastward
expansion, and had it not been for the laxity of Ivan II's control
over the lands of Smolensk during the early years of his reign,[2]

[1] Although Golubovsky, the historian of Smolensk, calls him Vasily
Ivanovich, thus making him the son of Ivan Romanovich, Dmitry's brother,
the chronicles make no mention of his patronymic. (*See* Golubovsky, *ISZ*,
p. 179. *See* also above, p. 204, note 1.)

As for Ivan Aleksandrovich, he was evidently reinstated in Smolensk in
1356. The Tver' Rogozhsky Chronicle states that in 1359 "Prince Ivan of
Smolensk died; his son Svyatoslav became prince." (*See* PSRL, xv (i), col.
67.)

[2] *See* below, p. 298.

it might have led to the permanent annexation of the economically important lands of the upper Dnepr and Desna rivers. As it was, even allowing for Ivan II's policy of appeasement with the west, Smolensk remained sturdily independent of Lithuania from 1352 to 1356, and there is nothing to show that troops from Smolensk took part in any Lithuanian military venture during this period.

Unfortunately the available Russian sources show no evidence of Tatar support for Semen's Smolensk operation of 1352. Indeed, we know that in the spring of that year "the Tatars, persuaded by Ol'gerd the duke of Lithuania with gifts and various promises, laid waste . . . the land of Podolia, which was subject to the kingdom of Poland".[1] However, the fact that the Tatars did not take part in Semen's campaign and the fact that they were fighting the Poles in 1352 need not lead us to think that the khan did not approve of, and indeed encourage, Semen's encroachment on the lands of Smolensk. The Soviet historian Cherepnin, in his analysis of the Muscovite grand-princely archives of the fourteenth century, writes: "Semen . . . undertook his campaign against Smolensk evidently in the interests of the Horde", and describes his Smolensk policy as "co-ordinated with the Horde".[2]

That no Tatar troops accompanied Semen in 1352 can be explained by the assumption that Semen, in view of the pre-occupation of Ol'gerd with his western and northern neighbours and the engagement of some or all of the Smolensk army on the Livonian front, foresaw few obstacles on the path to Smolensk. As for Tatar "co-operation" with Lithuania at the time, it should be borne in mind that the Smolensk campaign may well have taken place long after the Tatars' despoliation of Podolia— indeed, it may even have followed the peace which was concluded between Lithuania and Poland in the autumn of 1352 and which nullified the whole object of the anti-Polish Tatar-Lithuanian agreement of 1350. Even if the Tatar raid on Podolia and the Smolensk campaign were contemporaneous, there is no likelihood of there being any connection between the two: the Tatars were probably bribed by Ol'gerd's agents long before March 1352 and their raiding parties may well have wintered in the Black Sea steppes in anticipation of the Spring foray. In any case, by attacking Podolia, the Tatars were not necessarily

---

[1] See above, p. 200, note 2.   [2] See Cherepnin, RFA, vol. i, p. 22.

or consciously "strengthening" Lithuania; they were dealing a blow at Poland and at the same time enriching themselves with bribes and booty. There was in fact no reason why the Tatars' action in the south should have had any connection with Semen's plans in the north or should imply that the Muscovites did not enjoy full Tatar backing. Furthermore, it is unlikely that Semen would have undertaken so important a venture without first consulting the khan (or his representative) or without securing his blessing and moral support. Such behaviour would have been entirely out of keeping with what we know of Semen's policy towards the Horde.

One final consideration will strengthen the thesis that Semen enjoyed Jani-Beg's full support in 1352. If, as seems likely, Semen chose Vasily of Bryansk to replace Ivan Aleksandrovich on the throne of Smolensk in 1352, he chose a man with strong Tatar connections. Whether he was the son of Dmitry Romanovich or Ivan Romanovich of Bryansk, his family had close connections with the Golden Horde. Vasily Romanovich, his father's brother, had relied on the Tatars to oust Svyatoslav Glebovich from Bryansk in 1310;[1] Dmitry Romanovich had attacked Smolensk in 1333 with Tatar troops.[2] Still more significant is the fact that when Ol'gerd attacked him in Smolensk in 1356 and captured his son, he fled immediately to the Horde where he was given the *yarlyk* for Bryansk.[3]

While Jani-Beg was prepared to support Semen in the international conflict between Moscow and Lithuania, he was unwilling to allow the principality of Moscow to become unlimitedly strong at the expense of the other principalities of Suzdalia or of the semi-independent districts of Ryazan' and Murom. It would have been just as dangerous for the Tatars were Moscow to enlarge her territory by means of annexation or to increase her authority over her immediate neighbours in the north, east and south as if the grand principality of Lithuania were allowed to expand eastwards unhampered. The problem was how, without actually replacing the prince of Moscow on the throne of Vladimir by another Suzdalian claimant, to hold his position in check while

[1] *See* above, pp. 70–1.   [2] *See* above, p. 171.
[3] *See* above, p. 209.

at the same time keeping him sufficiently strong to resist Ol'gerd effectively.

The problem was solved with the customary shrewdness of the khans. No curb was placed on the traditional rights of the grand prince; he was able to maintain his nominal authority over the other Vsevolodovichi, that is to say he was able to command their obedience in time of war.[1] But while Semen and Ivan II continued to rule much as their father had, Jani-Beg saw to it that the combined strength of north-east Russia was kept under strict control by subtly interfering in the relations between Moscow and Suzdal', by fostering and supporting anti-Muscovite elements in Ryazan' and by contributing to the fragmentation of Tver'.

As has been mentioned above,[2] very little is known of the first decade of Konstantin Vasil'evich's reign in the principality of Suzdal'. He acceded to the throne in 1331 when his brother Grand Prince Aleksandr died. It seems likely that Ivan I claimed the Povolzh'e district, that is to say the basin of the Oka and middle Volga from approximately Yur'evets to the influx of the Vetluga, including the towns of Nizhny Novgorod and Gorodets, as part of the territory of the grand principality of Vladimir, and in fact succeeded in removing it from Konstantin's control.[3] As far as we know Konstantin offered no resistance to Ivan I: he probably took part in the campaign of 1333 against Torzhok and certainly marched under Ivan and Tovluby in 1339 against Smolensk.[4] It is only after Ivan's death in 1340 that we find Konstantin Vasil'evich attempting to assert his independence and perhaps even to rival Semen in the struggle for the throne of Vladimir.

Only one chronicle fragment of uncertain date[5] mentions

[1] In the campaign against Torzhok in 1340 or 1341, for instance, all the princes, with the possible exception of the prince of Tver', took part under Semen. (See below, p. 245.)

[2] See above, p. 179.   [3] See above, p. 179.   [4] See above, p. 173.

[5] An entry attached to the Voskresensky Chronicle. (See above, p. 181, note 2.) The Trinity and Rogozhsky Chronicles partly confirm this: on 2 May Semen and his brothers went to the Horde "and all the princes were at that time at the Horde" (i.e. they were there already). (See TL, p. 364; PSRL, xv (i), col. 53.) Cf., however, NL, p. 351, which indicates that they all went together.

THE PERIOD OF TRANSITION, 1340-1359

Konstantin Vasil'evich's first attempt to resist Muscovite hegemony. As soon as the death of Ivan Kalita became known, three
of the Suzdalian "vassal" princes, Konstantin Mikhaylovich of
Tver', Vasily Davidovich of Yaroslavl' and Konstantin Vasil'evich
of Suzdal', decided to dispute the retention of the *yarlyk* within the
family of the Danilovichi and its automatic transmission from
father to son. They reached the Horde before the Muscovite
princes and put their case to the khan. But when Semen and his
brothers arrived in Saray in the early summer of 1340, they had
no difficulty in persuading Uzbek to respect Kalita's wishes and
to hand over the *yarlyk* to Semen. The rebellion, if such it was,
was short-lived. A few months later, in early 1341,[1] all the princes
of Suzdalia were summoned to a great congress (*velik s'ezd*) in
Moscow. All, with the exception of the prince of Tver',[2] agreed
to march with Semen on his punitive campaign against Novgorod.[3]

Uzbek, no doubt, had made it clear to Konstantin Vasil'evich
that he was not prepared either to consider his candidature for
the throne of Vladimir or to sanction the return of the Povolzh'e
district to the princes of Suzdal', who justifiably considered themselves the rightful owners of Nizhny Novgorod and Gorodets.[4]
In 1341, however, Uzbek died. In the brief period following his
death, when his son Tini-Beg occupied the throne only to be
murdered and replaced by a second son, Jani-Beg, who then killed
yet a third son and rival, Khidr-Beg,[5] Konstantin took advantage
of the confusion in Saray and occupied Nizhny Novgorod and
Gorodets. He may even have obtained from whoever was khan

---

[1] Probably in February. The chronicles mention that Metropolitan
Feognost, who had been in Bryansk on 6 December 1340, was present at the
s'ezd and accompanied the expedition to Torzhok, which took place in 6848
(i.e. between 1 March 1340 and 28 February 1341). (*See TL*, pp. 364–5; *PSRL*,
xv (i), col. 53.)

[2] The Trinity and Tver' Rogozhsky Chronicles mention Semen, his
brother Ivan, Konstantin of Suzdal', Konstantin of Rostov, Vasily of
Yaroslavl' "and all the princes". (*See TL*, p. 365; *PSRL*, xv (i), col. 53.)
Neither mentions Konstantin of Tver', who, according to the Rogozhsky
Chronicle, "returned from the Horde to Tver'" in the autumn of 1340.

[3] *See* below, p. 245.   [4] *See* above, p. 113.

[5] *See* B. Spuler, *Die Goldene Horde*, pp. 98–9; *PSRL*, xv, (i), col. 54; xxv,
p. 173. *Cf. TL*, p. 365.

at the time the right to the title of "grand prince of Nizhny Novgorod and Gorodets": the only source to mention the episode, the Tver' Rogozhsky Chronicle, says that he "sat in Nizhny Novgorod [and] Gorodets upon the grand-princely throne".[1]

If we assume that Konstantin Vasil'evich, having occupied Nizhny Novgorod and Gorodets, acquired the right to rule them (perhaps from Tini-Beg himself), then it will be clear why Semen used no military force to dispossess him. Such problems could only be solved by disputation at the Horde. When Jani-Beg eventually established himself on the khanate in 1342, all the Suzdalian princes hastened to pay their respects and renew their patents. First to arrive were the three Konstantins—of Suzdal', Tver' and Rostov—and Vasily of Yaroslavl'.[2] Semen arrived at Saray later, together with Metropolitan Feognost, who was himself obliged to renew his *yarlyk* and those of his bishops.[3] The grand prince was unable to change the existing state of affairs: Konstantin Vasil'evich remained stubbornly master of the Povolzh'e. In the following year Semen tried once more to dislodge his cousin. This time he employed subtler tactics: he persuaded the fickle boyars of Nizhny Novgorod and Gorodets to transfer their allegiance to him.[4] "They opted for Semen," says the chronicler of Tver', "and went with him to the Horde."[5] The purpose of his second visit to Jani-Beg is explicitly stated: "Grand Prince Semen was in conflict with (*sper'sya s*) Prince Konstantin Vasil'evich of Suzdal' concerning the principality of Nizhny Novgorod [and Gorodets]."[6] With the local boyars to add weight to his arguments, he put his case before Jani-Beg. Konstantin Vasil'evich, however, had done his work well in the

---

[1] ". . . *sede v Novegorode v Nizhnem na Gorodtse na knyazhenii na velikom*" (*PSRL*, xv (i), col. 54).

[2] *See TL*, p. 365; *PSRL*, xv (i), col. 54. Both stress the earlier arrival of the four princes.

[3] *See PSRL*, x, p. 215.

[4] Note that some forty years earlier, at the death of Grand Prince Andrey, the boyars of Gorodets transferred their allegiance to the new grand prince. (*See PSRL*, xxv, p. 393.) There was also trouble with the boyars of Nizhny Novgorod. *See* above, p. 64. The boyars in question, however, may have been the personal followers of Andrey and not the local boyars.

[5] *PSRL*, xv (i), col. 55.   [6] Ibid.

previous year. Jani-Beg was impervious to the persuasion of Semen. Not only were the wretched boyars returned to their rightful master who confiscated their estates and had them publicly flogged, but once more Konstantin was confirmed in his owner- ship of the Povolzh'e district: "The rule over [Nizhny] Novgorod (*knyazhenie Novogorodskoe*) was granted to Prince Konstantin."[1]

1343 marks the beginning of the rise of the powerful new principality centred on the great trading city of Nizhny Nov- gorod, whither the capital was soon to be transferred from Suzdal'.[2] Four years later it acquired its own bishop when Feognost appointed one Nafanail bishop of Suzdal' and, presum- ably of Gorodets and Nizhny Novgorod as well.[3] The chronicle mentions the building activities of Konstantin in Nizhny Nov- gorod,[4] a sign of economic prosperity. None of this information, with the exception of the appointment of Nafanail to the see of Suzdal', was mentioned in the Muscovite chronicles: it was all contained in the Tver' Rogozhsky Chronicle, and was carefully expunged from the Trinity Chronicle. This is not surprising, particularly as far as Moscow's attempts to win back the Povolzh'e are concerned. The events of 1343 hardly reflected to the glory of Grand Prince Semen.

It might be asked why Jani-Beg in 1343 reversed the policy of his father and refused to allow Semen to regain control over the eastern Volga lands. The answer is that at this stage Lithuania had scarcely recovered from the death of Gedimin and presented nothing like the threat to Muscovy which she had in the past and which she was to in the near future. In 1341 Ol'gerd, prince of Krevo and Vitebsk, had failed in his attempt to recapture Mozhaysk from Moscow;[5] in 1342 the military intervention of Ol'gerd, his brother Keystut and his son Andrey in the Pskov- Livonian conflict—intervention which had been requested by the

[1] *PSRL*, xv (i), col. 55.
[2] *See* Presnyakov (*Obrazovanie*, p. 263), who dates the transfer of the capital 1350.
[3] *See TL*, p. 369; *PSRL*, xv (i), cols. 57–8; xxiii, p. 108; xxv, p. 176.
[4] In 1347 Konstantin had a "great bell" cast for the Spaso-Preobra- zhensky Cathedral in Nizhny Novgorod; the same cathedral was rebuilt in 1350 and Konstantin transferred to it the ikon of the Saviour from Suzdal'. (*See PSRL*, xv (i), cols. 58, 60; *Istoriya russkogo iskusstva*, vol. iii, pp. 16–17.)
[5] *See TL*, p. 365; *PSRL*, xv (i), cols. 53–4.

Pskovites because of the Novgorodians' unwillingness to help—had ended inconclusively with a reconciliation between Novgorod and Pskov,[1] in other words had ended in the failure of the Lithuanians to exploit a favourable situation. At the same time Semen of Moscow had considerably strengthened his own position by quickly settling affairs in Novgorod: by 1342 both the grand prince and the metropolitan seem to have regained control over the Novgorodians and their archbishop,[2] something which had rarely been achieved by Ivan I. Small wonder, then, that in 1343 Jani-Beg was not prepared to see Semen, who was in no danger on his western boundaries, strengthened by the reacquisition of Nizhny Novgorod and Gorodets, which Uzbek, it seems, had been ready to allow Ivan I to hold in compensation, one might almost say, for his inability to control Novgorod.

So far Konstantin and his family had in no way compromised themselves in the eyes of the khan, that is to say they had shown no overt pro-Lithuanian tendencies. The only dynastic marriage before 1352 was between Konstantin's daughter Antonida and Prince Andrey Fedorovich of Rostov in 1350.[3] What Andrey's political leanings were we do not know: he evidently shared the principality with his uncle Konstantin Vasil'evich of Rostov; beyond that nothing is known of him. In 1352, however, two of Konstantin of Suzdal''s children contracted marriages which were to have far-reaching results: his daughter Evdokia married Mikhail,[4] son of Aleksandr Mikhaylovich of Tver'—that same Mikhail whom nineteen years earlier Archbishop Vasily of Novgorod had demonstratively christened in Pskov,[5] whose sister was married to Ol'gerd[6] and who was later to prove the staunch ally of Lithuania and the bitter enemy of Moscow. In the same year Konstantin showed even more clearly his attitude towards Moscow by marrying his third eldest son Boris to a daughter of Ol'gerd, Agrafena.[7]

---

[1] See below, pp. 258 sq.   [2] See below, p. 248.
[3] See PSRL, xv (i), col. 60.   [4] See ibid., col. 61.
[5] See above, p. 142.
[6] Yuliania (Juliana) married Ol'gerd in 1349. (See TL, p. 370.)
[7] See PSRL, xv (i), col. 61. Cf. the Ermolinsky Chronicle and the Moscow svod of 1479, which date the marriage 1354 (PSRL, xxiii, pp. 111–12; xxv, p. 180).

In 1353 Jani-Beg was once again faced with the question of adjudicating between Moscow and Nizhny Novgorod-Suzdal'. This time the relative positions of the rulers of Lithuania and Moscow were very different from what they had been ten years before. By now Ol'gerd, having overthrown his brother Evnuty, Gedimin's heir, had made himself supreme ruler of Lithuania. After having successfully exploited Tatar aid against Poland, he had, in the autumn of 1352, made peace with King Casimir of Poland and was no longer on the defensive on his western frontiers. True, he had temporarily lost the initiative in Smolensk in 1352, but in the north he and Keystut were making up for the disaster of the Strava battle by carrying the war into the lands of the Prussians.[1] In Moscow, on the other hand, the plague had removed Semen and his sons, his brother Andrey and the metropolitan Feognost—all in 1353. His surviving brother Ivan had lost the control and support of Novgorod and was faced with the hostility of the remaining princes of Suzdalia, who naturally contested his right to the *yarlyk* at Saray.[2]

After the death of Semen and Andrey all the princes of north-east Rus' went to the Horde. Ivan, Semen's sole surviving brother, basing his claim no doubt on some agreement reached between Ivan I and Uzbek in 1339,[3] presented himself as candidate for the grand-princely *yarlyk*. His chief opponent was Konstantin Vasil'evich of Nizhny Novgorod-Suzdal'. But this time Konstantin enjoyed greater support than that previously afforded by the princes of Yaroslavl', Tver' or Rostov. The republic of Novgorod sent ambassadors to the Horde "requesting that the grand principality be given to Prince Konstantin of Suzdal'".[4] Jani-Beg refused. The *yarlyk* was granted to Ivan Ivanovich of Moscow. It was not so much because the combination of Nizhny Novgorod, Suzdal' and Novgorod the Great might prove too strong a political force in Eastern Europe[5] that the khan rejected the request of the republic; it was because Konstantin had

[1] *See* Paszkiewicz, *Jagiellonowie*, p. 396.
[2] "The princes went to the Horde to contest the grand principality" (*PSRL*, xxiii, p. 111; xxv, p. 179).
[3] *See* above, pp. 188–90.
[4] *NL*, p. 363; *PSRL*, iv (i), p. 286; xxiii, p. 111; xxv, p. 179.
[5] Such is Cherepnin's view. (*See Obrazovanie*, p. 534.)

virtually disqualified himself as candidate for the throne of
Vladimir by his dynastic links with Lithuania. It was decided to
continue to support the house of Moscow as the main bastion
against Lithuania.

The history of Nizhny Novgorod-Suzdal' during the rest of
the 1350's need not concern us here. The failure of Konstantin
Vasil'evich to get the *yarlyk* made little or no difference to his or
his successor's attitude towards Moscow; indeed, any misunder-
standings between the two principalities were cleared up in a
short time. In 1355 Konstantin drew up a treaty of friendship with
Moscow,[1] at the same time as Novgorod "made peace with
Prince Ivan".[2] He died in that same year, "having honourably
defended his patrimony against princes stronger than himself", so
runs the brief necrology in the Novgorod Fourth Chronicle
compilation.[3] His eldest son Andrey, who immediately obtained
from the Horde a continuation of his father's *yarlyk* for Suzdal',
Nizhny Novgorod and Gorodets,[4] ruled briefly and just as
peaceably. In 1356 he met Ivan II at Pereyaslavl' and drew up a
treaty with him. All we know is that the two parted on the best
of terms, Ivan having loaded Andrey with gifts in exchange for
the latter's recognition of the prince of Moscow as his feudal
superior, his "elder brother".[5] It was not until the end of the
fifties, at the time of the so-called "Great Trouble" in the Horde
(*velikaya zamyatnya*, in the Russian sources), when khan replaced
khan in rapid succession, that a brother of the gentle Andrey[6]
was able to put himself forward as successor to Ivan II and to
break the line of Danilovichi by becoming, albeit for only a short
time, grand prince of Vladimir.

[1] *See PSRL*, x, p. 227, the only source to mention the treaty, of which
there are no details.

[2] *See PSRL*, iv (i), p. 287.

[3] *PSRL*, iv (i), p. 287. "And against the Tatars" adds the Nikon Chronicle
(*PSRL*, x, p. 227). All the chronicles give 1355 as the year of his death except
the Ermolinsky Chronicle and the Moscow *svod* of 1479 which give 1354.

[4] *See PSRL*, iv (i), p. 286; v, p. 228.

[5] "In the year 6864 there was a congress (*s'ezd*) in Pereyaslavl' between
Grand Prince Ivan Ivanovich and Prince Andrey Konstantinovich; and he
(Ivan II) gave his younger brother many gifts and great honour . . ." (*PSRL*,
v, p. 228). This is only found in one copy of the Sofiysky First Chronicle.

[6] The Trinity Chronicle calls him "pious and humble" (*TL*, p. 381).

While Jani-Beg saw to it that Moscow did not expand eastwards
and acquire the Povolzh'e area and at the same time prevented
the princes of Suzdal'-Nizhny Novgorod from obtaining the
grand-princely *yarlyk*, he also concerned himself with Moscow's
southern borders. If Moscow-Ryazan' affairs were in the main
controlled by the Tatars, and there is good reason for believing
that they were, then it is clear that Khan Jani-Beg was attempting
to keep Moscow as weak in the south as she was strong in the
west. It was not that Tatar policy was in any way concerned with
strengthening the principality of Ryazan'—this would have been
of no advantage to the Tatars; it was merely a question of using
Ryazan' to limit Moscow's strength in certain directions, and,
strangely enough, to increase it in others.

There is very little information about either the government of
Ryazan' or the relations of Ryazan''s rulers with their northern
and western neighbours during the first forty years of the fourteenth century. Though technically independent—not ruled, that
is to say, by a descendant of Vsevolod III and thus paying tribute
direct to the Tatars—Ryazan' was clearly within Moscow's
sphere of influence for most of this time. Her troops were often
at the disposal of whoever was grand prince of Vladimir. But
Ryazan''s first allegiance was to the Tatars. Being physically
closest of all the north-eastern principalities to the Horde and
being virtually defenceless on the southern and eastern borders,
Ryazan' could offer little resistance to the demands of the Tatars.

During the 1330's there appears to have been some slight
revival of the political fortunes of Ryazan' under the energetic
Ivan Ivanovich Korotopol (1327-42).[1] A certain degree of freedom
from Muscovite and Tatar control may have been achieved
during his reign, but in 1342 he was ousted by his nephew,
Yaroslav Aleksandrovich. Yaroslav arrived in the capital Pereyaslavl'-Ryazansky with a Tatar army and a Tatar *posol*, who placed
him on the throne of Ryazan' and Pronsk.[2] It was partly an act
of vengeance on Yaroslav's part: Korotopol had murdered his
father at the beginning of the Smolensk campaign in 1339.[3] But
it was also an act of Tatar policy dictated by the khan. Yaroslav

[1] *See* above, p. 176.
[2] *See* TL, pp. 365-6; *PSRL*, xxiii, p. 107; xxv, pp. 174-5.
[3] *See* TL, p. 363.

of Pronsk, the chronicles stress, was "sent by the khan from the Horde". Of greater importance still is the fact that the new ruler of Ryazan' and Pronsk made his capital not Pereyaslavl' or his family town of Pronsk, but Rostislavl' on the Oka, Ryazan''s most northerly outpost on the border of the principality of Moscow.

It may well be that the establishment of the pro-Tatar Yaroslav in the border town of Rostislavl' was intended as the prelude to a combined Ryazan'-Tatar invasion of the trans-Oka districts of Kolomna-Serpukhov, which Moscow had seized from Ryazan' in 1301, and a weakening of Moscow's southern frontier. The time, however, for such a move had not yet come. The solution of the Povolzh'e problem in favour of Konstantin of Suzdal' was of greater importance to the khan, and even the most docile of grand princes would not have lightly put up with the seizure of part, or all, of the Kolomna district at the same time as the loss of Nizhny Novgorod and Gorodets. Besides, Semen was needed by the Tatars for other purposes at the time.

For ten years nothing happened. There are no recorded incidents which might indicate a strain or breach of relations between Moscow and Ryazan'. Yaroslav died in 1344 and was succeeded by his brother Ivan, about whom nothing is known. In 1350 or 1351 Ivan died.[1] His son Oleg, soon to become a thorn in Moscow's flesh, took over as ruler of Ryazan'. In the second year of his reign the Ryazanites invaded Muscovy.

It happened on 22 June 1353. Ryazan' troops entered Lopasnya, captured the Muscovite *namestnik*, one Mikhail Aleksandrovich, and occupied the area under his control.[2] Lopasnya had previously lain outside Ryazan' territory in the district of the princes of Chernigov but had presumably been annexed by Ryazan' in the second half of the thirteenth century.[3] In 1301 it was seized by Moscow together with Serpukhov, Khotun', Kolomna and the lower reaches of the Nara, Lopasna and Moskva rivers. What the size of the area under the command of the *namestnik* of Lopasnya was we do not know. We do not even know for certain

---

[1] See Baumgarten, *Généalogies*, vol. ii, p. 86.

[2] See TL, p. 374; PSRL, x, p. 227; xv (i) col. 63. For Mikhail Aleksandrovich, *see* below, pp. 293 sq.

[3] See Solov'ev, *Istoriya*, book i, col. 1142; Lyubavsky, *Obrazovanie*, pp. 7, 40.

where the town or settlement of Lopasnya was. If it was where the present town of Lopasnya (now called Chekhov) is, then it was due north of Serpukhov on the Lopasna river. The evidence of the various treaties between Moscow and Ryazan' in which Lopasnya is mentioned, however, would indicate that it was on the *south* bank of the Oka.[1] Wherever Lopasnya itself was, the area recaptured by the Ryzanites undoubtedly included that part of the Oka where the Lopasna river flowed into it. In other words, Moscow no longer controlled the whole of the Oka, from the influx of the Tsna to the influx of the Nara at Serpukhov. Her great natural southern barrier was now commanded in one place at least[2] by the Ryazanites and perhaps by the Tatars as well. It is quite probable too that the seizure of Lopasnya meant a considerable Ryazanite-Tatar bridgehead *north* of the Oka, between Kolomna and Serpukhov. In any case the southern frontier was seriously weakened as a result of the Ryazanite invasion of 1353.

Once again there is no positive information in the chronicles to prove that the Tatars had a hand in the seizure of Lopasnya, but, as was the case with the Muscovite invasion of Smolensk in 1352, there is much indirect evidence to indicate that they were behind Oleg Ivanovich's move. There is nothing in the sources to show that the Tatars in any way objected to the invasion and capture of Lopasnya, nor did Ivan II complain to the khan or attempt to win Lopasnya back; if he did, the chronicles are silent on the matter. Oleg's uncle Yaroslav, it will be remembered, had enjoyed Tatar support and had indeed ousted the rival branch

---

[1] See *DDG*, No. 10, p. 29 (treaty between Dmitry Donskoy and Oleg of Ryazan', 1382). In this treaty the boundary between Moscow and Ryazan' along the Oka is laid down. The relevant passage reads: "As for the places beyond the Oka on the Ryazan' side which were formerly dependent on (*potyaglo k*) Moscow, viz. the *pochen* (newly-established settlement?) Lopastna . . ." *Cf.* pp. 53, 84, 143. "Lopastna" was part of the district of Serpukhov left by Ivan I to his youngest son Andrey. *See* ibid., pp. 7, 9. Unfortunately the village of Talezhskoe on the Lopasna river (upstream from Khotun', which is not yet mentioned in the sources), which formed part of Andrey's *udel* in 1339 (*see DDG*, pp. 7, 9), is not mentioned again in the sources. (*See* Map B.)

[2] Note that Rostislavl', farther east, was also in Ryazan' hands. (*See* above, p. 220.)

of the family with the aid of Tatar troops. As will be seen later, after the murder of Khvost in 1357 the senior Muscovite boyars, whose policy was one of peaceful collaboration with the Horde, chose Ryazan' to flee to.[1]

Yet a further indication of possible military support afforded by the Tatars to Oleg is contained in the words of the reasonably unbiased Tverite Rogozhsky Chronicle, which describes the invasion in the following manner: ". . . on 22 June the Ryazanites took Lopasnya; Prince Oleg was then young, young in mind, harsh and fierce, and together with his Ryazanites and his helpers the *brodniki* (*s potakovniki emu sbrodni*) did much evil to the Christians . . ."[2] Who exactly the *brodniki* were is not certain. Cherepnin describes them as "Cossacks settled in the outskirts of the principality of Ryazan' and used by the Ryazan' boyars for their aims".[3] But judging from the context and taking into consideration the fact that the earliest Cossack bands in the Ryazan' area were of Tatar origin,[4] we may guess that the *brodniki* here mentioned, who caused so much distress to the Christians, were in fact Tatar troops of some sort or another, or perhaps mixed mobile forces of Tatars and Ryazanites.

The most convincing evidence, however, of the Tatars' approval of Oleg's action in 1353 is to be found in the subsequent redistribution of territory. Some time between the loss of Lopasnya and 1358, the probable date of the drawing up of Ivan II's will,[5] Ivan came to an agreement with the Ryazanites, and probably with the Tatars as well, on the readjustment of the frontier between the two principalities. We do not know when this took place or where. All we know is that Ivan II made good the loss of Lopasnya by adding to the estate of his nephew Vladimir certain new territories. "As for the Ryazan' districts on this side of the Oka which have come into my possession, I have given Prince Vladimir [Andreevich] Novy Gorodok on the mouth of the Porotl' (Protva) in lieu of Lopastna."[6] In other

---

[1] *See* below, p. 295.   [2] *PSRL*, xv (i), col. 63.
[3] *See* Cherepnin, *Obrazovanie*, p. 538.
[4] *See* G. Stökl, *Die Entstehung des Kozakentums*, pp. 44, 53 sq.
[5] For the question of the dating of the will, *see* Cherepnin, *RFA*, vol, ii, pp. 29–30.
[6] *DDG*, pp. 15, 18.

words, Ryazan' had clearly exchanged Lopasnya, or the district based on the mouth of the Lopasna river, for the town of Novy Gorodok on the influx of the Protva river into the Oka; the frontier had been shifted a few miles farther west to include the mouth of the Protva. But Novy Gorodok was clearly not all that Ivan II got from the negotiations. He also mentions "other Ryazan' districts which had been exchanged" and which he left "to [his] sons Prince Dmitry and Prince Ivan to be shared by them".[1]

What were these "other Ryazan' districts"? In the list of lands left by Ivan II in his will to his second son, Ivan of Zvenigorod, there is mention of the district of Borovsk on the Protva.[2] In a later treaty between Dmitry Donskoy and Oleg of Ryazan' (1382) there is mention of "Novy Gorodok, Luzha, Vereya, Borovsk and other Ryazan' districts"[3] as being Moscow territory. In other words, Ivan II acquired the entire basin of the Protva and Luzha rivers,[4] territory which had originally been part of the principality of Smolensk or Chernigov, but which had presumably been seized by Ryazan' in the second half of the thirteenth century.

Lopasnya was not all that Ivan II yielded to Ryazan' in exchange for the basin of the Protva and Luzha rivers. The same treaty between Dmitry Donskoy and Oleg defines the Oka basin territory, which was now considered to be in Ryazan' hands, in the following manner: "As for the places beyond (i.e. south of) the Oka which were formerly dependent on Moscow, viz. Lopasnya, the *uezd* of Mstislavl', the fortress of Zhadene, Zhademl', Dubok, Brodnichi and the places [attached to it?], as the princes of Torusa handed these places over to Fedor Svyatoslavich, these places [belong] to Ryazan'."[5] Where exactly these places were is not

[1] Ibid.   [2] Ibid., pp. 15, 17.   [3] Ibid., p. 29.
[4] Note that the source of the Protva river lay in Mozhaysk territory and had therefore been in Muscovite hands since 1304.
[5] *DDG*, p. 29; *cf.* pp. 53, 84, 143. Whether the words "as the princes of Torusa handed these places over to Fedor Svyatoslavich" refer to Mstislavl' *uezd*, Zhadene, Zhademl', Dubok and Brodnichi, or just to "the places [attached to Brodnichi]" is not clear from the context. The Fedor Svyatoslavich mentioned is presumably Fedor of Dorogobuzh and Vyaz'ma, who defected to Moscow in the early years of Semen's reign. (*See* above, pp. 205–6.)

known; but they were evidently somewhere in the neighbourhood of the Oka basin, between Novy Gorodok and Aleksin, and probably *east* of the Oka.

It would appear, then, that the result of Ivan II's negotiations with Ryazan' (and the Tatars) was as follows: Moscow agreed to yield to Ryazan': firstly, the district of Lopasnya, which may or may not have included territory north of the Oka along the Lopasna river, but which certainly was centred on the junction of the Lopasna and Oka rivers; and secondly, certain areas farther upstream of the Oka river, probably on the east bank, which had been temporarily conceded to Moscow by the princes of Tarusa.[1] In exchange Moscow gained Novy Gorodok at the mouth of the Protva and the entire course of the Protva and Luzha rivers. A glance at the map will show the strategic and political importance of the exchange. Moscow's southern border was considerably weakened, much to the advantage of Ryazan' and the Tatars. In the south-west, on the other hand, Moscow's frontiers pushed out still farther towards Smolensk, Vyaz'ma, Bryansk and the tiny principalities of the Upper Oka district. A further jumping-off ground for attacks on Lithuania[2] and a new belt of natural defences from attacks from the west had been acquired. That such a change in the relative strength of Moscow's frontiers was of immense value to the Tatars there can be no doubt. It was a case of the khan making use of Ryazan' to limit Moscow's strength in the south and increase it in the west.[3]

---

[1] The princes of Tarusa were descended from the dynasty of the Chernigov princes, and their land—the basin of the Oka from Novy Gorodok to Lyubutsk, and the Tarusa river—lay originally in the north-eastern corner of the principality of Chernigov. After the Mongol invasions Tarusa, as well as other Chernigov districts such as Kozel'sk and Novosil', became independent of Chernigov and appear to have maintained their independence throughout much of the fourteenth century.

[2] Note that at the beginning of his campaign against Smolensk in 1352 Semen had first of all marched to Vyshgorod (between Vereya and Borovsk on the Protva), then presumably in Ryazan' hands, and had then moved to the Ugra river. (*See* above, p. 208.)

[3] The final adjustment of frontiers, however, was not entirely to Tatar liking. In 1358 a *posol* named Makhmatozh appeared in Ryazan' and asked Ivan's permission to review the Moscow–Ryazan' frontier question. Ivan refused him entry. He was then called back to the Horde. (*See TL*, p. 376.)

During most of Ivan I's reign as grand prince of Vladimir, Tver' had been ruled quietly and sensibly by the husband of Ivan's niece, Konstantin Mikhaylovich of Tver'. The brief re-emergence of Aleksandr Mikhaylovich as prince of Tver' in 1338–9 had made little difference to the status of Tver' *vis-à-vis* Moscow, except for enabling Ivan to remove the outward symbols of Tver''s independence; it had also served to remind the people of Tver' of the misfortunes concomitant with the rule of a prince who enjoyed Lithuanian support.

During the twenty years which followed the death of Ivan I the fortunes of Tver' in no way improved. There was little sign of a revival of the political power of her princes or of an improvement in her economic situation. No ruler of Tver' during the depressed forties and fifties of the fourteenth century was able seriously to rival the prince of Moscow, or even the prince of Suzdal', militarily or economically. The house of the Yaroslavichi was for the time being out of the running.

The low ebb of Tver''s political fortunes can be ascribed largely to the disaster of 1339—the murder of Aleksandr at the Horde. Uzbek had shown the Tverites and the princes of Suzdalia just what could befall an unamenable ruler and the people he ruled. But there were of course other causes for the decline and atrophy of Tver' during the reigns of Semen and Ivan II. Chief amongst these was the fragmentation of the principality.

Unfortunately for Tver' Mikhail Yaroslavich left four sons, three of whom, Aleksandr, Konstantin and Vasily, each produced at least two sons of their own. The relative fertility of the Tverite princely family as well as the accident of their avoiding the ravages of the plague of 1352–3, which carried off four princes of Moscow to say nothing of the metropolitan, was to some extent Tver''s undoing. The land of Tver' had to be parcelled out amongst the sons and grandsons of Mikhail Yaroslavich. There was no reason, of course, why the four sons of Aleksandr who survived him (Vsevolod, Mikhail, Vladimir and Andrey), Konstantin and his two sons (Eremey and Semen) and Vasily and his two sons (Vasily and Mikhail) should not have lived in peace, had it not been for outside interference. Other large families in northeast Rus' had managed to avoid internecine war—the princes of Rostov, for example. But it was not in the interests of either the

H

Horde or Moscow that the princes of Tver' should remain united. Both the khan and the prince of Moscow saw to it that the house of Tver' was divided amongst itself during the two decades following the murder of Aleksandr Mikhaylovich. The full extent to which the Tatars (and with them the prince of Moscow) acted as an accelerator in the process of the fragmentation and consequent temporary decline of Tver' can only be understood if we examine what is known of the history of Tver' during the reigns of Semen and Ivan II, the period from 1339 to 1358.

When Aleksandr Mikhaylovich returned to Tver' in 1338 for the last months of his reign, his brother Konstantin, who had been quietly ruling Tver' in his place since the disaster of 1327, stepped aside and went into temporary retirement. The chronicles make no mention of his reaction to his brother's return to power. After the murder of Aleksandr and his eldest son Fedor at the Horde in 1339, Konstantin once again became the obvious candidate for the throne of Tver'. Aleksandr's four surviving sons were all under twelve, and in any case their turn to rule, according to the law of lateral succession, would only come when their uncles Konstantin and Vasily died.

Konstantin had previously ruled Tver' docilely and in obedience to the prince of Moscow. The murder of his brother and the obvious connivance of Ivan Kalita in the murder, however, made it impossible for him to continue his previous policy of amiable neutrality. Even if the people of Tver' were indifferent to the removal of their rulers, he could hardly sit by while his kinsmen were murdered and then continue his reign in submission to the prince of Moscow, who in his eyes bore equal blame for the tragedy of 1339. A sure indication of his unwillingness to associate himself and Tver' with Moscow or Tatar policies is the absence of troops from Tver' in the joint expedition of Tovluby and Kalita against Smolensk later in the same year: the chronicles list many of the major Suzdalian princes but significantly omit Konstantin and his army.[1] A still clearer sign of Konstantin's anti-Moscow orientation, however, is his opposition to the new candidate for the grand-princely throne in 1340. When Ivan I died, he hurried to the Horde with the princes of Yaroslavl' and Suzdal' to contest the succession of Semen.[2]

[1] *See* above, pp. 172 sq.   [2] *See* above, p. 181, note 2, 213.

Although the "rebellion" of the three princes proved a failure and although the other two members of the coalition were clearly brought to heel by Semen later in the same year, once again there is evidence that Konstantin managed to stand aloof from yet another Moscow-led Suzdalian military venture: the chronicles unanimously refrain from mentioning his participation in the great *s'ezd* of Moscow in 1340 and the subsequent campaign against Tozhok, while giving the names of the princes of Suzdal', Yaroslavl' and Rostov,[1] who were present at the *s'ezd* and who marched with Semen on Torzhok.

Just as Semen had been unable forcibly to remove Konstantin of Suzdal' from the Povolzh'e district which he had occupied in 1341,[2] so he was unable to take active steps against Konstantin of Tver'. When in 1342 Jani-Beg became khan, all the princes hastened to the Horde to congratulate him and renew their patents. Once again Konstantin of Tver' was in the group of princes who saw to it that they arrived at Saray before Semen.[3] This time, it is true, there is no mention of any struggle for the throne; but it may well be that the block of princes from Tver', Suzdal', Rostov and Yaroslavl' once more attempted to oust the prince of Moscow. Although they were unsuccessful, their patents were renewed. At this stage Semen, who was faced with the far more formidable problem of dealing with Suzdal', was unable to obtain permission from the khan to deal with Tver' or to persuade the Tatars to take steps themselves. He was, however, ably assisted by the ever-loyal Metropolitan Feognost, who, two years later, appointed one Fedor as bishop of Tver' in the place of the old bishop who had died in 1342.[4]

The choice of Fedor the Good, as he was later known, was not a fortuitous one. He came, so the Rogozhsky Chronicle informs us, "from the Holy Trinity in Kashin".[5] Now Kashin, the north-eastern portion of the principality of Tver', was the appanage

---

[1] *See TL*, pp. 364–5; *PSRL*, xv (i), col. 53.   [2] *See* above, p. 214.
[3] *See TL*, p. 365.
[4] *See* ibid., p. 366, for the death of bishop Fedor in 1342, and *PSRL*, xv (i), col. 55, for the appointment of the new Bishop Fedor.
[5] *PSRL*, xv (i), col. 55. His appointment, the first event of the "March" year 6852, took place on 8 February. It may therefore have been in 1343. For further details on Fedor, *see* Klibanov, *RD*, pp. 136 sq.

(*udel*) of Konstantin's sole surviving brother, Vasily, who was later to prove the staunch ally of Moscow against the sons of Aleksandr Mikhaylovich, the princes of Kholm and Mikulin in the south-west. Fedor himself, a man of considerable authority, influence and intelligence, remained bishop of Tver' for another sixteen or seventeen years. There can be no doubt as to his political allegiance: he was chosen for the see of Tver' by Feognost; he was close to Vasily Mikhaylovich; and he was later to be the firm supporter of Metropolitan Aleksey of Moscow. His appointment was to contribute indirectly to the fragmentation and weakening of Tver'.

The appointment of Fedor to the see of Tver' made little appreciable difference to the affairs of the principality during the early years of his bishopric. There are no signs of Konstantin changing his mind or his tactics, nor is there evidence of any activity on the part of Vasily Mikhaylovich of Kashin. It was only in 1346 that the feud which was to split Tver' began. It began, however, not between Konstantin and his younger brother Vasily, but between Konstantin and the family of his elder brother Aleksandr. Aleksandr's widow Anastasia had no doubt insisted on the territorial rights of her eldest surviving son Vsevolod, who had by now reached an age at which he was capable of taking an active interest in politics.[1] What the size of his appanage was and when in fact he had been granted it is not known.[2] But there seems to be little doubt that Vsevolod and his mother were settled in Kholm[3] in the extreme south-west tip of the principality, and that for some reason Konstantin took exception to their presence there. Only the Nikon Chronicle mentions the incident which sparked off the long feud between the different branches of the Tverite princely family. "In that year (1346) there was hostility between Prince Konstantin Mikhaylovich and Princess [A]nastasia (Aleksandr's widow) and Prince

[1] He was probably born not long after 1327 in Pskov. *See* Ekzemplyarsky, *VUK*, vol. ii, pp. 539–40 and note 1724.

[2] Presnyakov considers that the first division of Tver' into appanages was made by Mikhail Yaroslavich on the eve of his departure to the Horde in 1320. (*See* Presnyakov, *Obrazovanie*, pp. 191–2.)

[3] Kholm later appears in the sources as the *udel* of the descendants of Vsevolod.

Vsevolod Aleksandrovich." What happened is obscurely reported, but evidently Konstantin began to arrest their boyars and servants and to exert pressure on them.[1]

Konstantin's interference with his nephew's appanage had far-reaching results. The oppression of the local population of Kholm, or at any rate of Anastasia's and Vsevolod's retainers, was so great that Vsevolod had no alternative but to take his case to the grand prince of Vladimir. Either as a result of Semen's machinations at the Horde, or because he intended to forestall Vsevolod's accusations which he knew would eventually reach the khan via Moscow, Konstantin himself set off to Saray soon after Vsevolod's departure. When he got there he died;[2] although the Nikon Chronicle makes no mention of foul play, it is not improbable that he was murdered by the Tatars on the recommendation of Semen. Since 1339 Konstantin had hardly been behaving in a manner acceptable to the khan and the grand prince.

The death of Konstantin precipitated events in Tver'. Vasily of Kashin, as the last of the four sons of Grand Prince Mikhail, considered himself to be the rightful heir to the throne: by tradition he had precedence over the children of his brothers. Before setting off to the Horde he took steps to make his arrival there more acceptable: he sent his tax-collectors to Kholm to raise some tribute from his nephew's appanage. His delay, however, and the fact that his nephew Vsevolod left Moscow for Saray as soon as, or even before, Konstantin's death became known, cost him the *yarlyk*. Vsevolod, who had clearly spent his time profitably in Moscow ingratiating himself with Grand Prince Semen, had little difficulty at the Horde. As if in accordance with a preconceived plan, Jani-Beg, advised no doubt by Semen, granted him the patent for all Tver'. To add insult to injury, Vsevolod met his uncle Vasily on the Volga at a place called Bezdezh before the latter had reached Saray, defeated him in battle and relieved him of all the tribute levied from the inhabitants of Kholm.[3]

Vsevolod Aleksandrovich returned to Tver' with a Tatar *posol* and probably a Tatar army. Once upon the throne, he was master of the whole principality. Vasily was not the only one to

[1] *See PSRL*, x, p. 217.   [2] *See PSRL*, x, pp. 217–18.
[3] *See* ibid., p. 218. The location of Bezdezh is not known.

be vexed by the behaviour of Jani-Beg and Semen. Bishop Fedor, we can assume, can hardly have approved of Vsevolod's appointment. But the only person demonstratively to show his dissatisfaction was Metropolitan Feognost. When in the beginning of 1347 Semen clinched the agreement by marrying Vsevolod's sister—the arrangements for the marriage had evidently been drawn up by Vsevolod and Semen in the previous year while Vsevolod was in Moscow—he was obliged to conceal the fact from the metropolitan. Feognost was furious. Not for nothing had he promoted the cause of Vasily by appointing Fedor bishop of Tver' three years earlier—and now the grand prince was allying himself to the wrong branch of the family. He refused to give Semen and Maria of Tver' his blessing. He shut the churches of Moscow in protest.[1]

It was a marriage of considerable importance to Semen himself. Neither of his sons by his first wife had survived.[2] The frigid Evpraksia, who had been sent back to her father in 1346 for failing to perform her wifely duties satisfactorily with the grand prince,[3] had, not surprisingly, produced no children. Male offspring were essential. But the marriage was equally important as a demonstration of Semen's solidarity with Vsevolod.

It was evident that at this stage Semen had made a mistake in his policy towards Tver'. By appointing Fedor as bishop of Tver', Feognost had shown where his preference lay. If Semen were to continue his support for the Aleksandrovichi he would be risking a serious breach with the Church, and this he could ill afford. It was indeed the necessity of guaranteeing the continued co-operation of Feognost that obliged Semen radically to alter his attitude towards the princely family of Tver' and to persuade the khan of the need to support the prince of Kashin. The reconciliation between Semen and Feognost took place shortly after the wedding. According to the Nikon Chronicle "Feognost, metropolitan of Kiev and All Rus', took certain spiritual counsel with his son, Grand Prince Semen Ivanovich, and they sent to

---

[1] For the marriage of Semen and Maria, *see TL*, p. 368; *PSRL*, xxiii, p. 108; xxv, p. 176. For Feognost's reaction, *see PSRL*, xv (i), col. 57.

[2] Vasily, born 1337, died 1338 (*PSRL*, xxv, p. 171); Konstantin, born and died 1341 (*TL*, p. 365).

[3] *See* above, p. 206, note 2.

Constantinople to the patriarch for his blessing".[1] How exactly the quarrel between the grand prince and the metropolitan was made up is not known, but the results were spectacular. Not only did the patriarch give his blessing for Semen's third, adulterous, marriage,[2] but he also agreed, together with the emperor, to close once more the metropolitan see of Galich, which had last been closed by the efforts of Feognost in 1331 but which had since been reopened.[3] This latter decision of patriarch and emperor, facilitated by a timely bribe,[4] was of far greater political importance to Semen than his support for the Aleksandrovichi: it meant a decisive diplomatic victory over the Lithuanian Lyubart Gediminovich, prince of Volyn' and Galich, and a resumption of ecclesiastical control over districts which were now virtually part and parcel of the Lithuanian State. Small wonder, then, that Semen was prepared to jettison his brother-in-law, to reverse his policy *vis-à-vis* Tver' and to fall in with the wishes of Feognost.

The granting of the princely *yarlyk* to Vsevolod in 1346 led to a period of severe civil war in Tver'. Vsevolod and Vasily almost came to blows after their return from the Horde, so says the Nikon chronicler. That there was internecine fighting is evident from his remark: "The Tverites suffered sorely and many of them scattered abroad because of this derangement (*nestroeniya*)."[5] It may even be that Vsevolod and Vasily took their case once more to the Horde in 1347 or 1348 and that Jani-Beg confirmed his decision of 1346 by sending Vsevolod back in 1348 once more with the *yarlyk*.[6] The feud between the two branches of

[1] *PSRL*, x, p. 218.

[2] This is presumably the "blessing" asked for by Semen and Feognost.

[3] Golubinsky thinks that the metropolitan see had been reopened in 1337–8. (*See* Golubinsky, *IRTs*, vol, ii, book 1, pp. 157–8.) *Cf.* Paszkiewicz, *Jagiellonowie*, p. 382.

[4] The Byzantine historian, Nicephorus Gregoras, in book 28 of his history, mentions a large sum of money sent by Semen and other Russian princes to repair the church of St. Sophia in Constantinople. (*See* Nicephorus Gregoras, *Hist. Byz.*, vol. iii, pp. 199–200, 516.)

[5] *PSRL*, x, p. 220.

[6] The Nikon Chronicle—the only source to mention the details of the Tver' feud—first describes the clash between Konstantin and Vsevolod and the ensuing feud between Vsevolod and Vasily which began at the Horde,

the family was at length resolved in 1349. It was a year of considerable international achievement for Semen. After his great diplomatic victory over Ol'gerd at the Horde in 1348, he was able to force the Lithuanians to agree to what must have been a humiliating peace treaty. Furthermore in that same year Lyubart of Volyn' and Galich, prompted and prodded no doubt by Metropolitan Feognost, who was now master of the diocese of south-west Rus',[1] asked Semen for, and obtained, a peace treaty and the hand of his niece, the daughter of Konstantin of Rostov.[2] And to crown it all, Bishop Fedor the Good managed to oust Vsevolod Aleksandrovich from the throne of Tver'.

The Nikon Chronicle, again the only source to report on the events in Tver' of 1349, attributes the entire coup to Bishop Fedor. It was he who persuaded Vsevolod and Vasily to make peace and amicably to discuss the civil war and the dynastic problem. A treaty was drawn up and signed by both parties. Vsevolod put up no resistance; he yielded the throne of Tver' to his uncle and retired to his *udel* of Kholm, while Vasily of Kashin moved into the capital and began to rule the principality. The chronicler is at pains to stress the ending of the fratricidal strife and the benefit the Tverites acquired from the cessation of hostilities. "Vasily Mikhaylovich . . . began to live with his nephew . . . in peace and great love. And people came from all around to their cities, to their districts and to the land of Tver',

---

under 1346, ending with the words: "Prince Vasily Mikhaylovich of Kashin was grieved by his nephew Vsevolod Aleksandrovich of Kholm and Tver', because Jani-Beg had given him (Vsevolod) all the principality of Tver'." Then under 1348 the chronicler reports: "In that year Prince Vsevolod Aleksandrovich came from the Horde with the title bestowed (*s zhalovaniem*) and with great honour to the throne of Tver', and with him came a *posol* . . ." He then goes on to mention the strife in Tver' (*see* above). At first sight it looks as though this was a second trip to the Horde; but it may well be that the Nikon Chronicler, using two different accounts of the same event, muddled up his dates and made two encounters at the Horde out of one. It also seems unlikely that Vsevolod and Vasily spent two years litigating at the Horde, especially in view of the wedding of Maria and Semen, which took place in 1347. It is not clear why the account of Vasily's brief and catastrophic reign was excised from the Tver' and Moscow chronicles.

[1] Note that in 1347 (and 1348?) Feognost was in Volyn'. (*See PSRL*, x, p. 221.)

[2] *See TL*, p. 370.

and the people multiplied and rejoiced with great rejoicing."[1]

The fact that the chronicler stresses the major role of Fedor in the crisis of 1349 is of importance. The bishop, we may assume, was acting in the interests, not only of the prince of Kashin but also of the metropolitan and the grand prince. By now Feognost and Semen had made up their quarrel, and Semen, to recompense Feognost for his willingness to tolerate his third marriage and for his ecclesiastical victory over Ol'gerd in Volyn', was prepared to remove his support for the Aleksandrovichi as quickly as he had first given it. While he could hardly repudiate his third wife by sending her back to her family—especially in view of the fact that she was pregnant at the time[2]—he did the next best thing and married off his daughter in the following year (1350) to Mikhail, Vasily Mikhaylovich's son.[3]

There can be no doubt that the coup in Tver' of 1349 and the abrupt change in Semen's attitude towards the Aleksandrovichi were approved of, if not actually planned, by the Tatars themselves. There could be no question of exchanging *yarlyki* without reference to the Horde, and no amount of spiritual persuasion, even coupled with the threat of excommunication, could have urged Vsevolod of Tver' to abdicate had not the Tatars brought physical pressure to bear on him as well. Besides, the actual granting of the patent could only be done by the khan himself. From the scattered jottings of the Rogozhsky, Trinity and Nikon Chronicles it would appear that Feognost after the marriage of Semen and Maria in 1347 first convinced Semen that he had chosen the wrong branch of the family to support and that Semen, who twice visited the Horde between 1347 and 1350,[4] then convinced the khan of the need to transfer his support from Vsevolod to Vasily. The fact that in 1349 yet another sister of Vsevolod, Yuliania, married Ol'gerd of Lithuania,[5] albeit

[1] *PSRL*, x, p. 221.

[2] Maria of Tver' gave birth to her second son Mikhail on 7 September 1349. Feognost christened him. (*See TL*, p. 371.)

[3] *See TL*, p. 371; *PSRL*, xv (i), col. 60; xxv, p. 177 (under 1351).

[4] Semen went to the Golden Horde in early 1348 and returned in the same year (*TL*, p. 369); he went again in 1350 before marrying his daughter to Mikhail Vasil'evich of Kashin (*TL*, p. 371).

[5] *See TL*, p. 370. Permission was asked of Semen (he was Yuliania's brother-in-law); Semen reported the matter to Feognost who gave his blessing.

during a period of peace between Semen, Ol'gerd and Vsevolod of Tver', was probably one of the causes of the khan's willingness to listen to Semen and to back the house of Kashin rather than that of Kholm.

Although the Tatars had given their unofficial blessing to the agreement of 1349, official confirmation of the khan's approval did not materialize until 1352. In that year one Akhmat, a Tatar *posol*, arrived in Tver' and gave Vasily the *yarlyk*. His arrival acted as the signal for another outburst of civil war in the principality. Vasily, egged on no doubt by Akhmat, "began to bear a grudge against his nephew Prince Vsevolod Aleksandrovich of Kholm, recalling the robbery at Bezdezh (where Vsevolod had relieved him of the tribute in 1346)".[1] He took reprisals on the appanage of his nephew. Once again the unfortunate people of Kholm suffered as they had done twice in 1346.[2] "He began to offend the boyars and servants [of Vsevolod] with heavy taxation and there was lack of faith and hostility between them," says the Nikon Chronicler.[3]

The new phase of the civil war in Tver', sparked off by the agent of the khan, served to align the Aleksandrovichi with the enemies of Moscow. As has been mentioned above, one sister of Vsevolod had married Ol'gerd in 1349. Now in 1352 Vsevolod's brother Mikhail, the future defender of Tver''s independence against Moscow, married Evdokia, the daughter of Konstantin of Suzdal', who himself in that same year married off his son Boris to Ol'gerd's daughter.[4]

That this alliance of the Aleksandrovichi with the princes of Suzdal' and, through them, with Lithuania, was no accident but a deliberate act is shown by subsequent events. For the first four years of Ivan II's reign (1353–7), years during which the new prince of Moscow betrayed a remarkably conciliatory attitude towards the old enemies of his brother, there is no mention in the

---

[1] *PSRL*, x, p. 223. Again only the Nikon Chronicle reports the new phase of the civil war in Tver'.

[2] *See* above, p. 229.   [3] *PSRL*, x, p. 223.

[4] *See PSRL*, xv (i), col. 61. Note that in 1352 Vsevolod "sent off" (*otsla*) his wife to Ryazan'. She was evidently the sister of Oleg. Whether this action, which was presumably a method of divorce, meant an act of hostility between Vsevolod of Kholm and Oleg of Ryazan' cannot be said. (*See PSRL*, x, p. 224.)

chronicles of the civil war in Tver'. No peace was made. In 1357 Vsevolod of Kholm decided to bring his case before the recently appointed successor of Feognost, Metropolitan Aleksey. But Aleksey, the Muscovite boyar, the trainee of Feognost, was not prepared to listen to the complaints of Vsevolod against his uncle. Nor, on the other hand, was he prepared to treat with Vasily of Kashin before the latter had formally drawn up an alliance with Ivan II. Whether this meant that Ivan, during the first four years of his reign, had not wished to continue his brother's friendship and support for the house of Kashin or had even reversed Semen's policy to such an extent as to encourage the Lithuania-orientated Aleksandrovichi cannot be said. But it may well be indicative of a sudden change in Ivan's outlook following the murder of Khvost in 1357.[1] At any rate he was now prepared to resume the old Moscow-Kashin treaty of friendship, acting no doubt on the advice of Metropolitan Aleksey.

The resumption, or perhaps only the reaffirmation, of the Moscow-Kashin alliance in 1357 made no difference to the civil war in Tver'. Both Vasily and his bishop Fedor went to Vladimir on the Klyaz'ma to discuss matters with the supreme ecclesiastical arbitrator, Metropolitan Aleksey. The lengthy talks led to nothing. Vasily and Vsevolod returned home to continue their protracted squabble on Tver' territory.[2] If there had been previously any doubt about the international affiliations of either side, this was dispelled by the events of the next two years. Berdi-Beg's dramatic accession to the khanate in 1357 over the corpses of his twelve murdered brothers[3] meant that all the princes had to proceed to Saray to congratulate the new khan.

---

[1] See below, pp. 301 sq.

[2] The attempted reconciliation of 1357 in Vladimir is only mentioned in the Rogozhsky and Nikon Chronicles (the latter with slightly more detail). (See PSRL, x, pp. 229–30; xv (i), cols. 55–6.) Note that the previous detailed information on the history of Tver' for the years 1346, 1348, 1349 and 1352 is only given in the Nikon Chronicle. From this it is clear that the Rogozhsky and Nikon Chronicles were using the same source on Tver' affairs, but that the compiler of the former excluded from his text the events of 1346–52 as far as they concerned the quarrel between the two branches of the family. As has been pointed out above (p. 95, note 1), one of the sources of the Nikon Chronicle was the 1425 redaction of the Tver' Chronicles.

[3] See Spuler, GH, pp. 108–9.

Vasily evidently accompanied Grand Prince Ivan;[1] Vsevolod, however, who set off independently of his uncle—Vasily would not allow him to go with him—was stopped on the way by the grand prince's governors in Pereyaslavl'. They refused to let him go any farther. He could do nothing but turn back and either wait for his uncle to return to Tver' or take refuge in Lithuania. He chose the latter course.

In 1358 the rift between the rival branches of the family grew even greater thanks to the combined efforts of Moscow and the Horde. Vasily returned to Tver' in April with his title and patent renewed and confirmed.[2] Vsevolod of Kholm, determined to try his luck with the new khan and to contest his uncle's right to the throne of Tver', set off for Saray avoiding Muscovite territory. But once again Vasily Mikhaylovich forestalled him. His ambassador was already there and the new khan was ready for Vsevolod. He was unable to state his case. The khan arrested him "without judgment" and sent him back under escort to Tver', where he was handed over to Vasily. The civil war, if it had ever abated, began again. Vsevolod, his boyars and his servants—his retinue, which had been arrested with him—were ransomed at a great price, much to the distress and suffering of the "black people" of Kholm, who had to provide the cash.[3] So bitter had the struggle become that even Bishop Fedor attempted to resign from his troubled bishopric. Sickened by the family squabble which had now raged for over ten years, he begged the metropolitan to relieve him of his post. But Aleksey realized the importance of having a firm supporter of Moscow in this the most dangerous of all his dioceses. He begged Fedor to remain at his post. Fedor reluctantly agreed.[4] In the following year, 1359, shortly before Ivan II's death, Vsevolod of Kholm fled once more

[1] The Rogozhsky and Nikon Chronicles mention only Vasily by name among those who accompanied Ivan II: "Grand Prince Ivan and all the princes of Rus' and Prince Vasily Mikhaylovich went to the Horde" (*PSRL*, x, pp. 229–30; xv (i), col. 66).

[2] *See PSRL*, x, p. 230; xv (i), cols. 66–7.

[3] Probably the meaning of "*i boyarom i slugam prodazha dannaya velika, takozhe i chernym lyudyam*" (*PSRL*, xv (i), col. 67). *Cf.* the slightly expanded version of *PSRL*, x, p. 230. That Vsevolod was released is evident from his flight to Lithuania in 1359.

[4] *See PSRL*, x, p. 230; xv (i), col. 67.

to Lithuania,[1] there to strengthen his ties with his brother-in-law and to join up with the newly-appointed metropolitan of Lithuania, Roman, a Tverite by origin.[2]

By the end of Ivan II's reign the principality of Tver' was decisively weakened. Its political and economic fortunes had reached a lower ebb than at any time since the beginning of the fourteenth century. Not only was the country racked by civil war of a pernicious and senseless kind, which reflected in miniature the wasteful struggle between Lithuania and Moscow, but also the formerly unified principality was now split into a number of appanage (*udel'ny*) districts, each seemingly independent of the other and owing little allegiance to the senior prince of Tver', the holder of the *yarlyk*. True, there is not yet any evidence in the sources of the existence of the *udel* of Dorogobuzh in the northern districts of the principality,[3] which belonged to the children of Konstantin, nor were there any indications of the split of the Aleksandrovichi into the houses of Kholm and Mikulin. But, as has already been mentioned above, it is likely that the parcelling up of the district of Tver' had been carried out long before, perhaps even by Mikhail Yaroslavich.[4]

The history of Tver' during the 1340's and 1350's has shown that this enfeeblement of the principality was not a natural process; in other words, it was not merely the result of the low rate of mortality among the descendants of Mikhail Yaroslavich. It was a process which was deliberately hastened and encouraged by Moscow and the Horde. Semen and Jani-Beg welcomed and fostered the split between the Kholm and Kashin branches of the princely family, which itself accelerated the process of fragmentation. It is true that the quarrel appears to have been started by Konstantin Mikhaylovich in 1346 without any obvious prompting from Moscow or Saray, but this might well have been settled

---

[1] *See PSRL*, xv (i), cols. 67–8.

[2] *See* Presnyakov, *Obrazovanie*, pp. 196 sq.; Paszkiewicz, *Jagiellonowie*, pp. 390–1.

[3] Not to be confused with Dorogobuzh on the Dnepr in the district of Smolensk. The appanage principality of Tverite Dorogobuzh lay north of Tver' to the south of the Medveditsa river. (*See* Lyubavsky, *Obrazovanie*, pp. 116–17.) According to *Ocherki istorii SSSR*, ii, Map No. 1, Dorogobuzh may have been on the upper Shosha river.

[4] *See* above, p. 228, note 2.

had it not been for the immediate interference of Moscow. Semen's support for Vsevolod Aleksandrovich when Konstantin died was a flagrant breach of tradition; by arranging for an Aleksandrovich to acquire the patent in preference to the rightful heir, Vasily of Kashin, Semen was deliberately breaking the traditional order of succession, which, unless Vasily was prepared to submit, could only lead to civil war. When the tables were turned in 1349 and Vsevolod of Kholm was persuaded by the bishop of Tver' to hand over his throne to his uncle Vasily of Kashin, full approval was given to the new ruler by both Moscow and the Horde. The second bout of civil war, which began in 1352, was undoubtedly sparked off by the presence of a Tatar *posol* in Tver' and fanned to a flame, we may assume, by the Muscovites. By the end of the fifties the position had been still further aggravated by Moscow-Tatar action: the refusal of the Muscovites to allow Vsevolod to pass through Pereyaslavl' on his way to the Horde in 1357 and his ignominious arrest by the Tatars in the following year not only made it clear that the Tatars and the Grand Prince were still working in close co-operation and were not prepared to back the sons of Aleksandr, but also deepened the rift between the two hostile branches of the Tverite princely family and contributed still more to the enfeeblement of Moscow's old rival.

The results could have hardly been more gratifying to Moscow and the Horde. The once unified land of Tver' was split into two mutually hostile camps, one facing west and the other facing east; the senior prince, who owed his position almost exclusively to the good offices of the ruler of Moscow and was probably therefore under some form of military obligation to him,[1] was not able to control more than a third of his territory; an almost permanent

[1] In 1358 detachments from Tver' and Mozhaysk succeeded in temporarily driving out the Lithuanians who had occupied the border town of Rzheva in 1356. This was evidently an operation co-ordinated by Ivan II. The attack on the Lithuanian garrison in Rzheva is only mentioned in the Nikon and Rogozhsky Chronicles, both of which used the same source (*see above*, p. 95, note 1). The Rogozhsky (Tverite) chronicler, however, unwilling to associate himself with the pro-Moscow activities of Vasily of Kashin, replaced "Tver' army" (*Tverskaya rat'*) by "Volok army" (*volot'skaya rat'*). (*See PSRL*, x, p. 230; xv (i), col. 67.) For the Lithuanian occupation of Rzheva in 1356, *see PSRL*, x, p. 228; xv (i), col. 65.

state of civil war was sapping the economic and political strength of Tver'. The only appreciable disadvantage to Moscow and the Horde was the strengthening of the ties which bound the Aleksandrovichi to Lithuania. The support lent to Kashin and the encouragement of the civil war by Semen and Jani-Beg gave the princes of Kholm and Mikulin no alternative but to seek the aid of their father's old ally—the grand prince of Lithuania.

To summarize Tatar policy towards eastern Europe, more particularly towards north-east Rus' and Lithuania, during the forties and fifties of the fourteenth century, we can say that the overall attitude of the Horde appears not to have been in any way radically different from that of the previous decade. As has been pointed out above, the main element of continuity between the policies of Uzbek and Jani-Beg is to be found in the latter's realization of the danger of the growth of Lithuania and of the need to lend the principality of Moscow sufficient support for her to remain a bulwark against Lithuanian expansion eastward. Hence, throughout the reigns of Semen and Ivan II we find Moscow liberally aided by the Tatars in most, if not all, of her ventures into Lithuanian, or semi-Lithuanian, semi-neutral territory, and in her political clashes with the rulers of Lithuania. The principality of Moscow had to be, and was, kept sufficiently powerful to resist the wiles and strength of Ol'gerd and his brothers. At the same time Jani-Beg manifested great skill in restricting the prince of Moscow, in preventing him from growing disproportionately strong. By subtly interfering in the relationship between Moscow and Suzdal', the khan managed to stop the former from acquiring the economically important lands centred on the juncture of the Oka and Volga rivers and to build up the latter to the status of a potential political and military rival of Moscow. By affording Ryazan' timely moral and physical support, he contrived to weaken Moscow's southern boundary and thus to weaken her future defence against Tatar incursions from the south. At the same time he compensated Moscow for the humiliating loss of Lopasnya on the Oka by allowing her to acquire the Protva river basin, which was to prove invaluable for defence and aggression against Lithuania. As for Moscow's old rival Tver', Jani-Beg was ready to fall in with the plans and advice of the prince of Moscow. By granting now one branch of the princely family the *yarlyk*, now another, he was able to keep alive the civil war which started in 1346 and to encourage the fragmentation of the territory of Tver'.

Thus, broadly speaking, the Tatars saw to it that Moscow was purposefully strengthened, both defensively and offensively, against Lithuania, while at the same time her political power in Suzdalia itself was kept at much the same level as it had been in Kalita's days. The only difference was that the prince of Tver' had been replaced as potential political rival of Moscow by the ruler of Suzdal', Nizhny Novgorod and Gorodets on the Volga. From all this it might appear that the political and economic life of Moscow during the period under consideration was conditioned largely, if not solely, by the will of the khan and that Tatar policy regulated all Muscovite relations with Lithuania as well as her relative position among the principalities of north-east Rus'. This was of course true in so far as few major operations, especially those affecting foreign policy, could be undertaken without the sanction and assistance of the Horde. Yet it would be impossible to assess the growth or retardment of Moscow's power on the strength of Tatar policy alone, without considering her purely domestic affairs and her relations with Novgorod and Pskov. For, tied though the grand prince's hands were by unremitting Tatar control, there were of course a few spheres of activity where a certain independence of action and policy could be exercised. In order therefore to obtain as full a picture as possible of the principality of Moscow during this period of transition between the reigns of Ivan I and his grandson Dmitry Donskoy, we must now examine the problem of the position of Novgorod and Pskov on the border between the grand principalities of Lithuania and Vladimir, as well as the internal affairs of the principality of Moscow.

[ii] NOVGOROD AND PSKOV

The relations between Moscow and the two western republics of Novgorod and Pskov during the forties and the fifties of the fourteenth century are complex and unusually difficult to unravel.

The historian's task is not lightened by the nature of the sources. In most cases we have only the local chronicles of Novgorod and Pskov to consult; all other sources merely repeat, shorten or excise the information supplied by the Novgorodian and Pskovite chroniclers. Not that the information is scarce; on many occasions it is almost embarrassingly abundant. The difficulty is that it is often hard or impossible to assess the bias of the writer, to judge the time of writing and to establish which particular patron the chronicle was kept for. An event may have been originally described in terms calculated to please or flatter a particular incumbent of the see of Novgorod; but who can tell whether the text was altered by subsequent copyists in an effort to suit the needs of an archbishop ideologically or politically opposed to his predecessor? Only the independent evidence of non-Novgorodian, non-Pskovite sources can act as a corrective; and, alas, such corroborative evidence is sadly lacking for the history of Novgorod and Pskov in the reigns of Semen and Ivan II.

The situation is further complicated by the fact that the internal struggles in Novgorod can no longer be reduced to a conflict between two such plainly identifiable groups as the pro-Moscow and pro-Lithuania factions. That such factions still existed, of course, and that the majority of influential Novgorodians were committed one way or another in the conflict between Moscow and Lithuania there can be no doubt. But the struggle appears now to have been between groups of boyars intent on seizing and retaining power and possessions rather than between the supporters of Moscow and Lithuania. And in the turmoil of their squabbles it is difficult, sometimes even impossible, to estimate the political leanings of this or that group, or of this or that boyar. Indeed at times, when one realizes that a particular action was motivated largely by opportunism and self-seeking, the labels "pro-Moscow" and "pro-Lithuania" cease to have any real significance.

The basis of most of the conflicts between various groups in Novgorod during the reign of Semen the Proud was of course the quest for political power. By the beginning of the fourteenth century the foundations for what might be called oligarchic republicanism had been laid: the five administrative districts of the city (*kontsy*, singular *konets*) each elected one representative from their leading boyar clans as life member of the supreme governmental organ, the Council of Lords (*Sovet Gospod*). From these five members of the council one was elected annually as *posadnik*, the chief administrative post within the republic, second in authority only to the archbishop.[1] Had some degree of regular succession to the office of *posadnik* been observed—had there been, for instance some system of rotation for the *posadnichestvo* between the representatives of the *kontsy*—then perhaps some solidarity amongst the *boyarstvo* might have been achieved and the authority of the prince, which had been drastically reduced anyhow during the last decade of the thirteenth century, might have become still feebler. But there was no such system of regular succession. As far as one can tell, the office of *posadnik* passed to, or remained with, whichever of the contestants was powerful, cunning or rich enough to sway the electors.[2] Thus the first half of the fourteenth century witnessed a constant struggle between the leading boyar families: prior to Ivan I's reign this struggle can be identified with the conflict between the supporters of Tver' and of Moscow; during the thirties it largely reflects the dichotomy between Moscow and Lithuania; while during Semen's reign it becomes hard to distinguish between the "Lithuanian" and "Muscovite" tendencies of the various groups.

The political situation in Novgorod and Pskov at the end of the 1330's can scarcely have afforded Ivan Kalita much grounds for satisfaction. True, Pskov had lost her Tverite prince and had virtually severed political relations with Novgorod when the archbishop had fulminated his anathema in 1337;[3] but there is no evidence to show that Pskov had shaken off the Lithuanian protection which had surrounded her Tverite ruler or that the prince of Moscow had in any way increased his influence over the republic. As for Novgorod, almost the last recorded act of Kalita had been to remove his governors from the city and to leave Novgorod in a state of political suspension similar to that in which he had found her at the beginning of his rule as grand

---

[1] Up to 1316 five *kontsy* elected candidates. From 1316 to 1354 the *Lyudin* and *Zagorodsky kontsy* (together known as the Prussian Street—*Prusskaya ulitsa*) produced only one candidate for the *posadnichestvo*.

[2] *See* Yanin, *NP*, pp. 165 sq.

[3] *See* above, p. 160.

prince of Vladimir.[1] From 1333 to the end of his reign Ivan I had shown himself hesitant and irresolute when it came to taking decisions about Novgorod. Indeed the republic had maintained virtual independence thanks largely to the timidity of Moscow and the lethargy of Lithuania. In 1340 Novgorod presented a picture of a state lacking the military strength and organization to defend itself from its neighbours and poised between the greedy, growing powers of Lithuania and Moscow. What the relative strength of the political factions within the republic was we cannot say. All we know is that Archbishop Vasily, after seven years of skilled diplomatic tacking between East and West, had shown himself latterly to be more flexible than at first and more amenable to suggestion from the ruler of Moscow. He was no longer the unbending enemy of Kalita who had succeeded the pro-Muscovite Moisey in 1331.

No sooner had Semen returned from the Horde in the autumn of 1340 than he showed the Novgorodians that he was made of sterner stuff than Ivan. He set about establishing his authority with a decisiveness and energy which no prince of Moscow before him had manifested. The reasons for the vigour with which he engaged upon his task, and for the urgency of the operation which is evident from the various accounts found in the chronicles, are not hard to discover. It was not just a question of restoring the status quo which had been broken by Ivan I's recall of his governors and by the Novgorodians' refusal to accede to his request for additional tribute in that it constituted a breach of contract and tradition:[2] Semen's campaign was an act of retaliation against the Novgorodians for their interference with the allies of Moscow and for their raid on the politically dangerous district of Beloozero.

In the spring of early summer of 1340, at a time when Semen and "all the princes" were at the Horde negotiating the transfer of the grand-princely *yarlyk*, a Novgorodian force, described by the local chronicles as *molodtsy*,[3] attacked the town of Ustyuzhna

---

[1] *See* above, p. 157.

[2] *See* above, pp. 156–7.

[3] The word is only used by the Novgorodian chroniclers and usually designates raiding parties sent unofficially from Novgorod to the northern districts. The Muscovite chroniclers as a rule use the terms *razboyniki* or

in the extreme south-western tip of the principality of Beloozero. The raid, which was carried out by boat along the Mologa river from Novgorod territory, was not a success. Having burned Ustyuzhna, the raiding party was caught, presumably by troops of the prince of Beloozero, and relieved of its prisoners and loot. However, before returning home they managed to despoil "the district of Beloozero".[1]

The whole business might be written off as simply another piratical raid by the Novgorodians: the very words used by the chronicler are those normally associated with *ushkuynik*, or river pirate, activities.[2] But Beloozero was not the traditional raiding area of the *ushkuyniki*[3] who were normally concerned with securing the territorial possessions of this or that group of boyars in the Zavoloch'e district or in exploring the eastern reaches of the Volga. More important still, Beloozero may have been chosen by Novgorod for purely political reasons. In 1339, as has been mentioned above,[4] Yaroslavl' and Beloozero chose to rebel against Moscow. The princes of both districts refused to go to the Horde when summoned to appear there together with Aleksandr of Tver', and one of them, Vasily of Yaroslavl', even resisted a party of Muscovites sent to arrest him. There can be little doubt that Yaroslavl' and Beloozero were part of an anti-Moscow bloc with Tver'; indeed it is not beyond the bounds of possibility that Novgorod herself, was part of the coalition: her contemporary chronicler carefully notes the summons of Vasily, links his name with that of Aleksandr of Tver' and mentions Kalita's despatch of 500 men against him; what is more, Nov-

---

ushkuyniki for these semi-piratical groups of raiders. (*See* Bernadsky, *Novgorod*, p. 39.)

[1] Probably the stretch of the Mologa river downstream from Ustyuzhna to the Novgorod territory of Bezhetsky Verkh. The whole operation is described in the First and Fourth Novgorod Chronicles. The Moscow *svod* of 1479 mentions only the attack on Ustyuzhna. The Trinity, Ermolinsky and Tver' Chronicles are silent. (*See* NL, p. 351; PSRL, iv (i), p. 267; xxv, p. 172.)

[2] The chronicler talks of *molodtsy*, "bold men", and *lodeyniki*, "troops in boats".

[3] *See* Bernadsky, *Novgorod*, p. 39, for a list of all their objectives between 1320 and 1409.

[4] *See* above, pp. 179–80.

gorod's breach with Moscow in 1339 is clearly associated in the chronicler's mind with the summons of the princes to the Horde.[1] But whereas Novgorod's breach with Moscow lasted beyond Ivan's death, that of the princes of Yaroslavl' and Beloozero did not. They were temporarily reconciled with Kalita by means of dynastic marriages.[2] Of the two re-alliances, only that between Beloozero and Moscow appears to have been more than super-ficial, for in the list of princes who on Kalita's death dared to dispute Semen's right to the throne we find only the name of Vasily of Yaroslavl' alongside those of the princes of Tver' and Suzdal'.[3] Roman of Beloozero, it would appear, had broken with the anti-Moscow forces or had refused to renew his association with them. The raid on Ustyuzhna by the Novgorodians may be considered as an act of retaliation against the backsliding prince of Beloozero for his loyalty to Moscow.[4]

The action which the newly-elected grand prince took against Novgorod was swift and effective. Shortly after his official en-thronement in Vladimir on 1 October 1340, he summoned a congress of "all the princes" in Moscow. The semi-independent rulers of Suzdalia, with the possible exception of the prince of Tver',[5] agreed to join Semen in an expedition against Novgorod. Even the dissident Vasily of Yaroslavl' and Konstantin of Suzdal' were obliged to take part in the campaign against what they must have considered to be a former member of their anti-Moscow coalition. In late 1340 or early 1341 Semen decided as a preliminary measure to secure Torzhok, the eastern outpost of the republic. He sent his boyars there to "collect tribute" and to establish control over the town. As governor of Torzhok he appointed the brother of the newly-reconciled Vasily of

[1] The embassy of the Novgorodians to Ivan in 1339 is mentioned in the same sentence as Vasily's skirmish with the Muscovites: ". . . and Vasily of Yaroslavl' [went to the Horde] against whom Prince Ivan . . . sent 500 men to arrest him, but he fought his way off, for Prince Ivan had already returned from the Horde (*uzhe bo byashe knyaz' Ivan . . .*), and the Novgorodians sent envoys to him" (*NL*, p. 350).

[2] *See* above, pp. 180–1.   [3] *See PSRL*, vii, p. 237.

[4] It is interesting to note that the Novgorod First Chronicle does *not* mention Roman's name in connection with the summoning of Vasily of Yaroslavl'. (*See* above, p. 180.)

[5] *See* above, p. 227.

Yaroslavl', Mikhail Davidovich. The boyars of Torzhok, however, were not prepared to submit to what amounted to virtual occupation by the Muscovites. They sent word to Novgorod asking for help. Novgorod sent a powerful army,[1] which burst into Torzhok unexpectedly, seized and killed the *namestnik* and began to strengthen the city in anticipation of a retaliatory attack by the Moscow army. At the same time a delegation was sent from Novgorod to reason with the grand prince. They accused him of arbitrary and brutal action: "You have not yet been crowned prince of Novgorod, yet your boyars are already acting vehemently."[2] Semen was spared the task of taking retaliatory measures on Torzhok. The local population did the job for him. Not less than a month after the arrival of the Novgorod army in Torzhok the commonalty (*chern'*) rose up in a rebellion, armed themselves, freed the Muscovites who had been jailed and forced the Novgorodians to leave the city. The discountenanced boyars of Torzhok just managed to escape, though one of their number was killed by the mob.

Soon after the coup Semen and his army, which consisted of "all the princes" of Suzdalia, arrived in Torzhok. The seriousness of his intentions was evident to all, for he demonstratively included in his headquarters Metropolitan Feognost himself, who twelve years earlier had been used by Ivan I in just such an expedition against the rebellious prince of Tver'. The arrival of the Suzdalian army at Torzhok was sufficient warning for the Novgorodians. They took the precautionary measure of barricading their city in case negotiations should break down and sent off to Semen a deputation headed by Archbishop Vasily and Avram, the very same official who had been sent by the Novgorodians with Archbishop Moisey to talk the Pskovites out of harbouring Aleksandr of Tver' in 1328.[3] The Novgorodian delegation was negotiating from a position of weakness: the combined army of the mesopotamian principalities, the presence in Torzhok of Moscow's most destructive weapon, the metropolitan, and the unreliability of the populace of Torzhok were clear proof of the power of Semen's position; furthermore, the

[1] The size and strength of the army can be gauged from the list of commanders given in the Novgorod First Chronicle. (*See NL*, г. 352.)

[2] Ibid.   [3] *See* above, p. 115; *NL*, pp. 94, 341, 353.

Lithuanians, notwithstanding a foothold which they maintained in the northern "patrimonies" of Narimunt, showed no inclination, as usual, to provide Novgorod with encouragement or help. In spite of these considerations the peace conditions which were agreed upon were not unduly severe on Novgorod; indeed the Novgorod chronicler even went so far as to say that they "concluded a treaty according to the old documents, to suit the will of Novgorod (*na vsei voli novgorodchkoi*) and they kissed the cross [in agreement]".[1] The grand prince was given the right to levy a tax on the various districts of Novgorod (*bor po volosti*) and was granted a fine of 1,000 rubles from the inhabitants of Torzhok. At the conclusion of the negotiations Semen sent his governors to Novgorod. Once again the republic came under Moscow's control.[2]

Although the terms of the peace treaty of 1340 were not unduly harsh on Novgorod, at any rate according to the chronicler of Novgorod, nevertheless Semen established his authority as firmly as was permitted by the "old documents", in other words the contracts drawn up in the thirteenth century between Novgorod and the grand princes of Vladimir. The traditional formulae of the treaties allowed of no arbitrary behaviour on the part of the prince or his *namestniki*, no undue accretion of power or territory within the lands of the republic. Still, Semen, without even so much as setting foot in the city before 1346, managed to maintain a stricter control over Novgorod than any of his predecessors had done. More important still from his and the khan's point of view, he managed, if not to diminish the popularity of Ol'gerd within Novgorod, then at least to keep him at arm's length.

[1] *NL*, p. 353. Note that the words *na vsei voli novgorodchkoi* were deliberately omitted in the Moscow *svod* of 1479 as well as the Ermolinsky Chronicle. (*See PSRL*, xxiii, p. 106; xxv, p. 173.)

[2] For the fullest account of the events of 1340-1, see *NL*, pp. 352-3. The accounts found in the Ermolinsky Chronicle and the Moscow *svod* of 1479 (*PSRL*, xxiii, pp. 105-6; xxv, pp. 172-3) are slightly different and shorter, though both clearly use the Novgorod First Chronicle, or a version close to it, as their main source. The Trinity and Rogozhsky Chronicles merely mention the *s'ezd* in Moscow, the composition of the army and its seizure of Torzhok (after the upheaval of the *chern'* presumably). (*See TL*, pp. 364-5; *PSRL*, xv (i), col. 53.)

He was helped at first by the formidable figure of Feognost. The metropolitan, who entered the city soon after the signing of the treaty, immediately made his presence felt. Both the archbishop and the monasteries were obliged at great expense to support him and his large retinue for as long as he stayed there—and he remained there for the best part of two years.[1] If Archbishop Vasily was at first inclined to resist his influence, he was soon to work with him in close co-operation, and even harmony, it seems.[2] Thanks to Feognost's presence in the city Semen's task of restoring confidence in Moscow was considerably lightened.

Semen's task in Novgorod, however, was complicated and confused not so much by opposition to Moscow among the ruling classes—indeed, during his reign Semen maintained the strongest grip on the republic of any grand prince since the beginning of the century—as by the internal struggle for power among the boyars themselves. The best example of the conflicting interests of the various power groups with which Semen's representatives had to cope (or which they were obliged merely to witness) is afforded by the events of the year 1342. At the same time the reaction of "official" Novgorod to the affairs of Pskov in that year illustrates the strength of pro-Muscovite feeling in Novgorod during Semen's overlordship.

Ever since the crisis of 1333 and the re-establishment of Muscovite "control" in 1334 and 1335[3] the office of *posadnik* seems to

---

[1] He arrived in Novgorod in the beginning of 1341 (*NL*, p. 353) and was evidently still there at the end of 1342: Luka Varfolomeevich undertook his Zavoloch'e campaign "without the blessing of the metropolitan and the archbishop" (*NL*, p. 355)—i.e. they refused to sanction it. However, Feognost evidently went to the Horde in 1342 to pay his respects to Jani-Beg (*see TL*, p. 365; *PSRL*, x, p. 215).

[2] In 1341 the young Mikhail Aleksandrovich of Tver' was sent to Novgorod to be taught by his godfather Archbishop Vasily. In the spring of 1342, however, we find Vasily laying the foundation stone of a church on the site of the old Church of the Annunciation "which had been pulled down on the orders of Grand Prince Semen Ivanovich"; at the same time he orders a bell to be cast for St. Sofia and sends for a master-founder from Moscow. (*See NL*, p. 354.) As mentioned above, Feognost and Vasily jointly withheld their blessing from Luka's expedition in 1342.

[3] *See* above, pp. 142 sq.

have been confined to representatives of the two *kontsy* which constituted the eastern or "Trade" half of the city (*Torgovaya storona*)—the *Plotnitsky konets* and the *Slavensky konets*. From 1334 to 1342 there is no evidence to show that representatives of either the *Prusskaya ulitsa* or the *Nerevsky konets*, the two administrative divisions comprising the Cathedral Side (*Sofiyskaya storona*) of the city, ever became *posadnik*.[1] In 1340 Evstafy Dvoryaninets, the representative of the *Plotnitsky konets*, was *posadnik*; he was re-elected in 1341. In 1342 Fedor Danilovich, who represented the *Slavensky konets* from 1335 to 1350 and who had held the office of *posadnik* at least four times since 1335, was elected.[2] The events of 1342 can only be understood if considered in the light of the rivalry between the two halves of the city.

On 25 October 1342 Varfolomey Yur'evich Mishinich, the boyar representative of the *Nerevsky konets* since 1316 and many times *posadnik*, died. The Mishinichi, who had long been connected with the *Nerevsky konets* on the Cathedral Side, were one of the most powerful and wealthy boyar families in Novgorod. Twice during the rule of Ivan I, in early 1332 and in 1335,[3] the city had been on the verge of civil war between the Cathedral and Trade Sides, on both of which occasions the disputes are as clearly attributable to anti-Moscow or anti-Lithuania feeling among the ruling élite as to inter-boyar rivalry or discontent with economic conditions; and in both cases we may assume that Varfolomey and his family played a large role. It was his death, however, which sparked off the great disturbance of 1342. Once again the city was split into two seemingly irreconcilable factions. Immediately after his death his son Luka and grandson Ontsifor set off with an army to the Zavoloch'e region—the basin of the Northern Dvina river. What exactly the purpose of this expedition was is not stated in the only source to describe it, the Novgorod First Chronicle.[4] Certain historians consider that the main aim of the venture was to consolidate the possessions of the Mishinichi in Novgorod's northern "empire" or to combat independence

[1] *See* Yanin, *NP*, pp. 184–5.   [2] *See* ibid.
[3] *See* above, pp. 141, 150–1.
[4] *NL*, pp. 355–6. The story is reproduced in the Novgorod Fourth Chronicle. (*See PSRL*, iv (i), pp. 271–2.)

and separatist strivings among the local Dvinian *boyarstvo*.[1]
It seems more likely, however, that the purpose of the expedition
was rather to acquire possessions in the Dvina land or to seize
possessions there which were already owned by the Novgorodians and thus to strengthen the faction of the Mishinichi and their
supporters in Novgorod at the expense of their rivals. In the first
place, the activities of Luka and his son were clearly predatory
rather than consolidatory: Luka established the fortress of Orlets
on the Dvina;[2] from here he proceeded to range along the Dvina
river with a detachment of local inhabitants, which he had
recruited from the Emtsa river district, and seized the settlements
in the Dvina basin; his son Ontsifor meanwhile continued his
father's work along the Vaga river.[3] In the second place, the
campaign was carried out against the wishes of official Novgorod:
he left, remarks the chronicler, "disobeying (*ne poslushav*) Novgorod and [not having obtained] the blessing of the metropolitan
and the archbishop".[4] It was not only an act of defiance directed
against the representatives of Moscow in Novgorod but also a
challenge to the rivals of the Mishinichi on the other side of the
Volkhov river—the current *posadnik*, Fedor Danilovich, and
Evstafy Dvoryaninets of the *Plotnitsky konets*.

The essentially parochial nature of the conflict is illustrated
still better by subsequent events. Luka was killed in a skirmish
with the local inhabitants of the Dvina region—he was imprudent
enough to attempt further conquests with a band of only 200 men.
The news soon reached Novgorod, sped no doubt by Ontsifor,
and led to what the chronicler describes as a spontaneous uprising of the "black people" (*chornyi lyudi*) against the current
posadnik Fedor Danilovich. Fedor and his supporters—the name

[1] *See*, for instance, Bernadsky, *Novgorod*, pp. 17, 52; Rozhdestvensky,
"Dvinskie boyare", pp. 60–1. For the origins of the local boyars, *see* Rozhdestvensky, op. cit., pp. 56 sq.

[2] Note that Orlets became by the end of the century the chief Novgorod
administrative centre in the Dvina district. When the Novgorodians
attempted to capture it from the local boyars in 1397, it took them a whole
month and a number of siege-guns. (*See* Rozhdestvensky, op. cit., p. 50.)

[3] *See* NL, p. 355. One reading has "Volga"—clearly a misreading of
"Vaga", the western tributary of the Northern Dvina. The Emtsa is a
tributary of the Northern Dvina.

[4] NL, p. 355.

of one "Ondreshka", known to be connected with the *Plotnitsky konets*,[1] is linked with that of Fedor—were responsible for Luka's death: "They had sent men to kill Luka," claimed the rebellious mob.[2] Their houses and estates were plundered. To save their lives they were forced to flee to the provincial town of Kopor'e, one of the northern outposts which had been granted to Narimunt in 1333[3] and which, even after his enforced departure in 1335, still probably retained a Lithuanian garrison.[4] Although the chronicler makes no mention of the fact, it would appear that on Fedor's flight the office of *posadnik* was transferred to the only representative of the opposite Side of the river, the Cathedral Side (*Sofiyskaya storona*), namely the permanent delegate of the *Prusskaya ulitsa*, Matfey Koska.[5] When Ontsifor returned from his Dvina-Vaga campaign in the spring of 1343 he lodged a complaint against Fedor Danilovich and his accomplice, as a result of which they were brought back to Novgorod by an official delegation to answer the charges. They denied all complicity in the death of Luka. Once again the city was split into two. The two representatives of the Cathedral Side, Ontsifor and Matfey Koska,[6] summoned a *veche* "by St. Sofia"; their opponents, Fedor Danilovich and Ondreshka, summoned one on the other side of the Volkhov river "at the court of Yaroslav". At first an attempt was made to negotiate. Ontsifor and Matfey sent Archbishop Vasily to discuss matters with their opponents. But before he could cross the Volkhov with Fedor's reply, they decided to settle the matter by force of arms. They attacked the opposing *veche*. The assault, however, was a failure: Matfey and

[1] In 1329 "Ondreshka's house in Plotniki" burned. (*See NL*, p. 342.)

[2] *See NL*, pp. 355–6.

[3] *See* above, p. 131. Only half of Kopor'e was granted to Narimunt.

[4] The Soviet historian Bernadsky is of the opinion that Kopor'e "nourished" the descendants of Gedimin up to the days of Lugven', Ol'gerd's son, and that in the early fifteenth century it even served as a residence for the Gediminovichi. (*See* Bernadsky, *Novgorod*, p. 121.)

[5] Ontsifor Lukinich, who after the death of his father Luka had replaced his grandfather Varfolomey as representative of the *Nerevsky konets*, was still in the Zavoloch'e district.

[6] Matfey Varfolomeevich Koska, in spite of his patronymic, was probably not the brother of Luka Varfolomeevich Mishinich, as Yanin has convincingly shown. (*See* Yanin, *NP*, p. 181.) *Cf.*, however, Bernadsky, *Novgorod*, p. 17, note 6.

his son were arrested and locked up in a church; Ontsifor and his supporters fled the city. Novgorod was on the brink of civil war. Only the intervention of the archbishop and Semen's governor, one Boris, averted further fighting. The quarrel between the two most powerful groups of boyars and their supporters, the Mishinichi and Matfey Koska on the one hand and Fedor Danilovich and the boyars of the *Plotnitsky konets* on the other, a quarrel which once more resolved itself in a clash between the two halves of the city, had come to an inconclusive end.

Once again it must be stressed that the events of 1342–3 in Novgorod and the Zavoloch'e district had little or no connection with the major conflict between Moscow and Lithuania. True, there is some evidence to show that Fedor Danilovich and Evstafy Dvoryaninets, the representatives of the *Plotnitsky konets*, were inclined to support Moscow or at any rate to oppose an increase of Lithuanian influence in Novgorod—Evstafy indeed is reported publicly to have called Ol'gerd a "dog"[1]—and that Matfey Koska and the Mishinichi were opposed to Muscovite control.[2] Yet there is as much evidence to confound this view: after all, Fedor Danilovich chose to flee to Kopor'e, half of which, if it was not a residence of the Gediminovichi, at least contained a Lithuanian garrison; and Matfey Koska's predecessor as representative of the *Prusskaya ulitsa*, Fedor Akhmyl, was in all probability a strong supporter of Moscow.[3] At the same time the contemporary chronicler, who is moved to such righteous indignation at the treachery of the Pskovites in 1342 ("They surrendered to Lithuania, having rejected Novgorod and the grand prince"),[4] goes out of his way to pay tribute to the "servant of God" Varfolomey Mishinich and sympathetically—or at least

---

[1] *See NL,* p. 358.

[2] On the eve of the clash with Lithuania the office of *posadnik* was taken from Evstafy and given to Matfey (1345) (*see* ibid.). The Zavoloch'e expedition of the Mishinichi in 1342 was carried out in defiance of the *namestnik* of Semen.

[3] *See* above, p. 139.

[4] *NL,* p. 354. That the chronicler wrote at the same time as the events he described is shown, *inter alia,* by the invocation to God: "grant him (Archbishop Vasily) many years of life in this age . . ." under 1343. *Cf.* also the similar apostrophe under 1333. *See NL,* pp. 357, 345.

not hostilely—to report on the northern expedition of his son and grandson. The struggle, then, was not one between supporters of Moscow and Lithuania within the republic; it was between boyar groups fighting for power amongst themselves. Accordingly, the role of Semen's governor was one of gendarme, adjudicator and military defender. There was little he could do but witness the squabbles of the various factions and attempt to maintain a semblance of peace. Indeed there was little he need do so long as there was no sign of a pro-Lithuanian movement from within Novgorod or a Lithuanian threat from without.

Of course this does not mean that there was no opposition within Novgorod to the authority of the prince of Moscow. There was; but it was successfully held in check by Semen and his representatives in Novgorod during his reign. At the same time Semen's "rule" within the republic became perceptibly more popular than that of his father. Indeed, the strength of pro-Muscovite feeling in Novgorod as early as 1342 can be seen by the reaction of the city to the events in Pskov in that year.

During most of the reign of Ivan I Pskov had lain within the Lithuanian sphere of influence: from 1331 to 1337 Aleksandr Mikhaylovich of Tver' had ruled Pskov with the unconcealed support of his ally and relative by marriage Grand Prince Gedimin. In 1337, it will be remembered,[1] Archbishop Vasily of Novgorod had attempted to stop Aleksandr from quitting Pskov and as a result of his failure had broken off relations between the two republics. What happened immediately after Aleksandr's departure is not known: the chronicles make no mention of Pskov–Novgorod relations during the years 1337 and 1342; we do not know who replaced Aleksandr as prince—a representative of Lithuania or Moscow—nor do we know if and when the excommunication imposed by Archbishop Vasily in 1337 was removed. All we know is that in 1341 Pskov had as prince, that is to say as military defender of the district, one Aleksandr Vsevolodovich of unknown origin and unknown political affiliations.[2] It can be assumed, however, that he was

[1] *See* above, p. 160.
[2] He is only mentioned by the Pskov and Novgorod chronicles, and merely as "Prince Aleksandr Vsevolodovich". It is hard to see which Suzdalian princely family he could have belonged to, as there are no known

connected with Novgorod, and perhaps Moscow, rather than
with Lithuania, for in 1341, when he parted company with the
Pskovites, he proceeded to Novgorod.[1] It would seem, therefore,
most probable that Semen, in subjecting Novgorod to his power
in 1341, extended his control to the sister-republic of Pskov.

Whatever control Moscow or Novgorod exercised over
Pskov in the early months of Semen's reign, it was weak. Furthermore, as the events of 1341–2 show, it was opposed by the pro-
Lithuanian elements within the city. The crisis was precipitated,
as was so often the case with Pskov in the thirteenth and fourteenth centuries, by the aggressive behaviour of the Germans
on her western frontiers. After leading a retaliatory expedition
into the teritory of the Order in December 1341, Prince Aleksandr
"became angry with the Pskovites and fled from Pskov".[2]
The Pskovite chronicler makes no mention of the reason for his
dissatisfaction, but it seems likely that it was caused by political
friction, perhaps even by the opposition of the pro-Lithuanian
party in Pskov to Aleksandr's leadership in the war with the
Germans. But Pskov could not afford to be without a prince.
Like Novgorod she was unable to defend her frontiers against
foreign aggression without the support of a professional commander and a trained army of mercenaries. Consequently the
Pskovites, or at any rate the pro-Muscovite elements among
them, begged Aleksandr to return, and when their pleas failed,
they begged the Novgorodians to send a governor (*namestnik*)
and military aid.[3]

Characteristically, the Novgorodian and the Pskovite chroniclers give very different pictures of the reaction of Novgorod
to Pskov's plea for help. The chronicler of Pskov, anxious to
justify the subsequent reversal of policy and the attempt to seek
aid directly from Lithuania, merely states that the Novgorodians

---

Vsevolods who could have been his father and no Aleksandr Vsevolo-
doviches among the known Ryurikovichi in the fourteenth century.

[1] *See PL*, ii, p. 93. He first went south to the monastery of St. Panteleymon
at the confluence of the Cherekha and Velikaya rivers near Pskov, and thence
to Novgorod.

[2] *PL*, ii, p. 93.

[3] *See* ibid. *Cf. PL*, i, p. 18 (the Pskov First Chronicle), where the mission
to St. Panteleymon is not mentioned, only the plea to Novgorod.

refused to send either a governor or an army.[1] The chronicler of
Novgorod, on the other hand, desirous in his newly-found zeal
for all things Muscovite of stressing the heinousness of Pskov's
later treachery, gives a very different account of events. In
response to the Pskovites' plea for help, the Novgorodians
"delaying not, set off with speed, on Good Friday (29 March
1342) . . ." When they arrived at the village of Meletevo in
Pskov territory, they were met by ambassadors from Pskov,
who told them that there was no need for the Novgorodians to
continue their march as the Germans were not after all invading
but merely building a fortress on their side of the frontier.[2]
In spite of the Novgorodians' willingness to lend their military
support to Pskov, they agreed to accept the assurances of the
Pskovite ambassadors and to return home.[3]

Unfortunately there is no outside corroborative evidence to
show which of the sources is correct. The later Muscovite
chronicles make no mention of the earlier negotiations; they
merely echo the Novgorod chronicler's "the Pskovites . . .
rejected Novgorod and the grand prince."[4] However, from the
considerable detail with which the chronicler of Novgorod
described the expedition to aid Pskov, it seems more likely that
the Novgorodian version is correct and that the Pskovites in fact
rejected Novgorodian assistance as the result of an abrupt change
of policy; we can assume that the party which opposed Aleksandr Vsevolodovich in the first place gained power and took
over as the Novgorod army entered Pskov territory. Indeed it
would appear most improbable that the authorities in Novgorod
—and these of course included the Muscovite *namestnik*—would
have rejected out of hand Pskov's cry for help against the
Germans. A refusal could only mean that the door was open to the
Lithuanians.

Whatever the attitude of Novgorod to Pskov's request for

[1] See PL, i, p. 18; ii, p. 93.
[2] The Pskov Chronicle, after mentioning the Novgorodians' refusal to
help, states that "the Germans that winter came with all their army and
erected Novy gorodok on the Pivzha river in Pskov territory" (PL, i, p. 18;
PL, ii, pp. 24, 93). This was Novgorodok or Neuhausen (Estonian Vatse-
liina) on the Pizhma river, and *outside* Pskov territory at the time.
[3] See NL, p. 354.   [4] See PSRL, xxv, pp. 173–4; cf. xxiii, p. 106.

military assistance may have been, the outcome was a brusque reversal of Pskov policy. An embassy was sent to Ol'gerd, then not yet grand prince of Lithuania, in Vitebsk. "Our brothers the Novgorodians have turned us down," said the envoys; "help us, O master, at this time."[1] The response of the Lithuanians was for once swift and decisive. Sensing an opportunity to make good his losses sustained in the futile attempt to recapture Mozhaysk from the Muscovites in the previous year[2] and to gain a foothold in Pskov, Ol'gerd hastened to come to the aid of the republic, even though it meant a breach of the treaty which had been concluded between Lithuania and the Order in 1338.[3] His first action was to send a military commander, one Yury Vitovtovich, to take charge of the defences of Pskov and to conduct her war with the Germans until he could arrive in person. On 20 July 1342 he presented himself in Pskov. With him came not only Lithuanian troops—probably from Krevo, over which he had been appointed ruler in his father's will—and Ruthenian troops from Vitebsk, but also his brother and ally, Keystut, prince of Troki and Grodno, and his son Andrey.[4]

It was a formidably large army to deal with a situation which by mid-summer 1342 had clearly lost much of its gravity for the Pskovites,[5] and its purpose was purely political. As was so

[1] PL, ii, p. 93; cf. p. 24 and PL, i, p. 18 ("O master, Grand Prince Ol'gerd"). These three versions, the Third, Second and First Pskov Chronicles respectively, are much the same and are repeated in the Moscow svod of 1479 (with the significant addition "they lied against Novgorod") and in the Ermolinsky Chronicle. (See PSRL, xxv, p. 174; xxiii, p. 106.)

[2] On 1 October 1341 Ol'gerd attacked Mozhaysk and burned the posad, but was unable to capture the town. (See TL, p. 365.)

[3] See above, p. 155.

[4] At Gedimin's death his eldest son Evnuty had succeeded him as grand prince with his seat at Vil'na. Ol'gerd received Krevo and perhaps Polotsk (whence Narimunt appears to have been moved to Pinsk) and/or Vitebsk, though the latter may merely have been his headquarters in 1342. Keystut, with whom Ol'gerd may have concluded a treaty of alliance (against Evnuty and Narimunt?), received Troki, Grodno and perhaps Żmudź (Zhemaytia). (See Paszkiewicz, Jagiellonowie, pp. 359 sq., 379.)

[5] During the early summer months of 1342 the Pskovites appear to have coped quite easily with the Germans and even undertook successful campaigns in Livonian territory. The details of the fighting (April–June) are only given in the Pskov Third Chronicle. (See PL, ii, pp. 93–5.)

frequently the case with Lithuanian assistance to the opponents of Moscow throughout the fourteenth and fifteenth centuries, remarkably little seems to have been done to take full advantage of the situation and firmly to establish Lithuanian authority in Pskov. Military assistance was derisory: Ol'gerd dispatched his *voevoda*, Yury Vitovtovich, with an army to capture a prisoner from the newly-erected fortress of Novgorodok (Neuhausen) on the Pizhma; but Yury's army was defeated by the Germans, who proceeded to cross the frontier and lay siege to the second largest town in the district of Pskov, Izborsk. Unaware of Yury's defeat and the siege of Izborsk, Ol'gerd and Keystut demonstratively ordered their army, now consisting of "Lithuanians, Vidblyane (men of Vitebsk) and Pskovites" to cross the Velikaya river. But when they learned from a prisoner of the "great German force besieging the town of Izborsk", they gave orders to the main army swiftly to retrace its steps, recross the Velikaya and return to Pskov. The Pskovites were only too keen to accompany the Lithuanians, for as the Pskovite chronicler remarked, "they were anxious to protect their houses, wives and children from the Lithuanians." True, Ol'gerd and Keystut remained behind with a small part of the army; but after one of the Lithuanian commanders, Lyubko the son of Prince Voin of Polotsk, had been killed in a skirmish with the Germans, they decided that discretion was the better part of valour and, leaving Izborsk to cope with the siege by itself, returned to Pskov.[1]

The true nature of the mission of Ol'gerd and Keystut to Pskov became evident only after their return to the republic later in 1342. Negotiations between the Lithuanians and Pskov began in earnest. The Pskovites insisted that Ol'gerd, if he wished to become their prince and protector, accept baptism: a heathen ruler was unthinkable. But Ol'gerd prevaricated. As a Christian, his position in the struggle for power within pagan Lithuania would be considerably weakened, and he would need all the support he could get from the other Lithuanian princes to oust his elder brother Evnuty from Vil'na. A compromise was reached. He

[1] See *PL*, i, p. 19; ii, pp. 24-5, 95-6; *NL*, pp. 354-5. The Germans themselves raised the siege of Izborsk after ten days (five according to the Pskov Third Chronicle; eleven according to the Novgorod First Chronicle).

allowed his son Andrey to be baptized and to be nominated prince of Pskov.

Even with Andrey as prince of Pskov, the position of the Lithuanians in the republic might have been unassailable. Yet Ol'gerd and his son and brother went out of their way, it seems, to forfeit their advantage, as had so often happened in the past and was so often to happen in the future. Ol'gerd and Keystut withdrew from Pskov—perhaps in order to conduct a new campaign against the Livonian Order in a different sector[1]— and in so doing behaved in a manner calculated to distress and enrage the Pskovites: "They left with their Lithuanians and Vidblyane and destroyed the corn around the [Church of] the Holy Trinity (the cathedral church of Pskov) in the district of Pskov and also destroyed both grass and ploughland."[2] If this was not enough, Andrey soon quarrelled with the Pskovites, quit the republic and went home to his father.[3] There was nothing for it for Pskov but to return to the fold of Novgorod-Moscow; "The Pskovites, seeing that there was no help from any side . . . made peace with Novgorod."[4]

It must not be imagined that the breach with Lithuania was drastic or final. It was not. Nor did it mean that a state of war existed between the two. In fact Lithuania, even after the departure of Andrey, retained considerable control over Pskov: Prince Yury Vitovtovich still remained *voevoda*, and, to judge from the grief of the Pskovites at his death in 1348, enjoyed a rare degree of popularity;[5] furthermore, Andrey Ol'gerdovich had by no means left without a trace: as the Pskovites later complained, he still "ruled" Pskov from Lithuanian territory by means of governors (*namestniki*), a fact which considerably riled the Pskovites. Indeed the breach with Lithuania only occurred in

[1] According to the German chronicle of Wigand, "King Keystut and his brother Ol'gerd (*rex Kynstut cum fratre Algarto*) led three armies across the Dvina" in late 1342 or 1343. (*See* Paszkiewicz, *Jagiellonowie*, p. 370, note 4.)

[2] *PL*, ii, p. 96.

[3] This is only mentioned in the Pskov Second Chronicle. (*See PL*, ii, p. 25.)

[4] Only in the Pskov Third Chronicle. (*See PL*, ii, pp. 96–7.)

[5] He was killed defending Izborsk from the Germans in April 1349: "and there was great sorrow and grief in Pskov at that time; and all the clergy were present at his funeral and he was buried in the Cathedral of the Holy Trinity." (*PL*, ii, p. 99.)

1349 when after the death of the Lithuanian *voevoda*, Yury Vitov-tovich, the Pskovites broke finally with Ol'gerd and his son.[1] Nevertheless, in spite of the continued presence of Lithuanian officials and a Lithuanian defence-force in Pskov the reconcilia-tion between Novgorod and Pskov in the early spring of 1343 must be considered a success, if not a triumph, for Novgorod and the Muscovite authorities in Novgorod. There can be no doubt that Muscovite and Novgorodian officials were hard at work since the summer of 1342 persuading Pskov to renounce her Lithuanian alliance.

It was suggested above that there was little that Semen's repre-sentatives in Novgorod could do apart from attempting to keep the peace between the various squabbling factions, and little they need do so long as there was no threat from Lithuanian supporters within Novgorod or from the Lithuanians themselves. In the years which followed the internal upheavals of 1342, nothing happened to lessen the popularity of Semen's rule; but the Lithuanians themselves, or rather Ol'gerd and his brother Key-stut, by switching their attention from Pskov to Novgorod, forced Semen and his governor to tighten what can only be called their very loose control over the republic.

As prince of Krevo (and Vitebsk or Polotsk),[2] Ol'gerd was not in a position to do more than attempt to defend Pskov against the Order, and that on the insistence of the Pskovites themselves. To interfere with Novgorod at this stage would have meant involvement on an international scale with the grand prince of Vladimir. This he could hardly undertake without the power of all Lithuania behind him. In the winter of 1344–5, however, Ol'gerd and Keystut overthrew their brother, Grand Prince Evnuty, who fled via Smolensk to Moscow. At the same time yet another brother, Narimunt, the ally of Evnuty, fled to the Horde.[3] Ol'gerd established himself as grand prince of Lithuania.

[1] Ol'gerd's "dissatisfaction" with Pskov had started earlier, in 1346, when his troops, returning from a raid on Novgorod territory, suffered consider-able losses as they passed through the land of Pskov. (*See* ibid.)

[2] *See* above, p. 256, note 4.

[3] *See* NL, p. 358; *PSRL*, iv (i), p. 275; v, p. 224; xvii, cols. 71, 142–3, 153–4; xxiii, p. 107; xxv, p. 175. As for the dating (winter 1344–5), *see*

His surviving brothers, Keystut of Troki and Grodno, Koriad of Nowogródek and Black Rus', and Lyubart of Vladimir in Volyn', all appear to have given him support and to have recognized his suzerainty.[1] He was now in a position to extend his activities farther east, to Novgorod.

The first evidence of Lithuanian aggression against the territory of Novgorod is not found in the sources until 1346. But there are indications that Ol'gerd indulged in sabre-rattling as soon as he occupied Vil'na. In 1345 there was evidently yet another upheaval involving the two "Sides" of Novgorod and the boyar-contestants for the office of *posadnik*. The Novgorod First Chronicle merely reports that "they took the *posadnichestvo* from Ostafy (Evstafy) Dvoryaninets and gave it to Matfey Valfromeevich (Matfey Varfolomeevich Koska)." This might well imply a routine annual hand-over of the post from the representative of one *konets* to that of another, were it not for the words "and thanks to the grace of God there was no fighting (*likho*) between them" which were added to the entry.[2] If we take into consideration the fact that Ol'gerd motivated his invasion of Novgorod in the following year with an accusation against Evstafy Dvoryaninets ("He abused me (*layal mi*), called me a dog"), it will be clear that the transfer of the *posadnichestvo* was no routine matter but an emergency measure to avoid an imminent invasion.

The removal of the offending and offensive *posadnik* from the scene, however, was not enough. The archbishop and Semen's governor considered that the appointment of the less virulently anti-Lithuanian Matfey Koska was not sufficient in itself to avert an invasion. Threats could only be countered effectively by a show of strength in Novgorod itself. Consequently, towards the end of 1345 Archbishop Vasily set off to Moscow to request the

Paszkiewicz, *Jagiellonowie*, pp. 371–2; Berezhkov, *Khronologiya*, pp. 297, 345, note 25.

[1] Keystut's alliance with Ol'gerd is evident from his co-operation with him during the 1340's. Paszkiewicz thinks that Lyubart and Keystut formed an alliance before 1345 (*see Jagiellonowie*, p. 371). As for Koriad, he was sent by Ol'gerd to the Horde in 1348 (*see* above, pp. 198–9). Evnuty was baptized in Moscow (*see* TL, p. 367), but returned to Lithuania in 1347; Ol'gerd gave him the district of Zasław. (*See* PSRL, xvii, cols. 72, 143, 153–4.)

[2] *See* NL, p. 358; *cf.* PSRL, iv (i), p. 275.

grand prince to put in a personal appearance in the republic. He was received with great ceremony and an outward display of respect by the metropolitan, whose presence in Novgorod four years previously had caused such distress to the local clergy. Feognost not only gave him his blessing, but also bestowed upon him the right to wear a chasuble decorated with crosses ("*krestchatye rizy*"), which in all probability symbolized a measure of ecclesiastical autonomy and a degree of independence from the metropolitan.[1] On 5 March 1346 Semen himself arrived in Novgorod where at last he was solemnly enthroned.[2]

What exactly Semen did in Novgorod apart from having himself duly placed on the throne of Novgorod is not known. Tatishchev, the eighteenth-century Russian historian, talks of his popularity with the populace ("*a smerd' vsya ego lyublyashe*") and of his interference with the authority of the *posadnik* ("he removed much power from the *posadnik*").[3] Little credence, however, should be given to Tatishchev's unsubstantiated statements.[4] Semen came to Novgorod not so much to tighten his grip on the republic as to serve as a warning to the Lithuanians. His visit was of no avail. After three weeks he was obliged to return "to the Lower lands on the khan's business (*o tsesareve orud'i*)":[5] the sudden news of an imminent civil war in Tver', a war from which he could hope to reap immense benefits for the principality of

[1] See *NL*, p. 358; *PSRL*, iv (i), p. 276 (*not* in v, xxiii or xxv). That the right to wear the "chasuble with crosses" implied a degree of independence is evident from the fact that the patriarch permitted Vasily's successor Moisey to wear it, but obliged his (Moisey's) successor Aleksey to remove the crosses and to submit to the metropolitan. (*See* Sedel'nikov, "Vasilij Kalika", pp. 236–7; *cf.* Kartashev, *Ocherki*, vol. i, pp. 306–7.)

[2] See *NL*, p. 358. *Cf. PSRL*, v, p. 225; xxiii, p. 108; xxv, p. 176, in all of which the entry concerning Semen's enthronement in Novgorod is found *after* the description of Ol'gerd's invasion. Note that the Novgorod Fourth Chronicle makes no mention of Semen's visit to Novgorod; it merely mentions his summoning and the presentation of the "chasuble with crosses" to Vasily. For the dating of Semen's enthronement, *see* Berezhkov, *Khronologiya*, p. 297.

[3] See Tatishchev, *Istoriya*, vol. v, p. 99.

[4] *Cf.* his equally extravagant assertion that in 1340 Semen demanded that the Novgorod peace envoys appear before all the princes barefooted and on their knees. (*See* Tatishchev, *Istoriya*, vol. v, pp. 94–5.)

[5] *NL*, p. 358.

Moscow, seemed at the time more important than the possible threat of invasion in the west.[1]

The departure of Semen from Novgorod in 1346 acted, as it were, as a signal for the Lithuanians to invade. Ol'gerd, at the head of a large Lithuanian army consisting, according to the Novgorod First Chronicle, of "his brothers the princes and all the Lithuanian land",[2] marched along the Shelon' river as far as the mouth of the Pshaga. From there he sent his challenge to Novgorod: "I intend to fight you, to war on (or "take—*voevati*") your town and provinces."[3] As mentioned above, he stated that the reason for his aggression was the insulting behaviour of the ex-*posadnik*, Evstafy Dvoryaninets. Ol'gerd then proceeded to carry out his threat: one force overran the district on either side of the Shelon' as far as Golino (just west of Lake Il'men'); another moved along the basin of the Luga river to Sabel'sky Pogost at the southernmost bend of the river. Novgorod was within striking distance of the Lithuanian armies.

Why at this juncture Ol'gerd did not attempt to seize Novgorod is a mystery to which the chronicles offer no clues whatsoever. All we know is that the Novgorodians sent off an army to deal with the Lithuanian force on the Luga and that this army returned from its mission—"at the run", says the Nikon Chronicle[4]— having neither contacted the enemy nor achieved anything. When they reached Novgorod, a *veche* was summoned on the Trade Side ("at the Court of Yaroslav by the Church of St. Nicholas"[5]), at which it was decided to put Evstafy Dvoryaninets to death. "Because of you," he was told, "they have seized our province."[6]

---

[1] In 1346 Vsevolod Aleksandrovich of Tver' went to Moscow to complain to the grand prince of Konstantin Mikhaylovich's behaviour. This was evidently the reason for Semen's departure from Novgorod. (*See* above, p. 229.)

[2] *NL*, p. 358. Other chronicles (Sofiysky First, Ermolinsky, Moscow *svod* of 1479 and Nikon) all say that Keystut went with him. (*See PSRL*, v, p. 225; x, p. 217; xxiii, p. 108; xxv, p. 175.)

[3] *PSRL*, xxv, p. 175. The Novgorod First Chronicle is a little shorter and instead of "fight you (*s vami bitisya*)" has "see you (*s vami videtisya*)".

[4] *See PSRL*, x, p. 217. The other chronicles merely state that they returned to the city.

[5] *PSRL*, v, p. 225; xxv, p. 176.

[6] "*V tobe volost' nashyu vz yasha*". (*NL*, p. 358.)

No further fighting is reported. The Lithuanian army returned home with a large amount of loot and many prisoners,[1] opposed only by elements of the population of Pskov, in whose district, so Ol'gerd later complained, "many of my men and horses perished".[2] Shortly afterwards peace was made between Novgorod and Lithuania.[3]

As is so often the case, all the chronicle accounts of the invasion of Ol'gerd are incomplete: not one contains all the known facts.[4] The most incomplete, strange to say, is the version of the contemporary Novgorod First Chronicle, where one might expect to find the fullest account. The omissions, however, are by no means tendentious omissions, merely minor facts which increase the verisimilitude of the other accounts and add a certain amount of detail to the known facts of the case. From this, then, one may assume that a fuller version, or versions, originally existed, from which later compilers of other *svody* and chronicles borrowed information, but that the editor of the Novgorod First Chronicle decided then, or at a later date, to excise parts of his account for reasons of local pride or simply political tact. What else apart from the details found in other accounts was removed from the original version by the editor of the Novgorod First Chronicle we cannot tell, and we are left with a series of unanswered questions.

The most important of these questions is: why did the Lithuanian army decide to withdraw from the Novgorod theatre when it did? If we assume that the invasion was a serious one and that its aim was nothing less than the capture and occupation

---

[1] See *PSRL*, x, p. 217, the only source to mention the withdrawal of the Lithuanian expedition.

[2] See *PL*, i, p. 21; *PL*, ii, p. 99.

[3] The only source to mention the peace is the Novgorod Fourth Chronicle. (See *PSRL*, iv (i), p. 276.)

[4] The fullest version is that found in the Moscow *svod* of 1479 (and also in the Sofiysky First Chronicle), but it lacks certain information found in: the Novgorod Fourth Chronicle (the treaty between Novgorod and Lithuania); the Nikon Chronicle (the return of Ol'gerd and Keystut to Lithuania); the Pskov chronicles (Lithuanian losses on the way back through Pskov territory). The Ermolinsky Chronicle account is slightly shorter, though much the same as the Moscow *svod*. The Novgorod Fourth Chronicle is close to the Novgorod First Chronicle, but has certain additions.

of Novgorod,[1] then there must have been some serious reason for Ol'gerd's decision not to attack Novgorod when his armies were as near the city as Golino and Sabel'sky Pogost. Was it because of a threat in the rear from the Livonian Order or the Pskovites, through whose territory the Lithuanians would have to withdraw? Possibly yes; but there is no indication of any hostilities between the Germans and the Lithuanians before the battle on the Strava in early 1348, nor were the Pskovites, who were still nominally under Lithuanian control, likely to cause Ol'gerd any more than annoyance, certainly not alarm. Was it because of the strength of the defences of Novgorod, stiffened by a contingent of troops from Moscow which had been brought to the republic earlier in the year by Semen? If it was, the Moscow chronicles would probably have mentioned this as their share in the repelling of a Lithuanian invasion. Was perhaps a compromise reached between the *posadnik*, the Muscovite governor and the archbishop on the one hand and Ol'gerd on the other, when the Novgorodians marched out to meet the Lithuanians on the Luga? The subsequent execution of Evstafy Dvoryaninets might be an indication of the readiness of the Novgorodians to satisfy some at any rate of the Lithuanian demands; but we must be on our guard against inferring that the removal of one man was sufficient to satisfy Ol'gerd or that the expedition was merely an act of private revenge for the insults allegedly hurled at Ol'gerd by Evstafy.

While it is not unreasonable to suppose that all the above-mentioned hypothetical factors may have contributed collectively to the reasons for Ol'gerd's decision to quit Novgorod territory and withdraw, one further hypothesis must be considered. Given the strength of Novgorod's defences and the presence of a Muscovite garrison in the city, Ol'gerd's army could hardly have hoped to seize and occupy Novgorod without support from within. Only a strong pro-Lithuanian party willing to open the gates would have enabled Ol'gerd to achieve his undeniable

[1] This is clear from the size of the expedition ("Ol'gerd . . . Keystut . . . all the princes") and from the words of Ol'gerd's declaration of war ("I intend to fight you, to war on your town and provinces"). It seems most unlikely that Ol'gerd's expedition was simply an act of revenge for an ex-*posadnik*'s insults.

objective. Perhaps then the major cause of the change in Lithuanian plans was the realization that no such support was there within the city, that the pro-Lithuanian faction was not strong enough to overcome the support enjoyed by Semen and that the real battle which was being fought out in the republic was not between pro-Moscow and pro-Lithuania factions, but between groups of boyars struggling for power. The outcome of the events of 1346 was not so much a triumph for the partisans of Muscovite rule as a victory of the Cathedral Side over the Trade Side, of Ontsifor Lukinich Mishinich and Matfey Koska over Evstafy Dvoryaninets and Fedor Danilovich.

Strangely enough the year 1346 with its potentially dangerous invasion of Novgorod territory by Lithuania was by no means so critical a year in the history of Novgorod and of Moscow's relations with Novgorod as was 1348. Paradoxically, when Novgorod was under serious threat from either Lithuania or Moscow there is no evidence in the sources of any abatement in the inter-boyar struggle: it is only when the threat comes from a potentially less dangerous direction—from Sweden—that there appears to be a sinking of differences.

In 1348 King Magnus Eriksson of Sweden invaded Novgorod's northern territory. So detailed and full are the various accounts of the invasion found in the chronicles that we can with little difficulty reconstruct the courses of events during the years 1348-9.[1] Early in 1348, or even in 1347, Swedish envoys appeared in Novgorod to discuss with Archbishop Vasily the relative virtues of Catholicism and Orthodoxy, but in all probability to dispute the existing frontiers and to deliver an ultimatum.[2]

[1] There are four basic versions: (i) that found in the Novgorod First Chronicle (*NL*, pp. 359-61); (ii) that found in the Moscow *svod* of 1479 (*PSRL*, xxv, pp. 176-7), the Sofiysky First Chronicle (*PSRL*, v, pp. 225-6) and the Ermolinsky Chronicle (abridged) (*PSRL*, xxiii, pp. 108-9); (iii) that found in the Novgorod Fourth Chronicle (*PSRL*, iv (i), pp. 276-9); and (iv) the account of the Rogozhsky and Trinity Chronicles (*PSRL*, xv (i), cols. 58-9; *TL*, pp. 369-70). For a detailed analysis of the above, *see* J. L. I. Fennell, "The Campaign of King Magnus".

[2] The fact that the introductory episodes are virtually the same in all the sources which contain them (i.e. all but the Trinity and Rogozhsky Chronicles) shows that there was a common source for them.

In return the Novgorodians sent a delegation to discuss matters with Magnus, whom they found, ready to invade with his army, in the neighbourhood of Vyborg, just across the Novgorod–Swedish frontier. The talks broke down and the Swedes invaded the lands of Izhora and Vod', i.e. the basin of the river Izhora and the coastal district between the Narova and Neva rivers.[1] On hearing the news the Novgorodians despatched northwards a small force, 400 strong, under ex-*Posadnik* Varfolomey Mishinich's grandson, the redoubtable Ontsifor Lukinich; on 23 July 1348 Ontsifor defeated the Swedes at the battle of Zhabchee Pole (Toads' Field) in the Vod' district.[2] The main force, under command of the current *posadnik* Fedor Danilovich and consisting of "the governors of the grand prince, all the Novgorodians, a few Pskovites, the men of Torzhok and all the land of Novgorod",[3] went north to Ladoga. It was evidently a large army, but not large enough in the opinion of the Novgorodians to deal with Magnus's crusade. More help was needed, and an embassy was sent off to Semen of Moscow to ask him to "come and defend his patrimony".[4] Semen set off north-west, but shortly after leaving Torzhok was forced to abandon his project; news had just reached him of Ol'gerd's mission to the Horde and he was obliged to return to Moscow to deal with "the khan's business".[5]

[1] Note that all the sources mention Magnus's proselytism: "He began to convert the land of Izhora to his faith" (*NL*, p. 360)—thus giving his expedition the nature of a crusade. According to the accounts found in the Swedish Rhymed Chronicle and the Chronicle of Olaus Petri (*see Scriptores rerum Svecicarum*, vol. i, part 2, pp. 54–5, 267–8). The campaign had a proselytizing nature: the Swedes cut off the beards of their first prisoners, rebaptized them and made them promise "to convert their country to the Christian faith" (*see* ibid., p. 55). The size and seriousness of the campaign is indicated by the fact that Magnus "gathered a big army from Germany and Denmark, the Duke of Holstein and more such" (ibid., p. 54) and "had all the income from Peter's penny (*Romskott*) taken up in the country" (ibid., p. 268).

[2] For the date of the battle (*v kanon Borisa i Gleba*) and its location, *see PSRL*, iv (i), p. 277.

[3] *NL*, p. 360; *PSRL*, v, p. 226; xxv, p. 176. *Cf.* the different version of the Novgorod Fourth Chronicle ("The Novgorodians gathered in Ladoga awaiting Grand Prince Semen"—*PSRL*, iv (i), p. 277).

[4] *NL*, p. 360; *PSRL*, v, p. 226; xxiii, p. 109; xxv, p. 176. The request to Semen is omitted in the Novgorod Fourth Chronicle.

[5] I.e. to discuss the embassy of Koriad. (*See* above, pp. 198–9.)

Instead he sent an army under his brother Ivan to Novgorod.[1] Meanwhile, however, on 6 August Magnus captured the fortress of Orekhov (Oreshek, Orekhovets) at the eastern end of the Neva, which he had been besieging since the beginning of the operations in July. In the fortress was a governor, left there by Narimunt, and presumably a Lithuanian garrison as well as the members of the original Novgorodian embassy to Vyborg.[2]

The fall of the key-fortress of Orekhov was a matter of considerable concern to the Novgorodians. Built by Yury of Moscow in 1323,[3] it commanded the entrance to Lake Ladoga and the approaches to Novgorod. An enemy which held the entire Neva basin, as Magnus now did, was in a commanding position as far as Novgorod's possessions were concerned and was able to control the strip of land between Lake Ladoga and the Swedish frontier to the west—indeed, the Swedes occupied the outpost of Korela on the west bank of Lake Ladoga, as is evident from the thousand-man expedition despatched by the Novgorodians from Ladoga in August 1348.[4] The reaction of the allied force in Ladoga was to march immediately on Orekhov and lay siege to it.

The gravity of the situation appears to have been exploited to the full by the small Pskovite detachment which joined the Novgorodians earlier in the summer. The Pskovites agreed to accompany the army only on the condition that the Novgorodians regularized the equivocal relationship existing between the two city-states and granted Pskov her long-sought-after independence. On the march between Ladoga and Orekhov[5] the

---

[1] Also in the army, according to the Trinity and Rogozhsky Chronicles only, were Prince Konstantin of Rostov and Ivan Akinfovich, son of the Tverite boyar Akinf. (See *TL*, p. 370; *PSRL*, xv (i), col. 59.) For Akinf, see below, p. 272, note 2.

[2] For Narimunt's garrison in Orekhov, see above, pp. 131, 155. Note that the Swedish Rhymed Chronicle mentions that the force which later besieged the king at Orekhov consisted of "Russians, Lithuanians and Tatars (*Sold aff Ryssa, Lattoga ok Tattar*)". For the capture of Orekhov, see *NL*, p. 360 (no mention of Narimunt's garrison!); *PSRL*, iv (i), p. 277; xxiii, pp. 108–9; xxv, p. 177.

[3] See above, pp. 100–1.

[4] They defeated the Swedes, killed the commander, one Lyudka, and evidently recaptured the town. This is only mentioned in the Novgorod Fourth Chronicle (*PSRL*, iv (i), p. 278).

[5] "While the Novgorodians were marching towards Orekhovets, they granted a favour (*dasha zhalovanie*) to Pskov . . ." (*PSRL*, xxv, p. 177).

Novgorodians gave in and signed a treaty, the treaty of Bolotovo, with Pskov. The charter has not survived, but the terms of the agreement are mentioned in certain of the chronicles:[1] the *posadniki* of Novgorod were no longer to have any administrative or juridical functions in Pskov; the archbishop's law-courts in Pskov were to be run only by his representatives chosen from among the Pskovites themselves; the authorities in Novgorod were no longer to exercise the right of summoning Pskovites to attend trial in Novgorod; and the relationship between the two republics was to be that of elder brother to younger brother. In exchange for these privileges, which virtually amounted to a charter of independence for Pskov, Pskov evidently agreed to stand by Novgorod and defend her when attacked.[2] In fact the Pskovites refused to carry out their side of the bargain and assist the Novgorodians at the siege of Orekhov: in spite of being reproachfully reminded by the Novgorodians of their obligations, their detachment demonstratively departed to the accompaniment of trumpets, drums and fifes and the jeers and laughter of the besieged Swedes.[3]

[1] Curiously enough not in any of the Pskov chronicles, or in the Novgorod First Chronicle. (*See*, however, *PSRL*, iv (i), p. 278; v, p. 226; xxiii, p. 109; xxv, p. 177.)

[2] It would be tempting to dismiss the story of the chroniclers to the effect that the treaty of Bolotovo was signed while the Novgorodians and Pskovites were actually marching towards Orekhov and to treat it as an overdramatization of an event which took place six years earlier when the Pskovites are reported to have made peace with Novgorod after the Lithuanian intervention in Pskovite affairs of 1342 (*see* above, p. 256). However, the fact that one source actually mentions the name of the place where the treaty was drawn up as Bolotovo (*PSRL*, iv (i), p. 278) and the existence of a village of Bolotovo near Ladoga on the Volkhov (*see* M. Vasmer, *RGN*, vol. i, part 2, p. 458) make it reasonable to believe that the chronicle accounts are correct.

[3] This vivid episode is described only in the Novgorod Fourth Chronicle (*see PSRL*, iv (i), p. 278). Note that the Novgorodians begged the Pskovites to leave by night and not to shame them. The Pskovites, however, left at noon. Plausible as the narrative with all its details sounds, the reason for the Pskovites' departure was obviously not unwillingness to co-operate, as the anti-Pskovite Novgorodian author of the account found in the Novgorod Fourth Chronicle would have his readers believe. The Pskov chronicle makes it quite clear that the reason for the hurried departure from Orekhov was a renewal of the German offensive both north and south of Pskov: "and at that time the Pskovites were at Oreshek" (*see PL*, ii, p. 98).

Ivan Ivanovich's reaction to the fall of Orekhov was no less galling to the Novgorodians than the ingratitude of the Pskovites. He refused to march north to Ladoga and went back to the hower lands, "without accepting", so the Novgorod chronicles report, "the blessing of the archbishop or the petition of the Novgorodians". Muscovite aid was thus limited to the troops of Semen's *namestniki*, which had gone with the main body to Ladoga in the first place.

Unaided by the Pskovites or the reserve army of Ivan Ivanovich, the Novgorodians took nearly six months to recapture Orekhov. The siege was eventually lifted in February 1349 with minimal losses to the besiegers. The campaign was over. The threat from the north-west had dissolved.

The story of Magnus's crusade is of course of considerable interest as far as the history of Russo-Swedish relations and the question of Novgorod's north-west frontiers are concerned. But of still greater interest to the historian is the way in which some of the events described (or omitted) by the various sources throw light on Moscow–Pskov and Moscow–Novgorod relations. Two sections of the whole deserve particular attention in this respect: the account of the treaty of Bolotovo and the secession of Pskov; and the description of the behaviour of Grand Prince Semen and his brother Ivan.

Now the official (First) chronicle of Novgorod makes no mention of the Pskovites except briefly to report that there were a few men from Pskov among the troops who marched north to Ladoga. Nothing is said of Bolotovo or the withdrawal of the Pskovites from Orekhov. The version found in the Novgorod Fourth Chronicle, which is frankly anti-Pskovite and pro-Novgorodian, describes the affair in such a way as to ridicule the Pskovites and virtually accuse them of cowardice and treachery. The version which finally found its way into the Moscow *svod* of 1479 reports the treaty of Bolotovo calmly and dispassionately, giving the same details of the conditions as were found in the Novgorod Fourth Chronicle, but without the latter's (invented?) story of the Pskovites' departure from Orekhov.

The reasons for the inclusion of the story in the official grand-princely *svod* of Moscow are obvious: the incident in no way discredited Moscow or her prince; indeed, if in fact the outcome of the treaty was to the ultimate benefit of Moscow there was every reason for including it. As for its exclusion from the official Novgorodian chronicle, one valid reason is to be sought in Novgorod pride: the loss of a *prigorod* was a humiliating affair from a prestige point of view and hardly resounded to Novgorod's credit. Its exclusion, however, can also be explained away by a negative argument: if in fact the loss of Pskov made little difference to Novgorod–Pskov relations, then there was no point in mentioning it; on the other hand, had it led to a breach with Novgorod and a rapprochement with Lithuania, then the official spokesman of the republic might well have retained, or borrowed, the version which found its way into the Novgorod Fourth Chronicle and written up the event as illustrative of Pskovite treachery.

In actual fact the treaty of Bolotovo and the emancipation of Pskov neither led to a breach with Novgorod nor did it serve to push Pskov into Lithuanian arms. Pskov, in spite of the fact that prior to 1348 she was a province of Novgorod, had long enjoyed a considerable degree of autonomy and had been virtually free to invite *namestniki* from whatever source she chose. Nothing was easier for Pskov than to break off relations with Novgorod on the pretext that the latter provided no assistance in the seemingly endless wars with the Livonian Order, wars which many Pskovites must have suspected the Novgorodians of provoking.[1] And in the long periods of strained relations between the two city-states it is doubtful whether the *posadniki* of Novgorod exercised any real control over Pskov or whether the Pskovites in fact obeyed summons to appear at the law-courts in Novgorod. As for ecclesiastical relations between the two, these had been frequently ruptured before 1348, and in any case the treaty of Bolotovo in no way granted Pskov the ecclesiastical independence her clergy had so long wanted: after 1348 Pskov was no nearer to getting her own bishopric than she had been in 1332, when "envoys from Aleksandr [of Tver'], Gedimin and all the Lithuanian princes" appeared at Metropolitan Feognost's court in Vladimir Volynsky to request the establishment of a bishopric in Pskov[2]—and true political autonomy depended to a large extent on the freedom of the Church. In the long run, then, the

[1] *See* A. I. Nikitsky, *Ocherk*, pp. 104 sq.   [2] *See* above, pp. 130 sq.

independence acquired by Pskov at Bolotovo did not signify any appreciable slackening of the ties which had traditionally bound the two republics; it merely meant that in future there would be less interference by Novgorod in the internal administration of Pskov, that Pskovite citizens would technically enjoy a greater degree of freedom, and, most important, that Moscow need have no scruples in providing Pskov with a prince-mercenary to defend her frontiers.

Still less did the acquisition of political freedom by Pskov mean a rapprochement with the West. The relationship with Lithuania, ever since the departure of Ol'gerd in 1342, was equivocal and unsatisfactory from the Pskovites' point of view. Ol'gerd's son Andrey, who, it will be remembered,[1] had been christened and given the title of prince of Pskov in 1342, had quit Pskov for Lithuania shortly after his father and had continued to "rule" by means of *namestniki*, who were responsible to him alone.[2] The only crumb of comfort from this Lithuanian alliance was the presence in Pskov of Prince Yury Vitovtovich, an able and popular soldier, who appears to have been responsible for the defence of the republic. But when he died in April 1349 and when his widow and children left for Lithuania, the Pskovites decided to break off all relations with Ol'gerd and his son. They reproached Andrey for not bothering to reside in Pskov and informed him that he need no longer consider himself prince of Pskov. It was an act of calculated defiance and recognized as such by Ol'gerd, who, somewhat half-heartedly, declared war on Pskov. But there was little that Ol'gerd could do. His aggressiveness was limited to arresting Pskov merchants in his lands and sending his son Andrey on a raid against Pskov territory.[3]

One might well ask why Ol'gerd's reaction was so feeble or how Pskov found the temerity to issue such a challenge to Lithuania. Of course, much can be explained away by the fact that the years 1348 and 1349 marked the nadir of Ol'gerd's political fortunes—one has only to remember the crushing defeat on the Strava and the humiliation of Koriad and the diplomatic victory of Semen at the Horde in 1348—and by the fact that at the

---

[1] *See* above, p. 258.   [2] *See PL*, ii, p. 96.
[3] For the breach between Lithuania and Pskov and the subsequent beginning of hostilities, *see* ibid., p. 99.

time Ol'gerd, whether he liked it or not, was technically at peace with Moscow.[1] But the real answer is surely to be found in Muscovite support for Pskov. It is true that there is no mention in any of the sources of negotiations with Moscow or of the arrival of a Muscovite governor in Pskov at the time. But it would be difficult to see from where else Pskov could have received the military aid she so urgently needed to defend herself in the west: Novgorod was hardly likely to provide permanent assistance so soon after the treaty of Bolotovo and so soon after the refusal of the Pskovites to carry out their commitments at Orekhov. It seems likely, then, that the independence of Pskov in 1348 not only did not lead to a serious breach with Novgorod or a rapprochement with Lithuania, but may even have resulted in the spreading of Moscow's influence as far west as the city-state of Pskov. Whatever the chain of causes and results, by the end of the 1340's Pskov was at last within the sphere of influence of Moscow, which in view of the political proximity between Lithuania and Pskov during the past two decades was no mean achievement for Semen's diplomacy.

Still more light is shed on the relationship between Moscow and Novgorod in 1348 by the various accounts given in the chronicles of the events following Novgorod's appeal for additional military assistance. What happened is quite clear: Semen undoubtedly intended to afford substantial aid to Novgorod. He summoned a large army consisting, according to the Trinity Chronicle (which there is no reason to disbelieve in this case), of troops from Rostov and Tver' as well as from Moscow,[2] and was only deflected from his purpose by messengers from the khan, who desired that he return to Moscow to settle the more urgent question of Ol'gerd's brother. The command of the expedition was transferred to his brother Ivan, who proceeded to Novgorod, quarrelled with the Novgorodians, and returned to Moscow on hearing the news of the capture of Orekhov by the Swedes.

[1] *See* above, p. 200.

[2] This is evident from Semen's despatch of his brother Ivan, Konstantin of Rostov and Ivan Akinfovich to Novgorod. As Ivan Akinfovich's father had been a boyar of Tver' in the early fourteenth century (*see* above, p. 63), it is reasonable to assume that he, Ivan Akinfovich, commanded a detachment from Tver'.

What actually took place in Novgorod is relatively unimportant, as we know nothing concrete of the cause of Ivan's disagreement with the Novgorodians. What is important, however, is the attitude of the Novgorodians to the whole question of Muscovite aid, and this attitude can be, albeit partially, discerned from the remarks made by the various chroniclers. However disappointed the Novgorodians may have been at Semen's decision to attend to the "affairs of the khan", the author of the account found in the Novgorod First Chronicle is remarkably mild in his censure of Semen. In answer to the request of the envoys from Novgorod to "defend his patrimony" Semen is made to express pleasure at the thought of helping the republic: "I shall gladly go to you," he says.[1] The only slight note of criticism is struck in the next sentence: "but having tarried for a long time, the prince set off to Novgorod ..."[2] No mention is made of the reasons for Semen's decision to return to Moscow: we are simply told that "having gone from Torzhok to Sitno, he went back to Moscow." The (Novgorodian?) author of the version which found its way into the Novgorod Fourth Chronicle compilation is even more reticent. He makes no mention of the appeal for help; he simply states that the Novgorodians gathered in Ladoga, "waiting for Grand Prince Semen", but that Semen turned back at Sitno.[3] The version which finally appeared in the Moscow *svod* of 1479 follows closely that of the Novgorod First Chronicle, but, not surprisingly, seeks to justify Semen's behaviour by making him say, not "I shall gladly go to you," but "The khan's business has delayed me; when I have completed it, I shall quickly come to my patrimony."[4] Then, "having tarried *for a little*", Semen is made to set off to Novgorod and turn back at Sitno; and exactly the same terms are used as are found in the Novgorod First Chronicle.[5] At the other end of the scale, the tendentiously pro-

[1] *NL*, p. 360.   [2] Ibid.
[3] *See PSRL*, iv (i), p. 277.   [4] *PSRL*, xxv, p. 176.
[5] *See* ibid., p. 177. Clearly the redactor of the Moscow *svod* knew of the Trinity/Rogozhsky Chronicle version (according to which the khan's envoys catch up Semen at Sitno and tell him to go back) but utilized it to explain away Semen's delay, which he found, indirectly, in the Novgorod First Chronicle version.

Note that the Ermolinsky Chronicle, while including in a very abbreviated form the Novgorodians' request for help, simply omits all mention of

Muscovite Trinity Chronicle, showing a characteristic lack of interest in anything not directly related to Moscow's affairs, describes the business from a purely Muscovite point of view, makes no mention of Novgorod's appeal for help and has Semen spontaneously collect an army and march to Sitno where he is told to return by the khan's messengers.[1]

While Semen is virtually exonerated by the Novgorodian chroniclers for his decision to deal with the more pressing business of the khan rather than personally to go to the help of his "patrimony", the behaviour of his brother Ivan comes in for stiffer, though carefully camouflaged, criticism. From a first reading the note of censure is barely discernible: "But when he (Ivan) heard of that the Germans (i.e. the Swedes) had taken the town [of Orekhov], he did not even go to [the help of] the Novgorodians in Ladoga against the Germans, but marched back from Novgorod to the Lower land, without accepting the blessing of the archbishop or the petition of the Novgorodians."[2] The criticism, however, is there. Firstly, there is an obvious suggestion of cowardice or malice on Ivan's part in that he is made to leave Novgorod as soon as he hears the news of the fall of Orekhov, a setback of the first order for the Novgorodians and an event which made his presence in the north even more urgently needed than before. The chronicler's innuendo must have been unmistakable to his contemporaries. Secondly, there is a hint of considerable differences of opinion between Ivan and the republic in the mention of Ivan's non-acceptance of the "archbishop's blessing" and the "petition of the Novgorodians". Such words could only mean a complete rift between Ivan and the authorities in Novgorod, a serious quarrel. As might be expected, the compilers of the Moscow-orientated chronicles give quite a different picture. The Ermolinsky Chronicle account omits all

---

Semen's subsequent action—he is even silent on Ivan's trip to Novogrod. (*See* PSRL, xxiii, p. 109.)

[1] *See* TL, pp. 369–70.

[2] Such is the version of the Novgorod Fourth Chronicle. That of the First Chronicle is almost identical; only here the phrase "he did not even go to the Novgorodians in Ladoga" precedes the news of the capture of Orekhov by the Swedes, which itself is followed by Ivan's departure. (*See* PSRL, iv (i), pp. 277–8; NL, p. 360.)

mention of Ivan Ivanovitch. The Trinity and Rogozhsky Chronicles get Ivan to Novgorod "with many *voevody* and troops" and
then immediately report the recapture of Orekhov and the
triumphal despatch of the Swedish prisoners to Moscow[1] (needless to say, the Novgorod chronicles have the prisoners brought to
Novgorod); the innuendo, again, is obvious: Ivan and the forces
of Moscow were in some way responsible for the ultimate
victory over the Swedes.

From this analysis of the attitudes of the various chroniclers
to the behaviour of the two princes of Moscow it is clear that as a
result of the events of 1348 there was no diminution of the
popularity of Semen's régime in Novgorod. Just as in 1346 the
local chroniclers had shown no readiness to criticize Semen's
somewhat abrupt departure from Novgorod, an act which undoubtedly sparked off the Lithuanian invasion of Novgorod
territory, so in 1348 his decision to leave Novgorod to her own
devices was barely censured. It was only by Ivan's behaviour that
the people of Novgorod were riled. Indeed, they may well have
construed it as indicative not only of disobedience to Semen,
but even of active opposition and treachery. Five years later,
when on Semen's death Ivan became candidate for the title of
grand prince of Vladimir, Novgorod, remembering the events of
1348, sent an embassy to the Horde and asked the khan to grant
the patent to Konstantin of Suzdal'. And it is not surprising that,
when this failed, Novgorod, under her recently reappointed pro-
Muscovite archbishop Moisey, should have remained for the
first one and a half years of Ivan II's reign "without peace" with
the grand prince.[2]

In the description of the events of 1348 given in the various
chronicles there is little or no evidence of any sort of party strife
within Novgorod. We find Ontsifor Lukinich and the current
posadnik, Fedor Danilovich, representatives of opposite Sides
of the city, taking an equally active part in the defence of

[1] See *TL*, p. 370; *PSRL*, xv (i), cols. 58-9. The Moscow *svod* of 1479 tells
how Ivan departed from Novgorod on hearing the news of the fall of Orekhov,
but omits all mention of the archbishop's blessing and the petition of the
Novgorodians. (*See PSRL*, xxv, p. 177.)
[2] *NL*, p. 363.

Novgorod.[1] Evidently the danger from the north assumed more alarming proportions in the eyes of the people of Novgorod than the invasion of Ol'gerd and served to coalesce the mutually hostile boyar groups in Novgorod. Differences between the two halves of the town were temporarily sunk. It may well be that the victorious outcome of the Swedish war in 1349—a war which had been conducted largely by Novgorodian troops and Novgorodian efforts, and with little help from outside—gave Novgorod more confidence in her ability to deal with external enemies and convinced her of the need still further to lessen the authority of the prince-mercenary and his lieutenants. At the same time the realization that the efficient conduct of operations would have been impossible had the *kontsy* and their representatives been quarrelling among themselves at the time must have convinced public-spirited politicians, if any there were, that the time had come to put an end to inter-boyar conflict and to reorganize the internal administration of Novgorod on a more efficient basis. Only in this way could the republic bring about a more effective defence system and thus gradually diminish the need for a prince.

Relations between Novgorod and Semen for the remainder of the latter's rule seem to have been perfectly amicable. Semen never appeared again in Novgorod—he had neither the time nor the need to. During the seven years following Ol'gerd's abortive attempt to bluster Novgorod into submission, there was no hint of Lithuanian encroachment on to Novgorod territory. Semen's governors remained in Novgorod and took part in the successful retaliatory invasion of Swedish territory in 1351.[2] But during this period of outward harmonious coexistence momentous changes were taking place within Novgorod, changes which might well have altered the whole relationship between grand prince

[1] Ontsifor was in command of the detachment which beat the Swedes at battle of Zhabchee Pole (*see* above, p. 266); Fedor Danilovich led the army which collected at Ladoga and went to the relief of Orekhov (*see* above, pp. 266, 267).

[2] The Novgorodians, under command of the son of the *namestnik* Boris attacked Vyborg in March 1351 (for dating, *see* below, p. 277, note 2) and defeated the Swedes in a battle outside the town. As a result of the campaign the Swedes agreed to exchange prisoners in Yur'ev (Derpt) in the land of the Teutonic Order in May–June of the same year. (*See NL*, pp. 361–2.)

and republic, had they been carried to a logical conclusion.

As has been pointed out above,[1] the chief weakness of the *posadnichestvo* system in Novgorod during the first half of the fourteenth century lay in the failure to observe any regular method of rotation for the office of *posadnik*. The strongest of the representatives of the *kontsy* acquired or retained the office annually by a popular vote, which was dependent largely on his ability to amass sufficient supporters at the *veche*. Another weakness in the system lay in the exclusive authority of the *posadnik* and the relative impotence of the other representatives of the *kontsy* even though they were members of the oligarchical organ, the *Sovet Gospod*. In 1351, for the first time in the history of Novgorod, there is evidence of an attempt to change the old order, which had now been going on for half a century.

On 16 June 1351, one week after the return of the delegation from Yur'ev, where the exchange of prisoners with the Swedes had been successfully completed, the office of *posadnik* was taken from the current holder, Fedor Danilovich, and handed to Ontsifor Lukinich.[2] That this was no routine hand-over is evident from the date—the year of office normally began in March and ended in February. It is also evident from the events which followed. Shortly after the appointment of Ontsifor, "the people of Novgorod drove out [ex-]*Posadnik* Fedor and his brother Mikhail, and Yury and Ondreyan, and they plundered their houses and they pillaged all the *Prusskaya ulitsa* (i.e. the district on the *Sofiyskaya storona* comprising the *Zagorodsky* and *Lyudin kontsy*)".[3] As a result Fedor and his confederates fled, firstly to Pskov, then to Kopor'e, where Fedor Danilovich had taken refuge nine years earlier after a similar coup, also organized by his rival Ontsifor.[4]

At first sight the events of 1351 read like a repetition of the

[1] *See* above, p. 242.

[2] *See* NL, p. 362. The date given in the Novgorod First Chronicle is 1350 (6858); however, the day of the week given for the Novgorodians' arrival at Vyborg on 21 March is Monday, and 21 March 1351 fell on a Monday. There is no entry under 6859. Yanin gets the date wrong (*see* NP, p. 193), but *see* Berezhkov, *Khronologiya*, p. 298. *See* also Artsikhovsky's article on Ontsifor, where many of the dates are wrong (A. V. Artsikhovsky, "Pis'ma Ontsifora", p. 112).

[3] NL, p. 362.   [4] *See* above, p. 252.

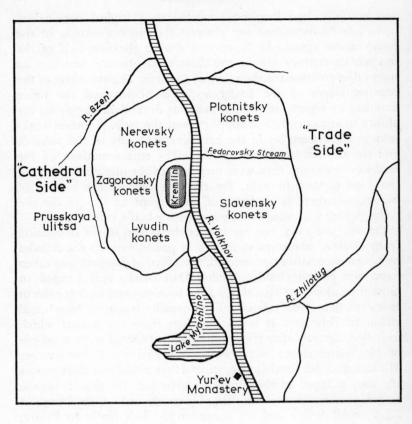

previous upheavals in Novgorod. But that this was no regular recurrent conflict between boyar representatives of the various *kontsy* is evident from the details of the narrative.[1] Yanin, the Soviet historian who has specialized in the history of the institution of the *posadnichestvo* in Novgorod, sees in the disturbances of 1351 "a revolt directed against *both boyar groups*, which had been the chief participants of the inter-boyar struggle. . . . The main blow was directed *against the very existence of an inter-boyar struggle*, which had led the republican régime to a protracted crisis."[2] In Yanin's eyes, the coup of Ontsifor, whom he describes as "the greatest statesman in the history of Novgorod", must be considered "the beginning of vital changes in the organization of the Novgorodian system of *posadnichestvo*".[3]

The reforms themselves only took place in 1354. During the intervening three years there is unfortunately no information at all as to the activities either of the chief reformer, Ontsifor Lukinich, or of his opponents who had fled to the north. Presumably Ontsifor himself remained at the head of the administration during most of this period (he was, it is known, *posadnik* in 1351, 1353 and 1354[4]) and was occupied in preparing the ground for the reforms. The fugitives in Kopor'e, we must assume, returned to Novgorod: no mention is made of them during the years in question. At last, in 1354, at a time when Novgorod was entirely free of either Muscovite or Lithuanian control, the reforms were carried out. An examination of the extremely complex evidence, which indicates that at this particular juncture the changes were

---

[1] Both Fedor and Mikhail Danilovichi were deputies of the *Slavensky konets*; "Yury" and "Ondreyean" can be identified with Yury Ivanovich and Andreyan Zakhar'inich, who in 1354 became *posadniki*-representatives of the *Nerevsky* and *Plotnitsky kontsy* respectively (Yury Ivanovich may have been *posadnik* earlier; the Novgorod Fourth Chronicle mentions a *posadnik* Yury who founded the Church of St. John Chrysostom in 1350; *see PSRL*, iv (i), p. 279. Yanin makes no mention of this). Even assuming that "Yury" was not the future representative of the *Nerevsky konets* (Ontsifor's own district), the events described could hardly denote a conflict between the Cathedral and Trade Sides—i.e. between Ontsifor representing the *Nerevsky konets*, and the Danilovichi and Andreyan representing the Trade Side—as the chronicler talks of the plundering of the *Prusskaya ulitsa* as well.

[2] Yanin, *NP*, p. 193 (the italics are mine).
[3] Ibid.   [4] *See* ibid., p. 203.

made, is beyond the scope of this book and need not occupy us here: suffice it to say that V. L. Yanin, in his capital work on the government of Novgorod, has convincingly and at great length demonstrated that the new system of collective *posadnichestvo* was initiated by Ontsifor in 1354.[1]

What appears to have happened is briefly as follows: Ontsifor, for reasons not stated in the chronicles,[2] resigned from the *posadnichestvo*. In his place were elected six permanent *posadniki*—the *Prusskaya ultisa* and the *Slavensky konets* each being split into two and providing two representatives each. These six *posadniki* were elected for life, while one of their number was annually appointed senior *posadnik*, or *stepenny posadnik*.

The virtues of the reform are not hard to see. Representation of the *kontsy* was increased from four to six, thus widening the number of boyar groupings seeking a share in the government of the republic. Authority was divided between six *posadniki*, even though one was *primus inter pares*. But above all, as Yanin says, the reorganization of the *posadnichestvo* meant "a complete renovation of all the ruling élite of Novgorod".[3] The six newly-appointed *posadniki* in 1354, as Yanin is at pains to point out, were new men, who were not linked with the devastating inter-boyar conflicts of the past.[4] By his reforms Ontsifor, temporarily at any rate, destroyed the main grounds for party strife and laid the foundation for "a new epoch in the development of the boyar republic. A new form of state organization was introduced in a place which had been specially cleared for it; its roots, which went deep into the rich soil of age-long conflict between the boyar groups, had been cut."[5]

The defects of the reform, however, are equally evident. Just as before 1354 there was no system of rotation for the office of *posadnik*, so now there was nothing to regulate the nomination to the supreme post of *stepenny posadnik*. The reform, in fact,

---

[1] *See* ibid., pp. 194 sq. *Cf.* Zimin, review of Yanin's *NP*, in *Sovetskaya arkheologiya*, No. 3, 1963, pp. 275–6.

[2] And not explained by Yanin either.   [3] *See* ibid., p. 200.

[4] Yanin, however, fails to mention that Yury Ivanovich and Andreyan Zakhar'inich, *posadniki*-representatives of the *Nerevsky* and *Plotnisky kontsy* respectively, were probably part of the group which supported Fedor Danilovich in 1351. (*See* above, p. 277.)

[5] Yanin, *NP*, p. 201.

though it greatly strengthened the oligarchical government of Novgorod and thus contributed to a weakening of the power of any prince who might be requested to "rule" the republic, nevertheless led to the ultimate enfeeblement of the governmental machine in that it did nothing to eliminate the element of competition amongst the aspirants for power.

Important though the great reform of 1354 was, it should not blind us to the events of the previous two years, which profoundly, though less lastingly than the reorganization of the internal government of Novgorod, affected Moscow–Novgorod relations. The plague which swept through the Russian lands in 1352 and 1353 carried away the three architects of Moscow–Novgorod solidarity, Semen, Feognost and Archbishop Vasily. It was as though their deaths acted as a signal for a general worsening in the relations between Moscow and Novgorod. However, that this was no repetition of the strain and tension which marked the relationship between the two states during the rule of Ivan I is evident from a consideration of the known facts.

On 3 July 1352, on his way back to Novgorod from Pskov where he had been performing what appear to have been purely ecclesiastical functions, Archbishop Vasily died of the plague. He had ruled his large diocese for twenty-one years with wisdom, tact and a rare sense of political responsibility. During the difficult days of the reign of Ivan I, though opposed to the overlordship of Muscovy and inclined to favour some form of rapprochement with Lithuania, he managed to steer the republic clear of a major war and to maintain a balance between east and west. During the 1340's the conflict between the pro-Lithuanian and the pro-Muscovite factions in Novgorod seems to have died down or to have been absorbed in the inter-boyar struggle for power. Taking advantage of the temporary lull, Vasily was shrewd enough to cast in his lot with Semen of Moscow and to persuade the Novgorodians that it was to their advantage to receive him as their prince and defender. His acceptance of Semen was bound up with the change in his relations with the metropolitan. And in 1345 the presentation by Metropolitan Feognost of the "chasuble with crosses" in all probability indicated the granting of a measure of ecclesiastical independence to the eparchy of

Novgorod.[1] By the end of Vasily's life Novgorod was closer to Moscow, and, paradoxically enough, to Pskov, than she had ever been.

On hearing the news of Vasily's death, the Novgorodians immediately sent to urge ex-Archbishop Moisey, who was living in semi-retirement in the Uspensky monastery at Kolmovo,[2] to return to his diocese. Not without resistance he allowed himself to be persuaded.[3] Moisey had first been appointed archbishop of Novgorod in 1325, at the death of David. For five years he showed himself to be the firm supporter of Moscow and the opponent of Tver' and Lithuania. He retired "voluntarily" in 1330, in spite of the efforts of certain elements, the pro-Muscovite elements in all probability, to retain him. In 1335, at a time when Ivan I was attempting to establish himself firmly in Novgorod, Moisey was prevailed upon to appear again in public and carry out certain functions as though he had been reinstated.[4] From 1335 to 1352 there is no information as to his activities: presumably he went back to his monastery at Kolmovo.

Ardent supporter of Moscow and of all that the prince of Moscow stood for though he had been, Moisey's reinstatement was followed by a sharp deterioration in Novgorod–Moscow relations. The fault, however, does not appear to have lain entirely with Moisey. Within a year of his appointment he sent a delegation to Constantinople to complain to emperor and patriarch of "unbefitting things which had befallen him forcibly at the hands of the metropolitan".[5] What precisely these "unbefitting things" were the Novgorodian chronicler forbears to mention; but from the timing of the mission—it was sent off *after* the death of Feognost (11 March 1353)[6]—and from the fact that in 1354 Moisey's envoys returned from Constantinople to Novgorod with "chasubles adorned with crosses and documents containing great favours from the emperor and the patriarch and

[1] *See* above, p. 261, note 1.

[2] Situated on the Volkhov just north of Novgorod. (*See* V. V. Zverinsky, *Materialy*, vol. ii, p. 390.)

[3] *See NL*, pp. 362–3; *PSRL*, xxiii, p. 111; xxv, p. 179.

[4] *See* above, p. 148.   [5] *NL*, p. 363.

[6] It is reported in the Novgorod First Chronicle after Semen's death (26 April 1353), and still later in the Novgorod Fourth Chronicle (*PSRL*, iv (i), p. 286).

a golden seal",[1] it is clear that Feognost, when appointing Moisey, had deprived him of the marks of distinction which he had bestowed on his predecessor. That the right to wear the chasuble implied a certain autonomy for the diocese of Novgorod is hinted at in the fuller description of the "documents" sent by the patriarch to Novgorod in 1354 contained in the sixteenth-century Nikon Chronicle: they concerned "ordination fees (*protorekh na postavleniakh*) and episcopal church taxes (*tserkovnykh poshlinakh svyatitel'skikh*)",[2] the right to determine and levy which was presumably entrusted to the archbishop independently of the jurisdiction of the metropolitan. Moisey was, not surprisingly, unprepared to forgo such hard-won privileges. It says much for the authority of the metropolitan that Moisey only dared complain to the patriarch after his death.

It was not, however, Moisey's protest to the patriarch that led to the breach with Moscow. The breach occurred when it became known in Novgorod that Semen had died and that his brother Ivan intended to replace him on the throne of Vladimir. The republic immediately sent a delegation to the Horde with instructions to request the khan to give the *yarlyk* to Prince Konstantin Vasil'evich of Suzdal'. Jani-Beg refused. Ivan of Moscow became grand prince and "the Novgorodians and the grand prince remained without peace for one and a half years".[3] There were no open hostilities, it is true; but it was not until 1355 that some sort of peace appears to have been patched up.[4] Whether this meant an acceptance of Ivan as prince of Novgorod we do not know; the official chronicler of Novgorod restricts himself to the barest details for the whole of the second episcopacy of Moisey: almost the only information we have of Novgorod's history during this period is of Moisey's church-building activities.

Novgorod's unwillingness to support the candidature of Ivan of Moscow, and the eighteen months of broken relations which followed, do not need to be explained by a change of heart towards Moscow on the part of Moisey. As has been pointed out above,[5] many historians have branded Moisey as "anti-Muscovite",

[1] NL, p. 364; PSRL, iv (i), p. 286.   [2] PSRL, x, p. 228.
[3] NL, p. 363.   [4] See PSRL, iv (i), p. 287.
[5] See above, p. 137.

basing their conclusions on the archbishop's quarrel with Feognost in 1352 and on the support of the Novgorod delegation for Konstantin of Suzdal' at the Horde. The events of 1353, however, are not in any way indicative of a change of attitude or policy on the part of Moisey and the rulers of the republic. The protest to the patriarch was motivated solely by the desire to recover the considerable ecclesiastical privileges enjoyed by Archbishop Vasily, and if the metropolitan-elect, Aleksey, ex-boyar of Moscow and firm supporter of the new grand prince, lost no opportunity himself to complain to the patriarch of Moisey's behaviour, it was not so much because of the subsequent action of the Novgorodians in supporting Ivan's rival as because of the request for the chasubles.[1] As for the Novgorodians' readiness to foster the cause of the prince of Suzdal', this does not mean either that Konstantin Vasil'evich had particularly endeared himself to the republic—there is no indication of any contact between Suzdal' and Novgorod—or that the feelings of the Novgorodians had undergone a drastic change towards Moscow. It simply meant that Ivan Ivanovich's refusal to come to the aid of the Novgorodian army which was besieging Swedish-held Orekhov in 1348 still rankled in the minds of the people of Novgorod. The republic was not prepared to lend its support to a prince who had left the Novgorodians to fight their own battles and who had abandoned them "without accepting the blessing of the archbishop or the petition of the Novgorodians".[2] It may even be that the archbishop and the government of the city were only too well aware that Ivan's political tendencies were very different from those of his brother.

As has been pointed out above, there is too little information in the chronicles or elsewhere to enable us to gauge the effect of the events of 1353-4 on the subsequent happenings in Novgorod.

---

[1] That Aleksey, who spent a year in Constantinople (1353-4) while his suitability as metropolitan was being examined, complained to the patriarch is evident from a document written by Patriarch Philotheos in July 1354 to Moisey enjoining him to obey Aleksey in all matters and not to have dealings with Constantinople without the knowledge of the metropolitan. (*See* Golubinsky, *IRTs*, vol. ii (Book I), pp. 185-7.)

[2] *See* above, p. 269.

The re-election of Moisey, the protest to the patriarch, the breach with Moscow and the reform of the electoral system to the office of *posadnik*, all these momentous events in the history of the republic are followed by five years of virtual silence in the chronicles. Whoever it was who had written with rapture and enthusiasm of the deeds of Archbishop Vasily and had praised his beloved pastor to the skies was now silent. All we have in the Novgorod First Chronicle between the return of Moisey's ambassadors from Constantinople in 1354 and Moisey's second and final retirement in 1359 is a dry list of churches built during the episcopate of Moisey and a curt note to the effect that Aleksey returned to Rus' in 1355 after his consecration in Constantinople. There is nothing even to help us speculate on the reason for the chronicler's stubborn silence. We merely know that the relations between Moisey and Metropolitan Aleksey were strained—after Aleksey had done what he could in Constantinople to limit Moisey's authority, the latter, not surprisingly, refused to acknowledge Aleksey as metropolitan[1]—and this undoubtedly did little to improve relations between Novgorod and Moscow. The best we can do is to assume that during the rule of Ivan II Novgorod and the archbishop managed to keep themselves apart from Moscow and to maintain a degree of independence which they had not known before. We may also assume that the government of the republic welcomed the respite as a period in which to reorganize its own internal affairs.

To summarize, then, the relationship between Novgorod and Moscow during the forties and fifties of the fourteenth century, during the transition period between Ivan I and Dmitry Donskoy, or at any rate during the reign of Semen of Moscow, we can say that Muscovite influence in the north-west Russian lands increased appreciably. In sharp contrast to the ineffectual rule of Ivan Kalita, Semen managed to establish a firm and popular position within the republic. His actual authority as prince, in terms of land, income and administrative control, may have diminished as the Novgorodians worked their way towards independence from the mercenary they hired to protect their frontiers; but the danger of an active pro-Lithuanian party, a danger which had bedevilled Kalita's attempts to keep Novgorod under his control, seems to

[1] *See* Presnyakov, *Obrazovanie*, p. 292.

have faded out almost miraculously during the 1340's. As the Lithuanians found to their chagrin in 1346, there was no longer an effective anti-Moscow party to open the gates to the invaders. The internal conflicts were no longer between supporters of the two rival grand princes of Moscow and Lithuania, but between groups of boyars fighting amongst themselves for power, and fighting with the ultimate aim of decreasing the republic's dependence on outside authority. That Semen managed to win and keep the respect and affection of the Novgorodians during this internal struggle, which had as its ultimate aim the weakening of his own authority, shows just how decisive and impressive was his attitude towards Novogorod early in the forties and just how shrewd were the tactics of his ally the metropolitan. An impressive display of military strength at the beginning of Semen's reign and an act of unprecedented generosity on the part of Feognost in granting Archbishop Vasily a modicum of ecclesiastical independence were sufficient to guarantee Moscow the support of the Novgorodians.

One of the most important results of Semen's policy of firmness and friendship with Novgorod was the neutralization of Lithuanian influence in the north-west Russian lands. The resoluteness of Semen and his readiness to demonstrate his strength in moments of crisis were enough to keep Ol'gerd at bay. Indeed, much of Ol'gerd's seeming sluggishness in his attitude to Novgorod may well be explained by the sound defence afforded by the troops from Moscow. The same can be said for Pskov. The seeming indifference displayed by Ol'gerd in 1342, when he threw away all the advantages at his disposal, was perhaps due to Moscow's strength; and the reconciliation between Novgorod and Pskov in the following year was undoubtedly a triumph for Muscovite diplomacy. Nor did Lithuania gain in any way from the treaty of Bolotovo in 1348, when Pskov formally acquired her independence from Novgorod. The semi-independence which in fact resulted meant that it was easier for Moscow to have a say in Pskovite affairs and effectively led to a breach of relations between Pskov and Lithuania. Thus at the beginning of the fifties it was Semen, and not Ol'gerd, who was, if not entrenched in the two western republics, then at least their popular partner and willingly-accepted defender.

[iii] INTERNAL AFFAIRS

Before we can begin to discuss the internal affairs of the principality of Moscow during the reigns of Semen and Ivan II, it must be pointed out that our knowledge of these is limited by the paucity of the sources to the relationship between the three brothers of the house of Moscow, to the organization of the first *udel*, or appanage, in Muscovite territory and to the first signs of what would appear to be a serious split in the ranks of the Muscovite *boyarstvo*. The extant sources give us practically no information on social and economic conditions within the principality; we know nothing of land-ownership, of agrarian conditions, of tax-collection, of legal administration. We must therefore confine ourselves to the question of inter-princely relationships and to what little is known of the senior advisers of the princes.

According to the will of Ivan Kalita, which was discussed in detail in a previous chapter,[1] each of the grand prince's three sons, Semen, Ivan and Andrey, was given a more or less equal share of the territory at the legator's immediate disposal. At the same time no attempt was made to stress the political seniority of the elder brother. Kalita's will, it seems, was a deliberately vague document, the main purpose of which was to convince the khan of the suitability of the three princes of Moscow as eventual holders of the grand-princely *yarlyk*. It was, as many princely wills were, merely the basis for future detailed agreements between the legatees themselves.

Only one compact between the three brothers has survived. That it was not the only treaty between them and that it was not the first is evident from a clause early in the agreement which talks of various fiscal and administrative privileges yielded previously to the grand prince by his two brothers.[2] Probably Semen, soon after Kalita's death, made his brothers agree to some arrangement whereby his seniority was established and the inadequacies of his father's will were redressed. The only copy

---

[1] *See* above, pp. 188 sq.
[2] *See* DDG, p. 11: "*A chto emu s'stupilisya tobe na stareyshinstvo . . . poltamgi . . .*", etc.

of the only extant treaty is unfortunately tattered, defective and without a date. Although the arguments of Cherepnin, who has carefully investigated the question of the dating of the document in question, are not always convincing, it seems likely from internal evidence that the treaty was drawn up late in the 1340's, at any rate not long before Semen drew up his will (spring 1353).[1]

The treaty between Semen and his brothers is of capital importance to the historian for two reasons: firstly, because it sheds light on the relations between the grand prince and his close relatives and can be said to establish the principles of appanage rule within the Muscovite state which were to remain more or less the same for two centuries; and secondly because it illustrates the initial stages of the feud between the "senior" and the "junior" Muscovite *boyarstvo* and gives us some idea of the position of Ivan Ivanovich before he acceded to the throne.

One of the first clauses of the treaty attempts to establish the seniority of Semen: "We shall hold and honour our elder brother in our father's place."[2] What precisely this clause meant in terms

[1] He considers that the words: "And those people who were captured in our territories now . . . war . . . (*A kotoryi lyudi po nashim volostem vyimany nyn . . . voyny . . .*)"—found *only* in the early printed edition (*SGGiD*, vol. i, p. 36; *cf. DDG*, p. 12, where the words "*nyn . . . voyny*" are missing) may refer to "the military activities of the Muscovite princes in connection with Ol'gerd's ravaging of the Muscovite patrimony" (*see* Cherepnin, RFA, i, p. 22). However, it is not entirely clear from the chronicle accounts of the requests and counter-requests made by Ol'gerd and Semen to Khan Jani-Beg in 1348 what exactly Ol'gerd's ravaging of Muscovite territory amounted to (*see* above, pp. 199 sq.); Semen's complaint might be a reference to the Lithuanian attack on Novgorod in 1346 (*see* above, pp. 262 sq.). Cherepnin also considers that the vague references in the treaty to the military failures of Semen and his *tysyatsky* in the struggle with Lithuania refer to the Smolensk campaign (1352). 1350–1, the probable date of the treaty settled on by Cherepnin, seems to satisfy neither of these suppositions. The most acceptable reasons for dating the treaty close to the end of Semen's reign rather than at the beginning seem to me to be (i) hints of a previous treaty and of conflicts between Semen and his brothers; (ii) proximity in style and content to Semen's will; and (iii) the fact that no living son of Semen is mentioned: by 1348 Semen's first four sons were all dead; his fifth son was born in 1350 or 1351.

[2] For this and all subsequent quotations from the treaty, *see DDG*, pp. 11–13.

of allegiance is specified almost immediately: in foreign affairs the roles of the three brothers were to be the same. All were to have common enemies and common allies, and no treaties were to be concluded unilaterally: "Whosoever shall be our elder brother's enemy shall also be our enemy; and whosoever shall be our elder brother's friend shall be our friend too. And you, O master (*gospodine*), Grand Prince, shall not make treaties with anybody without us." In military affairs, however, the senior prince was to take precedence—indeed, the only practical way in which Semen's leadership is evident is in his capacity as commander-in-chief. His was to be the leading role in questions of offence and defence, and the two brothers obliged themselves to submit to his decisions and orders. "Whenever I mount my horse, you are to mount with me. And should I not be able to mount my horse and should I have to send you [on campaign], then you shall mount your horses without disobedience."

So far there is little in the treaty to distinguish it from what we may assume to have been the typical form of inter-princely agreement for much of the preceding three centuries. Such formulae were probably used by the descendants of Yaroslav the Wise in order to regulate the relationships between the senior members of the family and his brothers, cousins, nephews, etc. What is new in the treaty, however, or at any rate what is here formulated legally for the first time, is the attitude of the contracting parties to the districts allocated to the junior members of the family.

Whereas in Kalita's will no mention is made of patrimonial possession, and the conditions on which the three brothers owned the lands left them are defined in the vaguest of terms, here the districts distributed by Ivan I to his sons are recognized as hereditary; furthermore, any acquisitions of land made by the individual princes after the death of their father and indeed after the conclusion of the treaty were to be recognized as hereditary as well, whether they were made by purchase or by any other means. The wording of the treaty is quite unambiguous:

Should God remove any one of us, then we shall protect that man's widow and children, after his death just as during his life. You (Semen) shall not offend them, nor shall you take

K

away from his widow or his children anything which our father bestowed upon him according to his distribution of territory.... And should any one of us have acquired or bought anything, or should any one of us henceforth buy or add anything to his possessions, then you should protect this too, and not offend....

Within these districts, now legally recognized as patrimonial *udely* or appanages, each of the two brothers of the grand prince appears to have been granted a considerable degree of autonomy. Although the relevant passages are so fragmentary as to be almost undecipherable, nevertheless it would seem that the rulers of the appanages were free to exercise a certain amount of administrative and legal control over those living within the boundaries of their lands; only the "boyars and free servants" had what was probably already the immemorial right to "serve" whomsoever they pleased, in other words to transfer their allegiance from one prince to another with impunity and presumably, although this is not stated here or elsewhere, to retain their landed estates in so doing. In an effort to guarantee the independence of their rule and to maintain the stability of their boundaries the princes saw to it that a clause prohibiting the purchase of land by any one prince in the *udel* of another was inserted in the treaty.

Semen's contract with his brothers is the first written evidence we have of the beginning of the so-called appanage system in the principality of Moscow. The principles contained in the clauses of the treaty were to be repeated again and again, often in identical terms, in subsequent treaties. Even in the late fifteenth century we find Ivan III reaffirming most of the basic tenets of appanage rule which were established in Semen's agreement with his brothers or even earlier.[1] The relationship between grand prince and appanage prince remained virtually the same.

However, neither Ivan nor his brother Andrey can be considered as more than a prototype of an appanage prince: certain modifications and additions had to be made to the formulae of Semen. From the point of view of the senior prince neither brother was sufficiently subjected to his authority. For an excellent example of the relationship between junior and senior prince we

[1] *See* J. L. I. Fennell, *Ivan the Great*, pp. 289 sq.

must look ahead to the treaty between Dmitry Donskoy and the only appanage prince in the family, his cousin Vladimir Andreevich of Serpukhov (c. 1367).[1] Here much of Semen's treaty was repeated, but there were significant additions. The independence of both Dmitry and Vladimir in the administration of their own estates is stressed: "You (Vladimir) are to manage (znati) your patrimony, and I am to manage mine." Vladimir, however, was in a position of far greater subordination to Dmitry than had been his father or uncle to Semen: "You, my younger brother, Prince Vladimir, shall hold my grand principality under me with respect and awe, and you shall wish me well in everything. . . . You shall serve me without disobedience." All negotiations with the Golden Horde were to be carried out by Dmitry alone. In a later treaty, dated 1374–5, Vladimir agreed to forgo all rights for himself or his successors to the throne of Moscow and even to the throne of Vladimir—a sign that by now the prince of Moscow considered the title of grand prince of Vladimir to be the exclusive preserve of the house of Moscow. "I shall not seek your patrimony, O master, nor the grand principality, either from you or from your children, nor shall my children seek the patrimony of your children."[2]

The treaty between Semen and his brothers is also of interest in so far as it contains the first hint of a serious rift both within the princely family and among the advisers of the senior prince. In the first place, it is evident that the treaty was concluded not only in order to repeat, modify or regularize a previous treaty or treaties, but also in order to resolve a conflict between Semen and his two brothers; the ringleader of this conflict had evidently been Aleksey Petrovich Khvost, a senior boyar at the court of the grand prince.

Towards the end of the treaty there is a separate clause relating to the seditious Khvost. "As for Aleksey Petrovich's conspiracy (koromola) against the grand prince, we, Prince Ivan and Prince

---

[1] When Semen and his two sons died in 1353, Ivan II added his (Semen's) "share", Kolomna and Mozhaysk, to his own of Zvenigorod. Serpukhov, the district of Andrey, passed to Andrey's son Vladimir when Andrey died (also in 1353). At his death in 1359 Ivan II left all his lands to his sons Dmitry and Ivan (the latter died heirless in 1364). The treaty between Dmitry and Vladimir (c. 1367) is printed in DDG, pp. 19–21. For the question of dating, see Cherepnin, RFA, vol. i, pp. 31 sq.

[2] DDG, p. 23. Cf. Cherepnin, RFA, vol. i, p. 36.

Andrey, agree not to receive him or his children into our service."
Only the grand prince, the clause continues, has the right to do
what he likes with him and his family (*"volen v nem knyaz' velikii"*).
On the strength of this alone it might appear that Khvost had
been found guilty of taking part in some form of conspiracy
directed against Semen Ivanovich; but other clauses in the treaty
can be taken to indicate that the brothers themselves were also
involved in a conflict with the grand prince. At the beginning of
the document it is laid down by the three brothers that "should
anyone cause us to quarrel (*nas svazhivati*) . . . then we should hold
an investigation . . . and punish the guilty one after the investigation"—an indication that there had already been some sort of
disagreement between the three. As a result of this disagreement
—assuming that the "conflict (*svada*)" and "conspiracy (*koromola*)" were one and the same thing—the grand prince had
confiscated all the possessions of Khvost and presumably distributed them among the brothers: at any rate we know that
Ivan Ivanovich had been given some of his possessions, probably
landed estates. At the end of the final clause we find Ivan swearing
not to return anything to Khvost or to his wife and children,
"and not to help them in any other way".

The information contained in the treaty is not of course
sufficient in itself to enable us to build up a picture of a revolt
headed by Ivan Ivanovich (and perhaps Andrey) and fostered by
Khvost; but later events concerning both Ivan and Khvost
indicate that the two were linked together and were perhaps
in some form of opposition to Semen at the time.

Khvost at the time of his murder in February 1357 occupied
the position of *tysyatsky*, or senior military commander, of
Moscow, a position of considerable authority and power. This
is evident from all the chronicles which mention the event.[1]
When was he in fact given this post? Certainly not during the
lifetime of Semen; not only do we know from the above-
mentioned treaty between Semen and his brothers that he was
in some form of disgrace during the latter part of Semen's reign,
but also we know that one "Vasily", who can without difficulty
be identified with Vasily Vasil'evich Vel'yaminov,[2] was *tysyatsky*

---

[1] *See TL*, p. 375; *PSRL*, xv (i), col. 65; xxv, p. 180.

[2] This identification is based on the information contained in the Trinity

of Moscow at the time of Semen's treaty[1] and presumably also up to the time of Semen's death, although he is not mentioned in the latter's will. The most likely time seems to be 1353, after Semen's death and the accession of Ivan II to the grand-princely throne, or in early 1354 when Ivan returned from the Horde. The Soviet historian Cherepnin has put forward the convincing theory that Khvost's rise to power was in some way connected with the invasion of the Lopasnya area by the Ryazanites and Tatars in June 1353, two months after the death of Semen.[2] The captured governor (*namestnik*) of Lopasnya was one Mikhail Aleksandro-vich, whom, Cherepnin thinks, it is reasonable to identify both with the Mikhaylo Aleksandrovich who together with Vasily (Vel'yaminov) was one of the witnesses of Semen's treaty with his brothers,[3] and with the Mikhaylo who was one of the murderers of Khvost.[4] If we bear in mind the fact that the chronicler also names Vel'yaminov as one of the boyars respon-sible for the murder and calls him Mikhaylo's brother-in-law (*zyat'*),[5] we may reasonably assume that Mikhail Aleksandrovich and Vasily Vasil'evich Vel'yaminov were closely associated and that they were the leading members of that section of the Muscovite *boyarstvo* which supported Semen and opposed the ringleader of the opposition to Semen, Khvost. If this is in fact the case, we may also suggest that what may well have appeared to Ivan II as a military and political disaster of the first order, namely the capture of Lopasnya and the resultant weakening of the southern line of defence against the Tatars, was sufficient stimulus for him to rid himself of his brother's senior adviser and *tysyatsky*, Vel'yaminov, whose brother-in-law he probably suspected of inefficiency and even responsibility for the loss of

---

Chronicle to the effect that in 1374 "Vasily Vasil'evich Vel'yaminov, the last *tysyatsky*, died in Moscow" (*TL*, p. 397). Dmitry Donskoy evidently abolished the office of *tysyatsky* in that year. (*See* Cherepnin, *Obrazovanie*, pp. 576–7.)

[1] *See DDG*, p. 13.

[2] *See* Cherepnin, *RFA*, vol. i, p. 23. For the Lopasnya raid, *see* above, pp. 220 sq.

[3] *See DDG*, p. 13.   [4] *See PSRL*, xv (i), col. 66; x, p. 230.

[5] *See* ibid. Note that Cherepnin considers that Vel'yaminov was also connected by marriage with Semen. He identifies him with the "my uncle Vasily" mentioned in Semen's will (*DDG*, p. 13). (*See RFA*, vol. i, pp. 26–7.)

Lopasnya, and to replace him with a man of a very different stamp, a representative of political views opposed to those of Semen and his advisers, Khvost.

The most striking evidence of a split within the *boyarstvo* and of a strong opposition party to Grand Prince Ivan is afforded by the events of 1357. In the early morning of 3 February, while the church bells of Moscow were ringing for matins, the corpse of Khvost was found "in the square" (presumably in the Kremlin). His death was a complete mystery to all. "His slaying", wrote one chronicler, "was somewhat strange and incomprehensible; it was as though no one had committed the deed. He was just found lying in the square."[1] The two Muscovite chronicles,[2] which repeat in an expurgated form the story found in its entirety in the Tver' Rogozhsky Chronicle, mention a current rumour to the effect that a secret council was held and that Khvost was murdered as a result of a conspiracy. "Some people said that a consultation was held in secret and that a plot was hatched against him; and that he was killed as a result of a general council of all the boyars."[3] They add that the murder was reminiscent of that of Andrey Bogolyubsky in 1176: "Just as God-loving Andrey was killed by his servants the Kuchkovichi, so too did this man suffer at the hands of his *druzhina*."[4]

The accounts of the murder found in these two basically pro-Muscovite chronicles are of little help in determining the true causes and results of the liquidation of Khvost. It was as though they carefully censored themselves in order to avoid any blame falling on those who opposed Khvost and who were patently responsible for the deed. The redactor of the Trinity Chronicle clearly entertained a deep respect for Vel'yaminov: his death in 1374 warranted an entry larger than the obituary notice given to Grand Prince Ivan II in 1359.[5] The author of the account found in the Rogozhksy Chronicle, however, leaves us in no doubt as to whom he considers to be guilty. He begins his account with a round condemnation of those responsible for the murder: "That

[1] *TL*, p. 375.   [2] The Moscow *svod* of 1479 and the Trinity Chronicle.
[3] *PSRL*, xxv, p. 180. *Cf. TL*, p. 375, where the words "of all the boyars" are omitted. The Novgorod chronicles (I and IV) make no mention of the murder.
[4] *PSRL*, xxv, p. 180; *TL*, p. 375.   [5] *See TL*, p. 397; *cf.* p. 376.

winter the devil instilled envy and insubordination into the boyars, and Aleksey Petrovich, the *tysyatsky*, was slain because of envy and the treachery of the devil."[1] After a factual description of the murder (which was later borrowed and inserted *in toto* into the two Muscovite chronicles) he goes on to put the blame, in somewhat less abstract terms, on the "elder boyars": "That same winter, using the last route (i.e. before the thaw in the spring of 1357), the elder boyars (*bolshii boyare*) of Moscow because of this murder departed (*ot'ekhasha*) to Ryazan' together with their wives and children."[2] The identity of the boyars who sought political asylum in Ryazan'—for such is implied in the term "departed" (*ot'ekhasha*)—is revealed in a later passage. In 1357 or early 1358 Ivan II, during his last visit to the Horde, was reconciled with "those boyars who were in Ryazan', Mikhaylo [*Aleksandrovich*] and his brother-in-law Vasily Vasil'evich [Vel'yaminov]".[3] The sixteenth-century Nikon Chronicle, which alone of all the sources mentions that "there was a great disturbance (*myatezh*) in Moscow because of the murder", adds that Ivan II, after his return from the Horde in 1358, "called back the boyars to his service".[4]

From all the evidence afforded by Semen's treaty with his brothers, by the murder of Khvost, by the flight of the "senior" boyars to Ryazan' and by their reconciliation with Ivan II in 1358, we can piece together a picture of a divided *boyarstvo* and a divided princely family during most of the two decades between the reigns of Ivan Kalita and Dmitry Donskoy. On the one side we have those representatives of the *boyarstvo* who supported Grand Prince Semen—Vel'yaminov and his brother-in-law Mikhail Aleksandrovich; on the other, Khvost, who headed that section of the Muscovite boyars which supported Ivan II.

If such a dichotomy within the ruling circles of the principality of Moscow existed, what were the political leanings and aspirations of both sides? Semen's overall policy is clear from his actions outlined in the previous sections of this book. It can be summarized briefly as follows: close co-operation with the Horde and strong resistance towards any increase in Lithuanian power. As for his supporters, there is little in the sources to show what their policy consisted of, except in so far as they opposed Khvost and

[1] *PSRL*, xv (i), col. 65.   [2] Ibid.
[3] Ibid., col. 66.   [4] *See PSRL*, x, pp. 229, 230.

his master Ivan II. But it is interesting to find that when the need arose for them to flee the principality of Moscow they chose Ryazan' of all places to seek refuge in—Ryazan', where Tatar influence and control was stronger than in any other Russian principality.

While there is nothing in the sources to show that Khvost was any more than a supporter of Ivan Ivanovich and an opponent of Semen and his clique, a careful scrutiny of the behaviour of Ivan Ivanovich over the years 1348 to 1359 gives us an inkling at least of his general policy. Of course the task of evaluating Ivan's attitude to such questions as the position of Moscow *vis-à-vis* the Horde and Lithuania is made very difficult by the reticence of the sources. This reticence was nothing more than an attempt to draw a discreet veil of silence over actions which in the eyes of later pro-Muscovite chroniclers may have been little short of treacherous and in any case quite out of keeping with the traditions of Kalita and Semen the Proud. Yet hints there are, indications of a policy so different from that of his predecessors and, in certain respects, from that of his successors, that it is no wonder the encomiasts of the glorious line of Daniil's descendants censored the record of most of his deeds.

Basically Ivan's policy, at least up to the year 1357, may be described as one of peaceful relations with Lithuania and, as a corollary, of hostility towards the Horde. Even before he became grand prince there is clear evidence of his opposition to the policy of his brother Semen. In 1348, it will be remembered,[1] his strange behaviour in Novgorod, which amounted to a refusal to do what Semen, and perhaps the khan,[2] had told him to do and go to the aid of the Novgorodians in the Orekhov–Ladoga theatre, was construed by the local chroniclers as disobedience to the grand prince and may even have been considered as treachery to the common cause. The antagonism between Ivan Ivanovich and the Novgorodians, who by the end of the 1340's had come to appreciate the advantages of stable Muscovite protection, was further evinced in 1353 when the popular Semen died: Novgorod, under her recently re-elected pro-Muscovite archbishop

[1] *See* above, pp. 274 sq.
[2] The Swedish Rhymed Chronicle talks of "Russians, Lithuanians and *Tatars*" besieging Magnus in Orekhov. (*See* above, p. 267, note 2.)

Moisey, immediately sent envoys to the Horde to support a rival candidate for the grand-princely *yarlyk*, and a period of hostility, or at any rate peacelessness, ensued.[1]

A glance at Ivan II's relations with other north-east Russian principalities, with potential enemies or with rivals of a strong Moscow, will show more clearly how he stood. There was no question of hostility with the powerful eastern principality of Suzdal'-Nizhny Novgorod-Gorodets, whose ruler Konstantin had been supported by Novgorod as a rival of Ivan Ivanovich for the patent in 1353. On the contrary, Ivan went out of his way to conclude treaties of friendship both with Konstantin (1355) and with his son and successor Andrey (1356). In view of the fact that in 1352 Konstantin Vasil'evich had married his son to a daughter of Ol'gerd and his daughter to Mikhail Aleksandrovich of Tver' (a brother-in-law of Ol'gerd), these Moscow-Suzdal' treaties can only be looked upon as indicative of a desire on Ivan's part to strengthen his ties with Lithuania.[2]

Still more striking is the attitude of Ivan to Tver'. During Semen's reign Tver' had been in the throes of a civil war skilfully fostered by the diplomacy of Semen and Jani-Beg. The principality had been split between two rival factions, one headed by the pro-Muscovite Vasily of Kashin, and the other by the pro-Lithuanian children of Aleksandr Mikhaylovich, notably Vsevolod of Kholm and Mikhail of Mikulin (that same Mikhail Aleksandrovich who had married the daughter of Konstantin of Suzdal').[3] For the first four years of Ivan II's reign as grand prince of Vladimir there is no mention in any of the chronicles of civil war in Tver'. Evidently Ivan refused to continue his brother's policy of supporting the house of Kashin: instead we can assume that he upheld that branch of the family which had closest links with Lithuania and the house of Suzdal', the Aleksandrovichi. It was only in 1357, after the murder of Khvost and the demonstrative flight of the "great" boyars to Ryazan', that Ivan changed his policy. In that year, it will be remembered, Vsevolod Aleksandrovich of Kholm went to Vladimir to the court of the recently-appointed metropolitan Aleksey to complain of his uncle Vasily, grand prince of Tver' since 1348.[4] No doubt Ivan's behaviour

[1] *See* above, p. 283.   [2] *See* above, p. 234 sq.
[3] *See* above, pp. 229 sq.   [4] *See* above, p. 235.

and attitude had led him to believe that Muscovite support would be forthcoming in the struggle with his uncle. But Aleksey, who may be described as a typical representative of the senior *boyarstvo*, would have no truck with Ol'gerd's brother-in-law. Instead, he obliged Ivan II to sign a pact of friendship with Semen's old ally, Vasily of Kashin.[1] This can only mean that Ivan had discontinued his brother's policy when he became grand prince and had in all probability supported the Aleksandrovichi.

As for direct relations with Lithuania, there are no signs of antagonism between Ivan and Ol'gerd during the first four years of the former's reign. There were no military clashes, no border disputes. Nothing was done by Ivan to strengthen the somewhat precarious control which Semen had won over the lands of Smolensk by his campaign of 1352; nor do we hear of Ivan showing any interest in his former father-in-law's border-state of Bryansk,[2] which since 1340 had evidently been in the sphere of influence of Moscow. So lax indeed was his control over these two vitally important semi-autonomous border-districts that Ol'gerd had no difficulty in attacking Smolensk and Bryansk in the autumn of 1356 and probably in resuming control over them.[3] No help came from Moscow; indeed it is significant that the "Vasily of Smolensk", whose son Ol'gerd captured in the attack on Smolensk, turned to the khan for help and not to Ivan of Moscow.[4]

Even more indicative of the friendly relations between Ivan II and Lithuania is the news that in the summer of 1356, before

[1] "Prince Vasily made peace (*vozma lyubov'*) with Prince Ivan Ivanovich according to the word of the metropolitan" (*PSRL*, xv (i), col. 66; *cf.* x, p. 229). "According to the word of the metropolitan (*po mitropolichyu slovu*)" must be taken to mean "on the instructions of the metropolitan".

[2] In 1341–2 Ivan had been married to the daughter of Dmitry of Bryansk; she died in 1343. (*See* above, p. 203.)

[3] *See* above, p. 204, note 1.

[4] *See* ibid. and p. 209. Whether in fact Ol'gerd resumed control over Smolensk in 1356 is not known. It seems, however, likely that the pro-Lithuanian Ivan Aleksandrovich, who had ruled Smolensk prior to 1352 as a semi-vassal of Ol'gerd, was reinstated in 1356. The Rogozhsky Chronicle states that in 1359 "Prince Ivan of Smolensk died and his son Svyatoslav sat upon the throne." (*See PSRL*, xv (i), col. 67.)

their attack on Smolensk and Bryansk, the Lithuanians had no difficulty in occupying and taking over the important border-town of Rzheva on the Volga, situated in Smolensk territory just to the west of Tver''s westernmost boundary. Rzheva had evidently come under Muscovite control in 1352 as a result of the treaty concluded between Semen and Smolensk, although there is no mention of it in the chronicles. The only two sources to mention the occupation of Rzheva, the Rogozhsky and Nikon Chronicles, describe it as though it was a purely peaceful operation: "In that summer Ivan Sizhsky settled in Rzheva with Lithuanians."[1] The verb used, *sede*, does not normally imply conquest or invasion, but colonization or the peaceful occupation of a throne. At the same time it is probable that the Lithuanians took over control of another Smolensk border-district, the town of Belaya on the Obsha river, south-west of Rzheva.[2]

Peaceful relations with a neighbour, however, were usually confirmed by a treaty or by a marriage. Although the one contemporary source to mention Russo-Lithuanian affairs in 1356, the Tver' Rogozhsky Chronicle, says nothing of a formal treaty, at least it reports the wedding of Ivan II's daughter with the son of Prince Koriad of Nowogródek, fifth eldest son of Gedimin.[3] That this was no love match, but a marriage of purely political convenience, is evident from the fact that Ivan's daughter cannot have been much over ten years old at the time.[4] The significance of the marriage becomes still clearer if we bear in mind the fact that Koriad was one of his brother Ol'gerd's most faithful allies and that he had assisted the grand prince of Lithuania both in

---

[1] *PSRL*, xv (i), col. 65; x, p. 228. Although the Rogozhsky Chronicle reports the occupation of Rzheva after the murder of Khvost (February 1357), it is more likely that it took place before (*see* the Nikon Chronicle), in the summer of 1356, and was misplaced by the editor of the Rogozhsky Chronicle.

[2] The chroniclers make no mention of its occupation; but in 1359, after the death of Ivan Aleksandrovich of Smolensk, when Smolensk evidently reverted to some sort of Muscovite control (Ol'gerd attacked it later in the year) "the men of Smolensk attacked (*voevali*) Belaya" (*PSRL*, xv (i), col. 68).

[3] *See PSRL*, xv (i), col. 65 (last entry under 1356). *Cf.* x, p. 228 (first entry under 1356).

[4] Assuming, that is, that she was the daughter of Ivan's second wife Aleksandra, whom he married in 1345 (*see TL*, p. 367).

his eastern and southern plans and in his anti-Tatar expansion of Lithuania.[1]

The picture of Ivan II which emerges from all these facts is a clear one. It is the picture of a prince who broke with the traditions of his elder brother and father and who revolted against the policy of servile submission to the Horde and its concomitant implacable hostility towards the West. In all Ivan's reported actions—and it must be repeated here that the majority of his deeds were probably expunged from the chronicles by later eulogists of the house of Moscow—there is evidence only of a complete reversal of Semen's policy. His actions speak for themselves: he flagrantly disobeyed his brother in 1348 by refusing to go to the aid of a Novgorod which was under pressure from the West; he allied himself to the princes of Suzdal', whose blatant links with Lithuania had made them even more unacceptable in the eyes of the khan than Ivan Ivanovich as candidates for the throne of Vladimir; he encouraged not the pro-Moscow, Tatar-sponsored house of Kashin in the quarrel which split Tver', but the sons of that great enemy of Moscow, Aleksandr Mikhaylovich, who like their father looked for support to the West and not to Moscow or Saray; he made no attempt to resist Ol'gerd's encroachments on the semi-aligned principality of Smolensk, which Semen had converted into an area of predominantly Muscovite influence in 1352—indeed the bloodless occupation of Rzheva looks as though it was carried out according to an agreement between the two grand princes; and, finally, he allied himself by marriage to a Lithuanian prince who not only was the faithful friend of his brother Ol'gerd but had been humiliatingly handed over by Khan Jani-Beg to Grand Prince Semen at the very moment when Ivan was performing his first recorded act of revolt against the accepted policy of the house of Moscow.[2] Small wonder that Ivan's friend and counsellor amongst the boyars, Khvost, was murdered by the exasperated "senior" boyars, who in the 1340's had been staunch supporters of Grand Prince Semen and who from 1353 to 1357 were obliged to witness the patient work of Ivan's predecessors being systematically undone. Only a drastic measure could save the principality of Moscow, indeed

[1] See Paszkiewicz, *Jagiellonowie*, p. 393, note 2.
[2] For Koriad's mission to Saray in 1348, *see* above, pp. 198 sq.

the whole grand principality of Vladimir; and the drastic measure taken, the murder of Khvost, acted as the necessary catalyst in the process of converting Ivan II from a policy of solidarity with the West and resistance to the overlordship of the Golden Horde to one of orthodox conformance not only with his immediate predecessors on the throne of Moscow but with most of the rulers of Vladimir over the last century.

From all the available information it would appear that the great change in Ivan's policy took place in 1357. It remains only to examine, firstly, the reasons for this change, and, secondly, what evidence there is of a new direction in the policy of the grand prince from 1357 to his death in 1359.

As has been said above, a powerful factor in the transformation of Ivan's government was the murder of Khvost. The rebellion and defection of part, perhaps most, of the senior advisers and administrators of the principality made a continuation of previous policy impossible. The "great boyars" could hardly be replaced in a hurry. Still more important, however, was the presence and influence of Metropolitan Aleksey.

Aleksey came from a boyar family closely connected with Moscow. His father, Fedor Byakont, had transferred his services from Chernigov to Daniil of Moscow in the thirteenth century. Aleksey was brought up at the court of the princes of Moscow (Ivan I was his godfather),[1] but took the tonsure at an early age in the Moscow monastery of the Epiphany, where he became closely associated with the abbot Stefan, the brother of St. Sergy of Radonezh.[2] He evidently attracted the attention of Metropolitan Feognost and Grand Prince Semen, for in 1352 the former appointed him bishop of Vladimir and designated him as his successor to the throne of metropolitan; indeed after his appointment to the see of Vladimir both Feognost and Semen sent envoys to Constantinople requesting recognition of him as metropolitan-elect.[3] When Feognost died in 1353, Aleksey went to Constantinople for consecration and returned to north-east Russia a year later as metropolitan.

The complex details of the first three years of Aleksey's metropolitanate need not concern us here; suffice it to say that they

[1] See PSRL, xxv, p. 194.   [2] See Presnyakov, Obrazovanie, p. 291, note 3.
[3] See PSRL, xxv, p. 179.

were years spent in trying to sort out what the Rogozhsky Chronicle calls an "unprecedented upheaval (*myatezh'* . . . *chego to ne byvalo prezhe sego*)"[1] resulting from the appointment of *two* metropolitans, Roman and Aleksey, by the patriarch. Eventually a compromise was reached whereby Aleksey was recognized as metropolitan of "the land of Rus'", while Roman, the candidate of Ol'gerd, received as his diocese "the land of Lithuania and Volyn'". We need not, then, wonder why pressure was not brought to bear on Ivan II during the first four years of his reign; during nearly half this time Aleksey was away in Constantinople pleading his cause for an undivided see. By 1357, however, the worst of the conflict was over and Aleksey was able to turn his attention to the errant prince of Moscow and Vladimir.

It is not surprising that Aleksey should have taken up a position politically and ideologically opposite to that of Ivan II and Khvost. He was, after all, a representative of the "old *boyarstvo*"; through Abbot Stefan, who was, according to Aleksey's *vita*, the father-confessor not only of Grand Prince Semen but also of Vasily Vasil'evich Vel'yaminov, Fedor Vasil'evich Vel'yaminov and "other senior boyars",[2] he was connected with the opponents of Khvost. His proximity to Semen is demonstrated not only by the fact that Semen supported his candidature in Constantinople, but also by the evidence of the grand prince's will: Aleksey headed the list of clergy who witnessed the signing of the document.[3]

A third and final reason for Ivan's change of heart in 1357 must be sought in the attitude of the Horde. After appointing Ivan Ivanovich grand prince in 1353 in preference to Konstantin of Suzdal', Jani-Beg seems to have had remarkably few dealings with north-east Rus'—it may well be that during the years 1353 to 1356 the Tatars were more concerned with the vast three-cornered struggle which was going on between Poland, Lithuania and the Teutonic Knights: we know of King Casimir's two embassies to the Horde in 1353 and 1354, as well as of the presence of "seven Tatar princes" and their armies who came to the help of the king in 1355.[4] In 1357, however, a "powerful envoy" (*posol silen*) by the name of Koshak arrived in Suzdalia and caused

---

[1] *PSRL*, xv (i), col. 63.   [2] *See* Cherepnin, *Obrazovanie*, p. 550.
[3] *See DDG*, p. 14.   [4] *See* Paszkiewicz, *Jagiellonowie*, p. 396.

"the Russian princes much suffering".[1] This, the first *posol* for many years to come on what seems to have been a purely punitive mission, may well have communicated to Grand Prince Ivan the disapproval of the khan.

With his advisory council of boyars debilitated by the self-imposed exile of probably at least half its members, browbeaten by the formidable figure of Aleksey and threatened by a khan used to subservience on the part of his vassals, Ivan II had little alternative but to mend his ways. That he did so there is ample evidence in the sources. The first act of conformity was the treaty of 1357 with Vasily of Kashin, a treaty signed on the insistence of the metropolitan. Later in the year Vsevolod of Kholm, who, it is reasonable to surmise, had enjoyed Ivan II's support from 1353 to 1357, was unceremoniously arrested by the grand prince's *namestniki* in Pereyaslavl' as he made his way to the Horde.[2] The sad history of war-racked Tver' during the years 1358 and 1359 is proof that Moscow and the Tatars were now again in close collaboration, purposefully working towards the enfeeblement of Tver': the prince of Moscow was once more firmly committed to the cause of the appanage of Kashin and just as firmly opposed to the Lithuania-oriented Aleksandrovichi, Vsevolod and Mikhail. Ivan himself, who presented his credentials to the new khan Berdi-Beg at the end of 1357, was formally reconciled with the recalcitrant boyars who had fled to Ryazan' earlier in the year: "He received them in the Horde," says the chronicle.[3] When he returned in the following year, he invited them to come back to Moscow.[4]

But for still more convincing evidence of Ivan's political *volte face* we must look to his relations with Lithuania. In 1358, for the first time in six years, the Muscovites made a vigorous attempt to check Ol'gerd's eastward expansion, which had been facilitated by Ivan's previous policy of friendship with Lithuania: a joint expedition from Mozhaysk and Tver' drove the Lithuanians out of Rzheva,[5] which they had occupied effortlessly two years earlier and which they had since held unopposed. When in the following year the pro-Lithuanian Ivan Aleksandrovich of Smolensk died,

[1] *PSRL*, xxv, p. 180.   [2] *See* above, p. 236.
[3] *PSRL*, xv (i), col. 66.   [4] *See PSRL*, x, p. 230.
[5] *See* above, p. 238, note 1.

the influence of Moscow was reasserted in his principality, for we find troops from Smolensk attacking Belaya, which had been occupied two years earlier by Lithuanians at the same time as Rzheva. This aggressive spirit shown by Ivan was answered by Ol'gerd later in 1359 when he attacked and regained control of Smolensk, occupied the town of Mstislavl' in the heart of the southern half of the principality of Smolensk, and reoccupied Rzheva in the east.[1] Once more we are witnessing, in the last year and a half of Ivan II's reign, the old hostility which existed between Lithuania and the Moscow of Ivan Kalita and Semen.

With Ivan II's brusque reversal of policy in 1357, his conversion, one might say, to the status of an orthodox Danilovich, we are back—in the sphere of foreign policy anyhow—to where we were in the reigns of Ivan I and Semen. It was not a case of Ivan II voluntarily changing his mind on realizing the danger of Ol'gerd and of his sympathizers in the north-east Russian principalities. It was a case of strong pressure being brought to bear on the grand prince by the most vigorous and powerful section of the community, the "great boyars", by the Church and by the Tatars. He was forced by those with vested interests to revert to the policy of his brother and his father.

What is important about Ivan's reign, however, is not so much that a grand prince should have enjoyed this brief period of what might almost be described as a revolt against tradition. After all there is very little to show that the events of the first four years of Ivan's reign had any lasting effect on Russo-Lithuanian relations or that any tenseness and disagreement between Ivan and Jani-Beg made much difference to subsequent relations between Moscow-Vladimir and the Tatars, for in any case these relations were entirely transformed by the internal disorders within the Horde and the period of civil war amongst the Tatars which followed the murder of Berdi-Beg in 1359.[2] What is of importance is the fact that the recorded events of Ivan II's reign provide us with the first evidence of a split in the ranks of the grand prince's advisers, between "senior" and "junior" boyars, who were fundamentally divided, not so much perhaps on the question of subjugation to the Horde, as on the question of relations with the

[1] See PSRL, xv (i), cols. 67–8.   [2] See Spuler, GH, pp. 109 sq.

West. In the succeeding two centuries this dichotomy becomes even more striking a feature in the political life of Muscovy. But curiously enough the roles change. It is the conservative "senior *boyarstvo*" of the fifteenth and sixteenth centuries, the Vsevolozhskys, the Patrikeevs and the Kurbskys, who press for a policy of peaceful relations with the West; while the "progressive" "junior *boyarstvo*" urge on the grand prince to assume an aggressive attitude towards Poland and Lithuania.

With the death of Ivan II in 1359 an age in the history of north-east Russia came to an end, an age of conflict, of struggle for supremacy amongst the toughest survivors of the descendants of Vsevolod III; and in the resolution of this struggle, as has been repeated many times above, one of the prime ascertainable factors was always the will of the khan. In other words it was an age of Suzdalian puppet-politics, controlled and dominated to a large extent by the supreme overlord, the ruler of the Golden Horde. Any attempts on the part of the grand princes to steer an independent course westwards, away from Saray, such as the brief but futile efforts of the early Tverite grand princes or of Ivan II of Moscow, were crushed by the khan, their instigators being either physically removed or forcibly persuaded to mend their ways.

Though the pattern of events of the succeeding reign of Dmitry Donskoy (1359–89) often bears a striking resemblance to that of the first sixty years of the fourteenth century, particularly where the relationships between the territories of north-east Russia and the unhesitating support lent by the Church to Moscow are concerned, nevertheless the thirty years following Ivan II's death are marked by changes so profound that one is justified in talking of a new era in the history of the principality of Moscow and the grand principality of Vladimir. In the first place Moscow consolidated her position as indisputable leader of the north-east Russian principalities. Proof of this hegemony is to be found not only in the impressive lists of princes who marched under the banners of the prince of Moscow in the wars against Tver', Lithuania and the Horde,[1] but also in the "gathering of the

[1] For an expression of the feeling of solidarity among the Russian princes under their military leader Dmitry of Moscow at the battle of Kulikovo

Russian lands" and in the conversion of the principality of Moscow into the grand principality of Vladimir *and* Moscow. Under Dmitry Donskoy there took place those vast annexations of territory which more than doubled the acreage of the districts directly under the control of the prince of Moscow (it will be remembered that the only incontrovertible annexation of territory by the rulers of Moscow during the preceding half-century was the district of Borovsk in the basins of the Luzha and upper Protva rivers, which had only been acquired at the expense of a valuable segment of the southern boundary on the Oka). And Dmitry Donskoy for the first time managed inseparably to identify the principality of Moscow with the grand principality of Vladimir by getting the Tatars and his Suzdalian cousins to recognize Vladimir, that is to say the title of grand prince and the territories dependent on Vladimir, as part and parcel of his own *otchina*, something which now belonged inalienably to the family of the Danilovichi. Already in 1371 the Muscovite authorities were able to talk of "our patrimony the grand principality"[1] in a treaty concluded with Ol'gerd of Lithuania; later in the 1370's, as has been mentioned above, Dmitry's cousin Vladimir Andreevich of Borovsk agreed not to "seek your patrimony nor the grand principality, either from you *or from your children*".[2] But the most vivid proof of the assimilation of the thrones of Vladimir and Moscow is to be found in Dmitry Donskoy's will of 1389 in which he *bequeaths* Vladimir to his eldest son: "I bless my son Prince Vasily with my patrimony the

---

(1380), see the following passage from the earliest extant version of Sofony of Ryazan''s "Tale of the Grand Prince Dmitry Ivanovich and his cousin Vladimir Andreevich" (Zadonshchina): "Then they flew together like eagles from all the northern land (i.e. Suzdalia). But these were not eagles that flew together, but all the Russian princes who assembled to help Grand Prince Dmitry Ivanovich, speaking thus: 'O Lord, Grand Prince, the pagan Tatars are already invading our fields and are taking our patrimony from us. . . . Let us cross the river Don, compose a wonder for other lands, a tale for old men to tell and young men to remember" (V. P. Adrianova-Peretts, "Zadonshchina", p. 233 (*Kirillo-Belozersky spisok*).

[1] "*v nashei ochine, v velikom knyazhen'i*", "*v nashyu ochinu, v velikoe knyazhen'e*" (*DDG*, p. 22; *see* Cherepnin, RFA, vol. i, p. 48).

[2] The italics are mine. (*See* above, p. 291.)

grand principality."[1] Not only the title of grand prince of Vladimir, but also the lands of Vladimir, Pereyaslavl' and Kostroma were now as much a possession of the Muscovite princely family as were the title of Prince of Moscow and the lands of Zvenigorod, say, or Mozhaysk.[2]

The period of thirty years following the death of Ivan II, however, not only differs from the period discussed in this book in the fact of Moscow's expansion and the final consolidation of her position as supreme leader amongst the principalities of Suzdalia, a position for which the ground had, after all, been prepared to some extent by the efforts of the earlier princes of Moscow; it is also remarkable for the complete change in the attitude of the rulers of Suzdalia towards the Horde. Diplomacy, strategy and morale underwent a striking transformation. The negative, defensive attitude adopted by the majority of the grand princes towards the Horde during the first sixty years of the fourteenth century, an attitude which was calculated to secure the position of the princes concerned and to guarantee for their lands safety from Tatar inroads, gradually changed during the sixties and seventies of the fourteenth century to one of resistance to the Horde and from defensive resistance to offensive aggression, culminating in the Russian victory over the Tatars on the Vozha river in 1378 and in the great battle of Kulikovo Pole in 1380. And although the sack of Moscow by Tokhtamysh in 1382 was a crushing blow to Dmitry Donskoy's aspirations as leader of the Russian liberation movement and led once again to a renewal of tribute-payment and an increase of Tatar pressure on the grand prince, we need not think that it meant an irreparable setback to unification or that it heralded a return to the age of Ivan I as far as relations with the Horde were concerned.[3] As Cherepnin has pointed out, "in the view of the government of Dmitry Donskoy the Tatar yoke and the obligation to pay tribute

---

[1] "*A se blagoslovlyayu syna svoego, knyaz ya Vasl'ya, svoeyu otchinoyu, velikim knyazhen'em*" (*DDG*, p. 34).

[2] According to his will Dmitry left his wife certain villages from the districts of Vladimir, Pereyaslavl' and Kostroma (*see ibid.*). Note, too, that when Ol'gerd's son, Dmitry of Trubchevsk, defected to Moscow in 1379 he was given "the city of Pereyaslavl' with all its revenues". (*See TL*, p. 419; *PSRL*, xxv, pp. 200–1.)

[3] Such is the view of Presnyakov. (*See Obrazovanie*, pp. 328–9.)

were merely temporary phenomena".[1] Kulikovo, although it could hardly be called a victory for the Russians, had indeed shown and convinced them that the Tatars were no longer invincible and that it was merely a matter of time and opportunity before the yoke was thrown off once and for all.

It is outside the scope of this book to discuss in detail the many complex reasons for this change of attitude towards the Horde, which so sharply differentiates Dmitry's reign from those of his predecessors. Suffice it to say that the two most powerful factors were firstly the enfeeblement of the Horde resulting from the internecine feuds and inter-khanate squabbles known by the Russians as the "Great Trouble" (velikaya zamyatnya), the beginning of which coincided with the beginning of Dmitry's reign; and secondly the growth and strengthening of Muscovy. The crisis in the Horde cannot of course be ascribed to Suzdalian intereference or diplomacy. But during the period described in this book much of the way had been paved by Dmitry Donskoy's predecessors for the ultimate strengthening of Muscovy and for her emergence as leader amongst the principalities of north-east Rus'.

[1] See Cherepnin, Obrazovanie, p. 651.

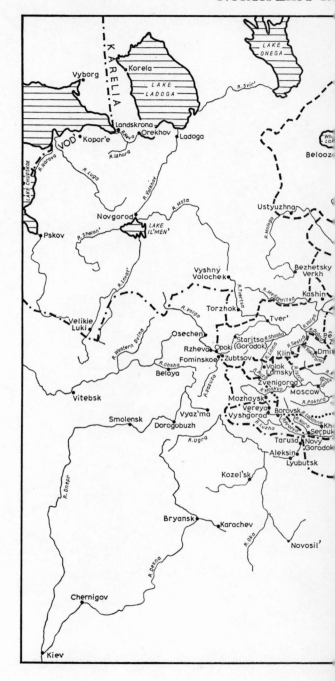

KARELIA

Vyborg

Korela

LAKE
LADOGA

LAKE
ONEGA

R. Svir'

Landskrona

VOD' Kopor'e Orekhov Ladoga

R. Neva

R. Izhora

R. Narova

LAKE CHUDSKOE

R. Luga

R. Volkhov

R. Msta

Beelooz

Whi
La

Ustyuzhna

R. Mologa

Novgorod

LAKE
IL'MEN'

R. Shelon'

Pskov

R. Lovat'

Bezhetsky
Verkh

Kashin

Vyshny
Volochek

R. Medveditsa

R. Tvertsa

Velikie
Luki

R. Valga

Torzhok

Tver'

R. Vazuza

R. Volga

Osechen

R. Western Dvina

Staritsa R. Shosha

Rzheva Opoki (Gorodok)

Fominskoe

R. Obsha

Zubtsov

Klin

R. Lama

Dmi

Volok
Lamsky

R. Sestra

R. Sestra

R. Istra

Pe
Z

Belaya

Zvenigorod

R. Moskva

MOSCOW

Vitebsk

Mozhaysk

R. Pakhra

Vyaz'ma

Vereya

Vyshgorod

Borovsk

R. Lopasna

Smolensk

Dorogobuzh

R. Ugra

R. Luzha

R. Protva

Tarusa Novy

Serpuk

Kh

Aleksin

Gorodok

R. Dnepr

Kozel'sk

Lyubutsk

R. Desna

Bryansk

Karachev

R. Oka

Novosil'

Chernigov

Kiev

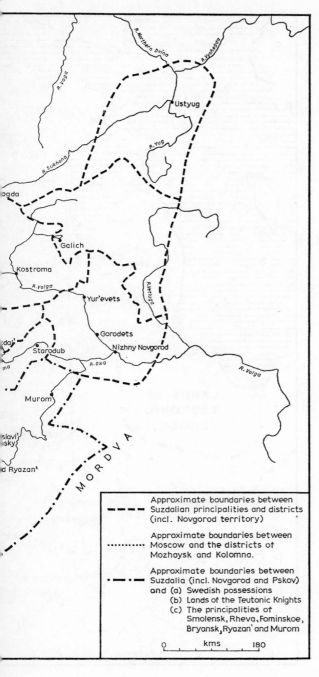

R. Northern Dvina

R. Vychegda

Ustyug

R. Yug

R. Vaga

R. Sukhona

ogda

Galich

Kostroma

R. Volga

Yur'evets

R. Vetluga

Gorodets

dai

Starodub

Nizhny Novgorod

ma

R. Oka

R. Volga

Murom

slavl'
sky

d Ryazan'

M O R D V A

Approximate boundaries between
— — — Suzdalian principalities and districts
(incl. Novgorod territory)

Approximate boundaries between
············ Moscow and the districts of
Mozhaysk and Kolomna.

Approximate boundaries between
—·—·— Suzdalia (incl. Novgorod and Pskov)
and (a) Swedish possessions
(b) Lands of the Teutonic Knights
(c) The principalities of
Smolensk, Rheva, Fominskoe,
Bryansk, Ryazan' and Murom

0   kms   180

R. Neva Orekhov

Kopor'e

AND OF NOVGOROD

Novgorod
LAKE
IL'MEN'

R. Lovat'

Torzhok   Tver'
R. Volga   PRINCIPALITY
OF TVER'

Velikie   Rzheva   Volok
Luki   Fominskoe   Lamsky
R. Obsha   Mozhaysk R. Moskva
NCIPALITY Western Dvina   PRINCIPALITY
OF POLOTSK   R. Mezha Belaya   OF MOSCOW
TY   R. Vazuza
Polotsk   PRINCIPALITY   R. Yaz'ma Vyaz'ma
Vitebsk   OF
Smolensk   Dorogobuzh
R. Dnepr   SMOLENSK
Drutsk   R. Drut'   Mstislavl'

Bryansk

CHERNIGOV
SEVERSKY   Trubchevsk

Novgorod
Seversky
'urov

Chernigov

INCIPALITY
OF
KIEV   Kiev

Appendix A: Sources

The following notes are not intended as an exhaustive study of the primary sources. They are intended rather as a general guide to the origins and history of those chronicles which I have used in this book as the main primary sources. Chronicles of later origin or those which I have only used rarely as sources (the Voskresensky, Nikon, Pskov First, Second and Third Chronicles, and others) have not been included: their reliability and their relationship to other sources are discussed, where relevant, in the footnotes.

[1] THE TRINITY CHRONICLE

In the fire of 1812 the only known copy of the Trinity Chronicle was burned. Karamzin, however, had used it extensively in his History and from his copious notes, in which he quotes it, and from the later Simeonovsky Chronicle (*PSRL*, xviii), which from 1177 to 1390 is very close to Karamzin's extracts, the Trinity Chronicle was reconstructed by the Soviet scholar M. D. Priselkov in 1950.

The Trinity Chronicle was compiled in 1408, probably by Metropolitan Kiprian, in Moscow. Priselkov reconstructs the history of the text as follows: from 1305 to 1327 a grand-princely chronicle was kept in Tver'. This Tverite redaction, or a copy of it, was evidently taken by Ivan I to Moscow in 1328 and re-edited to suit Muscovite ideology of the time. The chronicle was continued throughout Ivan I's and the succeeding reigns, and events were written or omitted purely to conform with the political tendencies of the princes of Moscow. The first *svod* or compilation was evidently completed in 1340.[1] From 1341 to 1389 the work

[1] *See* the words describing Ivan's death and burial (*TL*, p. 364). *Cf.* Priselkov, *IRL*, p. 124.

was continued in Moscow much in the same style as the earlier editions. The 1389 edition was known as the "Great Russian Chronicle".[1] The chronicle was then continued up to 1408. This latest edition Priselkov considers to have been an "all-Russian metropolitan *svod*", in other words a compilation carried out at the court of the metropolitan and not confined in interest or sources to one Russian district. Not only did the compiler (Kiprian?) use what must be assumed to have been the local, parochially Muscovite (and hence anti-Tver') "Great Russian Chronicle" of 1389, but he also incorporated into his text numerous other sources of information: in particular, a strictly censored Tverite continuation of the original *svod* of 1327; Novgorod information which had been carefully selected and pruned to conform with Muscovite political feelings; and news concerning the grand principality of Lithuania.[2] To what extent the last editor/compiler in 1408 altered what he found in his basic source, the compilation of 1389, or in his other sources cannot of course be estimated with any degree of accuracy; still less can one tell how the compiler of the "Great Russian Chronicle" of 1389 dealt with the work of his predecessor of 1340. Likhachev, however, is of the opinion that there was surprisingly little editing of the local chronicles which he used.[3]

To summarize, we can describe the history of the relation of events up to 1359 according to the Trinity Chronicle as follows:

Up to 1327: Tver' chronicle accounts strictly censored and/or remoulded by the Muscovite editor of 1328 (and probably by subsequent editors in 1340, 1389 and 1408 as well).

1328–59: Purely Muscovite chronicle-writing carried out in Moscow and, in its later stages at any rate, in the court of the metropolitan. Information from outside sources (Novgorod, Tver', Ryazan', Rostov, Suzdal', etc.) added probably only in 1408.

[1] For proof of the existence of the "Great Russian Chronicle (*Letopisets veliky russky*)" of 1389, *see TL*, p. 439. (*See* also Priselkov, *IRL*, pp. 121 sq.)
[2] Note that under Metropolitan Kiprian all the Russian and Lithuanian lands were united ecclesiastically.
[3] *See* Likhachev, *RL*, p. 297.

Thus the following basic stemma may be constructed (note that in this and in subsequent diagrams unshaded circles represent hypothetical redactions and sources):

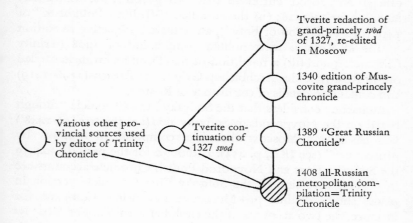

Tverite redaction of grand-princely *svod* of 1327, re-edited in Moscow

1340 edition of Muscovite grand-princely chronicle

Various other provincial sources used by editor of Trinity Chronicle

Tverite continuation of 1327 *svod*

1389 "Great Russian Chronicle"

1408 all-Russian metropolitan compilation=Trinity Chronicle

[2] THE NOVGOROD CHRONICLES

The earliest extant example of purely Novgorodian chronicle-writing is the Novgorod First Chronicle. The "older redaction" or *starshy izvod* (the so-called Sinodal'ny copy) takes the narrative up to 1330 and, for the first thirty years of the fourteenth century, can be considered as the official Novgorod chronicle kept at the court of the archbishop. After 1330 there are a few additional entries written in different hands (1331, 1332, 1333, 1337, 1345, 1353; see *NL*, pp. 99–100). The "later redaction" or *mladshy izvod* is much the same as the "older redaction" as far as the events of the first thirty years of the fourteenth century are concerned; for most of the period 1331–59 it also reflects the official attitude of the archbishop to contemporary events. In other words, both redactions of the Novgorod First Chronicle may be called the Novgorod archiepiscopal chronicle for the period 1304–59.

Both the Novgorod Fourth and the Sofiysky First Chronicles are later compilations and, as far as the events of the fourteenth century are concerned, both derive from a common source, a hypothetical *svod* of 1448.[1] This compilation of 1448 was, in the opinion of Priselkov and Likhachev, an amalgamation of three sources: (i) the so-called "Sofiysky vremennik" of 1418—the official Novgorod chronicle (i.e. Novgorod First Chronicle) taken as far as 1418; (ii) the so-called "Vladimir Polikhron" of 1418 (or "Polikhron of Foty"), an unbiased, objective re-edition of the all-Russian metropolitan compilation of 1408 (Trinity Chronicle); and (iii) a re-edition of the Trinity Chronicle carried out in Rostov under Archbishop Grigory of Rostov (1396–1419) and containing details of the history of Rostov.

Likhachev considers that the Sofiysky First Chronicle "though based on the Novgorodsko-Sofiysky *svod* (i.e. the '*svod* of 1448') was basically a Moscow chronicle, composed in Moscow by Muscovites" (see *IRL*, p. 453). Although for the period 1304–59 the Sofiysky First and Novgorod Fourth Chronicle accounts are in general very similar, the Sofiysky First Chronicle version in places shows distinct pro-Muscovite flavouring. Compare, for instance, the two accounts of the clash between Yury of Moscow and Mikhail of Tver' in 1317 (*PSRL*, iv (i), p. 257; v, pp. 206–7).

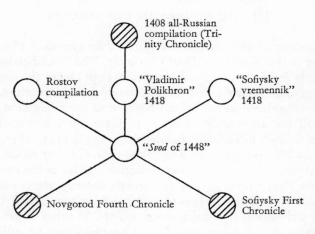

[1] Priselkov considered this to be a Muscovite metropolitan *svod*. Likhachev, on the other hand, not only considers 1448 to be the wrong date, but, together with A. A. Shakhmatov, thinks that it was a Novgorodian compilation ("*Novgorodsko-Sofiysky svod*). (*See* Priselkov, *IRL*, pp. 142 sq.; Likhachev, *RL*, pp. 446–9; A. A. Shakhmatov, *ORLS*, p. 155.)

[3] THE TVER' CHRONICLES

Tver' chronicle-writing in the fourteenth century is reflected in the Tver' Chronicle (Tverskoy sbornik: *PSRL*, xv) and the Rogozhsky Chronicle (*PSRL*, xv (i)). The latter is fuller and contains more detail than the former as far as events of the first sixty years of the fourteenth century are concerned, although from 1280 to 1327 the two are almost identical. As has been mentioned above (*see* p. 315), the grand-princely chronicle was kept in Tver' up to 1327. In spite of the disaster of 1327 and 1328 chronicle-writing evidently continued at the court of the prince of Tver' throughout the fourteenth century.[1] Later stages in Tver' chronicle-writing can be identified as follows: Bishop Arseny's *svod* of 1409; the grand-princely *svod* of 1425; the grand-princely *svod* of 1455.[2] The Rogozhsky Chronicle derived directly from the latter, but it also used as one of its sources the all-Russian *svod* of 1408 (= Trinity Chronicle) in a form re-edited in Tver' in 1412.[3] Consequently the events of the fourteenth century as given in the Rogozhsky Chronicle reflect not only Muscovite chronicle-writing, but also an *anti-Muscovite, pro-Tverite* point of view. The great value of the Rogozhsky Chronicle lies also in the fact that it apparently escaped later Muscovite censorship.[4] The later Tverskoy sbornik (*PSRL*, xv) derived indirectly from the grand-princely *svod* of 1455.

The striking amount of Tverite information found (sometimes exclusively) in the sixteenth-century Nikon Chronicle indicates that the latter used as one of its sources a redaction of the Tver' Chronicle. Nasonov suggests a Kashin redaction of 1425 which in its turn used as one of its sources the Tver' grand-princely *svod* of 1425.[5]

[1] Nasonov considers that the chronicle was transferred back to Tver' when the 1330's when the grand principality of Tver' was created by Tatar patent (Nasonov, "Letopisnye pamyatniki", p. 768). It seems, however, more likely that the *svod* was never removed and that it was continued in 1328 when Konstantin and Vasily returned to Tver' and re-established order there (*see PSRL*, xv (i), col. 44).

[2] *See* Nasonov, op. cit.   [3] *See* ibid.

[4] *See* Budovnits, "Otrazhenie", pp. 80 sq.; Likhachev, *RL*, pp. 458–60; Priselkov, *IRL*, ch. 5, 1; Shakhmatov, *ORLS*, ch. 24.

[5] *See* Nasonov, "Letopisnye pamyatniki", Section 4.

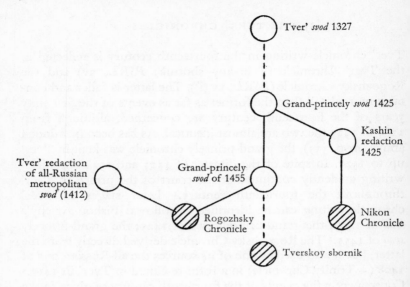

[4] THE MOSCOW SVOD OF 1479 AND THE
ERMOLINSKY CHRONICLE

The great Moscow compilation of 1479 (*PSRL*, xxv) presents
several complex textological problems. It was clearly the work of
laymen in the service of the grand prince of Moscow (and *not* the
metropolitan) and represents a major attempt to collate existing
chronicles and to edit them in conformity with the ideology of the
time.[1]

The most likely sources at the disposal of the compiler of the
svod of 1479 are as follows:

1   The previous grand-princely *svod* of 1472 (the Nikanorovsky
Chronicle which ends in 1471: *PSRL*, xxvii), called by Priselkov
"the first Muscovite grand-princely *svod*",[2] which in its turn
can be derived from the "*svod* of 1448" (the common source of

[1] This of course especially applies to the events of the fifteenth century.
See Ya. S. Lur'e, "Iz istorii", pp. 166 sq. A certain amount of tendentious
editing of the narration of events from 1304 to 1359 can also be detected,
but it is far less obvious. (*See* Priselkov, *IRL*, ch. 11, section 4.)

[2] Priselkov, *IRL*, ch. 10.

the Novgorod Fourth and Sofiysky First Chronicles; see above, pp. 317–18.)

2   One of the later redactions of the secular Muscovite "Great Russian Chronicle" of 1389 (*Letopisets veliky russky*, see above, pp. 315–16.)[1]

3   A Rostov edition of the Vladimir Polikhron of 1418 (*see* above, p. 318), carried out probably at the court of Archbishop Efrem (1427–53).[2]

4   An all-Russian *svod* (compiled probably in the 1450's or 1460's)[3] which contained certain information *not* found in the *svod* of 1448 (i.e. not found in the Sofiysky First, Novgorod Fourth, Novgorod First or Trinity Chronicles).[4] This *svod* in its turn derived from (i) the "*svod* of 1448"; (ii) the Vladimir Polikhron of 1418; and (iii) other sources (including one containing certain south-Russian information).

Now the Ermolinsky Chronicle (*PSRL*, xxiii) which at first sight looks like an abbreviation of the *svod* of 1479 (as far as the events prior to 1423 are concerned) is not, in fact, a contracted version of the *svod* of 1479, but a contracted version of 4 above. That the compiler of the Ermolinsky Chronicle did not use the *svod* of 1479 as his source and shorten it is evident from certain information it contains which is not found in the *svod* of 1479[5] (or in the Sofiysky First, Novgorod Fourth, Novgorod First, Trinity or Nikanorovsky Chronicles); and that the Ermolinsky Chronicle used as its main source a *svod* available only to the compiler of the *svod* of 1479 is demonstrated by frequent items

---

[1] *See* Priselkov, *IRL*, p. 174.   [2] *See* Priselkov, *IRL*, p. 182.

[3] It contained the story of the murder of Baty in Hungary (found in the *svod* of 1479 under 1247 and the Ermolinsky Chronicle under 1246, but not in the Sofiysky First, Novgorod Fourth, Novgorod First, Trinity or Nikanorovsky Chronicles) which was probably written by Pakhomy the Serb (active up to 1472). (*See* Nasonov, MSYuI, p. 361.)

[4] E.g. certain information on South Russia of the pre-Tatar period. (*See* Nasonov MSYuI.)

[5] *See* for example items contained in the Ermolinsky Chronicle on the events of 1317. *See* above, p. 84, notes 2 and 4.

For further convincing evidence to show that the Ermolinsky Chronicle did not abbreviate the *svod* of 1479, *see* Nasonov MSYuI, p. 359, and MSEL, p. 221. (*See* also above, pp. 105, note 4; 199, note 6.)

appearing only in these two works.[1] The Ermolinsky Chronicle, however, often shows similarity to the Trinity Chronicle and what we assume to have been the *svod* of 1448: this would indicate that these sources (i.e. the Vladimir Polikhron of 1418 and the *svod* of 1448) were either used by the compiler of 4 above, or, less likely, were available to the compiler of the Ermolinsky Chronicle.

The following stemma illustrates the main sources of the Moscow *svod* of 1479 and the Ermolinsky Chronicle.

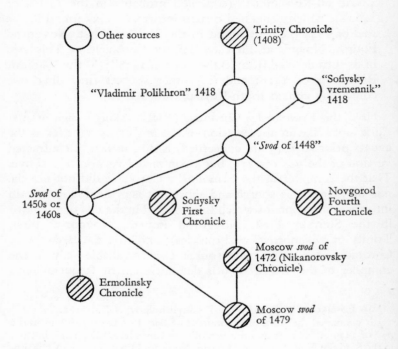

---

[1] E.g. the information that "Feognost set off for the land of Volyn'" in 1329, found only in *PSRL*, xxiii, p. 103 and xxv, p. 170, or the news of the murder of one Kruglets by Ol'gerd in 1347 (*PSRL*, xxiii, p. 109; xxv, p. 177). *Cf.* Nasonov, MSYuI, p. 359.

Appendix B: Genealogical Tables

(1) THE DESCENDANTS OF VLADIMIR I

Only those princes mentioned in the text are given in this Table

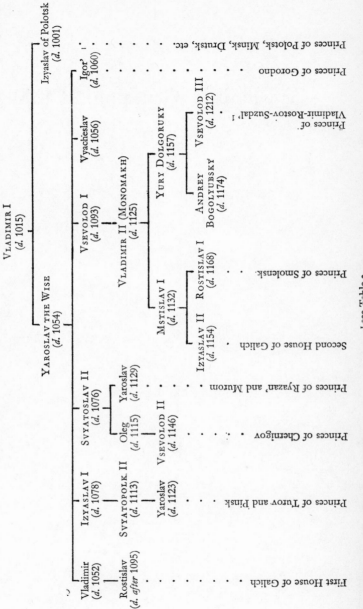

See Table 4

(2) THE DESCENDANTS OF VSEVOLOD III

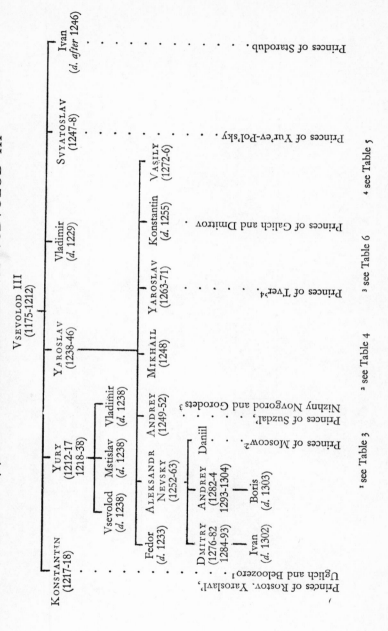

Vsevolod III
(1175-1212)

Konstantin (1217-18) — Yury (1212-17, 1218-38) — Yaroslav (1238-46) — Vladimir (d. 1229) — Svyatoslav (1247-8) — Ivan (d. after 1246)

Vsevolod (d. 1238) — Mstislav (d. 1238) — Vladimir (d. 1238)

Fedor (d. 1233) — Aleksandr Nevsky (1252-63) — Andrey (1249-52) — Mikhail (1248) — Yaroslav (1263-71) — Konstantin (d. 1255) — Vasily (1272-6)

Dmitry (1276-82, 1284-93) — Andrey (1282-4, 1293-1304) — Daniil

Ivan (d. 1302) — Boris (d. 1303)

Princes of Rostov, Yaroslavl', Uglich and Beloozero[1]

Princes of Moscow[2]

Princes of Suzdal', Nizhny Novgorod and Gorodets[3]

Princes of Tver'[4]

Princes of Galich and Dmitrov

Princes of Yur'ev-Pol'sky

Princes of Starodub

[1] see Table 3   [2] see Table 4   [3] see Table 6   [4] see Table 5

(3) THE DESCENDANTS OF KONSTANTIN VSEVOLODOVICH (PRINCES OF ROSTOV, BELOOZERO, UGLICH AND YAROSLAVL')

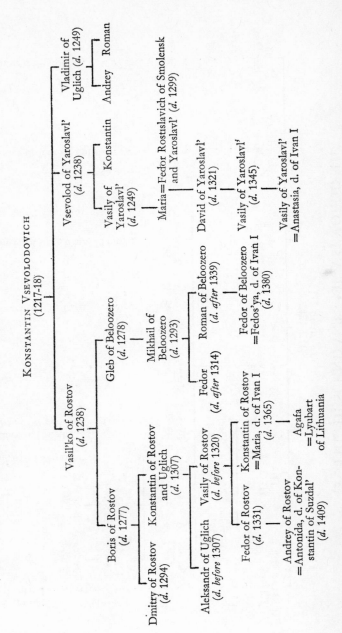

(4) THE DESCENDANTS OF DANIIL OF MOSCOW

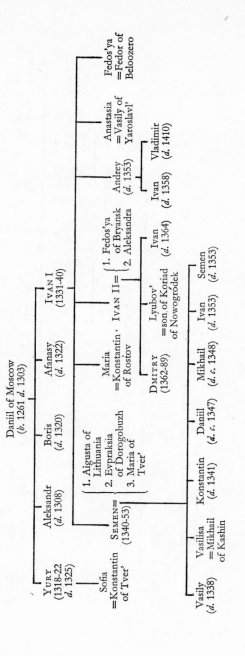

(5) THE DESCENDANTS OF YAROSLAV OF TVER'

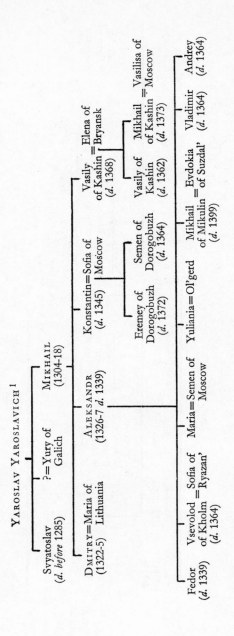

YAROSLAV YAROSLAVICH[1]

Svyatoslav (d. before 1285)

?=Yury of Galich

MIKHAIL (1304-18)

DMITRY=Maria of (1322-5) Lithuania

ALEKSANDR (1326-7 d. 1339)

Konstantin=Sofia of (d. 1345) Moscow

Vasily=Elena of of Kashin Bryansk (d. 1368)

Fedor (d. 1339)

Vsevolod=Sofia of of Kholm Ryazan' (d. 1364)

Maria=Semen of Moscow

Yuliania=Ol'gerd

Eremey of Dorogobuzh (d. 1372)

Semen of Dorogobuzh (d. 1364)

Mikhail=Evdokia of Mikulin of Suzdal' (d. 1399)

Vasily of Kashin (d. 1362)

Mikhail=Vasilisa of of Kashin Moscow (d. 1373)

Vladimir (d. 1364)

Andrey (d. 1364)

[1] see Table 2

(6) THE DESCENDANTS OF ANDREY OF SUZDAL'
AND NIZHNY NOVGOROD

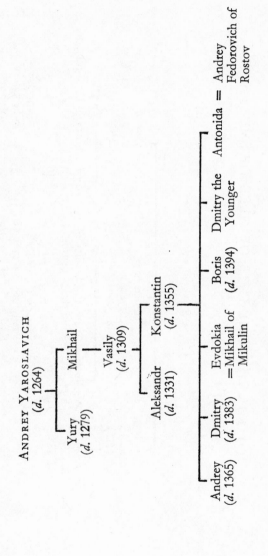

(7) THE DESCENDANTS OF GLEB OF SMOLENSK

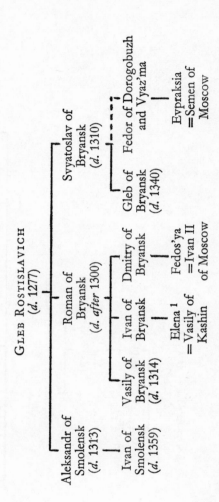

GLEB ROSTISLAVICH
(d. 1277)

Aleksandr of Smolensk
(d. 1313)

Ivan of Smolensk
(d. 1359)

Roman of Bryansk
(d. after 1300)

Vasily of Bryansk
(d. 1314)

Ivan of Bryansk

Elena [1]
= Vasily of Kashin

Dmitry of Bryansk

Fedos'ya
= Ivan II of Moscow

Svyatoslav of Bryansk
(d. 1310)

Gleb of Bryansk
(d. 1340)

Fedor of Dorogobuzh and Vyaz'ma

Evpraksia
= Semen of Moscow

[1] see Table 5

Glossary

baskak: Tatar overseer, official
boyar: nobleman, senior adviser of prince
boyarstvo: nobility, gentry
chern', chernye lyudi: commonalty, lit. "black people"
dar: tribute
dokonchanie: treaty
druzhina: bodyguard, detachment of troops, army
grivna: coin
izgoi: princes debarred from competing for title of grand prince
izvod: redaction
konets (pl. *kontsy*): city district of Novgorod
koromola: conspiracy, treachery, upheaval
koromol'nik: conspirator, trouble-maker
namestnik: lieutenant, governor
ostrog: system of fortifications
otchina: patrimony, estate or possession handed down by father
polk: force, detachment, regiment, division
pomest'e: land granted on precarious tenure in reward for service
posad: outskirts of a town
posadnichestvo: the office of *posadnik*
posadnik: annually appointed mayor (Novgorod and Pskov)
posol: Tatar official, envoy, representative of khan, plenipotentiary
prigorod: borough or town administratively dependent on larger town
pristav: police official
rat': army
ryad: contract, testament
seym: ⎫
s'ezd: ⎬ congress
snem: ⎭

Sovet Gospod: Council of Lords, senate (Novgorod)
Stepenny posadnik: senior *posadnik*
svod: chronicle compilation
temnik: Tatar commander of 10,000 men
tivun, tiyun: administrator, overseer
tysyatsky: local commander, judge and police chief
udel: appanage
uezd: district, administrative unit of land
ulus: nation, tribe, people (Tatar)
ushkuynik: river pirate (Novgorod)
veche: popular assembly
vechniki: participants at *veche*
vel' mozha: grandee
verst: measure of distance (about two-thirds of a mile)
voevoda: military commander
volost': district, area
yarlyk: patent to throne or diocese, Tatar document of privilege, charter

List of Works Cited and Abbreviations

Acta Patriarchatus Constantinopolitani (APC), ed. F. Miklosich and I. Müller, vol. i (Vienna, 1860).

Adrianova-Peretts, V. P., "Zadonshchina", *TODRL*, vol. vi, 1948.

A.N. SSSR—Akademiya Nauk SSSR

APC, see *Acta Patriarchatus Constantinopolitani*.

Artsikhovsky, A. V., "K istorii Novgoroda", *IZ*, book ii, 1938.

Artsikhovsky, A. V., "Pis'ma Ontsifora", *Problemy obshchestvenno-politicheskoy istorii Rossii i slavyanskikh stran. Sbornik statey k 70-letiyu akademika M. N. Tikhomirova* (Moscow, 1963).

Astrov, N., "Udel'ny knyaz' Fedor Yur'evich Fominsky", *ZhMNP*, vol. ix, 1872, pp. 61–75.

Bagaley, D., *Istoriya Severskoy zemli do poloviny XIV stoletiya* (Kiev, 1882).

Baumgarten, N. de, *Généalogies et mariages occidentaux des Rurikides Russes du Xe au XIIIe siècle (Généalogies, vol. i) (Orientalia Christiana*, vol. ix, No. 35, 1927).

Baumgarten, N. de, *Généalogies des branches régnantes des Rurikides du XIIIe au XVIe siècle (Généalogies, vol. ii) (Orientalia Christiana*, vol. xxxv, No. 94, 1934).

Begunov, Yu. K., *Pamyatnik russkoy literatury XIII veka "Slovo o pogibeli Russkoy zemli"* (A.N. SSSR, 1965).

Berezhkov, N. G., *Khronologiya russkogo letopisaniya* (A.N. SSSR, 1963).

Bernadsky, V. N., *Novgorod i Novgorodskaya zemlya v XV veke* (A.N. SSSR, 1961).

Blum, J., *Lord and Peasant in Russia from the ninth to the nineteenth century* (New York, 1964).

Borzakovsky, V. S., *Istoriya Tverskogo knyazhestva (ITK)* (SPb, 1876).

Budovnits, I. Yu, *Obshchestvenno-politicheskaya mysl' Drevney Rusi* (*OPM*) (Moscow, 1960).

Budovnits, I. Yu, "Otrazhenie politicheskoy bor'by Moskvy i Tveri v Tverskom i Moskovskom letopisanii XIV v.", *TODRL*, vol. xii, 1956, pp. 79–104.

Carr, E. H., *What is History?* (London, 1961).

Cherepnin, L. V., *Obrazovanie Russkogo tsentralizovannogo gosudarstva v XIV–XV vekakh* (Moscow, 1960).

Cherepnin, L. V., *Russkie feodal'nye arkhivy XIV–XV vekhov* (*RFA*), 2 vols. (A.N. SSSR, 1948, 1951).

Chodynicki, K., *Kościół prawosławny a Rzeczpospolita Polska (1370–1632)* (Warsaw, 1934).

Chteniya v imperatorskom obshchestve istorii i drevnosti (Moscow).

Danilevich, V. E., *Ocherk istorii Polotskoy zemli do kontsa XIV stoletiya* (Kiev, 1896).

Danilova, L. V., *Ocherki po istorii zemlevladeniya i khozyaystva v Novgorodskoy zemle v XIV–XV vv.* (A.N. SSSR, 1955).

DDG, see Dukhovnye i dogovornye gramoty velikikh i udel'nykh knyazey XIV–XV vekov.

Długosz, *Historia Polonica* (*HP*) (Leipzig, 1711).

Dukhovnye i dogovornye gramoty velikikh i udel'nykh knyazey XIV–XV vekov (*DDG*), ed. S. V. Bakhrushin and L. V. Cherepnin (A.N. SSSR, 1950).

Ekzemplyarsky, A. V., *Velikie i udel'nye knyaz'ya Severnoy Rusi v tatarsky period s 1238 po 1505 g.* (*VUK*), 2 vols. (SPb, 1889, 1891).

Fennell, J. L. I., *Ivan the Great of Moscow* (London, 1961).

Fennell, J. L. I., "The Campaign of King Magnus Eriksson against Novgorod in 1348: an Examination of the Sources.' *Jahrbücher für Geschichte Osteuropas*, Heft 1, 1966.

Fennell, J. L. I., "The Tver' Uprising of 1327: A Study of the Sources". *Jahrbücher für Geschichte Osteuropas*, Heft 2, 1967.

Fijałek, Y., "Średniowieczne biskupstwa kościoła wschodniego na Rusi i Litwie na podstawie źródeł greckich". *Kwartalnik Historyczny*, x, 3, 1896, pp. 487–521.

Filevich, I. P., *Bor'ba Pol'shi i Litvy-Rusi za galitsko-vladimirskoe nasledie* (SPb, 1890).

Goetz, L. K., *Deutsch-russische Handelsverträge des Mittelalters* (*DRHV*) (Abhandlungen des hamburgischen Kolonialinstituts, Band xxxvii, Hamburg, 1916).

Golubinsky, E., *Istoriya russkoy tserkvi,* (*IRTs*) vol. ii, book 1 (Moscow, 1900).

Golubovsky, P. V., *Istoriya Smolenskoy zemli do nachala XV stoletiya* (*ISZ*) (Kiev, 1895).

Gramoty Velikogo Novgoroda i Pskova (*GVNiP*), ed. S. N. Valk (A.N. SSSR, 1949).

Grekov, B. D. and Yakubovsky, A. Yu., *Zolotaya Orda i ee padenie* (A.N. SSSR, 1950).

Grekov, I. B., *Ocherki po istorii mezhdunarodnykh otnosheniy vostochnoy Evropy XIV–XVI vv.* (Moscow, 1963).

Grumel, V., "Titulature de métropolites byzantins II. Métropolites hypertimes", *Mémorial Louis Petit. Archives de l'Orient Chrétien,* I. (Bucarest, 1948).

GVNiP, see *Gramoty Velikogo Novgoroda i Pskova.*

Hrushevsky, M. *Istoriya Ukraini-Rusi* (*IUR*), 9 vols. (Kiev-Lwów, 1903–31).

Ilovaysky, D. *Istoriya Ryazanskogo knyazhestva*(IRK)(Moscow, 1858).

Istoricheskie pesni XIII–XVI vv., ed. B. N. Putilov and B. M. Dobrovol'sky (A.N. SSSR, 1960).

Istoricheskie Zapiski (*IZ*) (Moscow).

Istoriya russkogo iskusstva, vol. iii, ed. N. N. Voronin and V. N. Lazarev (Moscow, 1955).

IZ, see *Istoricheskie Zapiski.*

Kamentseva, E. I., *Russkaya khronologiya* (*R. Khr.*) (Moskovsky gosudarstvenny istoriko-arkhivny institut. Kafedra vspomogatel'nikh istoricheskikh distsiplin. Moscow, 1960).

Kamentseva, E. I. and Ustyugov, N. V., *Russkaya metrologiya* (Moscow, 1965).

Kartashev, A. V., *Ocherki po istorii russkoy tserkvi,* 2 vols. (Paris, 1959).

Kazakova, N. A. and Lur'e, Ya. S., *Antifeodal'nye ereticheskie dvizheniya na Rusi XIV—nachala XVI veka* (*AED*) (A.N. SSSR, 1955).

Khoroshkevich, A. L., *Torgovlya Velikogo Novgoroda v XIV–XV vv.* (A.N. SSSR, 1963).

Klibanov, A. I., *Reformatsionnye dvizheniya v Rossii v XIV—pervoy polovine XVI vv.* (*RD*) (A.N. SSSR, 1960).

Klyuchevsky, V. O., *Drevnerusskie zhitiya svyatykh kak istorichesky istochnik* (Moscow, 1871).

Klyuchevsky, V. O., *Sochineniya*, 8 vols. (Moscow, 1956–9).

Kochin, G. E., *Sel'skoe khozyaystvo na Rusi kontsa XIII–nachala XVI v.* (A.N. SSSR, 1965).

Kopanev, A. I., "O 'kuplyakh' Ivana Kality", *IZ*, vol. xx, 1946, pp. 24–37.

Kuchkin, V. A., "Skazanie o smerti mitropolita Petra", *TODRL*, vol. xviii, pp. 59–79.

Letopisets Pereyaslavlya-Suzdal'skogo, ed. M. Obolensky (Moscow, 1851).

Letopisi russkoy literatury i drevnosti (*LRLD*), ed. N. Tikhonravov (Moscow, 1859–63).

Likhachev, D. S., "Galitskaya literaturnaya traditsiya v Zhitii Aleksandra Nevskogo", *TODRL*, vol. v, 1947, pp. 36–56.

Likhachev, D. S., *Russkie letopisi* (*RL*) (A.N. SSSR, 1947).

LRLD, see *Letopisi russkoy literatury i drevnosti*.

Lur'e, Ya. S., "Iz istorii russkogo letopisaniya kontsa XV v.", *TODRL*, vol. xi, 1955, pp. 156–86.

Lur'e, Ya. S., "Rol' Tveri v sozdanii russkogo tsentralizovannogo gosudarstva", *Uchenye zapiski Leningradskogo gosudarstvennogo universiteta*, 1939, No. 4, pp. 85–109.

Lyubavsky, M. K., *Obrazovanie osnovnoy gosudarstvennoy territorii velikorusskoy narodnosti. Zaselenie i ob'edinenie tsentra* (Leningrad, 1929).

Lyubavsky, M. K., *Ocherk istorii Litovsko-russkogo gosudarstva do Lyublinskoy unii vklyuchitel'no* (Moscow, 1910).

Makary, Mitropolit Moskovsky, *Istoriya russkoy tserkvi* (SPb, 1886).

Milyutin, V. *O nedvizhimykh imushchestvakh dukhovenstva v Rossii*, *Chteniya*, vol. iv, 1859.

Mongayt, A. L., *Ryazanskaya zemlya* (*Istochniki istorii ryazanskoy zemli i istoriografiya*) (A.N. SSSR, 1961).

Monumenta Poloniae Historiae (*MPH*), ed. A. Bielowski, vol. ii (Lwów, 1864).

MPH, see above.

Nasonov, A. N., "Letopisnye pamyatniki Tverskogo knyazhestva", *Izvestiya A.N. SSSR, Otdel gumanitarnykh nauk*, 1930, No. 9, pp. 709–38, No. 10, pp. 739–73.

Nasonov, A. N., "Materialy i issledovaniya po istorii russkogo letopisaniya", *Problemy istochnikovedeniya*, vol. vi, 1958

Nasonov, A. N., *Mongoly i Rus'* (A.N. SSSR, 1940).

Nasonov, A. N., "Moskovsky svod 1479 i ego yuzhnorussky istochnik" (MSYuI), *Problemy istochnikovedeniya*, vol. ix, 1961, pp. 350–85.

Nasonov, A. N., "Moskovsky svod 1479 i Ermolinskaya letopis'" (MSEL), *Sbornik: Voprosy sotsial'no-ekonomicheskoy istorii i istochnikovedeniya perioda feodalizma v Rossii. Sbornik statey k 70-letiyu A.A. Novosel'skogo* (Moscow, 1961), pp. 218–22.

Nasonov, A. N., "*Russkaya zemlya" i obrazovanie territorii drevnerusskogo gosudarstva* (A.N. SSSR, 1951).

Nicephorus Gregoras, *Historiæ Byzantinae* (*Hist. Byz.*), vol. iii (Bonn, 1855).

Nikitsky, A. I., *Ocherk vnutrenney istorii Pskova* (SPb, 1873).

NL, see Novgorodskaya pervaya letopis'.

Novgorodskaya pervaya letopis' starshego i mladshego izvodov (NL) (A.N. SSSR, 1950).

Ocherki istorii SSSR, perioda feodalizma IX–XV vv., parts 1 and 2 (A.N. SSSR, 1953).

Pamyatniki russkogo prava, 8 vols. (Moscow, 1952–61).

Pashuto, V. T., *Obrazovanie Litovskogo gosudarstva* (OLG) (A.N. SSSR, 1959).

Pashuto, V. T., *Ocherki po istorii Galitsko-Volynskoy Rusi* (A.N. SSSR, 1950).

Paszkiewicz, H., *Jagiellonowie a Moskwa*, vol. i, *Litwa a Moskwa w XIII i XIV wieku* (Warsaw, 1933).

Paszkiewicz, H., *Polityka ruska Kazimierza Wielkiego* (Warsaw, 1925).

Pavlov-Sil'vansky, N. P., *Feodalizm v drevney Rusi* (SPb, 1907).

PL, see Pskovskie Letopisi.

Platonov, S. F., *Lektsii po russkoy istorii* (Petrograd, 1915).

Podmoskov'e. Pamyatnye mesta v istorii russkoy kul'tury XIV–XIX vv. (Moscow, 1962).

Podobedova, O. I., *Miniatyury russkikh istoricheskikh rukopisey* (Moscow, 1965).

Podobedova, O. I., "K istorii sozdaniya Tverskogo spiska khroniki Georgiya Amartola", *Doklady sovetskoy delegatsii, V Mezhdunarodny s'ezd slavistov* (Moscow, 1963).

Polnoe sobranie russkikh letopisey (PSRL).

Povest' vremennykh let (PVL), 2 vols. (A.N. SSSR, 1950).

Presnyakov, A. E., *Obrazovanie Velikorusskogo gosudarstva* (Petrograd, 1918).

Priselkov, M. D., *Istoriya russkogo letopisaniya XI–XV vv.* (*IRL*) (Leningrad, 1940).

Priselkov, M. D., see *Troitskaya letopis'*.

Priselkov, M. D. and Vasmer, M. R., "Otryvki V.I. Beneshevicha po istorii russkoy tserkvi XIV v." *Izvestiya Otdeleniya russkogo yazyka i slovesnosti Akademii nauk,* vol. xxi, 1916.

Pskovskie Letopisi (PL), ed. A. N. Nasonov, vol. i, 1941, vol. ii, 1955.

PSRL, see *Polnoe sobranie russkikh letopisey.*

PVL, see *Povest' vremennykh let.*

Ramm, B. Ya., *Papstvo i Rus' v X–XV vekahk* (A.N. SSSR, 1959).

RIB, see *Russkaya istoricheskaya biblioteka.*

Romanov, B. A., "Rodina Afanasiya Nikitina", *Khozhenie za tri morya Afanasiya Nikitina* (A.N. SSSR, 1948).

Rozhdestvensky, S. V., "Dvinskie boyare i dvinskoe khozyaystvo XIV–XVI vv." *Izvestiya A.N. SSSR, VII, seriya OGN,* 1929, No. 1, pp. 49–70.

Rozhkov, N. A., "Politicheskie partii v Velikom Novgorode XII–XV vv.", *Sbornik statey Rozhkova "Istoricheskie i sotsialogicheskie ocherki"*, part 1 (Moscow, 1906).

Russkaya istoricheskaya biblioteka (RIB), 39 vols. (SPb, 1872–1927).

Russkaya letopis' po Nikonovu spisku, vol. iii (SPb, 1786).

Rybakov, B. A., *Remeslo drevney Rusi* (Moscow, 1948).

Safargaliev, M. G., *Raspad Zolotoy Ordy* (Saransk, 1960).

Sakharov, A. M., *Goroda severo-vostochnoy Rusi (Goroda SVR)* (Moscow, 1959).

Scriptores rerum Prussicarum (Leipzig, 1861–74).

Scriptores rerum Svecicarum medii aevi, vol. i (Upsala, 1818).

Sedel'nikov, A. D., "Vasilij Kalika: l'histoire et la légende", *Revue des études slaves,* vol. vii, 1927, pp. 224–40.

SGGiD, see *Sobranie gosudarstvennykh gramot i dogovorov.*

Shakhmatov, A. A., *Obzor russkikh letopisnykh svodov XIV–XVI vv.* (*ORLS*) (A.N. SSSR, 1938).

Shaskol'sky, I. P., "Dogovory Novgoroda s Norvegiey", *IZ,* No. 14, 1945.

Shaskol'sky, I. P., "Novye materialy o shvedskom pokhode 1240 na Rus'", *Izvestiya A.N., seriya istorii i filosofii,* vol. viii, No. 3 (Moscow, 1951), pp. 267–76.

Sobranie gosudarsvtvennykh gramot i dogovorov (SGGiD), 5 vols. (Moscow, 1813–91).

Sokol'sky, V., *Uchastie russkogo dukhovenstva i monashestva v razvitii edinoderzhaviya i samoderzhaviya v Moskovskom gosudarstve v kontse 15 i pervoy polovine 16-go veka* (Kiev, 1902).

Solov'ev, A. V., "Velikaya, Malaya i Belaya Rus'", *Voprosy istorii*, 1947, No. 7, pp. 24–38.

Solov'ev, S. M., *Istoriya Rossii s drevneyshikh vremen*, ed. "Obshchestvennaya Pol'za" (SPb).

SPb, St. Petersburg.

Spuler, B., *Die Goldene Horde. Die Mongolen in Russland, 1223–1502 (GH)* (Wiesbaden, 1965).

Sreznevsky, I., "Svedeniya i zametki o maloizvestnykh i neizvestnykh pamyatnikakh", *Zapiski Akademii nauk*, No. 4, vol. xxxiv, 1879, pp. 1–192; Appendix, pp. 145–8.

Stagg, F. N., *North Norway, a history* (London, 1952).

Stökl, G., *Die Entstehung des Kozakentums* (Veröffentlichungen des Osteuropa-Institutes, Band iii, München, 1953).

Stroev, P. M., *Spiski ierarkhov i nastoyateley monastyrey Rossiyskoy tserkvi* (SPb, 1877).

Tatishchev, V. N., *Istoriya Rossiyskaya*, 5 vols. (Moscow-Leningrad, 1963–5).

Tikhomirov, I, "Torgovye snosheniya Polotska s Livoniey v XIV v.", *Zhurnal ministerstva narodnogo prosveshcheniya*, No. 12, 1887, pp. 232–9.

Tikhomirov, M. N., *Drevnerusskie goroda* (Moscow, 1956).

Tikhomirov, M. N., *Drevnyaya Moskva* (Moscow, 1947).

Tikhomirov, M. N., *Rossiya v XVI stoletii* (A.N. SSSR, 1962).

TL, see *Troitskaya letopis'*.

TODRL, see *Trudy otdela drevnerusskoy literatury*.

Troitskaya letopis' (TL). *Rekonstruktsiya teksta*, M.D. Priselko (A.N. SSSR, 1950).

Trudy otdela drevnerusskoy literatury (TODRL) (A.N. SSSR, Institut russkoy literatury).

UL, see *Ustyuzhsky letopisny svod*.

Ustyuzhsky letopisny svod (UL), ed. K. N. Serbina (A.N. SSSR, 1950).

Vasil'evsky, V., "Zapisi o postavlenii russkikh episkopov", *Zhurnal ministerstva narodnogo prosveshcheniya* (Feb., 1888), pp. 445–63.

Vasmer, M., *Russisches etymologisches Wörterbuch (REW)*, 3 vols. (Heidelberg, 1953–8).

Vasmer, M., *Russisches geographisches Namenbuch* (*RGN*) (Wiesbaden, 1962–).

Vernadsky, G., *The Mongols and Russia* (Yale University Press, 1953).

Veselovsky, S. B., *Feodal'noe zemlevladenie v severo-vostochnoy Rusi* (A.N. SSSR, 1947).

Voigt, J., *Geschichte Preussens*, 9 vols. (Königsberg, 1827–39).

Voinskie povesti drevney Rusi, ed. V. P. Adrianova-Peretts (A.N. SSSR, 1949).

Voronin, N. N., "'Pesnya o Shchelkane' i Tverskoe vosstanie 1327 g.", *Istorichesky zhurnal*, No. 9 (Moscow, 1944).

Vychegodsko-Vymskaya letopis', ed. P. Doronin, *Istoriko-filologichesky sbornik Komi-filiala A.N. SSSR*, vol. iv (Syktyvkar, 1958), pp. 257–70.

Winter, E., *Russland und das Papsttum* (Berlin, 1960).

Yanin, V. L., "Iz istorii vysshikh gosudarstvennykh dolzhnostey v Novgorode". *Problemy obshchestvenno-politicheskoy istorii Rossii i slavyanskikh stran. Sbornik statey k 70-letiyu akademika M.N. Tikhomirova* (Moscow, 1963).

Yanin, V. L., *Novgorodskie posadniki* (*NP*) (Moscow, 1962).

Zabelin, I. E., *Istoriya goroda Moskvy* (Moscow, 1902).

ZhMNP—Zhurnal ministerstva narodnogo prosverhcheniya.

Zimin, A. A., "Kratkoe i prostrannoe sobraniya khanskikh yarlykov, vydannykh russkim mitropolitam", *Arkheographichesky ezhegodnik za 1961* (Moscow, 1961), pp. 28–40.

Zimin, A. A., "Narodnye dvizheniya 20–kh godov XIV v. i likvidatsiya sistemy baskachestva v severo-vostochnoy Rusi", *Izvestiya A.N. SSSR, seriya istorii i filosofii*, vol. ix, No. 1, 1952.

Zimin, A. A., "Novgorod i Volokolamsk v XI–XV vekakh", *Novgorodsky istorichesky sbornik*, vol. x (Novgorod, 1961).

Zimin, A. A., "O khronologii dukhovnykh i dogovornykh gramot", *Problemy istochnikovedeniya*, vol. vi.

Zimin, A. A., "Pesnya o Shchelkane i vozniknovenie zhanra istoricheskoy pesni", *Istoriya SSSR*, No. 3 (Moscow, 1963), pp. 98–110.

Zimin, A. A., Review of Yanin's *NP* in *Sovetskaya arkheologiya*, No. 3 (Moscow, 1963), pp. 272–9.

Zverinsky, V. V., *Materialy dlya istoriko-topograficheskogo issledovaniya o pravoslavnykh monastyryakh v Rossiyskoy imperii*, 2 vols. (SPb, 1890, 1892).

Index